D0481330

AT EASE

THERE'S NO EXPERIENCE quite like life in the military—only someone who's "been there" can truly understand and appreciate it.

From basic training to mess hall chow to the people encountered and places visited along the way, veterans' memories of their service days always seem to bring a smile.

The personal recollections and photos in this book were shared by veterans who enjoy recalling the fond, funny and frustrating aspects of their days in uniform.

So, why not pull up a footlocker, relax and enjoy the memories in the pages that follow? They're sure to remind you of your own days in the service—and they're guaranteed to put you...*At Ease.*

☆ ☆ ☆

☆ ☆ ☆

Editor: Mike Beno
Assistant Editors: John Schroeder, Robert Fojut,
Henry de Fiebre, Terry Koper
Art Director: Bonnie Ziolecki
Production Assistant: Judy Pope
Photo Coordination: Trudi Bellin
Editorial Assistants: Barb Czysz, Blanche Comiskey,
Joe Kertzman
Publisher: Roy J. Reiman

Reminisce Books
International Standard Book Number: 0-89821-152-2
Library of Congress Catalog Card Number:
95-70942
All Rights Reserved
Printed in U.S.A.
Cover photo by Harold M. Lambert

For additional copies of this book or information on other
books, write Reminisce Books, P.O. Box 990,
Greendale WI 53129.
Credit card orders call toll-free 1-800/558-1013.

CONTENTS

Prologue

IN THE MONTHS before the 50th anniversary of D-Day, the editors of *Reminisce* magazine received a flood of fascinating memories from people who'd been in military service.

Most of this mail came from veterans who'd been "citizen soldiers"—those everyday people who never dreamed they'd end up becoming a soldier, a sailor, a Marine or part of an air crew.

They didn't see war from the perspective of a career military person or the detached viewpoint of a historian. The stories they sent weren't about bombs, bullets and blood. Instead, they were about the fond, funny and frustrating situations that military life seems so often to land you in.

These vets remembered the bewildering days of basic training, the organized insanity of service life (which became a lot funnier with the passage of time) and the eye-opening exposure to new places and faces.

Their stories were intensely personal and, from the standpoint of preserving history, a genuine national treasure.

Why Not Make a Magazine?

It seemed clear to us that these stories from veterans deserved the kind of wide audience that only a new national magazine could provide. So, we introduced the idea of *As You Were* and sat back to see what would happen.

Well, we got hundreds of enthusiastic letters, as well as mailbags full of great stories and photos, from veterans who wanted to share great tales of their days in stripes.

We produced the first issue of that unique ad-free military magazine—and had an awful lot of fun putting it together. Then we sent out sample issues and waited again.

Unfortunately, not nearly enough subscriptions came in to support a magazine which carried no advertising. So, after a lot of discussion here at *Reminisce*, we reluctantly decided not to continue publication of *As You Were,* giving the magazine an early but honorable discharge.

But that sure wasn't the end of it! We were flooded with letters from disappointed and—we might as well admit it—angry people who'd been waiting a very long time for a magazine devoted solely to veterans' memories. They had quickly subscribed when given the chance, and they didn't want a refund—they wanted *As You Were* to continue.

We did, too! All those stories we'd received were *too good* not to print. What was World War II really like in the eyes of a kid who hurried down to enlist before the smoke had cleared at Pearl Harbor? What was it like for the young woman who wanted to serve her country?

Stories *Had to* Be Told

Millions of words have been written about the Korean War, Vietnam and Desert Storm by war correspondents and military historians. But what about the common soldier's view of things? Didn't these stories deserve to be shared?

There was only one answer, and you're holding it in your hands. *At Ease* is a collection of some of the best yarns received from *hundreds* of service veterans.

Life in the military is about bewilderment and culture shock. It's about learning to bend to unyielding discipline. It's about discovering the folly of playing poker with a sergeant who has eight hash marks on his sleeve.

You learn things in the service that shape you forever,

"*T*hese veterans' stories were too good not to print..."

---

right down to the way you hang your shirts in the closet, even when you're into your retirement years.

You learn that when the drill sergeant asks if anyone in the platoon knows how to type, you shouldn't step forward unless you're prepared to spend the rest of the day unloading a semi full of typewriters.

You learn Rule Number One: If it moves, salute it. If it doesn't move, pick it up. If you can't pick it up, paint it.

Possibly most important of all, you learn that in the midst of insanity, your greatest friend is a sense of humor. No one demonstrated that better than Bill Mauldin, the talented cartoonist who irritated the brass but made the citizen-soldiers roar with laughter.

At Ease is dedicated to all the men and women who have selflessly served their country, whether in the armed forces or at home working in the shipyards...whether bravely bringing entertainment to outposts under shell fire or staffing urban USO clubs.

These are their stories, a priceless addition to American history. We thank all the men and women who shared their memories and photographs to make this book possible.

—*Clancy Strock*

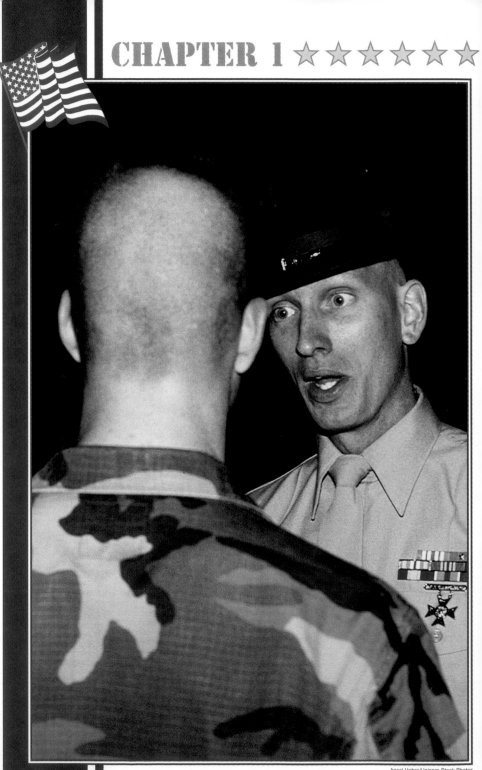

☆ ☆ ☆ BASIC STRAINING

We humans began trying to domesticate wild horses thousands of years ago. The process eventually came to be called "breaking" horses, a painfully accurate description of the way you teach a wild critter who's boss. Do it right, and the horse will go, stop, gee and haw, and pull heavy loads without much complaint.

In the military, this process is called "basic training" or "boot camp", and the results are amazingly similar. A once free-spirited person will, on command, go, stop, turn left, turn right and tote heavy loads without audible grumbling.

That same person will even unquestioningly walk into machine gun fire, man a deck gun as a kamikaze plane comes straight at him, jump out of a perfectly good airplane in the dead of night, or wade through frigid surf to reach a desolate beach on an island no one ever heard of.

I met the man assigned to break me to the ways of the military on a snowy, windy morning at Jefferson Barracks, Missouri in 1942.

He had the perpetually hoarse, raspy voice common to all drill instructors. Lean as a bullwhip, he came from the mountains of Kentucky and could trot backwards for miles even as I was going into cardiac arrest after the first lap around the parade ground.

Just like freshly captured wild horses, we stood wide-eyed and fearful in the company street that first day as he croaked out the news that we were now government property and our lives belonged not to Jesus but to him.

He woke us in the morning, roaring obscenities. He marched us to and from the chow hall, inspected our canvas-topped wooden huts and all our worldly possessions, taught us everything from personal sanitation to the Articles of War, "hawp-tawp-tree-hawed" us for hours in close order drill and tucked us into bed at taps.

He was a superhuman being who seemingly never slept, ate, or got tired. He did the impossible...he made soldiers out of us.

You never forget those first days in the service, or any further training you took, as the memories on the next several pages attest.

—*Clancy Strock*

Boat Crew Didn't Have All Oars In the Water

By Edward Withrow, Delray Beach, Florida

Newly arrived at the United States Coast Guard Receiving Station in Port Huron, Michigan, a fellow recruit confided he had never been *near* a boat, much less *in* a boat.

So when Arnold reported for lifeboat drill, he was nervous. In fact, when he tried to get into the boat, he tripped over his own feet and would have fallen overboard if one of the crew hadn't caught him.

The drill involved rowing 2-1/2 miles downstream on the swiftly moving St. Clair River (easy, with the current) and then back against the current (not easy).

As we slipped away from the dock, Arnold pulled weakly at his oar, "catching a crab" every other stroke, falling backwards off the thwart about a dozen times and having at least 100 other mishaps.

In spite of our sorry efforts, which the boatswain described as resembling "a centipede trying to walk with 75 broken legs", we made it back and were just a few yards from the dock.

That's when the boatswain saw our base commander, who had stopped to watch the drill's conclusion. The boatswain ordered the traditional boat salute, where each oarsman flips his oar up, blade facing fore and aft, and butt-end between his feet.

The command for this salute is "Toss oars". Eleven oars swept up in perfect unison. Arnold followed the command perfectly—he tossed his oar into the river!

EDWARD WITHROW in the North Atlantic in 1942.

In Boot Camp, Sailors Learned To Bare Arms

By Bob Belcher, Puyallup, Washington

I joined the Navy in 1951 to fight in Korea. I soon discovered it was a ritual on your first boot camp liberty to make a beeline for San Diego and seek out "Painless Nell", the tattoo artist on Broadway.

The enclosed photo (above) shows, left to right, Bill Carnes from Washington, Wayne Buchanan from Texas, me and Bob Hall from Arizona, the day after our trip to Nell's.

Another thing I learned from 39 years in the Navy and Naval Reserve was that whenever you asked a sailor how his duty had been, the answer always included a rating of the chow.

★

Hair Today, Gone Tomorrow

By Eugene Chatelaine, Inver Grove Heights, Minnesota

The first insult dealt to us new Air Force recruits at Lackland Air Force Base in June 1955 was the haircut.

At the time, we all proudly wore "ducktail" haircuts, long in the back with combed-back sides. Shortly after arriving at Lackland, we were marched to the barbershop.

With a smile, my barber politely asked me how I'd like to have my hair cut today. I told him to take a little off the sides, leave the back long and take nothing off the top. "Yes, sir!" said the good barber with a laugh.

He revved up the electric shears and suddenly raced down the middle of my head as though he were driving in the Indy 500. He made a right turn and nearly took off an ear.

Laughing insanely, he made two more runs down my head and three passes up. The deed was done in less than 15 seconds. When he got control of himself long enough to speak, he spun my chair to face the mirror and asked, "Is *this* how you wanted it, sir?"

I gasped at the sight—I looked like a bowling ball! Little did I realize that was just the first of many indignities to come, such as the "routine" physical...which, of course, is another story.

★

These Fleas Had a Right to Bite

By George Herbert, Camden, New York

I joined the U.S. Marine Corps in September 1942 and went to Parris Island, South Carolina for basic training.

A few days after arrival, we were doing close order drill when one of the recruits started scratching himself on the arm.

The DI immediately halted the platoon and asked the private what he was doing.

"I'm killing a sand flea that just bit me, sir," the private said.

"You do not kill sand fleas!" the DI barked. With that, he ordered the private to find the flea. The private got down on his hands and knees and picked up a dead sand flea.

"Is it the right one?" the DI demanded.

"Yes, sir," the private replied.

"Is it male or female?" the DI asked.

"It was a male, sir," the private replied.

The DI called over a corporal. They both examined the flea and determined it was a female.

For killing a female sand flea, the private was ordered to bury it. He had to dig a 2-foot-square, 2-foot-deep hole. When he was done with the burial, the private was told to never again kill sand fleas, as they had a right to bite.

We then went back to the drill as if nothing had happened.

Would 13th Jump Be His Last?

By Orville Dickerson, Canton, Michigan

H ey, Dickerson, watch out—you've got your 13th jump coming up on Thursday."

I'd been hearing those taunts ever since the jump schedule was posted several days before. I didn't think I was superstitious, but this barrage of "reminders" of bad luck was making me sweat this jump more than usual.

It was 1947 and I was a medic with the 188th Parachute Infantry Regiment stationed in Sendia, Japan. We were in the 11th Airborne, which was part of the Army of Occupation in Japan.

A bunch of nonsense, I told myself. The pre-13th jump hazing was traditional. Paratroopers were trained to believe they were the toughest men on earth, and no paratrooper would ever let anyone know he was even a little afraid.

The men scheduled for that "fateful" jump never talked about their feelings, not even to each other.

If they can do it, so can I, I told myself. I'm just as good a man as they are, I affirmed with all the courage I had amassed during my 18 years of life.

Thursday finally arrived, and when the company assembled for reveille, I felt the comforting warmth of the sun. At least the weather is good, I thought.

The next few hours were busy—30 minutes of calisthenics, morning chow and a 1-1/2-mile double-time march to the hangars. But even all this activity did not dispel the anxiety.

As soon as I was issued my chute, I rushed to be first on the "stick". There were three sticks of jumpers, 15 to a stick. The medic always jumped first or last, and I wanted to be first. If I froze, the guy behind me would push me out.

Soon we were airborne and over the jump site. "Hook up!" the jumpmaster commanded. "Move it up!"

I was propelled to the door by the 14 men behind me. "Go!" was the next command, and I'm not sure if I jumped or was pushed. The next thing I remember was the shock of the chute opening.

I looked up and saw one or two "blown" panels. Nothing to worry about, I thought. But other jumpers started yelling,

ON THE GROUND. That was where the training began, as these pilots learned. Orville Dickerson found all that training really pays off.

"Blown chute!" I thought it was just some more kidding.

"You blow it!" I yelled back. But as the words left my mouth, I realized I was falling too fast!

The ground was rushing up to meet me. The chute was collapsing, and I was lopsided and falling fast!

I yanked on the heavy metal handle attached to the rip cord on my emergency chute. The chute opened between my legs and flipped me right-side up. It slowed me, but I was still falling too fast.

Oh brother, I thought, I'm going to be one of those who lost it on the 13th jump!

I hit the ground hard. But all those landing drills in jump school paid off—I had made it alive.

I still had the rip cord handle in my hand. As the medics rushed toward me, I stuffed it in my boot. A quick examination showed I had suffered no broken bones.

A Jeep came speeding up, and a lieutenant jumped out. The first words out of his mouth were not "Are you hurt?" Instead, he demanded, "Where's your rip cord?"

"I don't know, sir," I lied.

"You dropped it, didn't you, private?" the lieutenant yelled. "Don't you know you could have hurt someone on the ground?"

I'm alive, I thought, ignoring the lieutenant's tirade. That handle will make a nice souvenir.

In all I made 22 jumps. Some were memorable, but none equaled the one on that Thursday in 1947. And ever since, I've been cautious about the number 13.

★

Sarge Cleaned Up On These New Recruits

By Bill Sadler, Brownsville, Texas

We arrived at Shepherd Field, Texas in February of 1943. A chill wind blew snow and sleet into our faces. We 254 former college students were addressed as "youse college brains" by our barracks sergeant.

On our second day, he informed us that life as we knew it depended on getting the barracks into spotless shape for inspection. We innocent lambs were about to get our first lesson in sheep shearing.

There was one problem, the sarge said—the Army hadn't provided the cleaning supplies we'd need. But he'd make the arduous trip into town to purchase brooms, mops, scrub brushes, buckets, bar soap and "stuff for da windows". All he needed was $2 from each of us. We ponied up.

Later, some quick math revealed we 254 lost sheep had just kicked in $508, a goodly sum for cleaning supplies in 1943. Of course, we later learned the sergeant simply went to Supply and requisitioned everything. But we were too terrified to complain.

Welcome to the Army, you poor little sheep!

'All Right,
I Need Some Volunteers...'

By Wally Pelchen, Brookfield, Wisconsin

At boot camp on Manhattan Island, New York, we were standing roll call in 20° January weather. The company commander asked if there were any enlistees who had typewriter experience.

I was new to the service and thrilled with the prospect of getting a typing job inside a warm building. So I took two steps forward to volunteer, along with six other recruits.

"Good," barked the CO. "We have seven typewriters that need to be carried across the drill field to the administrative building. Move it!"

★

Would-Be Drivers
Picked Up a Lesson

By Harold Crist, Arbovale, West Virginia

I was a green recruit at the Great Lakes Naval Training Center in Illinois during World War II and hadn't yet learned *not* to volunteer for anything.

So when our commanding officer came to the barracks one morning and asked if anyone could drive a pickup, I raised my hand, along with several others.

The four of us who were selected were excited—in the Navy only a week and already going to drive a pickup.

We were led to the drill field, where several sailors were busy digging a ditch and throwing the dirt into wheelbarrows.

"All right, you pickup drivers," the CO said, "I want you to pick up those wheelbarrows and drive them to that hole over there."

He left without saying another word. But I know he burst out laughing when he got out of sight. I never volunteered again.

"Okay, fellow," Dad said to himself. "I'll take this plane down. But if I die, I'm taking you with me."

Making what he considered the best maneuvers of his short flying career, Dad glided to earth, then eased back on the stick to soften the crash.

The plane hit the ground with a mighty bump, jumped back in the air, then came down again, bumping and flopping like a clumsy bird.

But he'd done it! He was on the ground—and alive!

Dad brought the plane to a stop, then jumped out of the cockpit, as mad as he'd ever been.

Out of his cockpit crawled the instructor. He jumped to the ground, shook his head and turned to walk away in disgust.

But Dad wasn't going to let him get away and shouted after him, "Sir, I haven't gone through landing instructions yet! I don't know how to land a plane!"

The instructor stopped, turned to Dad, shrugged his shoulders, and, with the hint of a grin, said, "Well, now you do." ★

Plenty of 'Training', No Boot Camp

By Leland Spore, Salem, Oregon

On June 26, 1943, about 50 of us boarded a train in Portland, Oregon headed for boot camp in San Diego, California...or so we thought. I had enlisted in the Navy only 20 days earlier, on my 17th birthday.

Things started to go wrong before we got out of Oregon. Somewhere around Klamath Falls, our car was pulled from the train. We were told the boot camp at San Diego was full.

We sat around a siding for a few hours until we were hooked onto another train. This time we were told we were going to Farragut Training Base in northern Idaho.

But before we got to Farragut, we learned that it, too, was full. Our car was unhooked again, this time in the tri-city area of Kennewick, Pasco and Richland, Washington. At least this time we got box lunches while we waited on a siding.

Eventually our car was hooked onto a third train. This time we were told our destination was Seattle, and we actually got there, although what should have been a 6-hour ride from Portland took 1-1/2 days!

We finally got off the train and were sent to the Navy shipyard in Bremerton, Washington, where we were quartered in the transient barracks.

As we had so far received no training and had no duties, the master at arms said all we had to do was make muster three times a day, keep the barracks clean and make our bunks.

So for 2 weeks that's all we did—eat, sleep and clean the barracks. But the first day of the third week, the picnic was over.

On the afternoon of that day, all of us were lying around on the grass in our civvies. We hadn't even been issued uniforms. A lieutenant commander drove by in his Jeep and saw us.

"What the hell are you men doing here?" he demanded.

A recruit jumped up, gave a sort of salute and explained our circumstances. Hearing that, the commander had us march to the small stores supply building, where they issued us uniforms.

But the supply room was not equipped to issue full seabags

to 51 men. So by the time I went through the line, all they had left were obsolete dress whites.

Next came work assignments. Mine was helping a civilian shipfitter in one of the dry docks where the *USS California* was being restored.

Later, still without having gone through boot camp, some of us were transferred to Sandpoint Naval Air Station in Seattle, where I was assigned to KP and washing cars at the base gas station.

I finally went to the personnel office and requested to be sent to boot camp. The officer there didn't believe me until he checked my service record. Then he told me I must be crazy to *want* to go to boot camp, which most recruits would gladly by-pass. Request denied.

So I took a test to determine what school I'd go to. Given two choices, I took Aviation Metalsmith School in Norman, Oklahoma... so, of course, I was sent to Radio Operating School, located in Boulder, Colorado.

The CPO I complained to about this (to no avail) had been a boxer and was a little "punch drunk". He said the prerequisite for being a radio operator was being a wee bit crazy.

He must have been right. I stayed at the job for 20 years...and never did like what I was doing! And I still think I was cheated by not being shipped off to boot camp!

BOOTED FROM BASIC? Leland Spore (right) did just fine in the Navy despite missing boot camp. He posed with friend Robert Lee Miller in Wakayama, Japan, 1945.

Clean Car Commendation Inspired Navy 'Boots'

By Bill Clark, Pearl River, New York

There was a lot of competition among the companies when I was in boot camp at Bainbridge, Maryland in 1956. Pennants were awarded for marching, athletics and weekly test scores.

But the bunch of "boots" in Company 188 (we were green kids mostly from New York and New Jersey) weren't doing very well at winning pennants…and that was deeply disappointing to our company commander.

Then one day about halfway through the 9-week training, Boatswain's Mate R.R. Rush appeared on the scene and started molding us into sailors.

Rush drove to our barracks each day in an old Pontiac that was always very dirty. Every time we asked him when he was going to wash it, Rush always replied, "When you clowns start looking like sailors, I'll wash my car."

I guess that was what we needed. We started winning pennants right up to and including the battalion drill flag, which entitled us to go right to chow without standing in line.

About 2 weeks before graduation, we looked out the barracks windows to see Rush's Pontiac sparkling in the winter sun. That bright, clean car meant as much to us as a presidential unit citation.

★

Student Pilot Got 'Snake Bit' On Flight

By Roger Markley, Nashville, Indiana

Once during training out in the desert of Arizona, I had just taken off in my twin-cockpit plane when I heard a noise in the rear cockpit.

I looked over my shoulder and saw that a rattlesnake had

PRIVATE PEAK. Clyde Becker of Coloma, Michigan took an elevated break from training at Camp San Luis Obispo in WWII.

climbed in the plane and was sunning himself on the seat!

Ignoring my training and the patterns I was supposed to fly, I headed straight down, landed without calling the tower, got out of my plane on the runway and ran.

For that I was grounded for several days and made to walk around the base in the hot sun 8 hours a day while wearing a parachute.

It was punishment for not flying the proper pattern and for not checking out my plane *before* taking off. Since then, I always check every airplane I get into.

Smoking Lamp Not Lit When This Boot Puffed

By Jim Talbert, Debary, Florida

I thought I'd be a wise guy and sneak a smoke on the way to the mess hall one very cold morning in 1942 at Great Lakes Naval Training Center.

I got caught and had to pull a week of the dreaded mid-watch—midnight to 4 a.m. on the top deck of the barracks.

After the fourth night I was so tired I thought I was going to die. My plan to "beat the system" was to sit on the top step. That way, if I went to sleep, I'd fall right down the stairs and wake up.

The problem was, I went to sleep and fell backwards, snoozing peacefully until the officer of the day nudged me awake with his foot.

They must have felt sorry for me. They only added 3 days to my mid-watch duty.

★

Private Peeled Spuds Where the Sun Didn't Shine

By Bill Williams, Louisville, Kentucky

We'd just gotten back from a 4-hour march in the hot Texas sun at Camp Wolters during basic training in 1941. The sarge barked, "Can anyone take shorthand?"

Seeing a chance to get out of the heat, I quickly raised my hand. The smiling sergeant ordered, "Get over to the mess hall—they're shorthanded in the kitchen."

Still, I had the last laugh. Peeling spuds in the shade was better than drilling in the hot sun.

TATER TRAINING. Caesar "Pat" Pasquesi of Highland Park, Illinois (right) peeled spuds in 1941.

★

These Soldiers Went Whole Hog in Training

By Gene Maggard, New Braunfels, Texas

Our Special Forces team had some slack time during a field training exercise in North Carolina. We were on a night mission to capture a bridge.

We bought a pig from a local farmer and, with his permission, set up camp and dug a roasting pit behind his pasture.

One of the exercise umpires came by with two soldiers, and they stayed to eat. After the umpire left, the soldiers got to talking and let it slip that *they* were guarding the bridge.

We took the bridge with no resistance and later told the umpire where he could find his tied-up guards.

WHEN DINING WAS A MESS

Here's one scene you can count on in every combat movie made during the World War II years. It's the one where a bunch of young servicemen are sitting around talking about home. What do they miss most of all? Of course! Mom's home cookin'...her apple pie...her spaghetti...her special meat loaf...

Somehow an out-of-sorts, potbellied mess sergeant couldn't measure up to Mom, even on her worst day in the kitchen.

The mystery meat and SOS he dished out were bad enough—but then things got *worse*...especially for the dogfaces and grunts.

Field rations didn't resemble anything you'd ever eaten in your life! You just knew that somewhere a dog food factory had, with minimum changes, been switched over to turning out K rations, 10-in-ones and C-rats.

Whoever first applied the term "mess" to military dining had it exactly right. What else could describe the contents of your greasy tin tray after you had miserably gone through the chow line?

It was simply amazing how the gravy ended up atop the ice cream, the string beans were buried beneath the mashed potatoes and the meat was revealed when you finished the Jell-O. A mess, indeed.

Of course some of the "mess" was a matter of pure malice on the part of the surly conscripts who were assigned to dish up what passed for food. Many were on KP as punishment. They had forgotten to salute a 90-day wonder, or perhaps they'd somehow offended the delicate sensibilities of their drill sergeant. Whatever...they were in a bum mood, and someone had to pay.

It should be no surprise then, as you read the following stories, that some of the most memorable feasts in our service days were the impromptu ones that ingenious GIs put together out of necessity...and far from the nearest mess hall.

—*Clancy Strock*

'We've Got 2,000 Coming for Supper!'

By Clancy Strock, Newberry, Florida

In a perverse way, I was one of the lucky ones. My mother was a wonderful, loving woman, but cooking wasn't her major strength. (Dad claimed that our dog committed suicide rather than face any more table scraps!)

That's why the guys around me thought I was Section Eight material when I raved about how good the food was during basic training at Jefferson Barracks, Missouri in 1942.

But why not? The gravy wasn't lumpy, the chicken wasn't burned black and the biscuits didn't have raw dough in the center. Heck, I even gained a few pounds while others were wasting away.

I didn't even mind KP all that much, except for reporting to work at 4 a.m. Peeling potatoes was a pleasant, mindless job, providing lots of time to swap stories with fellow peelers. It sure beat close order drill on the frigid, windswept parade grounds.

If you kept a low profile and didn't screw up, you could avoid the dreaded pots and pans detail. That was the ultimate punishment, reserved for those who were just one more mistake away from the guardhouse.

The mess sergeant, of course, was lord and master of his domain. Name me anyone else without stars on their collar who had more power.

Most mess sergeants took enormous pride in turning out decent meals and were legitimately offended by the complainers. After all, anyone who can whip up even a passable meal for several hundred men and women three times a day deserves a little respect.

I was particularly in awe of the ones who ran kitchens on troop trains. Fixing anything more than a bologna sandwich aboard a bucking, swaying train going 50 miles an hour was an impressive feat.

As a generality, it seemed Air Force and Navy people ate a bit better than the Army and Marine Corps.

Air Force folks always went "home" after work. The Navy took completely assembled galleys with them wherever they went. But Army and Marine mess operations were mobile and temporary and often hastily set up under field conditions.

You had breakfast beside the river, lunch 5 miles down the road and supper outside a freshly liberated village. If you were lucky.

Much of the time you carried all your meals with you. K rations or "10-in-ones" or "C-rats" sustained life, but that's the most you could say for them. Remember those little cans of scrambled eggs (made from dried eggs) with tiny chunks of mystery meat? What a way to start the day!

Sometimes the most tempting item in the package was the camouflage-colored toilet paper. I toyed with the thought of throwing it into a canteen cup of hot water, adding a little salt and pepper and seeing if it might not be better than the other stuff they claimed to be food.

There were two times of the year when you could count on great food, no matter where you were. Mess sergeants knocked themselves out at Thanksgiving and Christmas, even if it meant trucking hot meals through enemy fire right up to the front lines.

The secret was to squirrel away mess funds for months before the holidays. Sometimes that meant walking a delicate line that involved cutting back on chow quality in October and November just short of the point where you'd set off food riots. (You can only get away with serving SOS or boiled okra so many times.)

Thanksgiving and Christmas meals let the mess staff show just how good they really could be. I remember big, plump turkeys *and* hams *and* giant hunks of roast beef...candied yams *and* mashed potatoes *and* stuffing, plus a choice of vegetables and salads.

Later, there was pumpkin pie *and* mince pie *and* chocolate cake *and* ice cream. Sometimes they even passed out good cigars and chocolate mints.

During such feasts, the mess sergeant would stroll proudly among the tables, and the look

OH, MY. PIE! The squadron baker (above) served up a surprise in 1944 North Africa, says Robert Miley of Marion, Ohio.

on his face said it all: "Go ahead, I dare you to tell me your mom ever topped *this* spread!"

After nearly 3 undistinguished years as an enlisted man, I finally made it through OCS.

Besides more pay, one of the big lures for me was the chance to finally eat in the officers' mess. Like all enlisted men, I harbored the suspicion that officers enjoyed really great food.

Well, maybe *some* of them did, but not in any of the places I ever went. The only appreciable difference was that officers ate off china plates on white tablecloths. The food wasn't noticeably better.

Now if you can believe the movies of that era, things were much better in the Navy. Why, aboard the *Caine*, commanded by Humphrey Bogart, there were always plump, fresh strawberries in the refrigerator.

I was sure that the officers on every ship enjoyed snazzy dining rooms and were waited on by uniformed mess boys who brought them flagons of fine wine and rare old brandies to sip with Cuban cigars after dinner.

Meanwhile, 6 weeks after getting my gold bar, I was walking through an outdoor mess line on Leyte while a monsoon rain poured down on my miserable back.

I looked at the watery slop in my mess kit and did the only reasonable thing—continued on to the garbage can and dumped the works. I had lots of company.

But it didn't mean starvation. Someone in my outfit had discovered a circus-sized tent in nearby Tacloban filled with stacks of olive drab cans in all sizes and shapes, dented, squashed and mostly non-labeled.

You could take all you wanted, but with no guarantee against ptomaine poisoning. Four of us picked through the thousands of containers, not knowing for sure what we were grabbing, and took three gunnysacks of stuff back to our tent.

For the next 2 weeks, every meal was a gamble. I'll never forget one that consisted of string beans, baked beans, kidney beans and tomato juice.

No matter how often I tell that story, my wife still doesn't quite understand why I don't applaud when she announces that supper will be "noodle surprise casserole".

Fact is, the U.S. Army gave me more than enough supper-time surprises to last a lifetime.

This Marine Was Talkin' Turkey

By Philip Schwab, Arlington, Texas

I t was a few weeks before Thanksgiving 1943, and we Marines had had more than our fill of Spam.

We were manning an air base in the Solomon Islands, and our supply lines weren't functioning all that smoothly. This meant we'd been eating Spam three times daily for several weeks running.

With "turkey day" fast approaching, the scuttlebutt was that we'd be served a traditional turkey dinner with all the trimmings. For my part, I'd seen too much of the standard mess hall fare to put any stock in the rumor, and I couldn't help voicing my skepticism.

"If they serve us turkey dinner on Thanksgiving," I declared, in a voice loud enough for many in the mess hall to hear, "I'll be there in a top hat and tails!" Little did I know I'd end up eating those words.

Several days later, the officer who oversaw the enlisted men's mess stopped me on the street and asked if I had indeed made the crack about showing up in a top hat and tails.

When I told him I had, he smiled thinly and assured me that a full turkey dinner would be served to everyone in the squadron *except* me. That is, unless I showed up dressed as promised. "If you don't," the lieutenant said (without the thin smile), "your Thanksgiving dinner will consist of Spam, Spam and more Spam."

I knew I would not feel particularly thankful for such a dinner, so I got to work.

I received some help from a buddy in the quartermaster section, who supplied a gigantic khaki shirt. I cut off the shirttails in front, leaving two tails dangling behind.

The material I cut off was used to cover a makeshift top hat, and the shirtsleeves were long enough to permit me to improvise

"French cuffs" on my "tailed coat". The outfit was topped off with a "swagger stick", tipped with the copper point from a 50-caliber cartridge on one end, and the base of the brass at the other.

On Thanksgiving day, I showed up at the mess hall attired as shown in the accompanying snapshot.

The lieutenant was waiting for me with a can of Spam decorated with a length of ribbon.

When he got a load of my getup, he removed the ribbon from the Spam, tied it around my top hat and personally served me a dinner tray filled with turkey and all the trimmings. Believe me, that was the *only time* I ever saw a Marine commissioned officer wait on an enlisted guy like me!

That act, as well as the ridiculous top hat and tails, made Thanksgiving 1943 memorable for this gyrene…one who learned the hard way not to make any loud boasts he'd have a tough time backing up!

★

Weevils' Evils Were Stopped Cold

By Elliott Pilchard, Port Hueneme, California

Farmers have battled weevils in their fields for centuries. I recall one Navy cook who won the war against weevils a thousand miles out to sea.

At one time or another, most of us who served aboard Navy vessels have eaten weevils. These tiny insects thrived in the poor conditions where our food supplies were stored, such as warm, dank ship holds.

Put a cache of flour in a place like that and the weevils will make themselves right at home. Even worse, they multiply at a rate that makes rabbits look like pikers!

For almost 3 years aboard my first Navy ship, my crew mates and I ate weevils in bread, cakes, gravy…in short, *anything* made with flour.

They were so small it was impossible for the cook to sift them out, so we learned to live with "a little more protein" in our meals. We joked about it, and even made bets about how many we had in a particular piece of bread.

I joined my next ship just before the invasions of Iwo Jima and Okinawa, and, yes, we had weevils. This group of sailors, however, was not so tolerant.

The 2,000 men on board blamed the baker for the bugs, and they began giving it to him—and I mean *bad!* He knew he had to do something.

Late one afternoon he called out a work party and had the men load some flour bags into the meat freezer. The next morning, he cut open one of these cloth-lined paper bags and found *thousands* of frozen weevils trapped between the kraft paper and cloth.

When it got cold, they looked for a warm place. They were able to get through the fabric flour sack on the inside, but not the heavy brown paper on the outside, and froze right there!

The baker was vindicated and became our hero. He was even written up in the Navy journals and given a commendation. When asked how he came up with the idea, he said, "I put myself in the weevils' place and thought, 'What would I do?'"

★

Complaint Didn't Bug This Baker

By Mike Lacivita, Youngstown, Ohio

During World War II, we had a well-trained baker aboard our ship, and we received one slice of delicious homemade bread at each meal. It was so good that I permanently swapped my portion of mashed potatoes to a buddy for his ration of bread.

One day, however, I noticed tiny brown specks in that bread. A closer look confirmed my worst fears—the specks were bugs…I could even make out their little feet!

Meanwhile, my buddy Al was enjoying his double ration of mashed potatoes. What could I do? A deal is a deal.

The "buggy bread" continued, so I discussed the problem with our baker. He said, "Don't worry. I'll take care of it for you."

I figured he'd sift the flour and we'd have bug-free bread. Wrong! The next day we were served raisin bread. The bugs were still there, but it was a lot harder to see them.

From that day forward, I learned to like "raisin-beetle bread". Our baker was both a diplomat and an expert in camouflage.

'Hold the Bean Soup!'

By Clifford Brandenburger, Beecher City, Illinois

I t's a wonder I could ever eat another bean after serving in the United States Navy.

I was warned as a boy that if I went in the Navy I'd have to eat a lot of beans. Sure enough, my first boot camp meal at Great Lakes Naval Training Center was beans.

I eventually found myself on an LST (landing ship tank) crossing the equator in the Pacific. We'd been aboard for several weeks without enjoying a meal of beans, so they were bound to appear on our plates soon.

The cook sent a KP helper to the hold to bring up a gunnysack of dry beans. When the sailor opened the hatch, the aroma nearly decked him. Those beans were already "simmering away" down below!

Somehow the compartment had been flooded with about 2 feet of water, and the culprit never informed the captain. The beans had swollen, burst out of their gunnysacks and begun to sprout. Even worse, the tropical temperatures had the whole works fer-

James Stit/Jeff Ethell

menting, and the overpowering smell wafted from the hold and enveloped the ship.

The captain stopped the ship and ordered all hands to help clean up the mess. Since the "bean soup" would clog a pump, we had to form a bucket brigade and haul it all out by hand.

Two poor sailors stripped to their shorts, donned gas masks and went into the hold to hand up the buckets.

Of course, we weren't served any beans for the remainder of that cruise.

You'd think that episode would've ruined my taste for beans, but for some reason it didn't. I still love them!

★

For Navy Cook, Rough Seas Were 'Just Swell'

By Carl Stone, Cambridge Springs, Pennsylvania

The mess was often a *real mess* for Navy cooks at sea—I know, because I ran the galley on the *USS Chepachet*, a fleet oiler that cruised to Africa during World War II.

Rough seas were a constant problem in the galley. I recall the time two crewmen were carrying a 10-gallon pot of soup down a ladder when the ship rolled. A wave of soup splashed all over the place, but the men managed to save enough for me to start another batch quickly.

Trying to flip hamburgers could get interesting on the bounding main, too. The pan often seemed like a moving target, and it could be downright tough to keep those burgers in the skillet instead of on the deck.

But rough seas could be a blessing in disguise—when it got too bad, the amount of food I had to prepare for

200 men dropped drastically. Most of them would rather remain in the sack than eat.

Another problem I faced was cannon fire...not from the enemy, but our own! The galley was located beneath the ship's 5-inch gun. Whenever it went off, the blast sent stovepipe soot cascading over the meal I was making. At those times I'd tell the crew I had used "a little too much pepper".

Keeping a spotless galley under such conditions was impossible, but I never had to sweat inspections. Somehow, I always managed to serve spaghetti on the day before inspection.

A pasta-plugged drain guaranteed a flooded galley, and whenever the captain arrived, he'd simply bypass the area as we dealt with our "problem".

★

This Hungry Airman Got in His Licks

By Robert Longo, Woodridge, New York

Back in 1943 I was stationed at Laughlin Air Base in Del Rio, Texas.

We airmen rarely enjoyed desserts, but one day we were delighted to receive two cookies with our mess. What a treat!

With the treasured cookies on our trays, we went to our tables. Then a buddy remarked that he forgot his bread when going through the chow line.

He got up to get the bread, then took a look at us. He looked down at his cookies, then back at us. He knew his chances of seeing those cookies again were nil, so he picked them up and licked one side of each. Grinning smugly, he went back to the chow line.

When the airman returned, his cookies were still there. But just as he sat down one of us grabbed the cookies, licked the other sides, then put them back.

Our bread-bearing buddy was speechless, and the rest of us had a good laugh.

No one ended up eating those two cookies...but the rest of us shared ours with our buddy anyway.

Mama's Pepperoni Made This GI Popular

By Emanuel Carlo, Clifton, New Jersey

Mail call was a favorite time for all servicemen, and I still remember the special packages from home that made me the most popular soldier in Company B of the 87th Chemical Mortar Battalion.

It was about 2 months after D-Day and we were en route through Normandy, pushing the Germans toward Paris.

One day at mail call, a special bundle arrived. I opened it and found a letter, some family pictures...and Italian pepperoni. All the way from Jersey City, New Jersey, 3,000 miles to France, had come a thick stick of Mama's pepperoni!

"Long distance pepperoni?" my buddies snickered.

Why not? Its durability could match any fruit cake. I think the Army should have used it in their flavorless K rations.

PEPPERONI PALS. His buddies were grateful for the package Emanuel Carlo (above in St. Lo, Normandy, kneeling at left) got from home because it contained a big hunk of Mama's wonderful pepperoni.

Despite the teasing, I shared the pepperoni with my buddies. They were begging for more as we received our orders to move out.

I stuffed the pepperoni in my field pack and we boarded our jeeps. But one soldier who I'll never forget, Tony from Massachusetts, couldn't stop thinking about the spicy treat. He'd been on K rations since D-Day.

"Got any left?" he yelled from his vehicle. I began carving off slices with my trench knife and tossing them from jeep to jeep, yelling out friends' names as I tossed.

Artillery shells began flying as well, and I wanted to jump into the ditch. But Tony hollered, "Heck with the artillery. Throw me another slice of pepperoni!"

★

Sailor's Appetite Lost at Sea

By Dale Wilkins, Vale, Oregon

Backyard barbecues lost their flavor for me after a tour in the Navy. That's because every time I smell smoke, I think of our ship's only cook, a man we nicknamed "Scorchy".

Scorchy burned everything he served, and I think he was capable of burning water. How bad was his cooking? Try eating some burned butterscotch pudding sometime.

Scorchy's pancakes were like leather discs. He burned those flapjacks so tough that we could stand on deck and actually skip them across the ocean.

Luckily, we were able to have Scorchy transferred. But my memories of his cooking have a most durable aftertaste.

★

Airmen Enjoyed Old-Fashioned Thanksgiving in...New Delhi?

By Bob Lichty, Vacaville, California

Whether you served in the military or not, you have no doubt heard those sad stories about the lousy food endured by our armed forces.

But it wasn't all beans, Spam and C rations. I recall one truly excellent repast which I enjoyed at 10th Air Force Headquarters in New Delhi, India in 1943. This was our Thanksgiving menu:

Roast young turkey, old-fashioned dressing, giblet gravy,

NOT LIKE MOM'S. In spite of the mess hall Thanksgiving feast in New Delhi in 1943, this sergeant said he'd still rather be home.

snow-flaked potatoes, American creamed corn, buttered peas, Indian candied yams, Waldorf salad, cole slaw, mixed pies and cakes, assorted fruits, iced cocoa.

This was far from typical fare—especially at the front. When some of my friends heard about this headquarters feast, they asked me how I liked dining "up there on Per Diem Hill".

★

Phantom Friend Provided Breakfast

By Linwood Johnson, Menominee, Michigan

Our 474th Infantry Regiment was doing mop-up duty behind Patton's tank forces, which were sweeping east across Germany, outrunning their fuel supplies.

We'd appropriated an old building in a small German village as a temporary headquarters. I was on CQ (charge of quarters) duty there, and one day while at my desk, I saw out of the corner of my eye a little blonde girl of 5 or 6 peeking in our window. When I turned to look at her, she'd disappear.

So I opened the window, put a pack of gum on the sill and went back to my desk. Soon, a little hand came into view and the gum disappeared.

I felt good about making a friend of the "enemy". But the story doesn't end there. A little later I passed the window and there on the sill were two chicken eggs. I had been repaid!

How Far Would a Sawbuck Stretch?

By Donald Moore, Natalia, Texas

I n 1942 I joined the Marines and shipped out with the Sixth Regiment for New Zealand. Our 17-day crossing on a Dutch East Indies cattle boat was hardly a picnic.

Fresh water was scarce and food was in equally short supply, and not very good at that. By the time we landed at Wellington, we were one boatload of hungry Marines!

We were given liberty, so the first thing on our minds was finding something to eat. It was nighttime and the city was completely blacked out when we went ashore. A buddy and I stumbled around in the dark until we located a cafe.

My friend was broke, but I had $10 in my pocket. I told him not to worry, that we'd buy as much decent food as my sawbuck would get us—however much that would be. But we were so ravenous we didn't stop to ask questions.

We quickly ordered a pitcher of milk and a loaf of bread with butter and jam. While we dove into this "appetizer", the kitchen was preparing a grand main course of steak and eggs, tomatoes, and fried potatoes. By the time the main course arrived, we'd finished the bread and milk, so we ordered more.

The food was *heavenly*, and at the end of our grand repast, we walked up to the cashier just a little bit nervously. I gave her my $10 bill...and received eight American dollars and a handful of New Zealand coins in change! We had just eaten ourselves silly for less than a buck each!

All the Marines who did duty in New Zealand seemed to love the country, and especially its people. I'll never forget the way they treated two ravenous teenage boys a long way from home.

★

He Dined in the 'Proper Manor'

By Sam Hutchman, Norristown, Pennsylvania

A nyone who served in the military has heard of mobile hospitals and even mobile kitchens...but a mobile *mess hall*?

We had one in Casablanca, Morocco during World War II, and it was born of necessity.

We'd landed in North Africa after a long voyage featuring beans for breakfast and an occasional pig's knuckle. Once ashore our Army cooks worked out of a mobile kitchen—that is, a truck. It was fine for them, but *we* were eating outside.

One day an officer must have gotten as tired of swatting flies as we were, because the company carpenter, Will Schneider, was told to build a mess hall.

Will did it, using nothing but discarded packing crates left on the docks at Casablanca. It was appropriately named "Cratewood Manor". The structure had tables, benches and, best of all, screened windows.

We were eating the same old awful food. But without the flies, it somehow seemed to taste better.

Not only that, but the mess hall was easily dismantled and reassembled. We hauled Cratewood Manor all the way to northern Italy, where we finally bid it good-bye at war's end. Maybe it's still there!

CRATEWOOD MANOR. This mess hall might have been made from crates, but it had tables, benches and screens on the windows...and it was portable!

Once Through Chow Line Not Enough

By Wilbur Marrs, Boca Raton, Florida

Very thin turnip soup and rice was our diet for over 3 years as POWs in Japan. So when American bombers began to parachute food to us when the war ended, we began a feast that would take us across the ocean!

I was with the 4th Marines and became a POW when the Philippines fell. We had been working in the copper mines in the mountains at Akenobe, Japan when the war ended and the food started falling from the sky.

The first parachute I came to had a package of Lucy Allen candy bars. I ate 27 of them! Most of what was dropped was C rations, so we made sacks from the parachutes to carry the canned goods back to camp.

With all the food, candy and cigarettes, we had so much energy that first night, no one slept. We just ate and talked and smoked. Surprisingly, very few got sick on the rich food, in spite of our years on the bland POW diet.

We were eventually taken to a hospital ship in Yokohama for a checkup. There they served us sauerkraut and wieners. We ate all they would give us...and that was a lot!

THEN AND NOW. Wilbur Marrs (above left in 1941 and right in 1990) ate himself back to health after being held by the Japanese.

A day or two later, the 4th Marines put on a parade to honor us and, of course, had a big meal for us afterwards. We had steak, which was more meat in one meal than we had seen during our whole time in Japan.

About 300 of us POWs finally set sail for the States on the *USS Ozark*. All the Navy personnel on the ship were great to us, especially the crew in the galley. They let us go through the chow line, load up, eat up, then get back in line again.

About 3 days out, the captain got on the loudspeaker and told us to limit our trips through the line to one, or else we'd run out of food before we got to Guam!

They put us in a hospital on Guam for another checkup, and boy, was that soft living...beds and American nurses! When we went through the chow line there, we'd grab a bunch of bread, if they had extra.

After we ate the regular chow, we'd take the bread and pour milk and sugar on it. We got some funny looks about our "dessert", but it was *so* good!

By the time we got to Hawaii, we were allowed a little shore leave, just in the Navy yard. We had been paid on Guam, so when we came upon a canteen near our boat, we went in. We ate everything they had and put them out of business for the day!

Then four of us found a sandwich shop. We started eating again and this time drew a crowd of sailors.

When they found out we had been POWs in Japan, they started buying the food for us. We were there for 2 hours, and what we didn't eat, the sailors bought and gave us to take back to the other guys on the ship. The next morning was the first time I thought that one time through the chow line was enough.

We got back to the States about a month after our liberation. I started out at 116 pounds, and by the time we docked, I weighed 135.

Thanks, Navy!

★

Desire for Hot Meal Drove These Would-Be Chefs

By Melvin Lindahl, Fife Lake, Michigan

I drove a half-track through Germany with the 13th Armored Division during World War II. I also used the vehicle as a stove...but that's getting ahead of the story.

My buddies and I had just broken out some C rations and were getting ready to warm up a nice hot lunch. Just then our

CHOW TIME. This time it was K rations for Melvin Lindahl (above right) and Joe Ventrella, in 1945 Germany.

reconnaissance survey section officer pulled up with his jeep and driver.

"Mount up and follow me!" he ordered. We had to move out in a hurry, of course, so there went our plans for a hot lunch. But then I came up with a bright idea.

I opened the hood and put a can of C ration spaghetti on the engine exhaust manifold. My friends added assorted cans of their own. We closed the hood and got underway.

About 20 minutes down the road, an awful stench filled the vehicle. Something was burning, but I couldn't stop to check.

When we finally did stop, I opened the hood to find spaghetti, meatballs, beans and other assorted foods splattered all over the engine. All the cans had exploded from the heat—what a mess! Chunks of food were burning on the manifold, and the rest of our lunch was being baked to the underside of the hood.

Though we never did enjoy a hot lunch that day, I guess the story did have a happy ending. If this little episode had happened stateside on an army base, I'd *still* be out in the motor pool chiseling food out of that engine compartment.

★

'We'll Take 72 Dozen, Sunny-Side Up'

By Herman Sundler, Hayden, Idaho

The winter of 1944 I was assigned to the 363rd Combat Team, taking part in the assault against Hitler's Gothic Line in Italy.

Though qualified to wear a Combat Infantryman's Badge, I was a cook. For months I'd made powdered scrambled eggs for breakfast and the men endured them. But one afternoon we had an unbelievable stroke of luck—72 dozen fresh eggs arrived, all the way from Des Moines, Iowa.

I sure wasn't going to scramble real eggs! We'd been on the battle line for months, and I wanted to make the most of it. I decided to fry those eggs and some bacon at the front lines, right in the face of the Germans.

"Could you spare some extra mules to pack those eggs to the front line?" I asked my sergeant and the quartermaster. They quickly provided two mules, then asked how I intended to fry eggs without drawing enemy fire.

I told them I needed some men at the front to make a tent out of about seven shelter halves so the Germans couldn't see our cooking fires. My request was radioed ahead to the command post.

Another cook, Dick Webb, and I strapped two gasoline-fired field stoves to our packs and took off up the trail in the dark with our precious egg cargo.

We set up our stoves long before daylight and began frying breakfast. Soon our unit commander, Colonel McGill, came by and asked what we were frying.

"Fresh eggs, sir," I answered. "Are you going to stick around and have some?"

"Damn right!" he said. After all, we were the only frontline regiment cooking breakfast on that cold morning on a hilltop in Italy.

★

Generous Brits Made a Christmas to Remember

By Russell Hill, Dillwyn, Virginia

I n the bitter winter of 1944, just before Christmas and the Battle of the Bulge, I was in charge of a four-man outpost along the Maas River in an isolated part of Holland.

From our advanced position we reported the launchings of Hitler's buzz bombs, which were intended to destroy the port of Antwerp, Belgium. Our reports gave the antiaircraft gun crews time to get into action.

Our food rations came when they could be delivered, which wasn't often. We had plenty of coffee (snow was melted for the water) but little else. There were many days without food, and the food that did reach us was often spoiled and unfit to eat.

No food, frostbitten feet and having to fight German paratroopers made the upcoming Christmas look bleak indeed.

SPOILS OF WAR. Russell Hill's motorcycle might have been painted OD and with US Army stars, but it's a British bike.

On the day before Christmas, I went in search of food. I finally stopped a command car carrying a British lieutenant. I told him how we had been without food for several days, and he assured me he'd come to the outpost the next day with supplies.

On Christmas morning he brought a box of food. He asked me to select another man so the two of us could accompany him back to his headquarters for dinner. He also promised that the two men remaining on duty would be taken for a hot meal on our return.

Seven miles to the rear, the British mess hall was such a jovial place that we soon forgot the war. Candy, cigarettes, cigars and drinks were pressed upon us. When the signal was given to be seated, my buddy and I were put at the head of the table as guests of honor.

It was a memorable holiday feast, topped off with the traditional Christmas plum pudding.

When the kitchen crew came out to take a well-deserved bow, I told the mess sergeant that the plum pudding was the best I'd ever eaten. I'll never forget his reply:

"Aye, 'nd I put me bloomin' whiskey rations in that bugger."

What four hungry GIs thought would be a bleak Christmas alone at the front turned out to be one I'll never forget.

Farm-Style Breakfast Too Much to Resist

By Albert McGraw, Anderson, Alabama

We were on maneuvers in a swamp near Leesville, Louisiana in the winter of 1942-43. The weather was cold, and so was our food. For 3 months straight we ate either C or K rations, and we young soldiers were miserable.

Farmhouses dotted the landscape and we camped nearby some of them. Many times while we were eating our cold rations, we'd catch the tantalizing aroma of frying ham and boiling coffee drifting from a kitchen window. But we were under strict orders not to go near the farmhouses.

One bitterly cold Sunday morning, after marching more than 12 miles the previous night, we awoke to discover that we'd camped near another one of those farmhouses. And there came those maddening breakfast smells again—for *hours*, it seemed.

It was more than a buddy and I could stand. Hang the orders—we devised a plan to put our feet under the kitchen table in that farmhouse!

Soon we were darting from tree to tree, closing in on the source of those wonderful smells.

We made a mad dash to the back porch and peered inside. We were astonished to see a throng of soldiers sitting around a giant table. And on the floor were several more soldiers, plates in their laps and steaming coffee beside them.

A pleasant but unsmiling woman motioned politely for us to come inside. Her husband was busy at an old-fashioned wood-burning stove, stoking it with pine chunks. Sizzling on the stove were several pans of home-cured ham.

Two daughters were busy retrieving dirty dishes and silverware to wash in a giant dishpan.

At last it was our turn. I asked for four eggs, sunny-side up. When my plate came, it also contained two large pieces of ham plus three oversized scratch biscuits. It was the wonderful country breakfast I'd been dreaming about, but better.

As each soldier left, he placed a dollar bill beside his empty plate, despite protests from our hostess, who repeatedly said there was no charge.

We returned to our bivouac area undetected, only to learn that an impromptu inspection was imminent. I quickly checked my carbine for dust and rust, donned a fresh uniform and put on my well-greased combat boots.

The inspection was made by a colonel whose gruff, deep voice would put a bear's growl to shame. He grabbed my carbine, inspected it carefully and rubbed his white-gloved hand over the length of the barrel. I was positive I'd passed the inspection with flying colors.

But then the colonel stared straight at me for what seemed to be only slightly short of an eternity. It was the stare all soldiers dreaded.

At last he turned to our captain. "Captain Boyer, since when, pray tell, has the Second Battalion been afforded the luxury of eggs sunny-side up?"

Somehow in my haste, I hadn't noticed a tiny dried splotch of egg yolk near my mouth.

No matter. I'll never forget that sumptuous breakfast served up by a sympathetic farm family in Louisiana.

★

These Kids 'Got the Scoop'

By Bob Kufner, Boring, Oregon

While operating on the rivers in Vietnam one day in 1969, our ship's refrigeration system went on the fritz. The captain ordered the ice cream brought out for an "all-you-can-eat" party before the stuff went bad.

Three or four Vietnamese kids were watching us from the river bank. I got the captain's permission to take a 5-gallon cardboard tub of ice cream ashore to them.

I started with paper cups and a scoop, but after their first taste, the kids ran off yelling. I wondered what went wrong...did the cold stuff hurt their teeth? I was about to leave when I heard what sounded like 500 sea gulls.

Here came about 20 kids, all running and screaming to get a taste of the ice cream. The scoop was abandoned, as they reached over, under and around me, digging into the tub with their bare little hands.

'Monsoon Soup' Warmed Rainy Days in Vietnam

By Rod Hinsch, Beech Grove, Indiana

W hen monsoon season came in South Vietnam, we GIs would often catch up on sleep, write letters, read books, play cards or tell war stories.

Those torrential downpours also gave us the downtime we needed to get creative with our cooking...and nothing tastes better on a rainy day than a good bowl of hot soup.

So one rainy season, some friends and I concocted this recipe for "Asian Monsoon Soup".

You'd have a tough time making this at home, since the main ingredient is a steel pot full of monsoon water and the rest of the ingredients are C rations. Feel free to substitute as best you can using the suggestions below.

After catching about a quart and a half of rainwater, we'd rummage through a case of C-rats looking for: 1 can beef steak, 1 can sliced beef with potatoes and gravy, 1 can beef with spiced sauce and 2 cans beans with meatballs and tomato sauce. Then we'd cut the ingredients into bite-size pieces ("bite-size" being a relative term...one guy liked hunks the size of baseballs!).

Next, we'd combine all the ingredients in the helmetful of water and add whatever flavorings were on hand. Often, that was any kind of hot sauce, some soy sauce or even *nuoc mam*, a fermented fish sauce popular in Southeast Asia.

We'd simmer the whole works for an hour, then serve it in canteen cups with crushed C-rat crackers.

You may have to make a trip to the surplus store for the helmet, canteen cup and C rations. Try a Vietnamese specialty store for the *nuoc mam*.

This soup is guaranteed to keep you warm and smiling no matter how hard it may rain.

★

Marines' Clandestine 'Snack Bar' Invaded

By Donald Childs, Austin, Texas

ON BOARD. Donald Childs got to visit his old ship in New Orleans in 1989.

The food aboard the aircraft carrier I served on in World War II was very good. But it was nice to have a snack at night, so we Marines on board found a way.

On a short stop at Pearl Harbor to off-load planes, we bought and smuggled aboard a coffeemaker and hot plate. A little bribing in the aviation sheet metal shop got us a rack to hold the coffeemaker.

Coffee, sugar and cream were easily obtained by our Marines on mess duty. And what could be better than hot, fresh bread? As luck would have it, the cooling table for the loaves was just below a

FOOD AFLOAT. Don Childs and his fellow Marines ate well on the *USS Cabot*.

bakery porthole. When the cooks' heads were turned, we simply reached through the port and liberated a loaf or two.

Our food caches were stored in the ammunition magazines, behind the gun tubes. Empty ammo cans, which should have been disposed of, held the food. Of course, only we knew which

WELL-FED CREW. The contingent of Marines aboard the *Cabot* always found a way to have a snack. But they always made sure the brass got their share.

cans held goodies and which held ammunition.

We dined in a crew shelter which adjoined the ammo magazines. Entry to this tiny 8 x 10 room was gained through a low 4-foot door. The door was covered with a heavy curtain because of blackout conditions.

Anyone inside for a little snack and conversation would douse the lights when a new arrival rapped on the bulkhead. The hungry visitor would enter, put the curtain back in place, then give the OK signal—and then the lights were turned back on. Of course, all of this was going on right under the noses of our officers!

One night we accomplished a particularly successful "mission" to the bakery, netting us two huge sheet pies—one pineapple and one cherry. We were all sitting around inside the "diner" when we heard the familiar rap on the bulkhead.

Lights out. Visitor in. Lights on.

As our squinting eyes adjusted to the light, we began to make out the figure. Standing there before us in polished splendor, his silver bars shining in the dim light, was our executive officer! Mouths agape and eyes wide, we were a bunch of speechless 18-year-olds.

After what seemed an eternity, the exec said, "Isn't someone going to offer me a cup of coffee? And by the way...you can get a great piece of cherry pie over at gun four."

★

We Bartered Our Way to Better Chow

By John Woodward, Largo, Florida

In 1944, I was a radio operator and top turret gunner on a B-24 based in Italy near the Adriatic Sea. After flying missions three days in a row, our pilot passed along the welcome news that tomorrow we'd be standing down.

Just before we turned in, Shorty, our engineer, suggested we use our day off to travel to Altamura, where an elderly Italian signora always fed us when we stopped by hoping for a change in menu.

The chow at the base filled your stomach...but you had to stand upwind while eating it.

The next day after breakfast, we examined our meager supply of bartering goods. The signora was reluctant to accept scrip (invasion money)—it was too difficult to exchange for lira. No cigarettes, no soap, no chow!

Cigarettes were in short supply, and so was soap. But each of us had been hoarding our rations of Hershey bars, so we turned to them as a last resort for barter.

D.K., the tail gunner, suddenly discovered a problem.

"Oh, no!" he yelled, reaching into his footlocker. He then held up the limp, nearly liquid remains of his Hershey bars. They hung over his hand like a soggy brown handkerchief.

Each of us discovered the same thing. Some warmer-than-usual weather had turned all of our chocolate bars into a soupy paste, apparently beyond salvage. We resigned ourselves to another lunch of canned hamburger.

Our chocolate worries soon became secondary when the pilot stuck his head in the tent and said, "Tomorrow we fly. Long one!"

Our thoughts turned to our target, but our eyes remained on the mound of soft candy before us. It was Shorty who came up with the idea.

D.K. had a round cookie tin from home, empty now. Shorty suggested we scrape the chocolate from the wrappers into the tin.

"We'll smooth it out. Then we'll cut the Hershey's name out of a wrapper and lay it on top. Tomorrow, we'll take it up with us," Shorty said. "Secured in the bomb bay, it should be frozen good and hard when we land."

"But how do we keep it from re-melting?" D.K. asked.

"No sweat," Shorty replied. "We'll cadge a CO_2 cylinder from

BOMBER BUDDIES. Turret gunner John Woodward (right) and tail gunner D.K. Gunter ham it up while on leave in Cairo, Egypt.

the personal equipment tent and spray the tin occasionally."

It worked! When we landed, the chocolate was nice and firm and the wrapper had made a perfect impression in the center. The folks at Hershey would have been proud!

We re-froze the tin with pressurized CO_2 periodically after the flight, and we gave it one last long, cold shot to hold it for the trip to town.

We hopped a truck to Altamura. The tin was wrapped in an OD wool shirt for insulation, and we peeked at it from time to time. It was sweating profusely, and we urged the driver to hurry. When we finally got into Altamura, we hopped out and hurried to the signora's.

She let us in and we were seated in the over-furnished front room. We gently pried the cover from the tin, displayed our prize

and asked, "Pasta? Salada? Chicken?"

"Si, si," the signora nodded. "It's-a new candy?"

"Oh, yes," I assured her. "Special from America, just for you."

The signora supplied us with glasses of mouth-puckering Chianti while she began cooking. We loosened our ties, pulled off our shoes and relaxed.

When it came time to remove the chocolate from the tin, Shorty again had the solution. He had the signora warm the tin in a pan of hot water. We flipped the chocolate out, then over, revealing a perfectly labeled 8-inch circular Hershey bar.

Everything worked out just right. We left the signora's pleasantly sated and with her last request lingering in our ears, "You-a come again, and bring-a the new choc'lat. It's-a multo bono!"

Harold M. Lambert

The Last Thing She Wanted Was a German Meal

By Debbie McGrath, Rolla, Missouri

Tradition, especially on holidays, is a part of everyone's family. But why, I griped to my mother, was our Irish Catholic family eating sauerkraut and pork every New Year's Day?

The pork wasn't so bad. But the sauerkraut could stay with a person for days, in a manner better left unspoken. My griping led my mother to sit me down and tell me the story about how this German meal became part of our Irish family's holiday tradition.

It was November 1944. Mary Catherine (Kitty) was a 20-year-old informally engaged to Joseph Paul, a corporal in the 28th Infantry Division who was about to spend the holidays near Bastogne, Belgium, where the terrible Battle of the Bulge would break out on December 16.

Earlier that month, Kitty got the news from Joe's mother that he was missing in action, news that could dash the hopes and dreams of a lifetime.

As expected, Christmas passed in a blur. Weeks slipped by as Kitty waited, and prayed, with thoughts of despair beginning to cast their shadow inside her young heart.

On New Year's Eve, a friend convinced Kitty to eat a meal of sauerkraut and pork the next day. It was an old German tradition that guaranteed luck in the coming year.

Well, the last thing Kitty wanted to do was celebrate anything remotely German. But desperation breeds its own kind of religion. So on January 1, 1945, she ate sauerkraut and pork for supper.

Although Kitty didn't know it then, the day she was eating that good luck meal, Joe was recovering in an evacuation hospital from a concussion—and amnesia—suffered from the blast of a German railroad gun.

Joe had managed to escape from the Germans. But after suffering the concussion, he lay in a Belgian hospital, unable to remember his name and staring at a tattoo on his left arm

—a heart with the name of "Kitty".

It was spring before Kitty heard that Joe was back with his unit. By that time, he was on his way home. More months passed while Joe pieced together his identity. He was then honorably discharged, and he made it back to the States in time to celebrate V-E Day.

From that year on and ever since without fail, on New Year's Day, Kitty continued her good luck tradition as a way of honoring that fateful holiday.

But the story didn't end there. Twenty years ago my husband and I were stationed in Germany as newlyweds. It was my first Christmas away from family and I developed a case of homesick blues. There was something missing.

That's when I realized that the time had come for Eric and me to carry on our own traditions. So, on New Year's Day, when Eric came into the kitchen with, "What's that awful smell?", I just smiled and said, "Sit down and let me tell you a story about a young woman with a lot of heart, and a lucky guy I've come to know as Dad."

★

Now That's Convenience!

By Arthur Lee, Phoenix, Arizona

Being a good cook in the Army requires more than an ability to prepare tasty food. The man in charge of the mess must be equally adept at obtaining supplies. During World War II in the Philippines, our outfit was blessed with one of the best.

In 1944 our 25th Infantry Division reconnaissance unit was engaged in a particularly nasty skirmish on some grassy hills in central Luzon.

We were surprised in the middle of it all when a truck pulled up from the field kitchen. Out jumped the cook, who served us steak and ice cream right there in our foxholes!

Not only had he found some unusually good food, he got it to us on the battlefield. Now that's service!

Marines on the Move
Didn't Count Their Chickens

By Tim McCready, Salem, Connecticut

On Okinawa, a Marine buddy and I had time to thoroughly ponder the question, Which should come first, the chicken or the egg?

After landing on the island, our outfit was making good time, though much of it was spent slithering on our bellies. We'd far outpaced our supplies and were living on what we'd carried along, which wasn't much.

SANDY SUPPER. The desert of North Africa in 1943 was as good a place as any to set up for chow. No matter where it was, when it was time to eat, the GIs found the food.

When my buddy Avis came upon an abandoned farmhouse, he was delighted to find a hen on a nest. He immediately suggested a chicken dinner, with the leghorn as our "honored guest".

I stopped him with the reasoning that the two eggs beneath her would likely turn into more in the coming days. Then, just before we were to move out, we'd enjoy our chicken dinner. Avis agreed.

That evening, we fried fresh eggs in our mess kits...and just about the time we finished dinner, we were surprised to hear the fateful command, "Move out!"

No drumsticks for us, the hen got a timely reprieve.

From that point on, whenever our food supply began to dwindle, Avis never missed the chance to remind me about the chicken dinner we nearly enjoyed.

CHAPTER 3 ★ ★ ★ ★ ★ ★

SERVICE SILLINESS. There was nothing like a laugh to break up tedious military service. Three men from the 10th Air Force in India (right) react to a security briefing. (Photo from Bob Lichty of Vacaville, California.) Proving that the Allies could get along, Tom McLaughlin of Palm Bay, Florida sent photo below of his outfit stationed in Tiverton, England. At bottom, sergeants Bob Sand (right) of Bellingham, Washington and Russell Butts celebrated the Fourth in 1944.

Jeff Ethell

The captain, a direct descendant of Attila the Hun, summoned me to his desk. It seemed that a group of war correspondents and some showboating Congressmen had asked to visit Malinta Tunnel on Corregidor, now that we'd celebrated V-J Day and things were certifiably safe for important people.

I was the designated tour director. "Check out 50 flashlights from Supply," the captain commanded. "Everyone who goes into the tunnels must have one."

When we returned the next day, I dutifully lugged my box of 50 flashlights back to Supply.

"What's this?" grouched the supply sergeant, a 20-year man.

"The flashlights I checked out yesterday."

"You can't bring 'em back," said the sergeant. "They've already been written off. There's no way I can take 'em back. Once they're written off, they don't exist any more."

We argued a bit, but it was hopeless. Finally I asked what I was expected to do with 50 flashlights.

He rocked back in his chair, stunned and in shock. "How long have you been in this army, Lieutenant?"

Oh. At last I got it.

That afternoon 45 civilian Filipinos in our office went home with a barely used GI flashlight. They were thrilled. I was rid of the flashlights. The sergeant was happy.

The story has a bizarre postscript. Three days after our visit to Corregidor, a platoon of freshly barbered, fully armed Japanese appeared at the Corregidor boat dock ready to surrender. They hadn't gotten word that the war had ended 6 months earlier. Our party of civilian visitors was what tipped them off.

As the stories that follow make clear, a lot of things in military life didn't make much sense at the time. But they sure produced a lifetime's worth of offbeat stories for veterans to swap with friends.
                                                              —*Clancy Strock*

The Colonel Listened to the Plowboy

By John Deal, Wilmington, North Carolina

Sergeant Jimmy Bean was a good old "plowboy" out of the Ozarks and a darn good aircraft mechanic, too. I think it came from being raised on a tractor.

At Kirtland Air Force Base in Albuquerque, New Mexico back in 1952, Jimmy was always singing or whistling *Wild Side of Life* ("I didn't know God made honky-tonk angels, I might'a knowed you'd never make a wife").

Jimmy and I crewed a couple of F-84Es ("lead sleds") at Kirtland, where Colonel James Ritland was the base commanding officer. Like all "desk jockeys", Colonel Ritland had to maintain his flying status, and, for some reason, he'd only fly my plane.

One day my plane was out of commission for lack of a part. I talked the colonel into flying Jimmy Bean's, saying I had a great deal of respect for Jimmy's workmanship.

Jimmy and I buttoned the colonel into Jimmy's 84, opened the gate of the fenced-in area and watched him taxi to the end of the runway, where he locked the brakes and ran up the engine.

We heard the light "pop" as the emergency fuel pump was turned on and tested, but not the louder "Bang!" that's made when the pump is turned off.

"Uh-oh," Jimmy said. "He'll be back. Let's open the gate."

After the Colonel taxied back in, Jimmy and I went up the ladders on either side, rolled back the canopy and stuck our heads inside.

"Sergeant," the colonel said, "it won't come out of 'emergency fuel'."

Jimmy noticed that the colonel had inadvertently pushed the switch forward to the "steady on" position instead of pulling it aft to the spring-loaded "test" position. He reached down and popped it out, and we all heard the "Bang!"

In his best Ozark hillbilly drawl, Jimmy said, "There, Colonel. Now, if you'd jes' keep yer cotton-pickin' paws off'n them switches you don't know nuthin' about, you won't git yourself inta that kinda trouble."

I about fell off the ladder! I couldn't believe what I'd just heard a sergeant tell the base commanding officer!

But my fears were groundless. Colonel Jim just smiled and said, "Thank you, Sergeant." He closed the lid and taxied off.

About 10 years later I was in my second day on the job at North American Aviation Missile Division in Downey, California. I was in a narrow corridor when I saw a large group coming toward me.

The group contained the company president, the chairman of the board and some big-deal military brass. I was low man on the totem pole in the accounting department.

Suddenly the group parted and the center of their attention, a general, broke through and grabbed me like a long-lost son!

It was Colonel Ritland (now General Ritland), head of the Air Force's new Missile Command in San Bernardino—our biggest, most important customer!

I polished his star with the cuff of my sleeve and said, "Well, General, looks to me like you've been keepin' yer cotton-pickin' paws off'n them switches you don't know nuthin' about and stayin' outta trouble!"

We both laughed while the company brass stood around wondering what that was all about.

To this day I think of Jimmy Bean often. I'll bet he's still whistling *Wild Side of Life*. You can take the boy out of the Ozarks, but you can't take the Ozarks out of the boy.

★

Officer's First Salute Arrived With Zip

By Clancy Strock, Gainesville, Florida

Tradition had it that a newly commissioned officer, upon receiving his first salute, should give the one who saluted him a neatly folded dollar bill.

There I was, a freshly minted 90-day wonder walking down a company street at Fort Sill with a new dollar bill in my sweaty palm. I couldn't wait for that first salute!

At last it happened. Coming toward me was a potbellied master sergeant with hash marks up to his elbow. Target sighted!

But he didn't salute. Instead, he walked up to me and smirked, "Lieutenant, your fly is open."

Humility, thy lessons are many and varied.

This Breach of Security
Was Downright Alarming

By Robert Sturtevant, Santa Cruz, California

"The British are coming!"

Paul Revere's famous warning cry is familiar to every American. Too bad Paul wasn't alive in 1953, because we certainly could have used him.

I was stationed at the U.S. Air Force base at Sealand RAF Station in Wales. One day our brass decided to conduct a security check of our base and invited the local chapter of the British Home Guard to *try* to get onto the post. They accepted the challenge.

On the appointed day, Military Police were stationed strategically throughout the installation, especially watching nearby overpasses and remote gates.

All went well until about 10:30 a.m., when two fire engines came roaring up to the front gate, sirens howling and bells ringing. The MPs let them pass, thinking there must be a serious fire somewhere.

You guessed it. The "firemen" were the local Home Guard, who drove right up to base headquarters and captured it!

★

Recruit Spied a Chance
To Scope Out Scenery

By Roland Long, Ketchikan, Alaska

While serving aboard a destroyer in 1947, I was part of a crew taking a contingent of reservists on a training cruise from Seattle to Ketchikan, Alaska.

Ours was the flagship, and the commodore ordered the squadron to head up the beautifully scenic Inside Passage on the outbound trip.

Though many of the reservists were experienced sailors,

some were raw recruits who hadn't even gone through boot camp. I'll never forget one of those kids.

It was a lovely afternoon, and the commodore and a guest were on the bridge, viewing the scenery through a portable long glass.

The recruit walked up alongside the commodore, bumped his elbow and said, "Hey, mister, can I look through your spyglass?"

The commodore stepped back, his four broad gold stripes gleaming in the sun, and handed the glass to the kid with one tiny white stripe.

The kid scanned the beach, handed back the glass, said "Thanks" and walked away.

Of course, those of us who had observed all this were about to explode trying to keep straight faces. Recognizing this, the commodore walked by and said, "You know, I should have charged that guy a dime."

At that we let loose with torrents of laughter. But I'll bet there was no laughter on the bridge a few minutes later. Over the PA system, the commanding officer of the reservists was invited to "visit" the commodore—on the double!

★

Vietnam-Era Reservists May Have Met Gunga Din

By Edward McManus, Marlborough, Massachusetts

Our active reserve company trained in 1965 using manuals put together during World War II and supplemented up through the Korean War. They didn't include new sets of strategy and tactics learned in Vietnam.

One day a Regular Army captain recently back from Vietnam watched us attack a hill just the way our archaic manuals instructed. We softened it with rifle fire, then marched across the field shoulder to shoulder, firing as we advanced.

The captain shook his head sadly and sighed. "All you need now is a bagpiper and you're ready to take any hill in India."

'Splat Attack' Became Legend

By Ken Harrington, Boulder City, Nevada

Repeat a story often enough and it becomes fact, the saying goes.

Well, the story of the Battle of Suchow Creek went beyond mere fact. It became legend and was immortalized with a medal. Not bad for a battle that never happened!

The story was shared with me by my late brother, H.B. Harrington, who was a Marine sergeant when the tale was born.

Back in the early '30s he was with the Second Battalion, Fourth Marines, stationed in Shanghai, China. This was the home port for the entire Asiatic Fleet.

Suchow Creek is a small branch off the Yangtze River, just a few

SUCHOW CREEK VET. Marine Sgt. Hubert Harrington was there when the bombs hit the "honey barges" in a battle that everyone survived.

miles up from Shanghai. Back then it was used as a depository, so to speak.

The Shanghai sewage facilities were primitive at best. To deal with the problem, "honey barges" were used around Shanghai. A fleet of sampans would tow full barges up to Suchow Creek and dump them in a designated disposal area.

After a few years this site developed into quite a manure pile, which in time became a source of fertilizer for Chinese farmers.

One morning the Yangtze Patrol (part of the Asiatic Fleet) was passing the mouth of Suchow Creek when a squadron of

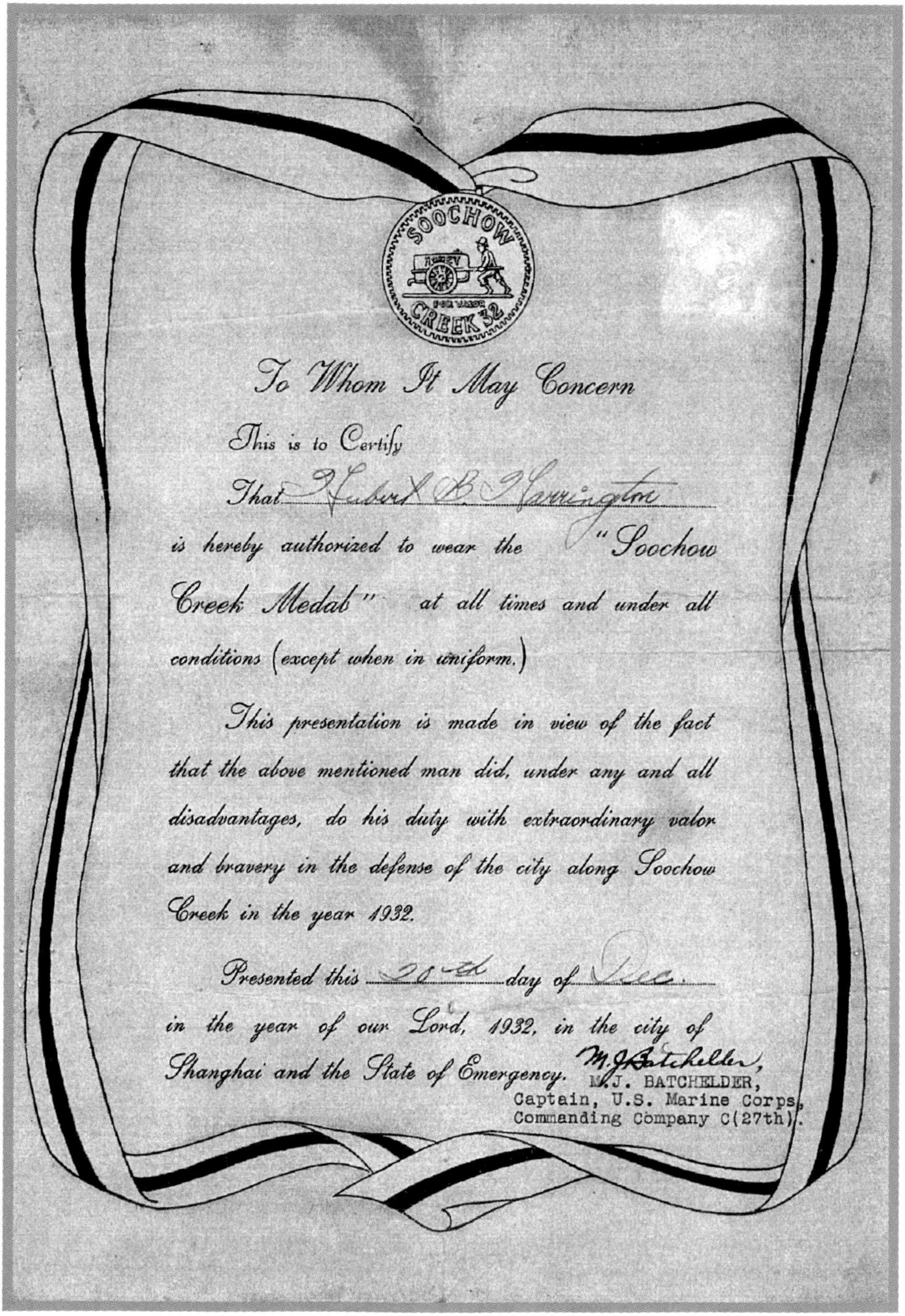

To Whom It May Concern

This is to Certify

That Hubert B Harrington

is hereby authorized to wear the "Soochow Creek Medal" at all times and under all conditions (except when in uniform.)

This presentation is made in view of the fact that the above mentioned man did, under any and all disadvantages, do his duty with extraordinary valor and bravery in the defense of the city along Soochow Creek in the year 1932.

Presented this 20th day of Dec in the year of our Lord, 1932, in the city of Shanghai and the State of Emergency.

M.J. Batchelder,
M.J. BATCHELDER,
Captain, U.S. Marine Corps,
Commanding Company C(27th).

Japanese planes flew by on their way to bomb Canton. As they passed over Suchow Creek, they dropped three bombs—probably by mistake.

The bombs hit dead center on the giant manure pile, splattering "fertilizer" everywhere. At first only the Yangtze Patrol claimed to be "hit". It wasn't long, however, before the whole fleet plus the Marines in the area also claimed to be splatter victims!

Eventually the "casualties" included the USS Augusta (a heavy cruiser) plus four destroyers, four submarines and several auxiliary vessels and patrol boats.

This "battle" was a main topic of conversation among the servicemen when they were on shore leave, and the stories grew in frequency and imagination. Finally, an enterprising Chinese businessman in Shanghai decided the Battle of Suchow Creek deserved its own commemorative medal.

A bronze disc was cast, showing a "honey barge" being towed toward a large pile of manure. "The Battle of Suchow Creek" was stamped around the edge of the disc, which hung from a white, purple and red silken ribbon to make it look official.

Only a few hundred were made at first. They went like hotcakes at 50¢ each (a pretty good sum at that time in China), so 3,000 more were cast!

These sold slower until the Chinese businessman printed an official-looking certificate to accompany the medal. That did it! Now everyone wanted one of the medals, and the enterprising fellow had no trouble clearing his shelves.

Men who were shipped stateside took their medals with them...some were even brazen enough to wear them on their uniforms. If questioned, they could show the certificate and launch into their version of the attack.

No doubt many of these impressive medals were stored away in old seabags or foot lockers, to be found a generation later by the descendants of those brave Asiatic sailors and marines and proudly put on display.

I hadn't thought about this story for some time. I was reminded of it recently at a local gathering place in Boulder City. Some war stories were being swapped, and someone mentioned that his uncle was aboard the USS Augusta during the Battle of Suchow Creek.

I was tempted to set the story straight, but I zipped my lip. After all, some legends can be fun, if not fact.

SHERMAN WAS RIGHT. These four Coast Guardsmen expressed their sentiments about war by using their heads just before crossing the English Channel on D-Day.

GIs Didn't Horse Around With Haircuts

By Donald Nelson, Blaine, Minnesota

The war had ended in Europe, but my outfit was snow-bound high in the Bavarian Alps in the little town of Ober-ammergau. We heard the news on the radio, but couldn't even go to town to celebrate.

When the snow finally melted, the first sergeant noticed a few of us were badly in need of haircuts. So he sent the company clerk into town to bring back a barber. The clerk didn't speak any German.

He returned with a protesting man who seemed a bit upset by all this. We handed him a pair of scissors and a hair clipper. He protested some more, then finally shrugged and gave all of us haircuts.

He cut each of our hair in the same style—it resembled an Iroquois headdress. We found out why later on when we got to town. The man wasn't a barber...our company clerk had found him working in a stable cutting horses' manes and tails!

There's a Right Way
And a Wrong Way

By Ron Sylvia, Santa Clara, California

During my younger brother's graduation from Coast Guard recruit training in the 1960s, we relatives were shown a film of what the trainees had learned, including the right and wrong ways to leave a sinking ship.

One of the wrong ways showed a sailor leaping from the bridge of a large cutter. His legs were spread, his arms were flailing and his mouth was wide open.

With horror, I recognized myself! When I was in the Coast Guard several years earlier, someone had snapped shots of a bunch of us fools leaping from lofty points of a weather cutter at sea during swim call. What an example I had set!

★

Chivalry Backfired
For 'Man Who Walked Alone'

By Dave McReynolds, Amarillo, Texas

We were just a mile south of the front lines on a cold winter day in Korea. I was sergeant of the guard and had just posted a newly arrived Marine PFC at the main gate guard shack.

The cup of hot coffee felt good in my hand, and I was anticipating how it would feel going down when the jangle of the phone interrupted me. It was the main gate.

"Sarge, come quick—something terrible has happened."

I yelled for the corporal of the guard and grabbed a relief PFC. We jumped into the jeep and flew to the main gate.

When we got there, a Korean "mama-san" was standing outside the guard shack crying. She was holding a large "honey pot" used to haul "organic fertilizer" to the fields.

Nothing else seemed amiss—no enemy, no second lieutenants, no nothing. I threw open the shack door and walked in...then quickly stumbled back out. It smelled like an open sewer.

The short of a long story revealed that the guard had seen the woman carrying a huge container on her head. She had stepped off the road to avoid a truck and ended up stuck with a foot on each side of the ditch.

The PFC had gone over to help. He didn't know the contents of the container and had no idea that it weighed close to 100 pounds. When he grabbed the pot, it tipped and the contents spilled all over him!

I posted the relief guard at the shack and made the poor stinking PFC walk back because I didn't want him smelling up the jeep.

The story doesn't end there. Because we were so close to the front line, a shower was something we only dreamed about.

It was 2 days before we could get that poor Marine back to division HQ and a shower. In the meantime, his tent mates made him sleep outside.

From then on, he was known throughout the outfit as "the man who walked alone".

★

These Allotment Requests Made News in Fresno

By R. Shelton Croom, Norfolk, Virginia

The Camp Dodge induction center received lots of mail from military dependents making application for allotments. A few of the more unusual notes were printed in the March 17, 1943 issue of *The Beam,* camp newspaper for Air Force Basic Training Center No. 8 in Fresno, California.

"In accordance with your instruction, I have given birth to twins in the enclosed envelope."

"Please send me my elopement as I have a 4 months old baby and he is my only support."

"I have had no clothing for one year and have been regular-

ly visited by the clergy."

"This is my eighth child and what are you going to do about it?"

★

He Was History's Only 'Draft-Dodging POW'

By Grant Wells, Vacaville, California

One day in December 1941, authorities knocked on my wife's apartment door. They were looking for me because:
1. I had failed to register for the draft.
2. I had failed to appear for induction into the armed forces.
3. I was considered a possible draft dodger.

My wife wasn't pleased. She'd just received word that Guam was under attack by the Japanese. I was at that time a mechanic on Guam, working for Pan American Airways, and had been there since July of 1941. Somehow the draft board had not received word.

After spending 3 years in Japanese prison camps on Guam and then in Japan, I was liberated by U.S. occupation forces and went back to work for Pan Am.

I think I was the first "draft-dodging POW" in history.

★

London Blitz Didn't Stop Die-Hard Golfers

Golf was not for the fainthearted at the Richmond Golf Club near London during World War II. These were some of the wartime rules:

1. Players are asked to collect bomb and shrapnel splinters to save causing damage to the mowers.

2. In competition, during gunfire or while bombs are falling, players may take shelter without penalty or ceasing play.

3. A ball moved by enemy action may be replaced. Lost or destroyed balls may be dropped not nearer the hole without penalty.

4. A player whose stroke is affected by the simultaneous explosion of a bomb may play another ball. Penalty one stroke.

5. The positions of known delayed-action bombs are marked by red flags at a reasonable, but not guaranteed, safe distance.

★

Alarming Distraction Gave Pilot a Bellyful

By Jake Hood, Gautier, Mississippi

Having just graduated from training in airplanes with fixed landing gear, my class of student pilots was learning to fly AT-6 trainers with retractable landing gear. We had to remember to put the wheels up or down.

To make sure we remembered, a very loud warning horn was installed directly behind the pilot's head. It went off if the gear wasn't down when you throttled back for a landing.

Our instructor emphasized this point with a story about a student who was in final approach to land. His throttle was fully retarded but the wheels were still up.

In spite of the tower's repeated radio instructions to put the wheels down, he continued his approach and belly-landed the plane, causing severe damage.

On the carpet in front of a group of angry officers, the pilot was asked why he hadn't put the wheels down as the tower instructed.

His reply?

"I couldn't understand what they were saying because a loud horn was blowing behind my head."

I Faked My Way
To a Commendation

By George Denardo, Camarillo, California

Back in 1958 I was a naive first lieutenant in the U.S. Air Force, flying as a "backseater" in the F-94C Starfire, an all-weather interceptor. I was thoroughly enjoying myself—until I was reassigned to a new position...make that, *several* positions.

A new squadron was being formed at Griffiss Air Force Base in upstate New York, and I suddenly found myself being made administrative officer, postal service officer, personnel officer and security officer.

It didn't matter that I had absolutely no training in any of those areas. I was second in command and that was that.

I quickly learned my duties. I *had* to—as security officer I was responsible for the special weapons area ("special" in this case meant "nuclear"). Another thing I quickly found out, however, was that the people at Group Headquarters wouldn't issue me a badge to get into the area I was in charge of!

So I went to see the group administrative officer.

"I'm not the smartest guy in the world," I told Captain Small, "but it makes sense to me that I have access—I'm listed on the orders as officer in charge."

"You won't have to go there," Small snapped back. "I'll do the going. That's final."

Well, it wasn't quite final. Two months later the division tactical evaluation team showed up for an unannounced inspection. This put everyone in a panic.

The inspection team chief, Colonel Waters, told my superiors he wanted the officer in charge to conduct the tour. That meant *me*. A shaken Captain Small called with the news.

"What?" I shouted into the phone. "I've never been to the area and don't even have a badge to get in!"

"Don't worry," Small reassured me. "I've called ahead and ordered the sergeant in charge to let you in."

"Then what am I supposed to do?" I asked. "I don't know anything about what goes on there."

"Fake it," Small said.

Fake it? I'd be showing the colonel some of the most important aspects of our air defense and I was going to fake it?

But there I was at 1230 hours at Base Operations to meet Master Sergeant Beamer, head of the flight line, who'd accompany me on the tour.

"Have you been there before, sergeant?" I asked hopefully.

"Many times, sir," he shot back confidently.

"Good!" I said. "You go in the lead vehicle, but don't drive

DREAMS OF GENIE. George Denardo's memories of his service days include the Northrop F-89J Scorpion. This plane carried the nuclear weapons George was in charge of. Two of those "Genie" rockets could be mounted under each wing of this plane.

fast. If I lose you, I've had it."

"Don't worry, sir," Beamer said.

Easy for *him* to say! I was going to conduct this tour and I didn't even know where the special weapons area was, much less what happened there.

The colonel's team arrived and off we drove to the special

weapons area. When we got there, the colonel asked me what the entry procedure was. I hadn't the slightest idea.

"Sergeant, please tell the colonel what the entry procedure is," I ordered. Of course, Beamer knew.

We got past the gate all right because the men had been told to allow me to enter without a challenge. But just to make it look official, I quickly flashed my *credit card* at the sentry.

The tour was moving along smoothly. When we reached the maintenance department of the weapons area, the sergeant in charge took over and conducted the tour. I was off the hook again.

I actually began enjoying the tour. I'd never seen nuclear weapons before and now here I was, with a chance for an up-close look at the "Genie" rockets I was responsible for.

Colonel Waters wanted to see the outer perimeter security, so we walked outside to the fence.

The colonel asked a few questions that, by a miracle, I could answer because I'd heard our commander discuss them at recent meetings.

Then the colonel hit me with a bombshell. "How many feet down are the chain link fences anchored?" he asked.

I glanced at Beamer for help, but the look in his eyes told me he wasn't familiar with this part of the security system.

I had to say something, so I shot back (with just about as much conviction as I could muster), "Sir, they are anchored at the 2-foot level."

"No, that's wrong," the colonel said. "According to regulations they should be anchored at exactly 2 feet, 3 inches. Make note of that and have it corrected before the next inspection."

"We will correct it, sir," I assured him.

When we returned to Base Operations, the colonel left his vehicle and walked toward me. I thought I'd had it.

"Lieutenant," he said, "I've conducted a great many of these inspections and I want to say this is the best one I've ever experienced. You and your men are to be commended. I will convey these thoughts to your commander."

Knowing when to leave well enough alone, I saluted and said, "Thank you, sir. I appreciate your comments."

Later, I thanked Sergeant Beamer for bailing me out...and then made sure my credit card was back in my billfold—in case I had to conduct another inspection tour.

Officer Needed to Have His Head Examined

By Donald Eggum, Waukesha, Wisconsin

One day, while acting as field duty officer at Fort Lee, Virginia, I got an urgent call from the commanding general. He had spotted an officer entering the main gate wearing a mixed uniform, needing a haircut and, worst of all, refusing to stop for the MP on duty. I was ordered in no uncertain terms to find that officer and get him to the post psychiatrist.

I found the officer. He *was* the post psychiatrist!

★

They Were in Hot Water When They Took This Bath

By Roger Markley, Nashville, Indiana

There were so many guys at our air base in England that there was never enough hot water for bathing. When we were restricted to the base for a mission, there just was no way to take a hot bath...until a buddy of mine found a solution.

He'd discovered a huge iron kettle in a shed. It was big enough for a man to sit inside, which is just what we did after dragging it outdoors, filling it with water and building a fire underneath. We even put boards on the bottom so we could sit down and not get burned on the hot metal.

But when we stood up, our feet would hit the metal and we'd have to jump out in a hurry...much to the amusement of a group of WACs who we heard giggling on a nearby hill as they watched us with binoculars!

"RHIP". Rank has its privilege, as Lieutenant Wallace Beardsell of Pacific Palisades, California proved when he got sprayed down by an enlisted man in North Africa in November 1942.

79

I Saw Pink Elephants in Vietnam

By Russell Hodges, Lompoc, California

I t was a beautiful day for flying, and I'd have been as happy as a pig in mud if it weren't for the fact that I could've been shot down at any minute.

The beautiful day was in Vietnam in 1966, where I was a forward air controller. My job was to fly over the Ho Chi Minh Trail and look for North Vietnamese trucks.

On this particular morning I took off as usual from the Special Forces airstrip at Kham Duc. I scanned the jungle for any signs of enemy activity in our area. If anything was brewing, I was to radio our camp commander.

Well, if I had radioed back the first thing I saw, my commander would have thought *I* was brewing something.

There in a small clearing, barely a mile from camp, were three elephants browsing just as casually as you please. Believe it or not, those elephants were bright pink!

I later learned from a Vietnamese counterpart that the pink elephants I'd seen were indeed real. When elephants wade or swim across streams in that region, leeches attach themselves to the animals' hide.

The elephants then roll in the dirt to get rid of the leeches. In our area there was a lot of red clay, and that stuff, when caked over the elephants' gray skin, creates a dusty rose coloring.

As it turned out, pink elephants weren't all I saw that day. Those son-of-a-guns on the Trail *did* shoot at me!

★

French Villagers Welcomed This 'Early Announcement'

By David Draves, Durham, New Hampshire

W e were tramping single file down a narrow dirt street in a small French village back in 1944. All the villagers

were hiding behind closed doors, occasionally peeking furtively from behind shuttered windows.

Our lieutenant sensed the need for more firepower at the head
of the column, so he sent the call back down the line for Feeny, our automatic rifleman, to hustle up front.

Down the line the call was loudly relayed: "Feeny! Feeny!
Feeny!"

Suddenly the doors and windows began swinging open and
beaming faces appeared everywhere. Turns out the French inhabitants thought we were chanting *Finis! Finis!*—announcing
at long last, the end of the war.

'You've Got How Many Passengers?'

By Robert Robeson, Lincoln, Nebraska

This classic "dust-off" yarn was spun during one of our helicopter rescue operations in Vietnam.

The incident I recall involves an outstanding aviator, Captain Richard Fox. He was a member of the 236th Medical Detachment (Helicopter Ambulance) situated on the edge of Da Nang Harbor at Red Beach in South Vietnam.

The unit has a long and distinguished history of dust-off duty. (Dust-off is a tactical call sign, originated because helicopters landing in dry areas tended to "dust off" the ground.)

Rich broke me in as operations officer when I first arrived. He taught me a great deal about flying, friendship, making split-

second decisions that would keep you alive…and humor, which can be an essential ingredient in tense situations.

One day, Rich was flying out of our field site to Landing Zone Baldy, about 25 miles south of Da Nang. He'd already been flying continuously for many hours in and out of insecure pickup sites.

A call came over his radio asking to evacuate a number of patients from Hiep Duc, a large Vietnamese village to the southwest. We called the location "Ulcer Alley" because it was one of the North Vietnamese army's infiltration routes.

We'd lost more aircraft over this dangerous stretch of real estate than anywhere else in our 5,000-square-mile area of operation.

But Rich did his duty. As often happened, however, there were more patients on the ground than the radio message claimed.

When Rich finished his tactical approach he saw what appeared to be an entire village waiting to be evacuated—and in typical Vietnamese fashion, they brought everything they could carry!

There was no time to haggle. Because of the insecurity of the area, the entire group was quickly loaded in the H-model Huey by Rich's medic and crew chief.

After a quick hover-check to make sure he had enough power for takeoff with that heavy load, Rich safely exited the landing zone.

The chopper was designed to carry 13 passengers plus the four-man crew. An in-flight head count, however, totaled 28 patients plus some extra "passengers"—four pigs and three chickens!

Our dust-off helicopters arrived at aid stations all over the country bearing loads of patients (and often their friends) with many devastating wounds or diseases. Whenever we could, we used humor to ease the tension.

Rich was ready to call his load in to the aid

HUMOR HELPS. Captain Richard Fox (left) and author (second from right) kept the gags coming to ease tense situations in Vietnam. Joining in were Lieutenant Rob Reidenbaugh (right) and CW2 Burlin Letcher at a unit awards ceremony in 1970.

station. Here is the one radio conversation I'll never forget:

"Charger [aid station call sign] Dust-Off, this is Dust-Off 6-0-7," Rich broadcast. "I'm about 15 minutes out. Request you have 10 open litters standing by on the pad. I have 10 Vietnamese litter, 18 Vietnamese ambulatory, plus four pigs and three chickens. How copy?"

"6-0-7, this is Charger. Would you say your last again? Over."

"Roger, Charger. I have 10 Vietnamese litter, 18 Vietnamese ambulatory, four pigs and three chickens. Over."

"Did you say four pigs and three chickens?"

"That's affirmative."

There was a long pause and then an ex-

CHOPPERS! A medical evacuation helicopter preparing to land with a load of wounded at LZ Hawk Hill, 36 miles south of Da Nang, in 1970.

asperated voice came back with the immortal words, "All right 6-0-7, what's wrong with the pigs and chickens?"

This story was shared over and over again with rookies and veterans alike—a story that could only have happened in combat, where a soldier fights off boredom and tragedy with humor.

In my opinion, it's a perfect example of how an enlisted radio operator and an experienced pilot could take a tough situation in stride and inject a small amount of humor to lighten their day.

Students Got a Kick Out Of Early 'Microwave Oven'

By Walter Raue, Merrillville, Indiana

I was a radar maintenance instructor for the Navy at Pearl Harbor during World War II...and one of the first persons to enjoy a hot meal "from the microwave".

We rigged up a radar antenna in the classroom so our students could gain some hands-on repair experience. The high-frequency waves the equipment generated were valuable for education—and recreation.

For instance, we always enjoyed the look of amazement on a visitor's face when we'd light up a fluorescent tube from the radiation, even as we stood in another room.

We instructed new students not to poke around in certain parts of the radar unit, but some of the more curious among them invariably did. Every now and then one would get a kick from the current and be knocked to the floor.

We began marking the spots where the students landed. When a visiting officer asked about the marks, we'd explain, with straight faces, that the marks helped us measure the voltage.

In the evenings we'd spear hot dogs with sticks and hold them near the parabolic reflector. Sandwiches and other snacks were held in place by squeezing them between two wooden rulers. We didn't know it then, but this was the beginning of microwave cooking.

★

'It's Regulations, Mister!'

By James Bently, Nampa, Idaho

All I needed were six rifle cleaning rods. As an assistant supply sergeant at Camp Drake, Japan during the Korean War, I thought I knew how to get them. But I found out you're never too old to learn about Army regulations.

I called the warehouse and was told the rods were in stock. I filled out the appropriate forms, in duplicate, borrowed a bicycle and pedaled the mile to Supply. But a sergeant told me I needed two more copies in case the rods had to be back-ordered.

I told the sergeant I'd checked and the rods were in stock. "Regulations say you must have four copies," he said.

So I pedaled the mile back to my office, made two more copies, rode back to Supply and handed the four copies to the sergeant. He stamped two of them "Approved" and threw the other two in the wastebasket.

I then pedaled to the warehouse and picked up the rods.

★

Just Mark His Package 'For General Delivery'

By Frank Havens, Rocky Hill, Connecticut

I was fresh out of OCS and didn't think I was ready for troop duty, so I asked to be assigned to a general staff. I was transferred to Fort Bragg, North Carolina. When I was ready to move on, the general there assigned me to one of his units at Fort Jackson, South Carolina.

I left, but forgot to first pick up my laundry. At my new post, a group of us was leaving the junior officers' club when the general pulled up in his command car and said, "Oh, Havens, I brought your laundry," then had his driver get it out of the trunk.

I had some wide-eyed buddies there for a while, wondering about a general delivering laundry to a shavetail.

★

If the Red Menace Came, These Troops Were Ready

By Delbert Lord, Shreveport, Louisiana

Things were so boring at our outpost in Iceland in January 1943, that we actually looked forward to attending the training film we were ordered to see one day.

The notice on the bulletin board said the film was *The Red Army*, and our CO decided it was so important, he gave us a lengthy discourse on the U.S.S.R.'s "Red Army" and the danger of communism. At that time, there were very few of us who knew what communism was.

When the CO had finished with his evaluation of the world situation, we settled back and watched 45 minutes of film about the proliferation and aggression of... *The Red Army of Ants*.

★

This 'Boot' Got the Message Via Telephone Pole

By Victor Root, Scottsdale, Arizona

My first day at boot camp at Great Lakes Naval Training Center in September 1942 was eventful, beginning with the issuance of my new Navy "blues". The supply clerk took one look at me (see photo) and told me to get over to the tailor building.

On the way, I encountered a chief petty officer. I said, "Hello", and kept walking. But I did an about-face when the chief stopped and called me over.

With his thumbs in his armpits, the chief said, "Don't you see this uniform?"

"Don't feel bad," I replied. "Mine doesn't fit good either."

I spent the next 24 hours (2 on and 2 off) walking around a block and saluting every telephone pole...with the chief walking right alongside me!

TREADING WATER? "Boot" Victor Root was "swimming" in his oversized uniform in September 1942.

Our SHELLter Hit Home

By Jim Warrender, Quimby, Iowa

It was fall of 1951 in Korea. As if facing the enemy wasn't enough, the guys in my outfit also faced the prospect of spending the coming winter in pup tents.

So, when we got a little downtime, we built ourselves a house—but not just an ordinary house, as you can see in the photos (at right).

The Second Infantry Division had just finished 3 months of savage fighting in what became known as the "Battle for the Hills". They'd been taken off the line for a breather, and that left our group of forward observers and wire men (who laid communications wire between the FOs and the gun batteries) with nothing to do.

Before long, someone discovered that the shipping containers for 105mm howitzer shells could be taken apart and fitted together to form logs. We pitched in and started work on a log cabin immediately.

With the material we had on hand, we were able to build 4-foot walls with a ridge almost 12 feet high. The ridgepole was a freshly cut tree, and the rafters were scavenged from the remains of a house.

The roof presented the biggest problem. Made of boards from ammunition boxes, it wouldn't shed water. We puzzled over this until someone suggested covering the roof with our tents—that worked like a charm!

We still had a standing problem, literally. With the wall only 4 feet high and most of us closer to 6 feet tall, too much time in the cabin would turn us unto a bunch of hunchbacks.

Solution? Simple—if you can't raise the ceiling, lower the floor! We dug down about 2 feet. Then we built seven double bunks along the walls.

We managed to scrounge up an oil stove for heat, but lacked lights...until a nearby outfit of engineers left a small gas generator very close to the road. It was their loss and our lights!

The cabin kept us warm and comfortable. We even gave it a name, as seen on the sign in the photos: "Old Soldiers" Home.

88

The "motto" we painted at the bottom is a takeoff on the famous quote from General MacArthur.

Not only did our cabin provide shelter, but building it helped take our minds off the war, at least temporarily.

I spent less than 2 months in the cabin before transferring to Japan, but I have many good memories of my cozy Korean

OLD KOREAN HOME. Author (standing far left) and his buddies in C Battery enjoyed the comforts of this log cabin in 1951, even after one comrade decided to "bomb" a rat with a hand grenade.

home...and one noisy incident of rodent removal.

One night, 13 of us had fallen asleep, but one man named Cunningham was reading. He heard rustling on the floor and spotted some rats.

Wanting to scare them away, he grabbed a hand grenade and screwed out the primer (the handle, the pin and the detonator charge that's normally inside the body of the grenade).

Cunningham pulled the pin and tossed the tiny bomb at the rats, not realizing that the detonator charge would be at least as loud as the report from a 12-gauge shotgun.

The blast pumped the 13 of us out of bed, every man certain the cabin had taken a direct hit. It was pure havoc as we scrambled to get out the single 4-foot door at the same time!

When we finally realized what had happened, we returned to the cabin for some good laughs before going back to sleep. Cunningham, however, was banished for the night to some cooler sleeping quarters on the front seat of a truck!

Christmas 1951
Kumwha N. Korea

Season's greetings

Jim Warrender

★

The Night Pest Control
Got Out of Control

By Herb Schmidt, West Union, South Carolina

We weren't the only occupants of our barracks in Laredo, Texas in 1952. Ants were all over the place, more than happy to take care of the crumbs from our "care" packages from home.

But one GI in our group couldn't get along with the insistent insects. He sprayed his bunk and area every night with a smelly insecticide.

He kept it up in spite of our repeated requests to cease. So one night, when he was out, we replaced the foul fumigant in his sprayer with Coca-Cola.

Later that night, the usual spraying routine took place. Sometime after lights out, we were wakened by a howl—as our fellow airman awoke to find himself a human anthill!

★

Guard Duty Was a Howling Success

By Eugene Bovee, Lawrence, Kansas

In the army, there's only one rank lower than private, and that's the officer candidate. At least that's what our small, 100-man group at Fort Washington, Maryland was told early in 1943.

"Men," said the commanding colonel, "there's nothing lower than the officer candidate. Yours is a short company, but you will do the duties of a regular 200-man company."

Did we ever! We pulled KP, guard duty and fire guard (stoking the barracks stoves on winter nights). We also policed the company area daily, scrubbed the barracks and ourselves for weekly inspections, did calisthenics, drilled, paraded, attended class and tackled field problems during our 5 a.m. to 10 p.m., Monday-through-Friday schedule.

It was "durance vile" for 13 weeks. But humor helped us survive.

I recall one cold, rainy March night when my buddy Frank and I pulled guard duty after serving the previous night as fire guards.

"What a night to walk the asphalt!" Frank grumbled. I echoed his sentiments in unprintable terms.

"Where's your post?" he asked.

"Around the junior officers' barracks," I replied.

"Ain't that next to the farmer's fence where those big dogs raise a racket?" Frank queried.

"Yep," I confirmed. "Why?"

"'Cause we can have a little fun keepin' them officers awake," said Frank with a grin. "I'll yodel like a coyote, and you answer. That'll set those dogs off and keep those lieutenants from gettin' much sleep until we go off guard duty at midnight."

"What if they come out to investigate?" I asked.

"In *this* downpour?" Frank laughed.

We were both already dead tired and pleased with the prospect of keeping the "shavetails" up with us. On my third trip around the barracks, Frank let go with a coyote wail and I answered with a full-out howl.

All four dogs went crazy! They barked and

COYOTE CAPER helped author (above in Normandy in 1944) get through guard duty.

dashed along the fence, and one answered the "coyote" with a deep moan of his own, ascending to a soprano howl.

Lights snapped on. A window opened and an angry voice bellowed, "What's going on out there, soldier?"

"Don't know, sir," I replied. "Some wild animal seems to have stirred up the dogs."

Slam! Down went the window.

Success so far. I smiled as I plodded through the rain.

About 11:15 p.m., Frank yipped again. I wailed an answer, and canine pandemonium again reigned along the fence.

More lights went on. More windows opened. More roars of "Shut up those dogs!"

At quarter to midnight, we gave it one more howl for good measure, with the same satisfying results. This time the headlights of a Jeep indicated that a complaint had been phoned to the duty officer.

"Halt and identify yourself!" I called as the Jeep approached.

"Duty officer," was the reply. "What's going on here?"

I snapped to attention and saluted. "Some animal in the woods, sir," I said. "It's keeping the dogs stirred up."

Just then Frank yipped and howled again from his post. The dogs erupted in noisy clamor, and the "songbird" among them once more lifted his own aria to the rainy sky.

"Well, whatever's going on, stop it!" snapped the duty officer.

"Yes, sir, if I can," I replied as the driver shifted gears and drove off.

Ten minutes later, Frank and I were relieved by the next two guards. We marched back to our barracks and tumbled into our cots to sleep happily for 4 hours until our next shift...with dreams undisturbed by "coyotes".

Archive Photos

★

This Young Lieutenant 'Led the Charge'

By Tom Curl, Brookfield, Wisconsin

My dad told me this story about the days when he served as a bomber mechanic in the Army Air Corps at Attleborough, England during World War II.

He was tending bar in the officers' club one evening when a serving tray came back with a broken wine glass on it. Dad emptied the pieces into the trash can.

A young lieutenant walked up. He was taking his responsibilities in club management very seriously.

"Sergeant, you'll have to pay for that broken glass," the rather self-important young officer announced.

"Sir, the glass was broken when it came back to me," Dad replied.

"That doesn't matter. You are responsible for it and you'll have to pay for it," the lieutenant insisted.

About that time, a bomber pilot who was not much older than

Dad or the lieutenant walked up to inquire about the problem.

"Captain, this man will have to pay for a broken wine glass," the lieutenent said.

"I told you I didn't break it," Dad replied.

"How much do wine glasses cost?" the bomber pilot asked.

"They're 3¢ each," the young officer answered.

The pilot thought for a few seconds. Then, with a sly grin, he reached for his wallet.

"Gimme $5 worth," he said.

Dad counted out 166 wine glasses. The pilot proceeded to throw them one at a time against the big stone fireplace.

When the captain had finished, Dad and another enlisted man cleaned up the mess with a broom and coal shovel...and the lieutenant never did come back to ask Dad for his 3¢.

★

Viet Officer in a Stew When Troops Opened Up

By Rod Hinsch, Beech Grove, Indiana

After a 5-day intelligence patrol, our team was tired and hungry for something even remotely resembling a hot meal.

The Vietnamese accompanying our team were on perimeter guard and we felt the area we were in was relatively safe, so we decided to make a fire to heat our C rations.

Our dreams of enjoying hot food abruptly changed to thoughts of self-preservation when the Vietnamese officer, Lieutenant Van, reached over to check his food and an explosion ripped through the fire pit.

The lieutenant screamed as he jerked back holding his face.

Seeing their commander hit, his men opened fire with everything they had. Machine gunners raked the surrounding jungle while a man crawled forward with a sack of grenades, hurling them at the unseen enemy.

Not until Lieutenant Van jumped up and ran around the camp shouting "Cease fire!" did things calm down. He then ordered his men to attention and chewed them out royally for firing indiscriminately and without orders.

All of this was done while Lieutenant Van's face was still covered with...the remains of his exploded can of C ration stew!

CANNED LAUGHTER. A warm meal really got hot for Rod Hinsch (right) and his campfire comrades.

★

My Colonel Finally Outshined Me

By David Willcox, Glen Ridge, New Jersey

Sometimes, even when there's a war on, there's nothing much to do in the Army but shine your boots.

That's the way it was in Korea in the early spring of 1953 when I, a green second lieutenant just off the boat, was on my way up to the line on a troop train.

I struck up an acquaintance with Lieutenant Colonel Bev Reed, and we started a friendly competition to see who could get the best "spit shine" on his boots. Little did I know then how serious Colonel Reed would take this competition.

I was pretty cocky, having just completed the infantry officers' candidate school. Colonel Reed, a product of the prestigious Military College of South Carolina—The Citadel—would later become my battalion commander.

I got up to the line and by late spring took charge of a platoon. In my own eyes I was by then a seasoned veteran. The rains

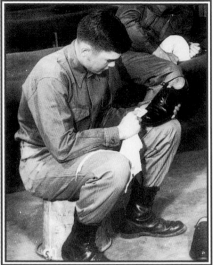

TAKING A SHINE to military life meant getting used to polishing those boots.

were constant that time of year, and so were skirmishes with the enemy, who always got active between 10 p.m. and 4 a.m. As a result, we got very little sleep.

Being the platoon leader, I had to resupply our unit and prepare for the next night before I could catch a few Z's. That was usually not until 7 in the morning.

We lived in trenches full of rainwater and mud. On one particular morning, I was finally able to hit the cot about 7 a.m. I hadn't shaved in days, and my boots were thick with mud. I quickly fell asleep in spite of my wet clothes.

Not 2 hours later, I was awakened from a sound sleep when my sergeant entered the bunker and announced, "The colonel is in the trenches and he wants you to report."

Now what? I groped for my muddy boots, pulled them on and just wrapped the laces around them rather than bothering to do it right.

I stumbled to the blanket that served as a door and pulled it aside to witness one of the most astonishing sights of my life.

There standing on top of the soupy mud was Colonel Reed! He was wearing spit-shined boots, sharply creased trousers ...and the biggest smile I ever saw!

My mouth just hung open, and my troops, who'd gathered around to watch, had a good laugh.

It turns out that the colonel had come up to our position in one set of clothes, then changed into the clean, freshly pressed clothes and shined boots in the bunker next to mine.

Then he'd had some of my men carry him to my front door and place him on sandbags that had been covered by a thin layer of mud.

It was the greatest morale booster we'd ever had. And, needless to say, Colonel Reed was proclaimed the winner of our boot shining competition!

Farewell Message From a Pal

By N.B. Kell, North Fort Myers, Florida

Sailing out of Tokyo Bay after World Ward II had ended, I looked back from the deck of our aircraft carrier as we turned to head toward the Pacific.

Along the shore were miles and miles of bombed-out buildings. But there was one that I'll never forget.

At the very top, in white letters 10 feet high, was painted a familiar message—KILROY WAS HERE.

★

Privy Poets Dueled in Rhyme

By Philip Beyers, Redford, Michigan

Finding a blank wall in the latrine, a GI couldn't resist scribbling a note:
Alas, Alack, I jump with joy,
I was here before Kilroy.
The next day he returned, and scrawled below his note was:
Sorry to spoil your little joke,
I was here, but my pencil broke.
KILROY.

★

Third Time's a Charm...I Hope!

By Gene Bilderback, Bloomington, California

We were high over Randolph Field, Texas, the "West Point of the Air", when I shook the stick and told my student pilot to come out from under the "hood".

It was 1944, and I was giving a lesson in instrument flying. The student wore a special visor that blocked his view of everything except the instruments. It could be pretty intense, so the student stayed under the hood for only about 15 minutes at a time.

We were in a BT-14, with me in the front seat and my student in the back seat. After I'd taken over the controls, I spotted another airplane below us and decided a 10-minute mock dogfight would be just the thing to relax my student.

I made a screaming dive and "attacked" the other plane, passing within a few feet of it. Usually fellow instructors were happy to engage in a make-believe battle...but this time, the dummy paid no attention.

I made another pass. No response. Finally I gave up in disgust and resumed the lesson.

When I landed later, my flight commander, Captain Paul Todd, was there to meet me. Something was up—exalted people of the high rank of captain did not routinely meet lowly second lieutenants at their airplanes. Had he come to tell me of my transfer to fighters? Not quite.

"Report to the stage commander's office on the double!" Captain Todd said tersely.

The stage commander, Major Disosway, was an aloof, almost mythical figure with a reputation sufficient to strike pure terror into the heart of a second lieutenant.

As I cooled my heels in his imposing outer office, I wondered what I'd done wrong...and envisioned myself being reprimanded and stripped of rank while standing at rigid attention.

With that thought, I was barely able to stand and walk the few steps into the major's inner sanctum. But he simply glared at me for a few seconds and growled something about never again trying to start a dogfight with him! I stuttered a "Yes, sir!" and he dismissed me.

Twenty years passed before our paths crossed again. I was then a colonel, and Disosway was a four-star general, commander of the Tactical Air Command. We were both attending a formal cocktail party at TAC headquarters.

We were dressed in white dinner jackets with epaulets, cummerbunds and dangling medals. I approached the general and asked him whether he remembered the dogfight incident.

"No," he laughed. "But obviously I intended for *you* to remember it!"

I laughed, too—and spilled bright-red shrimp sauce down the gleaming white satin lapel of my jacket! The general shook his head in disgust and turned away. I left the party in disgrace.

As fate would have it, our paths crossed again years later. Just plain Gabe Disosway was retired from the military and an executive vice president at LTV, a defense contractor. He had an office in the LTV Tower in downtown Dallas, where I happened to be one day.

I spoke with Gabe for a few minutes in the hall, then turned briskly to leave. That's when I smacked smartly into his private secretary, stretching her out on the carpet!

I haven't run into Gabe since. But next time I see him, I'll do what I should have done over 50 years ago—turn and fly away in the opposite direction!

★

Was This an Early Sighting of Bigfoot?

By Walter Ungerer, New Castle, Delaware

My fiance came to visit me on a Good Friday back in the '40s while I was stationed at Aberdeen, Maryland. The USO was scheduled to put on a show for us in which some of the performers dressed as animals.

When the cast went on a bus tour of the proving grounds, my girlfriend, who'd already taken the tour, stayed back to color Easter eggs. But she ended up getting "colored" herself when she encountered a skunk.

She took off her clothes and tried to get the smell off with a bath in the Bush River. I was not allowed into the guest house to get her a change of clothes, so I looked through the costumes of the USO troupe.

All I could find was a monkey suit, so she put it on. To this day, people who were there still tell the story of a strange, hairy and really bad smelling creature that came running out of the river on Good Friday!

This NCO 'Got to the Bottom of It'

By Herman Hoffman, Michigan Center, Michigan

During the Battle of the Bulge, I was part of a machine gun crew at an outpost in Luxembourg.

We would stand watch in our foxhole through the night, and our relief would come just before daybreak.

Since I was taller than average, my crew and I had dug the hole deeper so I wouldn't have to constantly stoop over. This caused a little problem one morning when our relief showed up.

Their NCO was a short fellow, and when we crawled out, he jumped in.

"Who stole the bottom of the hole?" he angrily yelled. "I thought I was airborne!"

He and his men worked the better part of a day putting the dirt back in so he could see out.

★

He Worried His Way To a Purple Heart

By Eugene Bovee, Lawrence, Kansas

Most soldiers I knew during World War II concealed their anxieties by using humor or griping about officers—Sheldon was the exception. He worried continually in a high-pitched nasal whine.

Sheldon was a well-educated big-city kid who accepted a commission in Military Intelligence. One requirement was 12 weeks of basic training. Sheldon made it, but he worried for 3 months straight.

He worried about his grades. He got straight A's.

He worried about the food. He ate heartily and never came down with the gastric afflictions others did.

He worried about blisters from hikes. He developed none.

He worried he wouldn't pass the physical tests requiring umpteen push-ups. He did.

He worried his rifle might backfire. He won a marksman medal.

In short, Sheldon worried about almost everything and almost

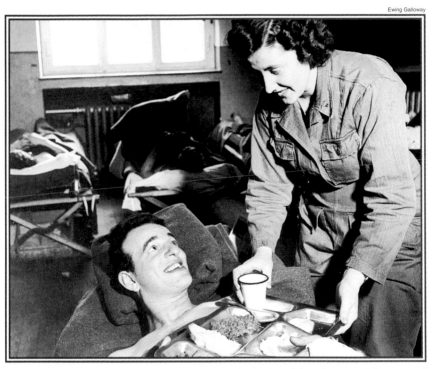

Ewing Galloway

NO WORRIES. Even when he was in the hospital, like the soldier above, Sheldon worried someone would find out why he was there and how he earned his Purple Heart.

nothing disagreeable happened. Still, most of his sentences began with the words, "What if...?"

Sheldon breezed through training, tanned, fit and in excellent health. Then our unit was shipped to London, where he really did have something to worry about—the V-1 "buzz bombs" and V-2 rockets!

Our unit worked in a building that was already badly bomb-shaken. Among the amenities was a rest room on the top floor. Its toilet was an ancient contraption. You flushed it by pulling a chain attached to a lever on a tank 6 feet above the stool. The tank and the stool were connected by a long brass pipe.

London's water mains were in constant need of repair because of the bombing, so water pressure was minimal. It was up to the one who pulled the chain to fill the elevated tank with water. This was done with a canteen as you stood on the rim of the bowl.

That's just what Sheldon was doing when a V-2 hit about 200 yards from the building. He howled as his left foot slipped into the bowl, twisting his knee.

Moaning and worrying, Sheldon was taken to the hospital. There his worries began anew, as we came to learn a few weeks later.

The rest of our unit shipped out to Normandy while Sheldon remained in the hospital. We later received a letter from him saying he'd arrived at the hospital at the same time as the wounded paratroopers from the D-Day drops. Sheldon was in the same ward and everybody thought he'd been injured in the Normandy parachute drops, too.

"I've been awarded the Purple Heart," Sheldon wrote. "And I couldn't bring myself to tell the other guys I wrenched my knee in the john!"

Sheldon's note ended with one final worry. He knew when the day came for him to be discharged from the hospital, he would be afraid to put on his uniform. When those paratroopers got a look at his shoulder patch, they might think he was a counter-intelligence spy!

★

Florida Heat Made Starch Unnecessary

By Addis Morgan, Woodbury, Connecticut

Shipping out of Fort Devens, Massachusetts to Miami Beach for Air Corps training during one of the coldest winters on record seemed like heaven to us.

We soon discovered that the heat and humidity of south Florida could cause some discomfort, too. When the perspiration on our shirts and socks dried, the clothes turned into board-like slabs.

Among the members of our "flight", the Air Corps equivalent of a platoon, was a recruit who wasn't inclined to move very fast under the best of circumstances. He found dashing out for reveille particularly distasteful.

One morning, when our friend made a belated appearance in the formation, the sergeant screamed, "What's your excuse?" and gave him a withering stare.

"Well, sergeant," the recruit drawled, "when the whistle blew and I jumped outta my upper bunk, I landed on one of my socks...and *bent* it." Even the crusty sergeant had to laugh.

★

This Bear's Roar Came in Staccato

By Harry Cook, Escondido, California

I n my company there was a soldier we nicknamed "Bear" because he was so big. But size wasn't the only thing unusual about Bear. He stuttered, too.

One Saturday morning, we were told a general was coming to inspect the troops. We made up our bunks, laid out our equipment in military fashion and got ready for a full inspection.

About 1000 hours, we fell out into formation and stood at

STANDING TALL, like these troops, was only one part of an inspection. Sometimes you had to talk, and that wasn't so easy for a stuttering soldier named "Bear".

attention, all spit and polish, our rifles at our sides. The general arrived and went up and down the ranks inspecting us and our rifles.

When the general approached, each soldier brought his rifle to "inspect arms". When he got to Bear, the general asked, "Where are you from, soldier?"

"B-B-Baltimore, s-s-sir," Bear replied.

"Soldier, do you always stutter?" the general asked.

"N-N-No, sir," Bear answered. "J-J-Just when I t-t-talk."

★

Last Day in Service Had Paratrooper in the Air

By John Sellers, Sunset Beach, North Carolina

Most of my last night as a paratrooper with the 11th Airborne Division in 1952 was spent in the NCO club at Fort Campbell, Kentucky.

I had my discharge, and my friends and I went out to celebrate. Let's just say we all celebrated a little more than we should have.

All that was left for me to do in the service was to catch a flight home, so I wasn't required to fall out the next morning. "Sleeping in" the following day, I was only vaguely aware of the rest of the company scrambling to get ready for early chow call. But I awakened a short time later to a burning sensation in my stomach.

Too much beer? No. It was a lightbulb. My buddies had placed my bunk on a stack of footlockers so high I was almost touching the ceiling light!

As if that weren't bad enough, when I attempted to get up to answer an urgent "call of nature", I discovered I was tied to the bunk.

I had to lie there in misery until my buddies returned, and then they just went about their business, ignoring my threats and insults.

I'm sure when my fellow paratroopers finally released me, I set a record in the 50-yard latrine dash.

Putting Skipper in the Pink
Led to Snappy Assignment

By Richard Miller, Kettering, Ohio

Our brand-new destroyer was built in a record 30 days and was about to sail for armed conflict with Japan. I was a pharmacist mate first class and assigned to the new sick bay.

The ship's captain was a 6-foot-5 former All-American tackle. Both his size and his gruffness left me a little terror-stricken. One day I was summoned to his cabin.

He explained that he'd been afflicted with stomach problems most of his adult life. A Navy doctor on his last ship had prescribed a miraculous pink liquid that instantly relieved the pain.

"Miller," the captain growled, "I want you to find out what was in that medication and get me some ASAP."

DOCTOR'S IN. When Richard Miller cured the skipper's tummy ache, he was rewarded.

"I'll do my best, sir," I replied, with little hope of surviving this assignment.

Then the captain abruptly changed the subject. "What do you know about photography, Miller?" he asked. My mind whizzed through this second hazard.

Before I could answer, the captain told me the ship had been assigned a motion picture camera and an expensive still camera, but no film and no one to operate them.

"You know anything about photography?" the captain repeated. I was on the spot in a big way.

"Yes, sir," I replied. (My photographic experience totaled three rolls of film.)

"Get me some of that medication and those cameras are yours for the duration of the cruise," the captain promised.

That would be great! Personal cameras were strictly forbidden on ships during wartime, and the only personnel allowed to take pictures were ships' photographers. I was itching to give it a try.

First, though, I had to find that medicine. I left the ship and headed for downtown Seattle. The only pink liquid stomach medication I could think of was Pepto-Bismol (what else?). I bought the biggest bottle I could find.

Back in sick bay, I poured the Pepto into a regulation Navy prescription bottle and plastered on a very official looking (and very illegible) label. I added some dosage instructions from the manufacturer, and ran to the skipper's cabin.

Praying to the patron saint of lost causes, I knocked, ever

FIRST PHOTO. Richard Miller's first shot with his new equipment was taken on commissioning day for his ship. His skipper with the stomach problems is standing in left foreground.

so lightly. The response was a gruff "Enter".

"Sir," I said, "I think I've unraveled the secret of your stomach medication." I handed him the bottle.

I held my breath as the captain took a healthy swig and licked his lips. "Hmmm," he mused. "It sure tastes like the stuff the doc prescribed. Check back in a week and I'll tell you if it worked."

Three days later I got a message to report to the captain.

"Hey, Miller," he growled, "you're all right. This stuff makes me feel like a new man. Make sure you can make enough of it for our trip to the war zone."

I made a mental note to buy, out of my own pocket, as much Pepto-Bismol as I could carry.

Then the captain handed me two boxes containing the cameras—one a good movie camera, and the other a top-of-the-line Kodak Medalist.

"Keep them locked in the sick bay safe," the captain cautioned, "and give me a copy of anything that turns out good."

I managed to finagle several cartons of film and got some great shots of our cruise to the South Pacific. I learned to operate those cameras so well that after the war I earned my way through college as a newspaper photographer.

Now, 50 years later, I still enjoy taking photos—all thanks to a few bottles of Pepto-Bismol.

★

I Once Built a Flying Outhouse

By Kenneth Stuber, Glenmont, Ohio

I guess the men in this artillery battery figured me for a country boy, because when I arrived they asked me if I knew how to build a decent outhouse.

Well, they were right. I was a country boy and had used an outhouse for most of my school days. I said, "Yeah, give me the materials and I'll have a go at it."

I'd been sent to LZ (Landing Zone) Don near Song Be, Vietnam just before Christmas 1969 for a week's duty as medic. There didn't seem to be many guys going on sick call, so I had plenty of time to try my hand at outhouse building.

The material was no problem. The guys took me to a spot where some lumber, tin roofing, nails, a ladder and a saw were all laid out like they'd just been special delivered by a lumber company.

I didn't see any toilet seats, though, and asked the men about them. They said they'd have them by the time I finished.

There was just enough material for the size outhouse the guys wanted—a three-holer measuring 4 by 8 by 8 feet. It took me 2-1/2 days to build it.

When I told the guys it was time for the final touch, they produced three hot pink toilet seats, still wrapped in plastic. Boy, I thought, these guys were good scroungers.

A few days later my time was up and I was heading back to my LZ. The guys thanked me for building the outhouse and told me if there was ever anything I needed, I should just get on the radio and call them.

The next day I was transferred to LZ Lee. That afternoon I was told to report to the radio tent, where I had a call from LZ Don.

It was the medic I had pulled duty for that past week. He was calling to tell me my outhouse had been stolen!

"How in the world could someone steal something that big without being caught?" I asked.

The medic said a helicopter passed over the LZ, then returned a short time later. Everyone assumed it was bringing late mail or someone coming back from "R&R".

But when the chopper hung real low over the shower buildings and outhouse, and there were bright lights and a lot of yelling, the medic ran out to investigate.

He got there just in time to see my outhouse sailing over the trees, firmly secured to the chopper with cargo straps!

It turned out the material I had used to build the outhouse had been scrounged from another battery a couple of days before I got there.

That battery soon found out who stole their lumber and figured the best way to get even was to let the outhouse be built, then pick it up, hot pink seats and all, and take it "home".

Oh, well, all's fair in war...I'm just glad no one was inside it at the time!

Upperclassman's Orders Made Him a Big Wig

By Jack Ralph, Enid, Oklahoma

Newly arrived cadets at Cimarron Army Air Field near El Reno, Oklahoma in 1942 were classified as "dodos" to distinguish them from the rest of us "birdmen" who'd been there all of 5 weeks. Each cadet was assigned an upperclassman. It was his job to make sure the dodo would learn all there was to know about being a proper upperclassman.

My friend "Pop" Purcell spied one of the new crop who was just as bald-headed as he was. This was a remarkable coincidence, since none of us was over 27 years old.

Pop immediately claimed the newcomer as his personal dodo, and their first conversation went something like this:

Pop: "Mister, do you have a girlfriend back home?"

Dodo (sweating profusely): "Yes, sir!"

Pop: "Mister, does she have beautiful hair?"

Dodo (wondering what this had to do with flying): "Yes, sir!"

Pop: "Mister, you and I need more hair. You write your girl and tell her she'd better send us some of her hair. Do you understand?"

Dodo: "Yes, sir!"

In about 10 days, the dodo received a letter from his girl containing a liberal sample of her fair tresses.

That night after study hour, Pop ordered his dodo to get

HAIR TODAY. But it was gone tomorrow, as "Pop" (left above) and unnamed "dodo" sport their tresses.

some tape. There followed a serious ceremony during which the hair was carefully divided into two little tufts and applied with the tape to the bald craniums of Pop and his dodo.

I then took a photo (on previous page) of the pair proudly displaying their new status symbols.

★

I Bugled My Way Through the Army

By Donald Cronan, Oswego, New York

I f you're in the Army with a bugle in your hands, you'd better have a lot of friends. Combat-ready men would rather be bounced from their bunks by falling bombs than roused at dawn to the strains of *Reveille*.

I found this out at Fort Dix when I played my first official call, *Fatigue*, which calls the soldiers to work. I'd only got out the first few notes when a couple of indignant recruits opened fire on me with lumps of coal. They almost scored a direct hit!

I went from Fort Dix to Fort Monroe, Virginia, where I was of-

REVOLTING REVEILLE was just one of the calls from buglers, like this one. But Donald Cronan remembers his days as a bugler when one call really did blow!

fered the duty of plotting ships entering the harbor. Instead I joined the buglers and was soon playing calls at the main fort.

Eventually I was pulling regular duty as bugler of the guard at the main post. This meant I had to wake up the MP who fired the cannon before I sounded *First Call*.

Now, this MP hated to get up early, so one day he asked me if I'd fire the cannon in his place. Would I? I jumped at this chance to get into the "artillery". Not only would I be waking up everyone on post with my bugle, I would be armed!

One morning, though, I more than woke up some hapless guy who came walking along the road just before I was to fire the blank round from the cannon. He was carrying a long ladder over his head, and his route looked like it would put him right in front of me about the time I was ready to fire.

Sure enough, as the second hand on my watch hit "60", the guy was in my "line of fire". I pulled the lanyard and "BOOM!"— I was engulfed in smoke that didn't clear until I was halfway through *First Call*.

When I was finally able to see the road again, the guy had disappeared! All that was left was the ladder, lying on the road. I never found out who the guy was or where he went.

After I made PFC, I tried to get transferred into aviation. But I didn't weigh enough. I was even lighter than the minimum of 114 pounds.

So before the physical, I went to town to buy some bananas. I knew that eating bananas and drinking water could give me enough weight to pass the test.

Bananas were hard to find during wartime, but I located a store that had a lot and I bought about 4 pounds. But I was called in for the test before I could eat the bananas and, sure enough, I weighed 110.

"Wait a minute," I said, and grabbed the bag of bananas and got back on the scale.

"You can't do that," the medic said. "You have something in your hand."

I explained that I intended to eat the bananas and be weighed again. About this time, the flight surgeon walked in and told me I'd probably get sick if I ate all the bananas.

"Bananas are hard to come by," he said with a smile. "If you'll give them to me, I'll pass you."

As it turned out, I was washed out of cadet training because of my eyesight and ended up in the infantry. Eventually I was shipped to Europe with the 63rd Division.

But my bugling experience still came in handy when one day I was asked to play *The General's March* for our division commander, General Louis Gibbs. At a division reunion 25 years later, the general told me he still remembered that day.

After V-J Day, I signed up for what I thought was a marching band. The interview was in the schoolhouse where the German surrender was signed.

But the band turned out to be a dance band! I stayed with bugling assignments until we headed home and I ended up where I started, at Fort Dix. My days as an Army bugler were over.

★

Dawdling Sergeant Got A Desert Dusting

By Frank Bever, North Manchester, Indiana

During desert training at Camp Coxcomb, California in 1943, we sweltered in the heat during the daytime and froze in our tents at night. As if that weren't enough, all of us had to stand reveille and retreat in between our training problems and other duties.

Most of the soldiers in my tent had the habit of waiting until the last second to fall out, not budging until the first sergeant blew his whistle. Then they'd grab their belts, rifles and helmets and run out to form up on company street.

One of those who *really* waited until the last second was Sergeant Hughes. I decided to "get" him one morning.

I figured the last thing he would do in his rush to get out of the tent was look inside his helmet. So I dumped in about a cup of foot powder.

The next morning, Hughes came rushing out of the tent covered from head to shoulders with foot powder. We all had a good laugh, including, thankfully, Sergeant Hughes.

Now This Was A Real Sight Gag

By Stanley Arvig,
Hacienda Heights, California

On leave during basic training in 1952, I acquired a fake plastic eye that made more than one person do a double take.

THE EYES HAVE IT. When Stan Arvig gave folks "the eye", they gasped and gaped. "Normal" Stan is below.

It was a hollow plastic half orb that fitted over my eyelid. When "scrunched" down on, the fake eye produced dramatic results, as you can see from the photo.

After I got back to camp, I had a great time with that eye. I gave people in cars an incredible stare, and they usually gave a relieved horn honk when I took it out.

Kids who witnessed my "eye washing" routine always asked me to "do it again".

But the best gag took place at Fort Lewis, Washington, when I was having some dental work done.

I was reclining in the chair with a trayful of dental tools arrayed before me. The dentist had his back to me as he waited for his assistant to prepare the filling material.

That's when inspiration struck! I quietly reached into my pocket, pulled out the eye and inserted it. Peeking through my half-closed other eye, I waited for the dentist to turn around.

When he turned back toward me and looked down, he came face to face with the eye. Just then I let out a *"Gaaah!"* that froze him to the spot.

He stared wide-eyed and openmouthed into my face, unsure of what had happened.

Seeing his shock, I couldn't hold the pose long. So I reached up, plucked out the eye and grinned as best I could around the hardware in my mouth.

The dentist slumped for a second, then quickly leaned forward and whispered, "Put it back in."

I did, and he turned to his assistant and said, "Helen?"

"Yes?" she answered.

When no further instructions followed, she turned from her mixing duties and came around to the other side of the chair.

She looked down at me, turned deathly pale, let out a piercing scream and ran out of the office, through the waiting room and down the hall.

This attracted attention. A line formed and for the next 15 minutes, "the creature" in the dental chair was on display.

Months later, while I was being given a dental check before discharge, I heard a familiar voice ask, "Hey, soldier, you still have that eye?"

"Yes, sir," I answered the dentist.

"Let's see it," he said.

After taking a long look, he said, "You really had me scared that day. I thought you'd had a novocaine reaction or died!"

★

Joe Louis' Exhibition Drew GI's Suggestion

By David Swaney, Girard, Pennsylvania

While I was overseas, we were entertained one day by heavyweight boxing champ Joe Louis.

A crowd had gathered around the makeshift ring, and Joe and another fighter climbed in. Joe's opponent, as it turned out, was his first sergeant.

The sergeant was much smaller than Joe, but he knew how to use his fists. They sparred a bit, and both landed some good body blows. But all the while, Joe was talking to the crowd.

"I gotta be careful with this guy," Joe joked. "He's my first sergeant."

That's when some GI out in the crowd yelled back, "I wish he was *mine!*"

This 'Dear John' Turned The Tables on His Ex

By Gerhard Windscheffel, Grand Junction, Colorado

Submarine Training School in New London, Connecticut was difficult under the best of circumstances. One of the young men in my class was suffering additionally from receiving a "Dear John" letter from his fiance. The girl said she'd found another boyfriend and wanted her photograph back.

As friends of the jilted party, we decided this sort of treatment deserved a response in kind. We collected every photo of a woman that each classmate had. We had photos of wives, girlfriends, daughters, mothers and grandmothers. They ranged from photos your mother would approve of, to those your kid brother would secretly enjoy.

We bundled up all the pictures and sent them off to the ex-girlfriend with the following note: "Sorry, but I've forgotten what you look like. Please pick your picture out of this bundle and send the rest back."

THE GIRL BACK HOME. This Marine is lucky to have a girl waiting. But "Dear Johns" could count on friends like Gerhard Windscheffel to ease the pain.

Ewing Galloway

CHAPTER 4

Bob Sand/Jeff Ethell

Howard Sayre

REMEMBER THESE FACES? In spite of the danger war presented, stars like Marilyn Monroe (above in Korea) and Bob Hope (right in England) gave servicemen and women a little bit of home. These were also times of famous—and infamous—leaders, as when Churchill, Roosevelt and Stalin (below) met in Yalta in February 1945.

National Archives/Jeff Ethell

All the wildest dreams of a "wanna-be" professional musician came true the night Louis Armstrong and his band arrived at Ellington Field, Texas.

These big-name musicians were on hand for one of the nightly *Coca-Cola Spotlight Band* network broadcasts from military bases. I was assigned to see that things were set up to their satisfaction. What more could an aspiring trumpet player ask for?

"Hey, Mr. Armstrong," I said. "Is there *anything* you need? *Anything* at all?"

"Mr. Armstrong was my father," he replied. "Call me Louis like the other cats do." What a guy! What a smile!

Many a serviceman came home with similar tales, as the biggest names in show business unstintingly turned over their lives to boost War Bond sales. They staffed crowded urban clubs like the Stage Door Canteen and popped up at remote USO outposts in far corners of the world.

Scores put themselves in harm's way, performing closer to combat zones than any prudent person would. They performed on makeshift stages, on carrier decks, in open fields and airplane hangars. They often performed for crowds of thousands, but worked just as enthusiastically for lonesome outposts of 50 men.

Comedienne Martha Raye was wounded twice during her trips. A fully qualified surgical nurse, she even pitched in to help the nurses when fresh casualties from nearby action were brought in. (It's one of many fascinating stories you'll find in this chapter.)

Nor were all the performers national celebrities. Dozens of traveling USO troupes were made up of talented singers and dancers and comedians who hadn't yet made it to the top, but wanted to bring some happiness to service people wherever they were.

The hours were grueling, the living conditions were deplorable and the pay was lousy. But never mind, there were troops who needed a few moments of entertainment and happiness.

Thanks to Bob Hope and his annual trips overseas to wherever Americans were stationed, the generosity of celebrities continued right on through Korea, Vietnam and Desert Storm.

—Clancy Strock

VERN AND 'THE MAN'. Author got to meet Musial in 1951.

The Day My Baseball Dream Came True

By Vernon King, Ashland, New Hampshire

It was tough being a St. Louis Cardinals fan while growing up in the small New Hampshire town of Ashland. Most kids were Red Sox or Yankees fans, and they could hear their teams on the radio.

Not me—I only heard the Cardinals on the radio if they got

into the World Series. During the season, I followed my idols by reading the scores in the newspapers. My dream, though, was to see them in person.

But the years rolled by. I graduated from high school and got a job. Shortly after that, the Korean War broke out and I enlisted in the Air Force.

As luck would have it, I was sent to Houston, Texas, home of the Houston Buffs, the Cardinals' AA farm team in the old Texas League.

My luck continued when I learned the annual preseason game between my beloved Cardinals and the St. Louis Browns was to be played in Buff Stadium! I would finally be able to see the Cards play in person.

The big day was April 10, 1951. Wearing my Air Force uniform, I arrived at the stadium entrance 2 hours early so I could watch the Cardinals' bus come in.

Soon they were there, the players who I had only been able to read about in the paper—Stan Musial, Red Schoendienst, Joe Garagiola, Solly Hemus, Harry "The Cat" Brecheen, manager Marty "The Octopus" Marion and all the rest.

I hadn't yet bought a ticket, but a kindly gatekeeper let me in to get some autographs. I went down near the dugout just in time to see the Cards coming in. I jumped onto the field and started collecting autographs.

I got one from every Cardinal including the trainer, "Doc" Werner, and even Fred Saigh, the owner. Then I walked over to Stan "The Man" Musial, my baseball idol.

As we talked, Stan asked if I'd like a picture of us together. He called over a photographer. I couldn't believe it—there I was, a 19-year-old kid from New Hampshire, standing next to Stan Musial.

But there was more to come. Someone asked if I'd like to sit in the dugout with the Cards during the game. Permission was granted by the Browns' manager and the umpire, and there I was, sitting in the dugout with my favorite team!

The great rookie "Vinegar Bend" Mizell came over, sat beside me and talked. In fact, the whole team was very nice to me.

My heroes lost 7-6 on a grand slam home run in the ninth by Browns catcher Sherm Lollar. But I did get to see Musial hit a three-run homer in the first inning.

By the way, I never did buy a ticket for that game!

Meeting 'Manassa Mauler' Was Knockout Experience

By Richard Peterson, North Fort Myers, Florida

THE CHAMP. Richard Peterson (right) finally got to meet his boyhood hero, Jack Dempsey, on Coast Guard duty in Hawaii.

One of my boyhood heroes was world heavyweight boxing champion Jack Dempsey. I agonized when he lost his title to Gene Tunney and was outraged in 1927 when Tunney won their rematch thanks to the controversial "long count".

Years later I entered the Coast Guard and eventually was made commanding officer of Coast Guard Unit 206, a LORAN station on the northern tip of the big island of Hawaii.

One day in 1945, Commander Jack Dempsey (also serving in the Coast Guard) visited our base in his morale-building capacity. What a thrill to finally have a face-to-face meeting with one of my boyhood heroes!

He spent hours chatting with my crew and having his picture taken with them. Later that day he invited me to join him at a luncheon with the general manager of a Hawaiian sugar company.

I'll never forget the pleasure of meeting the "Manassa Mauler" in person. He was a true champion in every way.

★

Frankly, King of Hollywood Was a 'Tenderfoot'

By Robert Campbell, Memphis, Tennessee

Clark Gable was a member of OCS Class 42D at Miami Beach in 1942, and so was I.

The enclosed photo (at right) was taken just after we came off of guard duty, during which we walked 2 hours, then had 4 hours off, repeating the sequence for 24 hours straight.

The tender feet we suffered caused Clark and many of the rest of us to wear bedroom slippers the next day. I'll never forget Clark's comment: "I wish I could have had a stand-in for that sequence!"

Martha Raye Was 'Colonel Maggie' to Me

By Rod Hinsch, Beech Grove, Indiana

COL. MAGGIE. Martha Raye (above with Rod Hinsch) proved she was a real trouper, as well as a trooper, during a firefight in Vietnam.

When most people hear the name Martha Raye, they think of a very funny lady who made millions laugh over several decades of movie and television performances.

But when I hear the name, I think of "Colonel Maggie", a nickname and honorary rank given her by the men of the Special Forces, the "Green Berets".

Besides being a talented entertainer, Martha Raye was a fully qualified surgical nurse. During her nine trips to Vietnam, she used those skills when some of the camps she visited came under attack.

When that happened, Maggie refused to be evacuated to safety and, while under fire and at great personal risk, gave medical aid and comfort to the wounded.

Maggie was herself wounded twice. But each time she stuck by the troops and continued to attend others until the battle subsided.

These acts of courage endeared her to the hearts of the Green

Berets, an elite, hard-fighting unit that Maggie adopted. In return we inducted her into the ranks of the Special Forces, gave her the honorary rank of colonel and presented her with our highest honor, the right to wear the coveted green beret.

My first encounter with Colonel Maggie was in 1967 when she came with a small troupe to entertain at our remote base located only a few hundred meters from the Cambodian border.

We didn't get the larger USO shows out there because of security. There was a rumor (later confirmed by military intelligence) that the communists had placed a $10,000 bounty on Bob Hope.

I was assigned as Maggie's bodyguard. I had never met the "Colonel", and when the middle-aged woman wearing fatigues and the green beret stepped from the helicopter, I was impressed...and intimidated.

When I stepped forward, saluted and introduced myself, Maggie looked me over and said, "Well, sergeant, why don't we go have a drink and talk more about protecting my body?"

This kind of humor was what we loved about Maggie. She was a very sharp lady, with plenty of wit. Very few of us could keep up with her in a match of repartee.

The show was performed on a makeshift stage, and Maggie started things off with a song. She then introduced each of the other performers as they began their acts. Song, dance and stand-up comedy were on the menu, and we ate it up.

But just to prove good things don't last, "Charlie" began a mortar attack. We quickly escorted Maggie and her troupe to a bunker designed for this sort of attack.

Fortunately the shelling was brief and casualties were light. But it didn't take Maggie long to jump into action cleaning wounds and bandaging those who lined up to be cared for by the most famous "nurse" in Vietnam.

I was among the "wounded" Maggie attended. While escorting her to the bunker, I slipped in the mud and slashed my leg on some barbed wire. Embarrassing as it was, I was thrilled to have Maggie as my nurse, although I tried hard not to show it.

I met Maggie twice more—again in Vietnam in 1968, then 23 years later in 1991 at the annual "Colonel Maggie's All Services Airborne Drop-In" at the American Legion post in Marina, California.

As I stood in line waiting my turn to talk to Maggie, I noticed how frail she seemed. She was by then confined to a wheelchair and affected by poor health.

When it was my turn, I pulled out a photo she had given me long ago in Vietnam, told her who I was and asked if she remembered giving me the photo.

Maggie took the photo, looked at it, then at me, cocked her head and said, "Still in the bodyguard business, sergeant?"

Maggie passed away October 19, 1994. But the memory of her will live on as long as one Green Beret who caught her act in the jungles of Vietnam remains alive.

★

Soldier Guarded the Infamous 'Tokyo Rose'

By Charles Herian, Melbourne, Florida

U.S. BOUND. Tokyo Rose was being turned over to escorts who would take her to trial in the States. Charles Herian is MP on left.

Sugamo Prison no longer stands, having been replaced in the 1970s by a shopping mall.

But after World War II, the prison, located in the suburbs of

Tokyo, was the temporary home of several infamous people, including Hideki Tojo, the general who, as premier, led Japan into war, and Iva D'Aquino, better known as "Tokyo Rose".

MONUMENT to peace at Sugamo site.

Tokyo Rose, who attempted to demoralize Allied troops with her propaganda broadcasts, was held at Sugamo for about a year right after the war and then released.

But she was arrested again in 1948, held at Sugamo for a short time, then transferred to the United States. The photo (on opposite page) was taken the day of her transfer.

Iva D'Aquino was an American and so was found guilty of treason. She served almost 7 years in a federal prison. Many years after her release, President Gerald Ford pardoned her.

★

He Joined Byrd's Last Migration South

By Rodger Crum, Bloomingdale, New Jersey

The Navy's Operation High Jump in October of 1948 was the largest Antarctic expedition ever undertaken.

There were 180 of us Seabees aboard the *USS Yancey* when it left for Antarctica. Our assignment was to establish a base camp and airstrip at Little America IV.

We sailed south for several weeks. The final leg of the journey was a hazardous push through 600 miles of pack ice in the Ross Sea. After we arrived, we worked 12-hour shifts (made possible by the fact that it was always daylight) and the base was quickly set up and made ready for use.

Shortly thereafter, the famous polar explorer Admiral Richard Byrd arrived by air from the carrier *Philippine Sea* in a ski-equipped R4D, the Navy version of the DC-3. The plane's tires protruded through the skis about 6 inches to allow for a carrier launch, the first for a plane of that size.

I had the privilege of meeting Admiral Byrd and finding out

BYRD'S DOG. Rodger Crum, shown with a puppy of Admiral Byrd's favorite sled dog, met the famous explorer in Antarctica.

how sentimental he was. He'd brought along "Ricky", an old husky who could no longer work with the other sled dogs.

Ricky had been born at Little America III during Byrd's expedition in 1933-34. He was from a litter of pups that are believed to be the first domesticated animals born in that section of Antarctica, and perhaps the entire continent.

The enclosed photo (above) shows me with an 8-week-old puppy of Ricky's, born just before Byrd's ship left the States.

Four-Star Car Meant Brass Aboard

By Eugene Bovee, Lawrence, Kansas

John Court

IKE'S PLATE got a salute, even on the car's trunk.

Second lieutenants rarely saw General Eisenhower unless they were attached to his headquarters staff. But as an office-bound "chairtrooper", I saw Ike at close range twice.

In England in 1944 as a Military Intelligence officer, I served in Cheltenham near a major troop marshaling area. Junior officers didn't merit cars, so we were issued bicycles to use on weekends for touring through the countryside.

On one such weekend, a camouflage-painted Cadillac bearing a red plate with four stars approached. I dismounted, stood at attention and snapped a salute, which General Eisenhower returned from the back seat.

Just a month later, I was transferred to London. One day three of us were walking to lunch and, as we turned a corner, nearly crashed into two senior officers—Generals Dwight Eisenhower and Omar Bradley!

We three lieutenants stood at attention and saluted. Bradley remarked dryly, "Well, gentlemen, you must have important jobs if you're in such a hurry."

"Yes, sir!" replied Lieutenant White, not known for his modesty. "We think so, sir."

"What's your assignment?" Ike asked, eyeing our "No Materials Branch" insignia, which was a cover for Military Intelligence.

"We're Military Intelligence, sir," I replied. "Assigned to Censorship Base overhead."

"You *do* have important jobs," Ike said. "And judging by the reports my headquarters gets from the Theater Censor's office, you're doing them well. Carry on, gentlemen."

127

He Found Shining Star
In Italian Mountains

By Ralph Lewis, Erlanger, Kentucky

Strict orders that my Special Services show should play at *all* hospitals, regardless of location, meant a trip to a remote section of the Italian Alps during World War II.

As if that weren't bad enough, no one at the hospital knew we were coming, and I got the old Army runaround. When I was finally referred to the Red Cross office, I was a bit irritated.

But when a gorgeous blonde smiled and very sweetly said, "Why, yes, we've been expecting you," things got better.

As we discussed the arrangements, I finally couldn't stand it any longer and said, "Maybe I've been overseas too long, but you look awfully familiar. Do I know you?"

She flashed that dazzling smile and said, "I'm Madeleine Carroll."

What was the beautiful star of *The 39 Steps* and many other movies doing there? Being a hardworking, wonderful Red Cross volunteer, I learned later from the men in the hospital.

The last time I heard about Madeleine, she was in southern France working with children orphaned by the war. She remains the most remarkable celebrity I ever met.

★

I Saw Stars During the War

By Joe Curreri, Philadelphia, Pennsylvania

Some well-known entertainers went off to fight during World War II, but others stayed home to entertain and build morale, a duty almost as important.

Many served at the Hollywood Canteen, which provided entertainment for troops on temporary leave from the fighting.

From the day it opened, the Hollywood Canteen—founded by

Bette Davis and John Garfield—was the best, most popular show in town. Just about every star in Hollywood showed up for duty—washing dishes, cooking, serving troops, scrubbing floors and, of course, entertaining.

I was a 22-year-old airman stationed at nearby Santa Monica who went there every chance he could get. I saw what I wanted to see—movie stars!

What a thrill to stand up close to them, talk with them, laugh with them. They were so real—Gary Cooper, so modest and shy; Basil Rathbone, so debonair; beautiful June Lang—she kissed me! Marlene Dietrich danced with me, and when other soldiers cut in, I cut right back. "You again!" she laughed.

Who would believe me back home if I bragged, "I held Marlene Dietrich and June Lang in my arms"?

The day Basil Rathbone was there, he signed autographs by the hour. When I went to him for an autograph, I asked, "Don't you wish you had a shorter name?" He laughed and said, "Yes, like 'X'."

Another time, John Garfield told us he had just finished working on love scenes with Ann Sheridan. "I had a tough day, a tough day," he said with a grin.

So many came and gave their time to entertain us—Edgar Bergen and Charlie McCarthy, Burns and Allen, Ginny Simms and Eddie Cantor, to name just a few.

I remember Red Skelton, who did his famous routine pretending to be a radio pitchman selling "Guzzler's Gin". "Ladies and gentlemen," Red would spiel, "try Guzzler's Gin, the college drink—one bottle and you're in a class by yourself."

Other unforgettable performances included The Andrews Sisters singing *Boogie Woogie Bugle Boy*, the popular song from the Abbott and Costello movie *Buck Privates*. Abbott and Costello themselves entertained us with their famous routine, "Who's on First?"

It was unreal. Here I was, a skinny kid from South Philadelphia, greeted at the door by Lana Turner, Deanna Durbin or Dinah Shore. Linda Darnell even served me dinner!

Servicemen could have a hamburger with John Garfield or dance to the music of Rudy Vallee, Tommy Dorsey or Xavier Cugat. George Raft washed dishes, and one day Vice President Henry Wallace joined the second shift in the kitchen!

Every Saturday night they'd have a bingo game. The emcee

was the "Old Puh-Fessuh" himself, a cackling Kay Kyser.

The popularity of the club inspired the movie *Hollywood Canteen* in 1944. The Department of Defense, which later decorated Bette Davis with a "Public Service" medal, said more than a million servicemen and women were entertained in the Canteen each year.

So many owe so much to these few men and women of the Hollywood Canteen. They entertained us, brought us a touch of home, built our morale and left us with lifelong memories.

★

FLASHY. The creator of Flash Gordon designed this patch.

Flash Gordon Creator
Left a Patch of Memories

By Carl Crumpton, Topeka, Kansas

When I was a boy in Ogden, Kansas during the '30s, my hero was the intrepid Flash Gordon.

So imagine my surprise and delight years later when Alex Raymond—the creator of Flash Gordon—joined my unit, Marine Torpedo Bombing Squadron VMTB-143, which flew from the escort carrier *USS Gilbert Islands.*

Captain Raymond was the combat artist for our flight group, assigned to paint pictures of life in a Marine Air Group flying from an aircraft carrier. A true gentleman, he often allowed us to watch him work.

We were one of the few squadrons to have two distinctly different patches during World War II. Alex Raymond created the second one for us (above) in 1945.

This Guy Played the Piano Just Like the Famous...

By C.C. Stewart, Mt. Nebo, West Virginia

During World War II, I was en route from Norfolk to Washington aboard one of the old Bay Line steamers. After dinner, I wandered into the dimly lit lounge.

A naval officer came in, went to the piano and began to play. The music was beautiful, so I sat and listened.

As the officer was about to leave, I went over to him and said, "Lieutenant, you play the piano just like Eddy Duchin."

"Chief," he replied with a smile, "I *am* Eddy Duchin."

★

He Helped Howard Hughes 'Spruce Up the Goose'

By Marvin Kiel, Marshall, Minnesota

Back in 1947, my ship, the *USS Jason*, pulled into Long Beach, California. I was coxswain on a 40-foot launch used to transport sailors and pick up and deliver freight.

On one trip, we were asked to deliver a box of flight instruments to an enormous "flying boat" being built in the harbor.

We got a big surprise when we tied up to the plane and the builder came out—it was Howard Hughes! That dapper young man in a short-sleeved shirt and wide-brimmed fedora invited me and my three-man crew aboard his *Spruce Goose* to take a look.

The huge flying machine was made mostly of plywood, and once inside, we had to wade knee-deep through wood shavings. We really enjoyed chatting with Hughes, who was very friendly and thanked us profusely for delivering his parts.

Several months later, we had the great privilege of watching as Hughes took the *Spruce Goose* on its first and only flight.

Yankee Doodle Dandy
Came to My Town

By Ed Knapp, Three Rivers, Michigan

That red hair...that unmistakable face—they could belong to nobody else but James Cagney!

It was September 8, 1942, a Tuesday. The government had designated September as "Salute to Our Heroes" month, kicking off a war bond effort in Hollywood with such stars as Greer Garson, Hedy Lamarr, Irene Dunne, Ann Rutherford and Martha Scott.

And in Kalamazoo, Michigan, we were getting James Cagney, the hard-boiled gangster from *The Public Enemy*, the six-shoot-

ing cowboy from *The Oklahoma Kid* and, most recently, that *Yankee Doodle Dandy*, George M. Cohan.

Back then, James Cagney was among the 10 most popular movie stars. He was to appear on the steps of the county building in Kalamazoo, and I was going to be there.

My father, well aware of my keen interest in the movies, got me excused from school. I was also interested in cameras and brought along my Argus in hopes of getting a photo of Jimmy.

My excitement built as I waited with the large crowd, but being young, I soon grew impatient. Just as my enthusiasm began to wane, a group of smartly dressed people came out of the building, and with them was James Cagney!

My first impression was one of disbelief. Oh, it was Cagney, all right...but he seemed much shorter than his larger-than-life image on the silver screen.

I was so enthralled I almost forgot I had my camera along.

But I was soon busy snapping pictures to record this historic moment.

At first Jim seemed a bit uneasy. He fiddled with his wristwatch and even tripped over the microphone cord. But he soon warmed up to the occasion, and his speech was vintage "tough guy" Cagney:

"This month, a billion dollars worth of war bonds and stamps must be raised for the effort. As for Hitler, Hirohito and Mussolini, we'll blow their brains out—that is, if they ever had any!"

The speech was followed by several patriotic songs, including *You're a Grand Old Flag* from Cagney's latest feature, *Yankee Doodle Dandy*.

I became even more aware of the necessity of those war bond sales when, less than a year later, I entered the service in the Army Signal Corps and served in the European and Asian theaters.

I played my part in history by fighting for my country, just as I felt a part of history the day that great entertainer and patriot James Cagney came to town.

With Two Broken Legs
Pilot Glided to Stars

By Roger Markley, Nashville, Indiana

My glider was shot down on D-Day while I was carrying a 57 mm cannon and some men from the 101st Airborne. I ended up in a hospital in England with two broken legs.

Assigned to a C-47 for a flight back to the States, I was surprised to find that my fellow passengers were a USO troupe.

I became well acquainted with Pat O'Brien, Ann Miller and Buster Keaton. All three walked over and shook my hand good-bye when we landed.

Pat O'Brien promised to kiss that good old American soil when he got back, and he did just that in front of a crowd and the press.

★

Buddy Ernie Was a Novel Character

By Vince Klinefelter, Loomis, California

My friend Si was a carefree GI who was never without a grin on his face, even when he was in hot water—as he was the day he skidded to a muddy stop on a French motorcycle he'd found somewhere that morning.

The lieutenant chewed out Si, who was supposed to have been there 2 hours earlier.

"Heck, I was having a drink with Ernie," Si grinned. He had long ago forgotten to say "Sir" when talking to an officer. "You gotta know Ernie—everybody does."

Si finally got the lieutenant curious enough to drive back (in a Jeep) to the German cottage where they found a group of men gathered around a table.

"Hello, Si," said one of them.

"Guys, meet my lieutenant," Si said.

"Let me introduce you," said one, shaking the lieutenant's

hand. "This is Al Smalley, reporter for the *St. Louis Post-Dispatch*. Next is Bob Capa, who shoots all the war pictures you see in *Life*. This is Hank, our correspondent for a bunch of English papers. My name is Groth. I paint scenes for *Parade*. Ernie just stepped out."

Just then, Ernie returned.

"Ernie, this is Lieutenant Lewis," Groth said. The lieutenant just stared. "Lieutenant, I suppose you already know Ernie Hemingway."

★

I Had a Royal Christmas in Monaco

By Steve Pozar, Butler, Pennsylvania

Like many other servicemen, I was faced with spending the holidays miles from home and family. What I didn't know was that by Christmas, I'd be dining with royalty!

Thanksgiving, 1967, was approaching, and I was assigned to the Sixth Fleet in the Mediterranean Sea. It was the worst winter in recent memory, and my ship, the *USS Seneca*, a 200-foot oceangoing tug, was bounced around enthusiastically by the severe storms.

Only two men out of a crew of 81 didn't get seasick, and to top it off, we passed Thanksgiving shadowing a Russian trawler in the western Mediterranean. Being a small ship, we were junior to just about everything larger than a whaleboat, and so we were kept pretty busy for the next several weeks.

But Christmas week found us in the snug harbor of Monaco, where the *Seneca's* small size was finally an advantage. We tied up between two yachts that were almost as big as we were.

Because of the company we were now keeping, the captain ordered a full scrub-down, fore and aft. We hopped to it.

It was the middle of the scrub-down when I got word the captain wanted to see me. This is not what a sailor wants to hear. I squared away my white cap, rolled down my sleeves and headed toward "officers' country".

As it turned out, I had nothing to worry about. Just the opposite, in fact— the captain asked if I wanted to have Christmas dinner at the palace of Prince Rainier and Princess Grace!

Par ordre de Leurs Altesses Sérénissimes
le Gouverneur de la Maison a l'honneur d'informer
Stephan M. Pozar qu'il est invité à un Déjeuner qui sera
Offert au Palais, le Dimanche 25 Décembre 1966, à
13 heures.

Tenue: Uniforme.

R.S.V.P.
au Gouverneur

INVITATION to a royal
Christmas in Monaco for a lucky sailor.

136

I quickly replied, "Yes, sir!" The captain explained the drill and concluded by ordering me not to make a fool of myself.

Thinking I could handle that, I said, "Aye, aye, sir!" and was dismissed.

Six of us were invited to the palace, two from each U.S. Navy ship in Monaco. The royal family did this every Christmas, we learned. We were greeted at the palace by the captain of the guard, who checked our invitations and turned us over to the "majordomo". He was decked out like a fleet admiral, and we treated him accordingly.

We were eventually ushered into a large, high-ceilinged room with a fireplace at one end and a huge Christmas tree in one corner. Before we knew it, the Prince and Princess had shaken our hands, introduced us to their children and invited us to sit by the fire.

Princess Grace did most of the talking until we found our tongues. She asked about our homes and families, and before long we were at ease.

After Caroline, who was about 10, played the piano for us, Princess Grace suggested we play a game with a toy bomb the children had received for Christmas. It was a black sphere with a large red wick. When wound up, it ticked, then "went off" with a loud CLACK!

We were to toss the bomb around the room, and whoever was holding it when it went off had to crawl through a long toy tunnel, another of the children's gifts.

The game ended when the bomb went off in Prince Rainier's hands. He went into one end of the tunnel, and Princess Grace sent Stephanie, then just a toddler, into the other.

The two met in the middle and enjoyed a good laugh. I had the feeling Princess Grace had this in mind when she started the game.

After a turkey dinner, complete with wine poured by attentive servants, we adjourned to the recreation room, where Princess Grace proved what I had heard about her prowess at a table-soccer game. She beat me 5-1.

The evening passed all too quickly, and as the Prince and Princess saw us out of the palace, they gave each one of us a gift in remembrance of the day. As we walked back down the hill to our ships, we agreed among ourselves that this was a Christmas we would long remember.

USO Shows Caught Up With Him

By Jack Ritzma, Pollock Pines, California

T he first night I was in the service, I enjoyed a Spike Jones USO show at Fort MacArthur, California. But for the next 3-1/2 years, I missed every other USO performance in my area, sometimes by just 2 or 3 days.

Then, 2 months before my discharge, I lucked out—I was at the Santa Ana, California military hospital when Joe E. Brown and Jack Haley showed up to entertain us.

Some of us even wound up on the stage singing with them.

GREAT THERAPY. With Joe E. Brown and Jack Haley, hospitalized GIs (author is fourth from right) had a healthy time harmonizing.

★

Farmer John Cut a Lonely Figure

By Max Harrington, Calistoga, California

S everal of us in a submarine reserve contingent were hanging around the Baltimore airport in the summer of 1966, waiting to proceed to Norfolk, Virginia. It was 6 a.m.

One of our group who had been wandering the concourse hurried back with big news. "I think I spotted a famous actor."

"Yeah, who?"

"I don't know his name, but I've seen him in the movies."

We followed him to where a solitary figure was slumped on a bench. He was wearing a faded blue checkered shirt, a sweat-stained felt hat and a pair of old bib overalls with yellow straw clinging to them. All we could see was a craggy face with a deep-cleft chin.

He looked up. "Hi, boys. You lost?"

I said, "Uhh, you sure look a lot like Robert Mitchum."

He grinned and glanced around the huge, empty terminal. "Yeah, don't spread it around, but I'm Bob Mitchum. Why don't you sit for a while and we'll talk. Gets lonely here at this time of the morning."

We talked for an hour and a half. He was on the way to his ranch and traveled late at night to avoid autograph seekers. "The Farmer John look helps, too," he admitted. "Fools most people."

Finally our flight was called. We shook hands and hurried away. Glancing back, I saw him framed against windows glowing with dawn. He waved, a lonely gesture from a lonely figure.

★

Sailor Heeded Admiral's Advice During Career

By Doug Adams, Gulf Breeze, Florida

In April 1947 I was assigned to the Naval Communications Headquarters in Washington, D.C.

Although the war had been over for some time, we still had to wear our uniforms on liberty. So I found myself swaggering into town on an autumn afternoon, all of 7 months in the Navy (none of it afloat), with my sleeves rolled up, cap on the back of my head and neckerchief two-blocked at the neck.

Unfortunately, my stroll took me past the headquarters of the

Navy Department, where I heard someone call for a "sailor" to stop. It must have been me, because the other guy in uniform had gold from his wrists to his armpits!

I came to attention and gave him a salute, only to be told I wasn't dressed suitably to salute him. My sleeves were quickly rolled down, neckerchief brought down to the "V" in my jumper and cap squared away.

I was then told I could salute, which I did.

He returned it, adding, "Now that you're in the Navy, why don't you join it?"

I took the advice of Fleet Admiral Chester Nimitz to heart, followed the rules, and retired a commander 28 years later.

★

Frozen North Thawed When Stars Came Out

By Orville Duke, Mesa, Arizona

Bob Hope's Christmas show came to Goose Bay, Labrador in 1961 while I was stationed there with a communications squadron. The group needed escorts, and I jokingly said I'd volunteer only if I got to escort Jayne Mansfield.

JAYNE AND MICK (left) in Orville Duke's photo.

Well, was I ever shocked when I learned that's exactly who I would be escorting! I was assigned a staff car and was at Jayne's beck and call during her stay in the VIP quarters.

Jayne and her husband, Mickey Hargitay, were both just as nice as they were good looking. Some other officers and I even had Christmas dinner with them.

Jayne said we could take all the pictures of her we wanted, just as long as we let her know when we were doing so.

Hero Takes Time for Admirer

By Mary Lou Jones, Gainesville, Florida.

I'll never forget September 28, 1946. It was the day General Jonathan Wainwright, the "Hero of Bataan" was coming to our town of Starke, Florida. Our county was having a "Homecoming Veterans Celebration" that started with a motorcade to Jacksonville to greet the general. There was also a parade and a reception for the general at the local USO club.

GENERAL came to Mary Lou (above) as she sat curbside.

At the time, I had an attack of rheumatic fever and was unable to walk. If I left the house, my dad had to carry me. But I still wanted to join in the celebration.

We attended the parade and cheered as General Wainwright came by leading the procession. I wanted to attend the reception, but my dad thought it would be too crowded.

That night, Dad consented to take the family downtown and park across from the USO club. I could see the people coming and going, and that satisfied me. But not my mother. "I'm going to see the general," she said to Dad, "and tell him about Mary Lou and ask if he'll speak to her if you carry her in."

The rest of us laughed when Mother got out of the car and walked into the club. But in a short while, we sat there flabbergasted as Mother, and the general, walked up!

The general opened the door and we visited for several minutes. He gave me some encouraging words, then leaned down and kissed me on the cheek as we said good-bye.

Mother said later that when she asked the general about talking to me if Father carried me in, the old soldier replied, "Why, no indeed. I'll go out and see her."

At the time, I was merely excited to meet such a famous person. Now, years later, I realize I met that night not only a very brave leader but also a caring and compassionate man.

His gesture of tenderness, after what had probably been a long and tiring day for him, will always be a treasured memory.

CHAPTER 5 ★★★★★

SHE PROUDLY SERVED.

Since World War II, women in stripes have valiantly served their nation—as WACs, WAVEs, WAFs, WASPs, SPARs and Woman Marines. Outside the service, Red Cross volunteers and "Rosie the Riveter" also played important roles.

Harold M. Lambert

Ewing Galloway

Archive Photos/PopperFoto

OUR PROUD WOMEN IN STRIPES

U ntil recently, war was an enterprise for men only. You got a bunch of guys together and went off on a Crusade or sacked Rome or tried to conquer the entire known world. Women stayed home.

But World War II changed that forever, when the military welcomed women enlistees. Some joined out of sheer patriotism. Others were looking for adventure or romance. More than a few enlisted after a brother or father was killed in action.

Some took along their secretarial skills and worked in offices. Others became mechanics or ordnance specialists. As the old military cliche went, "Their duties were many and varied."

They suffered the rigors of basic training just the way the men did...but had to put up with the wolf whistles and sardonic cries of "You'll be SOR-eeee."

In combat zones they lived in leaky tents, endured hordes of pesky insects and hunkered down in foxholes during air raids. Many never made it home.

I met "Mac the WAC"—an inevitable nickname because of her Scotch ancestry—in the Philippines, where we worked together. She was one of the many who enlisted early out of a strong sense of patriotism rather than a yearning for adventure.

But she'd had more than her share of adventures, too. They started when she was shipped to New Guinea, where Atabrine tablets quickly turned her peaches-and-cream complexion to a sallow yellow.

Later she hop-skipped along with MacArthur's Pacific campaign—Bougainville, Biak, Hollandia, Leyte and finally Manila. She was every inch a soldier and was justifiably proud of the contribution she made toward winning the war.

Thousands like her served with distinction, proving beyond argument that there was a place in the military for women who wanted to serve their country. They were truly trailblazers for the proud women who serve our country today.

—*Clancy Strock*

So Much for Chivalry

By Midge Brubaker Ahrendt, Calabasas, California

After 27 days at sea, we WACs were happy to feel firm ground under our feet when we landed at Hollandia, New Guinea.

Typically, however, the military had issued us heavy winter clothing before sending us to this steamy "tropical paradise". We faced a steep uphill climb to where trucks were waiting to take us to Far East Air Force Headquarters.

I was struggling with my duffel bag full of winter gear when a soldier walked up and said, "Here, let me help you."

Hooray, he was going to carry it up the hill for me!

Wrong! He merely picked up the duffel bag and threw it over my shoulder. I fell flat on my stomach. So much for chivalry.

PALM BALM. Relaxing against a tree in the Philippines in 1944, Midge managed a smile.

★

The Enemy Was One Step Away

By J.G. Anderson, Sun City, California

They crested the hill, silhouetted by a full moon—Japanese soldiers coming down the narrow path that led...straight to us! It was 1944 in New Guinea. I was one of the first WACs to arrive and was serving in a radar countermeasure unit.

Because Japanese stragglers were still in the area, military women were never allowed out of the compound without an armed soldier. It seemed a little silly, but the protection was welcome.

Tom, my companion, spotted the soldiers at the same time I did. There was no time for heroics—besides, we were outnumbered. The only thing to do was hide.

Tom rolled to the left and hid under low scrub. I flattened myself and rolled to the right. My brush was so scrawny that I had to depend on my green camouflage clothing for concealment.

The Japanese came nearer and nearer. I could even smell them—a sort of boiled rice aroma. Heart pounding, I fervently wished to be back in the States within the dull safety of my parents' home, leading a well-ordered and terror-free life.

The platoon passed right on by us. When their footsteps died in the distance, Tom and I emerged from hiding.

"What's that on your sleeve?" he asked. It was a muddy footprint from the cleft shoe of one of the soldiers. He'd nearly stepped on my arm!

Suddenly the moonlight and the flowers and the ferns had lost their appeal. We called it a night and returned to our respective quarters.

★

Burner Blew Lid Off Savory Secret

By Helen Anderson Glass, Tucson, Arizona

Cooking a tasty alternative to our bland mess hall fare nearly got me in a stew with the top brass!

I was a mechanic at the Naval Air Station in Opa-locka, Florida from 1943 to 1945. Sometimes I'd go to a nearby store and buy enough food to make a lunch for the guys and gals who worked with me in the hangar.

One day I'd purchased some corned beef, cabbage, potatoes,

onions and carrots and put together a good old-fashioned Irish lunch. The whole works was simmering away in a large well-cleaned can with some Bunsen burners beneath it.

Suddenly an announcement boomed over the loudspeaker: "Now hear this! The captain and staff officers will escort a group of officers from Washington through the hangar for inspection. All Navy and Marine personnel present will stand at attention when the inspection team arrives in each section of the hangar."

I quickly covered the bubbling can with a lid and hoped they wouldn't notice. However, just as the inspection team approached our group in Engine Overhaul, the lid blew off the can and the hangar wall was showered with cabbage, potatoes, onions and broth.

NON-EXPLOSIVE LUNCH was enjoyed by this Red Cross worker dining alfresco in Mindoro, Philippines.

"Who's responsible for this?" our furious commanding officer roared.

Shaking and scared to death, I meekly stepped forward. "Anderson, sir. I am responsible."

At that, my chief and all his buddies stepped forward, too. "We are also, sir," they admitted.

The visiting vice admiral from Washington walked up to me and said, "Smells great! Wish I could stay for lunch." With that, he led the inspection team away from the food-splattered area.

We never heard another word about the incident, and it made me feel good that my comrades would stand by me when I was in a jam.

I felt so good about the whole thing, in fact, that I eventually married the chief!

WAC Kept a Secret Under Her Hat

By JoAnn Hannum, Yakima, Washington

One of my barracks mates at Fort Oglethorpe, Georgia in 1943 was Marion Giovonii. We bunked across from each other, which gave me a front row "seat" one Saturday when a surprise inspection was called.

Marion found herself with an apple she didn't know how to get rid of. So she hid it under her "hobby" hat, the duck-billed uniform hat we wore, and put it back on the shelf.

The inspecting officer came in and started down the aisle—looking under each hat for hidden items! Since Marion was facing forward, she couldn't see what was happening.

And she also didn't know why I was having so much trouble keeping from laughing. Being across the aisle, I could see what was going on and was having visions of the officer getting beaned with that apple when she lifted Marion's hat.

But just before she reached Marion's area, the officer stopped checking under the hats! Marion and I had a good laugh after the inspection when I told her how close she came to getting into trouble.

CAPPED COUPLE. WAC buddies JoAnn (right in both photos) and Marion always enjoyed a good laugh.

Wearing Your Heart on Your Sleeve Is One Thing...

By Lona King, Kalkaska, Michigan

We were having a commander's inspection one sunny spring morning in the early 1960s at Camp Pendleton Naval Hospital, where I was a WAVE. It's a good thing our CO "had a heart".

We were standing in open ranks, and the CO stopped to look at the back of a young sailor standing in front of me.

The sailor was wearing whites, as were the rest of us. But those white trousers made it plain to see he was also wearing a pair of heart-decorated skivvies! (He'd obviously received them from his girlfriend for Valentine's Day.) Those of us behind that sailor were having a tough time keeping straight faces.

Before we were dismissed, the CO made a remark about the "lovely hearts" a certain sailor was wearing. That was all we needed to hear. The whole formation exploded in laughter...all but the sailor, that is, who turned as red as his hearts.

★

The 'Blue' That She Sought Turned Out to Be Briney

By Jane Romig Smith, Allentown, Pennsylvania

I signed on with the Army Nurse Corps in hopes of going off into the "blue yonder". But my poor eyesight shot that idea down in flames, and instead I ended up on the blue ocean, assigned to the 201st Hospital Ship Complement.

We sailed out of Charleston, South Carolina in January 1945 and headed for Italy and North Africa. We were to pick up wounded soldiers and bring them back home.

On shore leave we had the opportunity to visit Sidi-bel-Abbes, the home of the Foreign Legion, and got to Naples, the Isle of Capri, Pompeii and Rome. We usually traveled in "luxury" aboard 2-1/2-ton trucks.

The other side of the coin was returning to the States with 400 or more wounded boys. We learned how wonderful the American GI can be—no whining, no griping. I've never forgotten a brave 18-year-old double amputee who joked that he no longer needed to trim his toenails.

They played tricks on each other, and on us. But they also helped each other, and the nurses, with daily care. It was an experience I've never regretted.

SALTY FLIGHT. Jane Smith (above) hoped to fly, but settled for sailing, on the Army hospital ship *Seminole.*

★

The '20th Century Limited' This Wasn't

By Ann Mays, Quincy, Illinois

Editor's Note: When Ann Mays left basic training at Fort Dodge, Iowa to attend medic school at Brooke General Hospital at Fort Sam Houston in San Antonio, Texas in 1945, she got a memorable train ride that she wrote home about.

We left Des Moines at 2000 hours. Our duffel bags had been packed since 0730 hours! We hung around the barracks until 1945 hours, when the trucks came to take us to the station.

The train cars were old-timers with 52 of us in each coach—

sitting up all the way, of course. The windows were wide open. We'll be picking out cinders and washing the soot from our hair for the next week.

The mess car was next to ours. We ate off paper plates, but the food was excellent.

In Kansas City we sat for 2 hours. For the first time I get the "urge" and we're not allowed to use the "biff"!

Oklahoma looked just like any other state...except for the cowboys and oil wells.

I sat guard duty last night for 2 hours. We had to sit in the

ALL CLEAN. Ann Mays (second from right) and her group of "Cinderellas" at Fort Dodge before their 54-hour train trip.

kitchen and see that the stove fire didn't go out. The kitchen was made over from an old baggage car, with counters on one side. The cook and four other girls slept on the counters!

It was nice, though, having people wave at us as the train rode along. In all the times I waved at troop trains, little did I think that some day I'd be on the receiving end.

By the time we got to Fort Worth, we were calling ourselves the "Cinderellas" of the armed forces. My hair feels like Brillo! Good thing it was dark when we finally got in.

We went right into our barracks—beds and *baths*! Lord, what a sight we were, after 54 hours on that train.

Boot Camp Taught This WAVE Lifelong Lesson

By Beverly Johnson Wesling, Eustis, Florida

What am I letting myself in for now?" I asked myself as I raised my hand and took the oath at the WAVES recruiting office.

My fiance, Bill, was off to sea, so I decided I could do my bit by joining the Women Accepted for Voluntary Emergency Service. If I had second thoughts that day, it was too late...we were on our way to boot camp at Hunter College in New York.

Jessie, a girl I met when I enlisted, met me at Grand Central Station. We took the

NO REGRETS. The first day in the WAVES was an experience for Beverly Wesling.

subway to Hunter College, where we joined a throng of green-horns. We eyed each other warily as a sharp-looking lady in a WAVES uniform guided us through various routines, all the while smiling encouragement to one and all.

"Hey, this looks like it might be fun," I said to Jessie, grinning excitedly, "and everyone seems so nice."

At that very instant another uniformed woman, barely 5 feet tall, shouted, "Now hear this! Line up in rows of two and follow me!"

Wide-eyed, Jessie and I grabbed our stuff and joined the wobbly line that was forming. "Gosh," I said to Jessie, "I hope we don't regret what we've done."

"Pipe down!" the "little" woman shouted at me.

That's when I found out I was in the Navy. Before the day was out, I had been drilled in Navy lingo and discipline. Most of all, this Yankee girl learned that "Yes, sir" and "No, sir" were not just terms used by Southerners.

Praying Babies and Young Mustaches

By Asta Ostlind Chase, McPherson, Kansas

My days as a Navy nurse in the San Francisco Bay area and as an instructor in the Hospital Corps School in San Diego provided me with many unforgettable memories...like the "praying" baby who had no name.

I was put in charge of a new maternity ward where one baby boy, born prematurely, stayed in the nursery for a few weeks. His parents hadn't named him yet, so I called him "Pedro".

Pedro developed a habit of putting his little hands together when he saw his bottle. It looked almost like he was praying.

After a while, as I would sit in a rocking chair to feed Pedro, I'd look up to see two or three sailors or Marines, patients from my previous ward, looking through the nursery window. They'd heard about Pedro—the baby who said grace before meals!

Then there was the blond teenager in one of my classes who was desperately trying to grow a mustache. Each day he'd come up, show me his profile and ask if his mustache was visible yet. Finally I told him that I'd bring some mascara the next day and help him out.

A few days later I was told to report to the commanding officer. "Lieutenant Ostlind," he asked, "is it true you used mascara on one of your students to enhance his mustache?"

"Yes, sir," I admitted.

"How do you expect to maintain any sort of discipline in your class with carrying-on like that?" he demanded.

"Sir," I replied, "you may enter my classroom unannounced at any time when I'm teaching. If you find any lack of order or discipline, I'll accept your reprimand."

I was dismissed without a reprimand, and as I went out the door, I was sure I saw the captain trying to hold back a smile.

In another class, I was going over "Special Watch" and emphasized that while on that duty, the corpsman is not to leave the patient under any condition until he's properly relieved.

As I expected, one hand shot up, followed with, "What if you really, really have to go bad?"

"I suppose in that case," I replied seriously, "you would have to use your head."

After a moment of stunned silence, the class erupted into wild laughter...and I joined them.

★

Being 'Lost' in Kansas Was Great Time for WAC

By Helen Horvath Ellis, Pompano Beach, Florida

'd been on leave from my duty in the intelligence office at the Pecos, Texas Army Air Base and visiting my family in Michigan. On the way back to the base, I was directed to the wrong train and ended up in Lawrence, Kansas.

There was no train to Texas for 2 days! Fortunately, a teacher at the station took me to her home, where I phoned my commanding officer .

WONDERFUL AWOL. An unavoidable delay en route left Helen Ellis stranded in Kansas...but she loved every minute of it.

The teacher invited me to spend the 2 days at her house, and the people of Lawrence couldn't have been nicer—I was treated to free meals in restaurants, free magazines and books and even free laundry service. I guess there's something about a uniform! When I got back to Texas I was confined to my barracks for a week. Quite a change from that good Kansas hospitality!

★

This Son Outranked Mom

By Donald Rohde, Los Osos, California

n September 1944, while in the western Pacific serving as lieutenant commander on a light cruiser, I received a letter from my mother that began, "Dear Don, Sir..."

Mother had tried to enlist in the Navy as a WAVE, but was overage. So she joined the Army Air Corps as a private.

Stationed at the Air Photo Reconnaissance Base in Coffeyville, Kansas, Mother worked in an office for a second lieutenant who called her "Mom".

In January 1945, after 18 months at sea, I was home on leave and staying with my in-laws in Peoria, Illinois. Mother came to see me, and a *Peoria Journal Transcript* photographer came out and took this picture of "Private Mom" and her officer son.

SON...SIR. Army private E.M. Rohde (right) ranked with Navy officer son, Donald.

★

This Navy WAVE Is Still a Flag-Waver

By Helen Anderson Glass, Tucson, Arizona

My life in the U.S. Navy WAVES helped make me the person I am today. I've been a member of the American Legion for 50 years and am also a member of the VFW, Order of the Purple Heart and other vet groups. I volunteer at the V.A. Medical Center in Tucson.

Does that sound like bragging? Sure it does...I'm a flag-waver!

I was stationed at Terrace Barracks in Opa-locka, Florida, outside the naval base there. This was Al Capone's former gambling joint!

Victor Mature was in the Coast Guard, and he helped our group put on a show, *Tar and Spars*. We had a lot of fun.

SALUTE from WAVE Helen Glass shows her pride 50 years ago—it continues to this day.

I met wonderful men and women in the service. They were all dedicated, patriotic young people, wanting to give our country their best.

★

Mess Line Didn't Help Uniform Shortage

By Virginia Kelly Homan, Denver, Colorado

One of the first indignities suffered in boot camp is being issued ill-fitting clothes. Back in 1943, my WAVES unit was spared that humiliation—but the alternative was worse!

We were going through our indoctrination at Hunter College in the Bronx, New York. For the first 5 weeks, the Navy didn't have uniforms for us, so we had to wear our civilian clothes. We wore them *constantly*, with no chance to have them cleaned.

The mess hall didn't help matters by making a mess of our single change of clothing.

The problem was, the KP crew worked very fast, slapping down huge helpings as we walked through the chow line.

Signs were posted everywhere warning, "There's a war on! Don't waste food!" So we had to eat everything that was placed on our trays.

We learned to pull our trays toward ourselves quickly to avoid any unwanted servings. This didn't always work, and we were often spattered with soup, oatmeal, spaghetti and runny eggs.

When we finally got our uniforms, a roommate and I were boxing up our "civvies" to send them home. As she tried to scrape 5 weeks' worth of food remnants off her tweed coat, she remarked, "What a shame to waste all this food!"

FINALLY. Virginia Homan was glad to be in uniform.

CHAPTER 6

John Court

Just a few months ago, the most exciting thing in your life was cruising Main Street on Saturday night with buddies you'd known since kindergarten. Hey: *"bo-orrr-ing!"*

That's nothing compared with finding yourself at an airfield in Goose Bay, Labrador, preparing to fly across the Atlantic Ocean, for Pete's sake!

Or, hitting the beach in Saipan...or being temporarily quartered in a luxury hotel on a Miami beach...or going to school in Biarritz, France. Wow!

This chapter is filled with interesting military tales that are so unusual they defy categorization. These "general" tales from veterans are so good, we just had to share them, so we decided to put them all in one place—this chapter.

Underlying all the diverse stories in the following pages is the abrupt way the military jerked us from our comfy, familiar lives and popped us down in every imaginable part of the world—Eniwetok, Frankfurt, Okinawa, Auckland, Stalag Luft 1, the remote mountains of India, Vietnam's jungles, Korea, North Africa, or the frigid seas off Manchuria.

For that matter, Harlingen, Texas sure wasn't anything like back home in Sheridan, Wyoming. Nor did South Dakota in January vaguely resemble Jackson, Mississippi.

Okay, some places were considerably better than others. But what are the chances we veterans would have learned so much about our planet any other way? What an education!

We learned smatterings of foreign languages, developed a taste for strange cuisines, lost our fear of "foreigners", got to share a tent with an honest-to-goodness Cajun, had dinner in a Jewish home, got through O.C.S. thanks to the help of the first black man we'd ever known, and picked up a case of "itchy feet" that still gives us the urge to travel.

We returned home with an enlightened appreciation of what "The Good Old U.S. of A." really meant. Doggone, we hadn't realized just how *good* it was. We saluted the flag with new pride and recited the Pledge of Allegiance with an informed heart.

Yes, after our stint in the service, the old home town looked surprisingly good, too.   —*Clancy Strock*

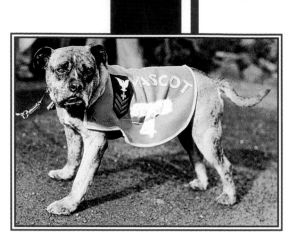

TOP DOG. With a collar, Churchill was a real leatherneck.

Churchill Was a Doggone Good Marine

By Joseph Siwinski, Cocoa Beach, Florida

Before he arrived in Auckland, New Zealand, Churchill took part in the initial landing at Guadalcanal. In fact, the story was he had been wounded there and received the Purple Heart.

Not bad for a 12-year-old bulldog! Yes, Churchill, named perhaps for his resemblance to the famous British prime minister, was our mascot, and a real traveler.

Churchill was brought overseas from the U.S.A. by some of the Marines who landed at Guadalcanal. Later, he accompanied the Marines to Auckland. Somehow he wound up at the naval hospital there, where he acquired his name and was adopted as the hospital mascot.

Exactly how Churchill got to that hospital isn't known for sure, but it was probably on an open garbage truck, his favorite mode of transportation.

Churchill was notorious for mooching rides. He'd jump into any moving vehicle he could catch up with (garbage trucks moved slowly). And, of course, just about everyone tried to steal him for themselves.

Churchill was a joy, and a problem. We had to keep an eye

on him whenever a truck drove into the compound. Anyone who was around at such times would have to run out and grab Churchill before he "hitchhiked" to another post.

Another bad habit of Churchill's was falling asleep when we showed movies. He'd doze off in the aisle, all four paws in the air...and he snored! Those who came late to the show usually tripped over Churchill.

Churchill slept like this all the time, and he slept soundly. This led to a gag some corpsmen would often pull on a sailor who went to town on liberty, especially a sailor who slept in an upper bunk.

They'd lift Churchill into the bunk. It took two men to do this, not only because of the height of the upper bunk, but because of the bulldog's weight.

Once "tucked in", Churchill assumed his usual four-paws-to-Heaven position and snored away peacefully.

When the hapless sailor got back off liberty, there was no way he could single-handedly remove the snoozing Churchill. Besides, Churchill had been given the rank of boatswain's mate second class!

There was nothing for the bunkless "libertarian" to do but sleep on the deck until morning when he could get help to move the massive mascot from his bed.

Churchill was responsible for spreading a lot of joy around Base Hospital 4. But the day came when, we assumed, an inviting garbage truck pulled into the compound and no one was watching Churchill.

We hope he brought as much joy—and some loud snoring—to some other lucky sailors and Marines.

★

The Hits Just Kept on Coming For These POWs

By Michael Pappas, Calimesa, California

On May 3, 1945, Stalag Luft 1 held about 10,000 downed Allied airmen, and exactly no German guards. They had abandoned the camp the night before, anticipating the advancing Red Army.

It didn't take long for some of our fellow inmates to break into the camp headquarters office, where they hooked up the radio to the loudspeakers on the fences.

That night, the radio picked up the BBC from London, which was broadcasting the U.S. Armed Forces Radio Hour. Featured this night was a recording of the *Lucky Strike Hit Parade*.

We'd been out of circulation for so long, these new songs were unfamiliar to us. But still we listened and cheered at each announcement of a song's position. After all, this was America we were listening to, and we'd soon be home!

But the biggest cheer—pandemonium really—came when the number one song on the hit parade was announced—*Don't Fence Me In*!

★

Oklahoma Kids Bombed Enemy With a Message

By William Woolman, Shell Knob, Missouri

Our Marine Corps B-25 was chosen for a rather special mission in May 1944 in the Pacific Theater.

We were part of a medium bomber squadron which normally hunted submarines, searched for downed aircraft, made chow runs to Australia and did some "skip bombing".

But this day we'd been elected to drop a different kind of bomb. Back home in Oklahoma, some 35,000 schoolchildren had each donated a dime to buy a new transport plane for the Marines.

They'd also signed their names to a 65-foot-long scroll and attached an ultimatum to Hitler and Tojo. Our mission was to drop this "bomb" on Japan.

BOMBER BOY. After the run.

Our commanding officers thought it would be fitting to have an all-Oklahoma crew deliver the bomb. Since Lieutenant Dick Morgan and I were the only two "Okies" on our crew, we adopted the other four as "Okies for a Day".

We flew from our base on Green Island to Piva on Bougainville, where we picked up the scroll. We attached a large flare parachute to it, then rolled the scroll around a burned-out machine

SCROLL AWAY. Before dropping the scroll on the Japanese air base, crew members check it out (top photo). General Ralph Mitchell added his name (bottom photo).

gun barrel to give it a little weight for proper descent.

With four Marine Corsair fighters flying cover, we dropped a load of bombs on Rapoppo Air Field on Rabaul Island. I had the honor of tossing out the scroll.

After we dropped the bombs, we circled to observe the results. The bombs left several craters on the airstrip, and the scroll floated gently down onto the middle of the airfield.

For all these years I've wondered what the Japanese thought when they got that message from 35,000 kids in Oklahoma.

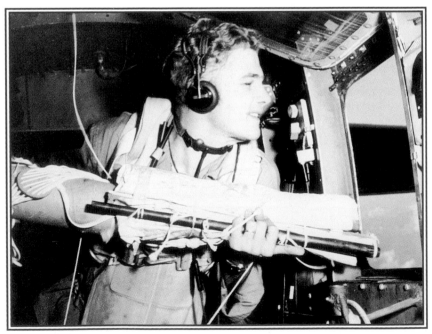

SCROLL AWAY! General Ralph Mitchell gives scroll to Lieutenant Dick Morgan (top photo). Bill Woolman had the pleasure of dropping it (bottom photo).

B-17 Waist Gunner Learned on the Fly

By Jim Burleson, Garland, Texas

Back in 1944, skydiving was not a sport. But I had a chance to try it on April 27, 1944 when our B-17 was shot down over Cherbourg, France.

The plane went into a spin and we were pinned to the floor. The autopilot was switched on and the plane pulled out of its spin briefly. I didn't hesitate to put on my chest chute and crawl to the back door. But I didn't know how to leave the plane.

When my ball turret gunner yelled at me to get out, I simply leaped, spinning end over end.

We were at about 18,000 feet, and I soon learned I could control my spinning and descent by using my arms and legs.

GERONIMO! Jim Burleson's first try at skydiving landed him in a German stalag. "Before" picture above, his POW photo's below.

I rolled over, faceup, so the chute wouldn't open in my face. But occasionally, I'd roll back to face the ground. It actually began to seem peaceful and quiet...especially since I didn't realize I was traveling over 100 miles per hour!

We had been taught to delay opening our parachutes until we were close to the ground, to avoid being strafed by fighters. They said we should look for windows in houses to determine our altitude.

I looked for windows. Guess what?...no houses. The ground was getting closer and closer, so I pulled the rip cord. Nothing.

I pulled again, harder. Seconds seemed like minutes, but finally the chute opened. Good thing I didn't wait any longer, because I made about two swings and hit the ground.

That was the end of my skydiving, and, for me, the fighting. I fell right into the arms of the Germans and spent the balance of the war at Stalag 17B in Krems, Austria.

Writin' About Fightin'

By Howard Sayre, Parker, Colorado

TYPE FIGHTER. Howard Sayre covered Korea.

I can't complain one bit about my military career. In Korea, I had travel orders equivalent to a field-grade officer's...and since I wore no rank insignia, I didn't have to salute anyone.

Of course, it didn't start out that way. I was trained as an artillery fire direction specialist and sent overseas in 1952 to Camp Drake in Tokyo. Once they found I could type—all of 30 words a minute—I was sent to join the First Cavalry Division in Hokkaido.

There I typed documents for court-martials. But since I was living in the same barracks as the guys who put out the base newspaper, I quickly let them know I'd done a little newswriting and was interested in working with them. A month later, orders came through assigning me to the First Cav's newspaper.

I always liked writing feature articles, so a Signal Corps photographer and I went around looking for stories. I did one on the Ainu people of Hokkaido, and the staff at Pacific *Stars and Stripes* in Tokyo saw it and liked it.

Stars and Stripes sent a reporter to do their own story on the Ainu. After I met the reporter and showed him around, he said he thought he could get me transferred to *Stars*

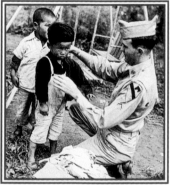

WET SUIT, DRY CLOTHES. Howard Sayre would go to any depth to get a story (left). But he also made friends with the local kids (above) when his mother and her friends collected children's clothes at home and sent them to Howard in Korea, where they were welcome.

SHOOTING STARS. Howard Sayre photographed and wrote about famous folks in Korea, like President Syngman Rhee (above) and legendary newsman Edward R. Murrow (below).

MRS. DIMAGGIO. An appearance by Marilyn Monroe (above) took the boys' minds off the war.

and Stripes if I wanted to try it.

"My bags are packed!" I said. In a short time I was back in Tokyo working for *Stars and Stripes*. Later I had the chance to go to Korea, and that was where I pretty much had free rein to go where I wanted and write about it.

The photos here were taken to go with some of the stories I wrote. I snapped some of the pictures, others were by Signal Corps photographers. I'll never forget my first ride in a jet or my brief stint as a deep-sea diver!

My "gravy days" with the Army in Korea had to end sometime. My wife was living alone in Tokyo, so I eventually took advantage of an early out and we headed back home.

His Ship Was the First Home After Armistice

By William Dietzman, Milwaukee, Wisconsin

In World War I, I was on a gun crew aboard a Navy transport that crossed the Atlantic 14 times taking troops to Europe. The trip took from 10 to 15 days, on a zigzag course, with our crew on watch for 4 hours, then off 4 hours.

We left Brest, France November 6, 1918 and headed back to New York for more troops. Five days later, while we were trying to get some sleep during our off hours, we heard an awful noise in the mess hall below our quarters.

"I wish those cooks would learn to hang on to their pots," my bunkmate complained.

Shortly, one of the guys in our division stuck his head into our quarters and announced, "The war's over, boys!"

My bunkmate threw a shoe at him and said, "Get out of here. We're trying to sleep."

But 2 hours later, we got orders to knock off the 4-on, 4-off shifts. It really *was* over!

We were the first armed ship into New York Harbor after the Armistice. There was no welcome. We just moved up the river and tied up at our pier.

★

Joining the Reserve Could Be Dangerous

By Dale Withem, Ashdown, Arkansas

After World War II, I found myself suffering from "post-service syndrome"—civilian life seemed boring to me.

I joined the Army Reserve so I could

DOUBLE VET. Dale Withem wasn't popular with his buddy when they both ended up in Korea.

meet with other veterans, share war stories and take a little more time to readjust.

My good friend LeRoy was a veteran, too. With much persuasion I convinced him to join. Shortly afterward, the Korean War began, and we "part-time soldiers" were called up to active duty.

LeRoy was furious! He swore that if our paths ever crossed in Korea, he'd shoot me on sight! I only half-believed him, but you can be sure I watched my back.

After the war I went to see LeRoy to try to bury the hatchet. He assured me that his anger had been only temporary, and we became good friends again, sharing Korean war stories.

After that, military life lost its appeal and I was happy to become a full-time civilian again.

★

Mid-Pacific Furlough Got Stretched

By Charles Boyer, Cape Coral, Florida

During World War II, I was the commanding officer of a Marine unit on an island in the Pacific.

Things had quieted down and it actually got rather boring. One day a young man in my outfit came in, said he had a 15-day furlough coming and insisted on taking it.

It didn't matter that we were in the middle of the Pacific—he just wanted to have his own time, with no roll calls or duties for 15 days.

That sounded reasonable, so I signed the necessary papers and he disappeared. I hadn't reckoned with the fact that we were in aviation and these kids knew their way around.

Fifteen days later, the boy was reported missing from muster. But he showed up on day 16 with quite a story. He had hitched rides on a number of airplanes and made it all the way back to Brooklyn to see his girl!

The only glitch was that he had missed a connection in Chicago, and that had made him one day late. No punitive action was taken.

Women on Board Were Good Luck

By Richard Amos, Akron, Ohio

I t took some doing considering the ancient naval taboo, but we finally convinced our skipper and executive officer that allowing girls aboard would boost the morale of the crew on the *USS Luzon.*

It was March of 1946 and the "Mighty Lu" was in port near Orange, Texas. With liberty every other night and weekend, four

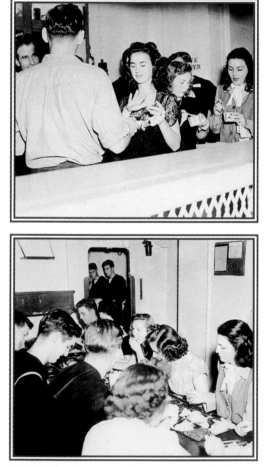

buddies and I spent a lot of time at the Orange USO. The girls there made us feel so welcome, we wanted to show our thanks.

My buddies—Jerry O'Rourke of Flint, Michigan, Bob Horne of Pittsburgh, Dick Dunnigan of Syracuse, New York, Dick Reed of Detroit—and I were a particularly close and imaginative group. What one of us didn't think of, another would.

One day we decided it would be a great idea if we each invited a young lady from the USO aboard for dinner.

It was no easy task getting the brass to suspend the rule against women on ships. But we finally convinced them it would be a great way to thank the USO for providing a place for sailors to enjoy liberty, and it would also

WAVE OF WOMEN. All eyes were on the ladies when Richard Amos and his buddies brought them aboard. The author is standing at left in the chow line in photo on opposite page.

168

build up the crew's morale to see beautiful young women dining with us.

All eyes were on us and our dates as we came aboard and went through the chow line. The girls enjoyed the meal, and the admiring glances.

After dinner, we took our dates to the ship's commissary for "pogie bait" (ice cream), then escorted them to the USO for an evening's entertainment.

We were grateful to the skipper and the exec for giving us permission to bring the young ladies on board, and for helping us gain a reputation as a group who could pull off anything.

★

A German Guarded Our Army Post

By Donald Lang, Kane, Pennsylvania

He didn't understand English and he often slept on the job. But he was the best guard we had at the 255th Ordnance Company just after World War II.

The day I met Hektor, I was in a bad mood. The war had ended and all my buddies were headed home. I had enough points to join them, but at the last minute was assigned to be commanding officer of the 255th, an outfit I'd never heard of, in a small town in the middle of Germany.

"Can I keep my dog?" asked Lieutenant Ray Cumb as he saluted and laid his transfer orders on my desk.

"The dog will probably be more welcome than you are," I joked. As I said, I was in a bad mood.

"*Hier, Hektor, kommen sie hier,*" Lieutenant Cumb called as he turned toward the open door behind him. Through the door came a big, beautiful German shepherd, limping slightly as he walked over to his master.

"Hektor, er ist der kommandant," Lieutenant Cumb said, pointing at me, *"und er ist gut."*

Cumb then asked me to come over, shake hands with him and pet Hektor. Then he asked me to let Hektor look me over real good. As soon as he did, I knew I had a canine friend for life.

Hektor was a German-trained war dog that didn't understand English. Cumb found him on the battlefield with a piece of shrapnel in his hip. The lieutenant rescued Hektor, nursed him back to health and kept him until the war ended.

Once Hektor joined our company, he made himself useful. Each night he slept with his back to the orderly room door. Any soldier coming late off pass would find Hektor frightfully near his throat.

A simple *"Hektor, platz!"* from me or the charge of quarters was all it took for Hektor to end the attack and lie back down as if nothing had happened.

One time an artillery observer flew in for an overnight visit and wanted a guard on his plane. I wasn't anxious to assign any war-weary soldiers to additional duty, but it seemed unavoidable. Then Lieutenant Cumb and Hektor came to my rescue.

We took Hektor to the field, opened the door of the plane and had him hop in the back seat. With another *"Hektor, platz!"*, we left him on his own. The next morning Hektor was asleep beneath the plane, which was, of course, just as we had left it.

Another time, when Hektor was staying with me, I left him in the house when I went to pick up the company payroll. But just as I got into the Jeep, I felt it shake. There was Hektor in the backseat.

I put Hektor back in the house, closed the door again, got back in the Jeep and this time watched the door. Soon a shadow appeared in the frosted glass window, the door handle turned down and the door opened just enough for Hektor to get his nose through. I took Hektor with me.

It worked out all right. I parked the Jeep, gave Hektor the usual *"Platz!"* and went in to get the payroll. I checked out the window occasionally to see Hektor sprawled out on the backseat, but alert. Everyone gave the Jeep a wide berth.

Hektor stayed in the rear seat on the ride back, just like a general on parade. And why not? He deserved a salute!

My First Car Was a Military Transport

By Edward Mullendore, Hagerstown, Maryland

SITTING PRETTY was author at end of Coast Guard motor trip.

At the end of Coast Guard boot camp at Curtis Bay, Maryland in 1947, just about everyone was being transferred to posts in other parts of the country.

I was put to work in the base fire department and hadn't yet received my assignment. Each day cars would come up for sale by those who were being sent too far away to take their old clunkers.

One day a '33 Chevrolet coupe came up for sale. She was black and sporty looking, with a rumble seat, yellow wheels and a louvered hood. She was beautiful!

I bought her for $75 and when I got my next pass, drove her home to Hagerstown. On the way the throttle stuck, the engine caught fire and I had to sit on a seat full of broken springs. I didn't care...she was still gorgeous!

My father and my girlfriend didn't see it quite the same way. "A fool and his money are soon parted," my father said.

My girlfriend shared that sentiment, especially when the car caught fire again on a date.

When I returned to base, my orders came through assigning me to Mayport, Florida. I pondered selling my beauty, but I just couldn't.

Instead, I received permission to drive to my new base, and learned I'd be paid 3¢ a mile! On top of that, two sailors who were taking their motorcycles to Mayport paid me $5 each to haul their gear. I had $20 of my own, so now I had $30 for the trip.

My father was certain I wouldn't make it. He had four new tires installed on the car and wished me luck...lots of it.

The first day, I rolled into Richmond, Virginia, where I stopped for gas. The station owner noticed my Maryland tag, and when I told him where I was headed, he called all his people over to look at "the crazy sailor and his rattletrap".

But he gave me a tank of gas and everyone wished me luck.

By that afternoon, all the truckers knew me because they'd passed me on the hills. If I stopped to eat, they'd buy my meal. One even offered to haul my car as far as Georgia!

In Florence, South Carolina, I stopped for gas just as the owner was closing. He had me drive the car into the garage, raised it on the lift and let me sleep in it for the night! The next morning, he also filled my tank, fixed a leaking water hose and bought me breakfast.

I made it to Jacksonville, Florida and stopped at a gas station to get directions to Mayport. The owner couldn't believe I'd made it all the way from Maryland. He also filled the tank, and he had his people give the car a wash job.

That night, when I arrived at the gates of the Mayport Coast Guard station, I was swamped with well-wishers. But the best thing was, I still had that $30!

I sold my beautiful Chevy a few months later for $275. That wonderful car had not only given me a great adventure, she gave me my first bank account.

MAN AND HIS CHEV. It was a '33 Chevy coupe like this one that gave Ed Mullendore (inset) a great adventure, a profit on the sale of the car, and his first bank account. Ed's dad wished him good luck, and Ed had it!

Beacon Duty Appreciated
By Both Sides

By B.J. Whitley, Alief, Texas

he recruiter had promised this Texas boy he'd serve in the sunny Gulf of Mexico. But the man must have forgotten to tell anyone else in the Coast Guard. I realized that when I found myself aboard a cutter bound for an isolated rock near St. Bride's, Newfoundland. We ended up snowed in all winter.

Six of us lived in three Quonset huts out there. Our only duty was to make sure an automatic radio beacon sent out the Morse code signal for the letter "C" for 4 minutes, followed by a minute of silence, repeating the sequence continuously.

This gave passing ships a signal they could use to get their bearings. We never knew when a ship was doing that.

One day we were put on alert because a Nazi sub had been detected offshore. Aware that our total arsenal consisted of one M-1 rifle, the boatswain had me call the operations office for instructions.

"Sit tight," Operations advised us. "The Nazis use you for bearings just as much as we do. They don't want you knocked out!" Which led me to wonder, isn't giving aid to the enemy considered treason?

★

We Went From Bullets to Books

By William Draves, Fond du Lac, Wisconsin

lthough some 4,000 enrolled for the first 8-week term, and about 12,000 graduated, the Biarritz American University, called by some a "noble experiment", lasted only 6 months.

Biarritz is a picturesque and fashionable resort town in southwest France, located on the Bay of Biscay, just a few miles from the Spanish border. But when World War II came to a close, this storied European resort town was turned into a university with a

SEASIDE U. GIs lucky enough to get in, got an education in one of the world's more scenic spots when they attended American University in Biarritz, France on the Bay of Biscay. It was "Camelot", one ex-GI said.

"campus" that included 90 villas and 40 hotels.

The university was created to give military personnel the opportunity to get started in a civilian career while still in uniform. For the 12,000 who eventually attended BAU, it was also an unexpected break from military routine, a chance to take up textbooks instead of arms.

Biarritz wasn't the only place this happened. There was a similar university in Shrivenham, England, and there was an Army University Study Center in Florence, Italy.

But in Biarritz we had classes in seaside villas, civic buildings and hotels. GIs who had gone through years of war now found themselves sleeping between sheets, eating French cuisine served by waiters, socializing with bikini-clad girls on the beach and taking part in drama, music and sporting events.

While some of the faculty were drawn from the armed forces in the European Theater, another 200 or so professors from the United States got off a troop ship at Le Havre and suffered a 10-hour ride in Army trucks to Biarritz.

In addition to the studies, a troupe of soldier dramatists presented *The Front Page*, *You Can't Take It With You* and *Richard III*. Between terms, the cast took *The Time of Your Life* to Paris for five performances.

There was a full symphony, a 60-voice chorus and a radio station that was on the air 20 hours a day. Athletes formed two basketball teams that beat the best in Europe, a fencing team and a track team. And there were side trips to Bayonne, Lourdes and the Basque country.

We GI journalists produced a daily newspaper, *La Banniere de Biarritz*, on an ancient French press, and I recall writing up the World Series finale, a 9-3 Detroit victory over the Cubs on October 10, 1945, from radio broadcasts.

An editorial in *La Banniere* after the first term said, "Biarritz has been more than just another assignment to us. It has given us a chance to act like human beings.

"The full significance of BAU cannot be noticed immediately. It will come to us many years from now when we sit with our memories and cherish them like rare gems."

Hugh Mulligan, an Associated Press feature writer who attended BAU as a GI, went back to Biarritz in 1965. He wrote:

"A Camelot of sorts once thrived there, a bright and shining city of the intellect. For some of us, there will never be another alma mater."

And now, 50 years later, with Biarritz American University surviving only in the archives of the Army Historical Section, I believe BAU was one of the nobler experiments of the war.

★

Marine's Seabag Got a Late Discharge

By Dale Young, Palm Harbor, Florida

I was with the Second Marine Division during World War II. Before going into battle, we'd pack all our belongings into our seabags for storage. After the battle, they'd be returned to us. That didn't quite happen for me.

I was wounded during the taking of Saipan in June of 1944 and spent 14 months in a hospital. I was discharged in 1945 and got married in 1946.

One day in 1949, there came a knock on my apartment door...special delivery. You guessed it—my seabag had finally caught up with me.

The things inside were mighty moldy, but I had a good time going through them and recalling my Marine Corps days.

My Chilly Trip 'Across the Pond'

By Charles Hoover, Sebring, Florida

When I was issued my first parachute, I promptly picked it up by the convenient big red handle.
Unfortunately, that was the rip cord. The parachute billowed

READY FOR TAKEOFF on this B-24 Liberator was Sergeant Charles Hoover, in England, 1944.

out all over me and my surroundings, to the great annoyance of the parachute riggers who had just issued it to me.

Fresh out of radar mechanic school in April 1944, I'd been ordered to England with the Eighth Air Force. I'd be crossing the North Atlantic in a B-17 "Flying Fortress".

We left Goose Bay, Labrador on a beautiful moonlit night. I carried a copy of the flight instructions, which told the pilots how to conserve enough fuel to make the long transoceanic flight.

The tips urged pilots not to mistake the northern lights for clouds and try to fly over them, and never to test their landing gear over the mid-Atlantic and have it freeze in the down position.

The instructions concluded, "A plane and crew in the ocean is of no use against Jerry."

We flew all night. As a passenger, I was back in the waist, which was unheated. When it came time to sleep, I went up near the radio, where there was a heater. The radio operator, navigator and I lay down on the floor like sardines.

The heater gave off fumes that made us drowsy, and soon we were out. The pilot couldn't raise us on the intercom, so he sent the copilot back along the catwalk through the bomb bay to wake us.

After that, I went back to the waist. It was very cold, but the air was fresh and wholesome.

Through my headphones I heard the navigator tell the pilot he thought we'd passed Iceland and that we should turn back. The pilot said we couldn't have passed Iceland and refused to turn.

"Let's get busy and find out where we are," the pilot said. By then it was daylight, but we were in a pea soup fog. After a long time seeing nothing but fog blowing by, the pilot ordered the radio operator to send out a Mayday.

There was a long silence, and then the pilot asked, "What about that Mayday?" The radio operator said all he heard was another plane sending out a Mayday.

"Come on, guys, this is getting serious," the pilot said. Shivering back in the waist, I agreed.

We slowly descended through the fog, hoping we wouldn't find a mountain in Greenland or Iceland. We saw nothing but the cold, gray waves of the North Atlantic.

I remembered what my dad had told me—the life expectancy of a man in the frigid water of the North Atlantic was about 20 minutes.

The seriousness of the situation intensified when the pilot said we were getting low on fuel. He ordered me to open our emergency kit from under the escape hatch.

There above the North Atlantic, somewhere near Iceland, I opened the kit designed to help us in this unforgiving environment. It contained a machete for hacking our way through the jungle, mosquito netting, insect repellent, sunglasses and chocolate that wouldn't melt at 120°!

I reported this "good news" to the pilot, then started praying while I awaited his order to abandon ship. But a short time later, the pilot suddenly announced he was picking up a station in Iceland on our radio compass and was homing in on it.

You can imagine how happy we were to land at Keflavik, Iceland. As we left the airfield in an open army truck, we waved to some native Icelanders, who in turn shook their fists at us. They didn't care much for the American "occupation", but we were mighty glad to be there just the same.

Oh, yes...I still have that machete on display in my home.

★

Hardened POW Really a Soft Touch

By Hal Lynch, San Antonio, Texas

My escape from the Germans and travels through enemy territory on the way to the Allied lines were exciting and, at times, *more* than exciting.

But the memory that stands out above all others is of an incident that took place after I had made it back into Allied territory.

During my 2-week trek across Germany, I realized I had crossed the lines only when I heard artillery fire behind me, directed east. I hadn't contacted any Allied troops, but something told me it would happen soon.

Sure enough, one day coming down the road toward me were two Sherman tanks and about 30 GIs. They gave me a loaf of bread and some K rations and told me to keep walking west. They didn't have time to talk.

"We have to take this town by 3 this afternoon," one said. "Just keep walking west toward Frankfurt. Someone will take care of you sooner or later."

They were right. About a half hour later, an Army truck came up behind me. In my best imitation of Clark Gable in *It Happened One Night*, I stuck out my thumb.

It worked! The truck stopped and the driver leaned out the window. "Hop in back," he said. "You'll have plenty of company."

How true. The truck was packed with German POWs! I worked my way to the front, sat down and looked at my fellow passengers. They were either very old, or very young. Some appeared to be as young as 14.

Suddenly, I was feeling mighty arrogant. After all, for so many months I'd been *their* prisoner. They fed me

KIND SOLDIER Hal Lynch (above) met German POWs...and a moral dilemma.

only a bowl of potato soup every other day and I'd lost 30 pounds.

Now I was in charge—and I had the food. Bumping along in the truck, I had a vengeful thought. I'd pull out my loaf of bread, take a bite, then throw the rest over the side as that woeful lot watched me. Then I'd have a good long laugh at them.

I took out the loaf and my eyes met those of one German boy who said, *"Nicht essen drei tagen."* (I haven't eaten in 3 days.)

It was then that the guidance of my wonderful parents came back to me. In this boy's eyes I no longer saw the enemy. I saw instead my old high school classmates and the kids I knew at the Central Queens YMCA in New York.

Always a soft touch for someone less fortunate, I handed the bread and the K rations to the boy. He shared the food with the others, and *"Danke, danke"* was repeated over and over from young and old alike.

World War II is long over. My hope is that the boy I met in the back of that truck in early 1945 never forgot the kindness of one American, and returned it to someone else.

When the Cold War Heated Up, It Was Time to Dial Direct

By Gary Zimmerman, Salem, Virginia

I n late 1965, I served aboard the destroyer *Alfred A. Cunningham* off the coast of Vietnam. We'd been supporting the Marines with our 5-inch guns when we got a better assignment—shadowing a Russian naval force. Little did we imagine that combat would turn out to have been less tense.

We'd been enduring oppressive heat while remaining constantly alert for probing enemy submarines. The tension and conditions put us at the limit of physical endurance.

But now, as we followed the Russian force in the northern Sea of Japan, cool breezes swept over us. Further north, the breezes turned to icy winds blowing at us from Manchuria. As we once fought the heat, now we fought the cold.

Our mission was no secret. We soon received a message

WARM SMILE and a sunny disposition look evident on Gary Zimmerman, back in August of 1965...and why not? In this photograph, he's seen steaming his way to Hawaii! He got a much chillier reception later on, in the northern Sea of Japan.

from the Russian ships welcoming us to their northern waters. The Russian naval force was no longer our primary adversary. We were about to learn what Napoleon learned—to engage Mother Russia is to engage Mother Nature.

Snow came at us in blinding swirls. Vapor rose from the churning sea like steam from a bubbling cauldron. And ice...the ice was everywhere.

Stanchions the size of water pipes in a house now strained under 6, 8 and even 10 inches of gleaming ice. The ship slowed and groaned under the deadly weight.

The inclinometer tracked the ever-increasing list to both starboard and port. The crew was strangely silent. Everyone knew the ship was getting dangerously close to the point where we'd capsize.

I was manning the equipment in the sonar room. Everything that would generate heat was turned on or in its standby position. The lead torpedo man came into the room, and I could see fear on his face.

He was the typical American sailor—big, strong, a stern leader. We knew that if our torpedo decks should be called into action, they'd be ready.

"Don't you think you should say something?" he asked.

The question puzzled me. "Say something?" I replied. "What do you want me to say?"

"Don't you think you should pray?" he said.

If things were so bad this hardened veteran thought prayer was necessary, I guess I did, too. So you bet I prayed, and not a child's "Now I lay me down to sleep" either. This was a person-to-person prayer, a direct line!

Finally, we broke off shadowing the Russians and eased into a protected bay. There we donned our Arctic gear and, tethered to strong lines, started beating on the ice with anything we could find, including broom handles.

Each man spent only 15 minutes or less in the deadly cold. After several hours of very dangerous work, the ship was able to swing south, where days later the ice began to melt in the warmer waters.

The lead torpedo man was still the stern leader, but I think we both learned a valuable lesson—in times of peril, even the strongest reach out, and up.

I Kept My Head in India

By Marshall Wikey, San Jose, California

I went to India in 1942 as part of the 10th Air Force. I was a P-40 mechanic, so, naturally, they made me a combat photographer.

My assignment was temporary—a Signal Corps unit was due to arrive in the next convoy. But photos were needed right away, and since I had some experience behind a camera, I was selected to stand in.

My job was to photograph the bombing raids in the China-Burma-India Theater. Since I was the only photographer, I went along on every mission.

On one such sortie, one of our B-25s went down somewhere in the Naga Hills near Dinjan, in the northeast corner of India. It was a mountainous area of extremely dense jungle.

That plane was equipped with a top secret Norden bombsight, and we couldn't allow it to fall into enemy hands. A lieutenant, another enlisted man and I were assigned to retrieve it.

Giant? No. At 5 feet, 11 inches, author towered over one of his Naga bearers. The Naga were at home in rugged country.

We flew to Calcutta, took a train, then drove a jeep as far into the bush as the trails would allow. We rode on elephant back until we got near the crash site, then organized a search party.

We used two native Naga bearers, who carried supplies and led the way. We didn't know where the plane was, but the Naga did, and they navigated our way through the jungle by relying on the native drum communications system.

Small in stature, the Naga had extremely powerful legs from climbing up and down the mountains with heavy loads. They could

BEARING UP. The Naga bearers, in front, didn't even breathe hard toting loads in the hills.

go to the top of a hill without stopping, then look back and laugh at us lagging far behind and panting from exertion.

The Naga were not warriors, but they did practice head-hunting. Great Britain, which controlled India, assigned overseers to circulate among the tribes to discourage the activity.

We paid the natives in Indian coins. They had no use for money since they used a barter system, so they'd turn the coins into pendants to wear around their necks.

We traveled for 2 days in jungle so thick we had to hack our way through with machetes. There were times the foliage was so dense we could see neither ground nor sky.

We covered less than a mile a day. Not only was it tough going, but we had poisonous pythons to contend with as well as a smaller snake whose venom was said to be so potent that once bitten, a man would be dead before he hit the ground.

We finally arrived at the crash site late one afternoon and camped overnight. Chattering monkeys and unknown animals constantly spoke out in the darkness, making sleep a real challenge.

The plane had fallen in a ravine so deep we had to use ropes to slide down to the bottom. The craft had apparently ricocheted off the sides of the ravine, scattering pieces all over.

None of the crew had survived. We buried the remains, then made preparations to blow up the wreckage. We dismantled the bombsight, taking all the parts we could carry. I took the photographs we needed, then we armed the bombs.

When we set them off, pieces of debris rained all around us. The lieutenant was on all fours, digging a hole as fast as he could!

The return trip took half the time because we could follow the tunnel-like trail we'd cut on our way in.

In spite of the grim aspects of the mission, it was a complete success. We'd accomplished all our objectives, thanks to our friendly aborigine allies.

★

Local Boy Returns Home In a Big Way

By Marshall Stelzriede, Alhambra, California

Although I had my share of thrills during 25 missions over Europe as a B-17 navigator, an even bigger air thrill happened before I ever left the States.

I was assigned to a combat air crew at Dalhart, Texas. After many training missions, we went to Scott Field, Illinois and picked up our brand-new B-17.

We had to calibrate its navigational instruments in the air, so we flew over a farming area about 20 miles southeast of Scott Field. Earlier I'd told the pilot my hometown of Orient was only another 50 miles in the same direction.

After the calibration, the pilot asked for a compass heading back to Scott. I gave him a heading southeast. He soon called me back and said, "We're headed for your hometown, aren't we?"

I confessed we were, to which he replied, "Well, let's give them a show."

We made four passes over Orient, so low we were almost down to the top of the 100-foot smokestack at the edge of town. The town only had about 800 people, so most of those who came out to watch were people I knew, including my parents who were in the backyard waving!

Everyone in town knew it was me—I was the only one from Orient serving on a B-17. To this day, whenever I visit there, someone brings up the excitement of the time we buzzed them.

The pilot had his day, too. On our way to Bangor, Maine, we went out of our way to fly over Elizabeth, New Jersey, where he saw his apartment building and high school.

★

Stranger's Helping Hand Helped Soldier in a Jam

By Ray Webber, Lindsay, Oklahoma

I finished basic training in December 1944 and had 10 days to report to Fort Mead, Maryland. On the way, I stopped at Baltimore and swung by a post office to send a package to my wife in Oklahoma.

I left the post office and strolled downtown, just killing time. I stopped in a cafe to get a bite to eat and discovered I'd left my wallet at the post office! It held $7, all the money I had.

I ran a mile to get back there, but found a locked door—the post office had closed. I banged on the door until a worker let me in. Another man there said a soldier had found my wallet and taken it with him. He left his address, which was Fort Mead.

That was where I was headed, but now I had no money to get there. I was leaving when a woman stopped me. She'd been mopping the floor and overheard the discussion.

"Soldier, what are you going to do?"

I told her not to worry, I'd make it there just fine.

She reached into her apron pocket, pulled out a little snap purse and gave me $5. It was all she had, and *a lot* of money back then. I tried to refuse, but she insisted, so I accepted it on the condition she give me her name and address so I could repay her.

The money got me back to camp, where I wrote my wife and asked her to send the kind woman her $5. Oh, yes. I found the soldier with my wallet—the $7 was still in it.

I Served Aboard a 'Large Slow Target'

By Michael Lacivita, Youngstown, Ohio

Evansville, Indiana and Ambridge, Pennsylvania as vital shipyards during World War II? Hard to believe today, but it's true.

And how the entire history of that war would have been changed had the mighty Mississippi River suffered the disastrous flooding of 1993 back in those years!

I learned all about it as a 19-year-old sailor. In October 1943, I was assigned to the newly commissioned LST 494. "LST" was a newly hatched term for a newly hatched ship, the "Landing Ship Tank". Or, as it became known, the "Large Slow Target".

BEER AND LEATHERNECKS were some of the cargo Michael Lacivita (right) had on LST 582.

186

Ours was the 49th ship built by the Evansville yard, out of an eventual total of 167. The overall length of an LST was 328 feet, with a width of 50 feet. It could carry 2,302 tons of cargo.

Each LST also carried anywhere from two to six "Higgins Boats", officially called Landing Craft Vehicle Personnel (LCVP), and had a modest ability to defend itself against enemy aircraft.

The flat-bottomed craft was built to hit the beach, lower its ramp, and spew out tanks, trucks, heavy equipment, artillery, troops and other cargo.

We sailed down the Ohio River, entered the Mississippi at Cairo, Illinois and arrived in New Orleans a week later. It was a shakedown cruise for our crew of 110, so we traveled by day and tied up at night.

I trained with the 494 for 5 months, but left it when the ship sailed for Europe. After some additional training, it was back to Evansville to pick up LST 582 and repeat the same trip.

As we approached the high bridge over the Mississippi at Memphis, two hot-rodding P-40 fighter planes roared out of the sky, flew under the bridge and buzzed our ship. Little did we know it was a preview of things to come.

Eventually the 582 proceeded through the Panama Canal and on to San Diego to pick up vital cargo—38,000 cases of beer destined for Pearl Harbor!

At Pearl Harbor we picked up our second cargo, a large contingent of gung ho Marines headed for the Admiralty Islands in the Pacific.

LSTs were also built in Jeffersonville, Indiana; Pittsburgh, Pennsylvania; and Seneca, Illinois. None of them could have made it into combat without the Mississippi River.

Name an invasion and LSTs were there—Normandy, Southern France, Africa, Italy, the Philippines, Iwo Jima, Okinawa ...the list goes on. In all, more than 1,000 LSTs saw service, many of them destroyed during invasion landings. They did their part in winning "The Big One".

Our 582 received two battle stars, one for the invasion of Lingayen Gulf in Luzon and the other for the 1945 invasion of Okinawa. Ironically, after being decommissioned on January 29, 1946, she was turned over to the Japanese Merchant Marine.

I served on the 582 from the beginning to the end. Those were the most memorable days of my life.

This 'Recruit' Learned Career Skills in Military

By John Hanson, Morton Grove, Illinois

The boy was barely alive when I reached out to him deep in a cave on Saipan. It was months after the invasion, but there were still snipers harassing our efforts to secure the island for the construction crews.

But this native boy was no sniper. In fact, he'd prove to be a big help in ridding the island of the snipers. A native work crew foreman told me the boy was 12, an orphan living with relatives, and that his name was Emmanuel.

When I next saw Emmanuel, he recognized me and wrapped his thin arms around me. I asked him to come along when I picked up the work crew. I started by taking him to the company mess hall where he devoured everything in sight, much to the delight of the cook. Then we worked on his English by taking him to the beach.

I drew pictures in the sand and slowly repeated the words for Emmanuel to mimic. He was eager to learn and soon mastered those words that were important.

We were making good progress on the construction projects in spite of the Japanese snipers. Dogs and tear gas were used, but we still couldn't root all of them out of their caves.

The native work crews were doing such a good job, I decided to reward them. I had sent Emmanuel to a Signal Corps outfit where he learned to operate a film projector. He proudly showed me his genuine Signal Corps projectionist card.

So we decided to give the crew a picnic and a movie. We picked a spot on top of a mountain overlooking Magicienne Bay. The new road the crew built made the area accessible.

The afternoon of the picnic, we loaded three trucks with the crew and supplies—bread, Spam and beer—and headed up the winding road to the mountaintop. At dusk, Emmanuel climbed a tree to hang the screen, then set up the projector. When it got dark, the crew began clapping eagerly for the movie to start.

It was a big success, but when the movie was over and the crew back in the trucks, Emmanuel came over and told me, "There's more people than came up in the trucks." At the time, I paid little attention.

But when the MPs told me the next day that they had picked up a number of Japanese in the village, all wearing native clothing, it dawned on me what had happened.

During the movie, Japanese hiding on the mountain mingled with the crowd. They were near starvation, so the bread, Spam and beer were powerful incentives. They then went back to the village in our trucks, having found an honorable way to surrender.

What a great way to clear out the remaining Japanese on the island, I thought. We'd have another picnic and take extra trucks!

Sure enough, at the next movie, more Japanese came out of hiding. The natives were in on the plan and made room for their "invited" guests, who could now surrender with dignity, while watching Hopalong Cassidy!

Years later I learned from a friend who visited Saipan that Emmanuel finished school on Guam, then returned to Saipan and became a businessman. He operated the only movie theater on the island!

★

Never Too Busy to Say Good-Bye

By John Schroeder, Waukesha, Wisconsin

I t was something of a tradition at Panzer Kaserne, home of the 97th Signal Battalion, near Boeblingen, Germany, to turn out, even when on duty, to say good-bye to a buddy.

"Short-timers" were the envy of everyone, as they called out the number of days they had left to every new arrival. In the photo, Mike (in dress greens), our company armorer, was as "short" as you could get...he was going home this day in 1964.

Mike would soon take a troop ship home. The four of us there to see Mike off would have our days soon enough.

Me, Sarge and the Invisible Man

By Jerome Chaney, Martinez, California

My father was about to ship out for Korea. I watched anxiously as he adjusted the jacket on his uniform and my mother straightened the knot of his tie and kissed his cheek.

In a few hours Sergeant First Class Edward Chaney would be gone. It was 1952 and the war in Korea was in full swing. My mother was about to experience the loneliness she'd felt as a young bride of only a few months. Back then it was World War II.

Sergeant Chaney would answer his country's call, as his service stripes, campaign ribbons and Purple Heart medal showed. But he was not quite ready to say his good-byes.

Kneeling down to me, he said, "Go get your cap, sport. We've got a matinee to catch."

Only moments before I was filled with despair. Now it was delight, as I dashed to my room, grabbed my cap and headed for the door.

We hopped in our '49 Chevy and headed for the State Theatre, where the marquee read *Abbott and Costello Meet the Invisible Man*.

JODY AND SARGE. In 1952, author and his dad (above) shared a special day before "Sarge" had to go off to fight again.

As my father stood there paying for the tickets, he seemed 20 feet tall and made of leather and brass. I delighted in soaking in the wondrous sight and smells of this man.

We sat amid hundreds of screaming, excited children. When the lights went out, my father reached over and placed his beefy hand on my shoulder. I don't think I ever felt so secure in my life.

Nothing could frighten me now, not even the Invisible Man. This time, I promised myself, no matter what came on the screen, I *wasn't* going to close my eyes.

It worked! I braced myself for the scary scenes, forcing myself to watch. After each scene, I'd glance victoriously at my father to see if he'd witnessed my heroics.

He had been watching me, and not just during those few isolated incidents. Apparently, he'd been watching me at length, and during the film's brightly lit scenes I'd catch the face of a smiling, but teary-eyed sergeant.

To make matters worse, my father began furtively checking his watch, calculating his remaining time. I began leaning my head on his chest, hoping he'd develop a pouch where I could jump in and remain forever.

But the movie ended and soon we were back in the Chevy, driving home. Dad tried to make conversation, while I sat, glumly grunting on occasion.

As we turned into the driveway, I saw my mother on the porch with duffel bags piled behind her. She was talking to a man in uniform I'd never seen before.

"Are you ready, sarge?" the stranger called as we got out of the car.

Before answering, my father reached down, lifted me up and hugged me. As I burrowed my head into his neck, I could feel him nodding to the other soldier.

At the car, he kissed my mother, then bent down to me for a final embrace. "Jody, you're the man of the house now," he said. "I watched how brave you were in the movie today. Not once did you close your eyes, not even when the Invisible Man appeared. If you weren't afraid of him, then imagine how easy it will be for you to handle the bad things that you *can* see."

With that, he kissed me on the forehead, came to attention and snapped me a salute. Then he was gone.

Sergeant Chaney came back all right, in a year. And although he shipped out again from time to time, I had the honor of knowing a father whose love of family and dedication to country made him a most visible man indeed.

A Heartfelt Letter to Say 'Thanks'

By Nickolas George Taminich, Buena Park, California

I was born in 1943 at the height of World War II. My father, Nick A. Taminich, did his part as officer in charge of the Army Air Command base in Coolidge, Arizona. After the war, it was up to him to close the base down.

I served in the Navy during the early '60s. Recently, I began to reflect on who I am and how lucky I am to be here. And I thought long and hard about the unselfish people to whom I owe a debt of gratitude.

My father and everyone else who served in World War II gave me and all Americans the chance to live a good life, in freedom.

That's why I sat down and wrote these lines to express my sincere thanks for what my father—and all the others—gave to those of us in my generation.

Dear Friends:

When I was born, the whole United States was at work for me. Fathers, uncles, brothers and young sons stood in lines to join

the war effort. To this day I don't know very many of you, because after the war you blended without fanfare into the new and progressive population of today.

Quiet though you've been, we must never forget the gift you've given us. The adrenaline produced within you pushed the United States so very far ahead, and thanks to you, I've grown up wanting for nothing.

You paid in advance for my freedom. I've been given a free ride at your expense, and at your families' loss.

After your job was finished, you returned to your old-new world and melted into its fabric, asking for nothing after having given your all.

To all of you I say *thank you*. Please accept my thanks for giving me the chance to live my life in freedom.

P.S. I'm sorry I was too young to help, and very sorry it took me so long to express my gratitude.

★

IN MEMORY of his father (right), author (left, on Okinawa in 1962) wrote this letter. Elder Taminich is honored at service (below).

CHAPTER 7

G. I. JOE'S
BEST COFFEE
BETWEEN HERE AND C.B.I.

ARMY NURSES in Europe in 1944
enjoyed hospitality of the Red Cross.

John Court

My mother, like so many mothers of servicemen, was determined to do something on behalf of the war effort during the 1940s. So she worked long hours in our small town's Red Cross office, helping young wives cope with life as single mothers, rolling bandages, making home calls and doing a host of other much-needed chores.

But her major contribution to the war effort occurred during a train trip to visit me. It was, beyond argument, the biggest personal sacrifice she made for her country.

To appreciate it, you need to understand one thing about Mom. When it came to alcoholic beverages, she was miles to the right of the WCTU. Whiskey was, as the old Roy Acuff song went, "the devil in liquid form". She actually crossed the street to avoid walking past the only tavern in our town's business district.

So here she was on a crowded train. Frantically shoving their way through the jammed aisles came two sailors. Entering the car in hot pursuit were two Shore Patrolmen.

One of the sailors thrust a pint bottle of booze into Mom's hands and gasped, "Quick, hide it!" and then continued his flight.

It posed a moral dilemma of monstrous proportions to Mom, the lifelong foe of Demon Rum. She had to make a snap judgment. Reluctantly she hid the pint under her skirts.

"They seemed like such nice young men, and I didn't want to get them in trouble," she explained later. "It wasn't the right thing to do—but, you know, those boys *were* serving their country."

A half hour later, the sailors returned to retrieve their treasure. I'm sure Mom gave them a tight-lipped, halfhearted smile when they thanked her. Little did they suspect she had just made what was by far her biggest sacrifice on behalf of winning World War II.

Meanwhile, hundreds of thousands of other home front Americans were making their own contributions, each in their own way, to hasten victory. Some of their stories are recalled on the pages that follow. —*Clancy Strock*

'I Pedaled Hard for Western Union'

By Patricia Calvert Collins, Bend, Oregon

In the early '40s when World War II began, I was 16 and working as a carhop at a drive-in. Before long my brother was sent overseas with the 82nd Airborne Division, and my boyfriend went with the 101st.

Many of my friends were enlisting, and I wanted to do my part. So I quit my job and became the only messenger girl for Western Union in Merced, California.

My "uniform" was a Western Union cap, and my transportation was a "victory bike"—no frills, thin-tired and lightweight.

I still recall how proud and important I felt as I pedaled furiously to deliver telegrams to families whose sons and daughters were in the service.

PEDALING FOR VICTORY. In 1943, Pat Collins was the only messenger girl at the local Western Union.

In many cases the messages were good news. But other times my heart was heavy as I handed a parent or wife an envelope stamped with a star—the dreaded symbol that meant "missing" or "killed in action".

I recall listening for the train to come into town with soldiers aboard. I'd zip over to the depot and slowly ride my bike past the open windows, picking up mail they had written along the way. I'd then rush to the post office so their mail could get on its way just a little sooner.

Even though safely stateside, I was once "wounded in action".

One stormy night I had a telegram from a service boy who was on his way home and wanted his folks to pick him up at the station early the next morning. I was pedaling as fast as I could to get it delivered.

Suddenly I heard the air raid sirens that signaled "lights out". The next thing I knew, I was flying down the road in total darkness. I hit a bump, flipped off my bike and was knocked out.

When I came to, I was on a sofa in a strange house. "You all right, honey?" asked a sweet woman peering down at me with anxious eyes. I said I was, but didn't know how I had got there.

She explained that her husband had been on his way home when he heard the sirens and decided to park the car and walk. Along the way, he tripped over me in the middle of the road! He picked me up and carried me to their home.

That wonderful man had then gone back to get my bike and was in the garage fixing it when I regained consciousness. When the "all clear" sounded, he drove me to deliver the telegram and then took me home. That was a perfect example of the neighborly attitude of the time.

Reflecting back on those days, I miss them so much. We were a nation who cared for one another then, a loving, sacrificing family with one goal in mind—to bring an end to the war and get our fighting men and women safely home once again.

I was proud to do my part by helping people keep in touch with their loved ones.

★

I Was the USO Hostess For a Whole Troop Train

By Marilyn Keller, Ogden, Utah

I was only 17 when I was called to "frontline duty" at the Ogden, Utah USO, where I was the secretary. The workday began at 10 a.m. But I came in at 8 to get started on my secretarial duties, and I usually got a lot done before anyone arrived.

Union Station was just 3 blocks from the USO. One spring

morning in 1943, a train stopped and unloaded a bunch of hot and grimy men who'd been aboard for 3 days. They were directed to the USO for showers.

On the way, a butcher gave the servicemen a couple of boxes of hot dogs and a baker gave them some buns. Into the USO they trooped.

This happened before the rest of the USO staff arrived, so I was completely on my own. I handed out towels until we ran out. I handed out soap until we ran out. Then the hot water ran out. With nothing left to hand out, I started cooking the hot dogs and left the boys to figure out how to shower with cold water and no soap, and dry themselves with wet towels.

We did have some fresh apple pie and ice cream on hand, so when the hot dogs were gone, I served apple pie a la mode. I dipped ice cream until I felt, and looked, like a big sticky ice cream bar.

The friendly soldiers talked and laughed and flirted with me. I loved it!

At exactly 9:45, the person in charge of the troops came in and sent everyone marching back up the street to the train. At 10, my boss came in and launched into a lengthy dissertation on how bad the USO and I looked that morning. After a lot of explaining, I was allowed to go home, take a hot bath and change my clothes. That was a morning I'll never forget!

★

Crop Corps Gal Knew Beans About Home Front Service

By Dorothy Brockhausen, Waianae, Hawaii

As the summer of 1945 rolled around, we patriotic girls were "gung ho" to do our duty. After all, most of us had boyfriends in the service.

So a bunch of us from my all-girl high school in New York City signed up as "Victory Farm Volunteers" in the U.S. Crop

GET A GRIP. Dorothy Brockhausen (right) and sister Victory Farm Volunteers Dotty (left) and Barbara get ready to grab their grips in Geneva, New York in July 1945.

Corps. Part of the USDA's War Food Administration, the program was put in place to help bring in the summer harvest.

Early in July, the nearly 100 girls in our group met at Grand Central Station. Suitcases in hand, we were ready to begin our harvesting adventure.

We "shipped out" by train to Geneva, New York, in the Finger Lakes region, to pick string beans.

We stayed in the local high school gym and were trucked to the field each day. Our pay was 50¢ a bushel, but our room and board was $10 a week! We had to pick fast to cover our costs.

The trucks that took us to the fields had open beds with planks around the sides for seats. Each truck carried the day's essentials—water, lunch and the various toilet articles.

One August afternoon there was a great commotion at the weighing station where we checked in with our bushels of beans. The war was over!

Of course, no more picking was done that day. As we rode through town singing and laughing, we festooned Main Street with toilet paper. It was the only confetti we had!

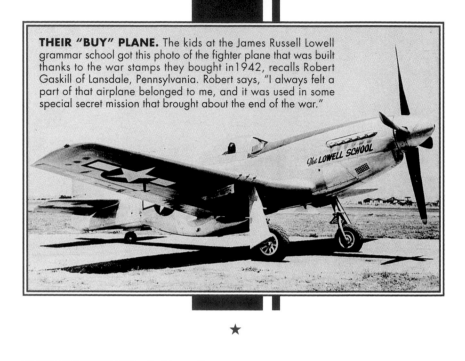

THEIR "BUY" PLANE. The kids at the James Russell Lowell grammar school got this photo of the fighter plane that was built thanks to the war stamps they bought in 1942, recalls Robert Gaskill of Lansdale, Pennsylvania. Robert says, "I always felt a part of that airplane belonged to me, and it was used in some special secret mission that brought about the end of the war."

★

'I Served With the Tin Cannoneers'

By Sharon Ritter, Pekin, Illinois

I'd almost forgotten about my years of service in the old outfit. But then I happened across a memento in a box of school photos while I was cleaning out the attic.

There it was, tucked carefully away between some fourth and fifth grade "mug shots". It was that precious symbol of my childhood—the stripes I earned as a sergeant in the ranks of the "Tin Cannoneers".

Just about every grade school kid I knew enlisted in the Cannoneers during World War II. We fought on the scrap metal front lines by doing door-to-door duty.

After school and on weekends, we collected empty tin cans. My sister Elaine and I ran a regular patrol up and down the seven-block length of our street in Peoria, Illinois.

The cans and pieces of scrap metal we collected were recycled into material needed for the war effort. Our collected metal was weighed, and each Cannoneer was given a credit for pounds delivered.

Cannoneers started out as privates, then advanced through the ranks according to the accumulated weight of their metal. It took at least a million tons to earn a set of sergeant's stripes...or so it seemed to me then!

I never met anyone above the rank of sergeant, although it was rumored some "higher-ups" were around. But that would have been tough, because metal cans were more scarce then.

Most housewives used canning jars over and over, buying metal-canned goods as a last resort. I was convinced that earning a lieutenant's rank in the Cannoneers would have required a raid on a Del Monte factory!

Just collecting the cans was hazardous duty. Most had jagged edges where they were opened (no neat electric can openers in those days). Plus, we had to cut the bottoms out and place them inside before we could mash the cans flat.

Then there was the dreaded KP pulled by a dedicated Cannoneer when someone donated a whole sack of empty cans that still contained food residue. Such cans were often inhabited by enemy invaders of the insect variety, and this was in the days before chemical warfare fought with products like Raid.

But despite our casualties, we marched on, undaunted, until the end. And where are all those gallant comrades in arms today? I'd like to meet some of them again, especially anyone over the rank of sergeant.

I'd like to find out where on earth they found all those cans!

★

'I Had 20,000 Dance Partners'

By Jean Carroll, Carlsbad, California

The swing era was a terrific time for a teenage girl to grow up. I remember those days well because I was lucky enough to have a father who led a Big Band...and we lived on a naval base with 20,000 sailors. There was never a lack of

dance partners for me!

My father was Chief Musician Guy Lyda. He was bandmaster on the carrier *USS Hornet* when it was attacked by Japanese kamikazes. Dad was helping tend the wounded during the battle when he was knocked overboard. A Marine risked his life by jumping in and saving him.

After the *Hornet* was sunk, Dad was transferred to San Diego. It was there, at the Pacific Ballroom, where I first danced to the Big Bands.

Every Sunday my father would take me to the ballroom. I met Red Skelton, Glen Gray, Jimmy Dorsey, Bob Crosby and others. I even danced cheek-to-cheek with Rudy Vallee while the band played *Sentimental Journey!*

From 1944 to 1946, Dad directed the band at the Sampson Naval Training Center near Geneva, New York. Though I was just in high school, I attended dances every night.

I never had to worry about a dance partner at Sampson. Sailors were lined up waiting to grab a girl for the next dance. The ratio was something like 50 men to one girl.

The dance floor was huge, so there was plenty of room to boogie-woogie or do the lindy. Sometimes a partner would spin me onto the floor where we'd

LEADER OF THE BAND. Jean Carroll (top) was dolled up and ready to dance in this photo. Her father, Guy Lyda, led the band (above in 1945) at Sampson Naval Training Center.

find ourselves dancing alone, surrounded by clapping hands.

That big dance floor came in handy when things started jumping and I'd find myself lifted high over heads or tossed under legs! But when we danced to the slow tunes, like *Stardust* or *That Old Black Magic*, I was able to talk to my partners and find out where they were from.

My father's band played for most of the dances. When one of my partners would remark that the band was great, I'd proudly say, "That's my dad."

Dumbfounded, the sailor would stare at me and say, *"He's your father?* Wait till I tell the guys I danced with the Chief's daughter!"

But Dad's band wasn't the only entertainment at Sampson. A number of USO bands played there, as did the great Artie Shaw. He came to Sampson frequently, and I got to dance with him, too. I even met my future husband there. It was a great place to be!

I can truthfully say of all the bands I danced to, my dad's was among the best. But my favorite was the Glenn Miller Or-chestra, so you can imagine what a thrill it was to meet Glenn Miller himself.

Dad introduced me to Glenn at the Sheraton Hotel in Washington, D.C. I was so proud when Glenn greeted my father with, "Hi, Chief, it's good to see you again."

And my heart nearly stopped beating when Glenn turned to me and said, "Hello, young lady, I'm glad to meet you."

They were great times and I have great memories of them. Perhaps some ex-sailors reading this share the same memories and maybe even danced with me way back when.

ANNIVERSARY WALTZ. Still tripping the light fantastic, Jean and husband Ed led the way to the dance floor on their 44th anniversary in 1991.

Unscheduled Stop Got Sailor Home

By Tim Sedman, Gainesville, Virginia

After 2 years on a destroyer in the South Pacific, I was going home on leave. I found myself on a long train ride from Seattle, Washington to Dayton, Tennessee.

I'd been aboard for 3 days and the train had just crossed into Tennessee. It was late at night and I was sitting alone when the conductor came by and asked where I was going.

When I told him I was going to see my parents in Dayton, he said, "You've traveled far enough"—and arranged for the train to make an unscheduled stop!

My ticket was to Chattanooga, the nearest destination to home. At Chattanooga I was to hop a bus back to Dayton, a backtracking trip of 3 hours. With that kind conductor's help, I was home in 10 minutes.

★

This Liberator Had Her Name on It

By Betty Small, Manteca, California

When the 5,000th B-24 Liberator rolled off the line at the Consolidated Vultee Aircraft Corporation in San Diego, California, it had my name on it—in lipstick!

All employees who had worked on the historic B-24, nicknamed *V Grand*, were invited to sign the plane before it was flown overseas for duty in World War II.

It happened in June 1943, when I worked at the plant along with my husband, Lee, and my mother and father. I was a blueprint file clerk and joined with hundreds of others who lined up to sign the Liberator.

I happened to be standing next to the plane when a Fox Movietone News photographer walked up and asked me to sign the B-24 so he could film it.

I was thrilled, of course, but replied that I had nothing to sign with. He suggested I use lipstick, if I happened to have any.

I did have a tube—it was a cardboard container, because all metal was being used for the war effort. I wrote my name in lipstick on the big white star painted on the plane's side. Today, I still have what's left of that lipstick.

I later learned that this Liberator flew in the Mediterranean Theater with the 15th Air Force, and all of our names remained in place while the bomber was in combat.

There were 18,000 B-24s built during the war. There is only one still flying, and I've seen it twice at the Stockton, California airport near my home. It's exciting to see, bringing back memories from the days when they flew B-24s I helped build.

In more recent times, my family continued helping to "build" B-24s. My nephew, Gary McElfresh of Flagstaff, Arizona, is a volunteer fire watch ranger and often hikes the trails in the San Francisco Mountains near Flagstaff.

Over the years, he has found many parts from bombers that crashed during training flights.

Gary donated some of those parts to help restore the only flying B-24. Now when the plane is flown to Arizona, Gary often hosts the crew.

STICKING IT TO THE AXIS. With a swirl of her lipstick, Betty Small autographs the B-24 Liberator she helped build in San Diego in 1943. She's still got the lipstick!

Blacked-Out Bus Rang With Song

By Kenneth Bowers, Mount Pleasant, Texas

My family moved from Texas to San Diego at the start of World War II so my dad could work in the Consolidated Vultee defense plant as an airplane assembler.

We lived in Linda Vista, a settlement of prefabricated houses built for the influx of workers. We commuted to San Diego by bus for work, church, shopping and an occasional movie. We spent a lot of time on the bus—and it was *always* packed.

People from all walks of life had moved to the West Coast to work or serve in the armed forces. The bus was filled with people from many different states.

After nightfall, you never got a look at your fellow passengers' faces on the bus. A wartime blackout rule decreed that no lights were to be on inside the bus once it was away from the city. We rode in total darkness from the time we left San Diego, through all our stops, until we finally reached home.

But as it began to get dark, a wonderful thing would happen. From a corner of the bus someone would start singing. He or she wouldn't get out more than two or three notes before everyone on the bus would join in—even the driver.

We'd roll down the road happily belting out the tunes of the day, *Mairzy Doats, Bell Bottom Trousers, Don't Fence Me In*, and even *White Christmas* when it was brand-new.

When one song ended, it was a race to see who could start the next. Sometimes there were two or three tunes going at the same time.

The strongest voices would win out, but there were no hard feelings. In fact, the drowned-out song was usually sung next.

My favorite song was *Deep in the Heart of Texas*. We sang it at the top of our lungs and clapped our hands so hard they'd sting. Sometimes we sang it two or three times, depending on how many Texans were on the bus.

We'd roll along in song, oblivious to the world's troubles. After we turned onto the Linda Vista road, we would start making stops to let people off. The volume of our sing-along would drop a little at each stop until the main stop at Linda Vista, where there would be a mass exodus.

That was where most of the best singers got off. There'd be only a few of us left, but we didn't stop singing. Even when we got to our stop, which was the end of the line, and there were only a half dozen of us left, we'd keep singing until the driver opened the door to let us out.

By that time, my throat was parched and my head so full of tunes I could hear them buzzing around as we walked the two blocks to our house, usually with me atop Dad's shoulders.

In a way, it was sad when the war ended. Not because the war was over, but because when the lights came back on, the music stopped. It was as if everyone was worried someone would know who was singing.

But for several years we enjoyed the anonymity the dark afforded and the courage and camaraderie gained from it. Never since have I felt as safe and peaceful, or as friendly toward my fellow man, as I did as a little boy on a dark bus, singing joyfully with people I'd never met.

★

Wartime Train Trip Was Friendly Fun

By Bette Johnson, Amarillo, Texas

I'd never seen so many people! It was 1944 and the Amarillo station platform was crowded with soldiers and their families. Our annual auto trip to Grandma's house had been canceled because of gas rationing, so we were traveling by train instead. I was 9 years old and excited about the adventure ahead.

Father was in the lead, gripping my hand and pulling me along after him. I held my mother's hand tightly as she followed. If we got separated in this mass of humanity, we might not find one another again.

We stepped up to the coach, handed our tickets to the conductor and climbed aboard.

The coach was as crowded as the station platform had been. When they saw Mother and me enter the car, two soldiers gallantly rose and gave us their seats. It was quite a sacrifice, since there was no place else to sit down except on their suitcases in the aisle or perched on the arms of other seats.

Finally the Atchison, Topeka & Santa Fe locomotive huffed and groaned as we pulled out of Amarillo.

The young servicemen around us were chatty and friendly, especially to me. "I've got a little sister about your age," said one. Another complimented my mother on her "pretty child". I enjoyed the attention and flattery.

Despite the crowded conditions, there was almost a party atmosphere. My father, a magician, never left the house without some of his tricks in his pockets. It didn't take long for him to fish them out. Since he didn't have a seat, he performed in the aisle.

As night fell, he traveled the length of the car, amazing and amusing the soldiers.

One of them had a harmonica and began to play. Soon we had an old-fashioned sing-along in progress. We sang old-time favorites like *Oh, Suzanna*, *Clementine*, *My Wild Irish Rose* and many others. I knew most of the words and sang right along with the grown-ups.

The train carried no dining car, so everyone had come prepared with food for the evening meal. It turned into a giant picnic as we all shared cookies and sandwiches. I especially recall how difficult it was to carry little paper cups from the water dispenser at the far end of the car back to our seats.

As I looked outside into the darkness, I could no longer see the countryside flying by. We had become a little world all our own, hurtling through the night.

One of the soldiers, Eddie, turned out to be good at drawing portraits. He would sketch a face and then tint it with his colored pencils. Soon everyone wanted to have their portrait done.

By the time he got around to me, he discovered he was out of paper. But he had a solution. He sent me to the ladies' restroom for paper towels. I remember trying to sit very still as the train swayed and bumped.

Eddie's finished job was excellent, and I still have the tattered paper towel with the likeness of a little girl with a big blue ribbon in her hair. I had a crush on Eddie for years.

We reached our destination in the wee hours of the morning. My granddaddy was there to meet us. I stood on the platform and waved good-bye to my new soldier friends until the red taillight on the caboose dimmed, then winked out of sight.

I often think back over that night so long ago. I wonder about the soldiers we met. Did Eddie survive the war? What became of the harmonica player? Are there veterans who remember my father's magic tricks?

What did the future hold for all those young men on that wartime train that sped through the night?

★

Airmen's Trip Home
Was a Real Sleeper

By John Woodward, Largo, Florida

WELL-RESTED. Author (right) and his buddy, Shorty, got a good night's sleep on their train ride home in 1944, thanks to a grateful conductor.

November 8, 1944, was election day—but my buddy and I weren't thinking about politics. Shorty and I were jubilant that we'd survived our 50-mission tours as turret gunners aboard a B-24 in Europe. We were going home!

At the Philadelphia train station, we waited to board the *Limited*, bound for Chicago and furlough processing at Fort Sheridan. We had a long ride ahead, but it had taken a lot longer to get this far. Our liberty ship crossing from Italy was 23 days.

When the *Limited* rolled in, we boarded a standard coach and settled into facing seats at the front of the car. The train left Philly just before twilight and we reveled in the sights of our country rolling by the window until they became lost in nightfall.

The call for dinner broke up our gin rummy game. Dinner in

the diner was finer than the chow overseas...but not by much.

Back in our coach, we realized it was going to be a long night. Anyone who recalls the rock-hard seats of World War II passenger trains knows what I mean.

We sat down again, figuring we'd do the best we could, using our musette bags for pillows and our heavy wool overcoats for blankets.

Our friendly conductor stopped on one of his tours and told us the lights would be dimmed in 15 minutes. He returned moments later, sat on the arm of my seat and said, "Tell me where you've been and what you saw...and tell me about your decorations."

That unleashed a veritable waterfall of stories from Shorty and me. We told him about everything, both the good and the bad. The conductor seemed genuinely interested and showed a fatherly concern at our accounts of the difficult times.

He finally rose and said, "Goodnight and lots of luck to you. I must dim the lights now."

But just as we were pulling our overcoats snugly around our necks, the conductor returned and had me move my feet so he could sit down.

"Be quiet while I tell you something, and when I finish, don't make a fuss," he whispered.

He told us there was a spare sleeper compartment in the following car and he'd made arrangements with the porter for us to occupy it that night.

"When you pick up your luggage, do it casually and go to the sleeper," he said. "Just one thing—be sure to tip the porter a couple of bucks for remaking the beds."

We found it difficult to thank him without arousing the curiosity of our fellow travelers. He had to hush us.

The three of us stepped out of the car. The wind blew hard and the clanking coupling plates shifted beneath our feet. The noise made normal conversation impossible.

As we thanked him and shook his hand for the umpteenth time, he said, "It's nothing. I'm happy to be able to do something for you."

I turned to go and he pulled me close, "I have a boy in the service," he said, "and I hope someone will do something like this for him."

★

Yearning for the Land

ALSO BY JOHN WARFIELD SIMPSON

Visions of Paradise:
Glimpses of Our Landscape's Legacy

YEARNING
FOR THE LAND

A Search for the Importance of Place

JOHN WARFIELD SIMPSON

Pantheon Books New York

Some portions of this book were previously published in
Visions of Paradise: Glimpses of our Landscape's Legacy.
Copyright © 1999 by John Warfield Simpson.
Reprinted by permission of the University of California Press.

Grateful acknowledgment is made to the following for
permission to reprint previously published material.
OXFORD UNIVERSITY PRESS, INC., AND FABER AND FABER LTD.:
Poem "The Debtor" from *Collected Poems* by Edwin Muir.
Copyright © 1960 by Willa Muir. Reprinted by permission of
Oxford University Press, Inc., and Faber and Faber Ltd., London
WISCONSIN HUMANITIES COUNCIL: Excerpt from a pamphlet by
Wallace Stegner. Originally published by the Wisconsin Humanities
Committee, republished in the book *Where the Bluebird Sings
to the Lemonade Springs: Living and Writing in the West* (New York:
Random House, 1992). Commissioned and published
by the Wisconsin Humanities Committee with support
from the National Endowment for the Humanities.
Reprinted by permission of the Wisconsin Humanities Council.

A cataloging-in-publication record has been established for
Yearning for the Land by the Library of Congress.
ISBN: 0-375-42086-X

www.pantheonbooks.com

Book design by M. Kristen Bearse

Printed in the United States of America
First Edition
2 4 6 8 9 7 5 3 1

To

KATHERINE ANNE

AND

EDWARD WARFIELD

Breathes there the man, with soul so dead,
Who never to himself hath said,
This is my own, my native land!
Whose heart hath ne'er within him burned,
As home his footsteps he hath turned,
From wandering on a foreign strand!
If such there breathe, go, mark him well;
For him no Minstrel raptures swell.

SIR WALTER SCOTT, *The Lay of the Last Minstrel*

CONTENTS

EAST LOTHIAN REGION, SCOTLAND

Anstruther

Firth of Forth

BASS ROCK

North Berwick

Atlantic Ocean

North Sea

SCOTLAND

Edinburgh

Glasgow •

Area of Detail

Berwick-upon-Tweed

IRELAND

ENGLAND

A198

Peffer Burn

John Muir Country Park

Binning Wood

Belhaven

New (Victoria) Harbor

Old (Cromwell) Harbor

Tyninghame Estate House

Belhaven Bay

Tyninghame

St. Baldred's Church

A1

Dunbar

Broxmouth Estate House

East Linton

West Barnes

Catcraig

River Tyne

Hedderwick Burn

Biel Water

Brock (Spott) Burn

△ *DOON HILL*

Skateraw Harbor

△ *TRAPRAIN LAW*

Dry Burn

Cove

Cove Harbor

Dunglass Collegiate Church

Pease Bay

Dunglass Estate House

Siccar Point

DUNGLASS DEAN

Cockburnspath

PEASE DEAN

Lammermuir Hills

A1

0 Miles   4   6   8   10

0 Kilometers   10

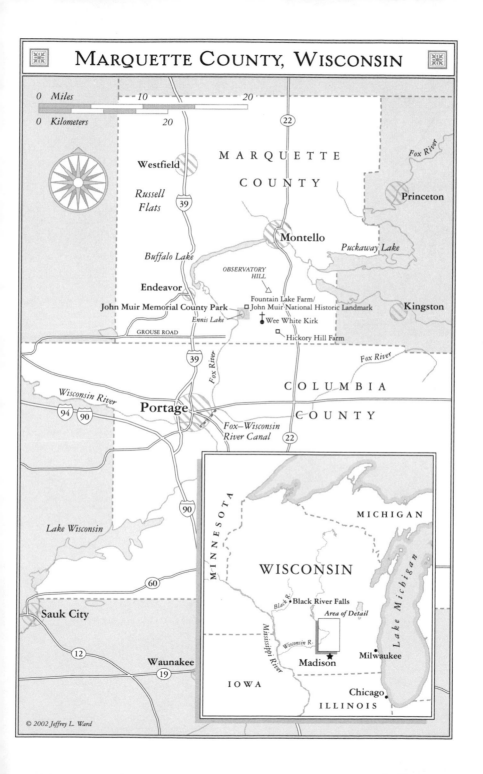

MARQUETTE COUNTY, WISCONSIN

0 *Miles* --- 10 --- 20

0 *Kilometers* --- 20

M A R Q U E T T E

C O U N T Y

Fox River

22

Westfield

Princeton

*Russell
Flats*

39

Puckaway Lake

Buffalo Lake

Montello

*OBSERVATORY
HILL*

Endeavor

Fountain Lake Farm/
John Muir National Historic Landmark

Kingston

John Muir Memorial County Park

Ennis Lake

Wee White Kirk

GROUSE ROAD

Hickory Hill Farm

39

Fox River

Fox River

C O L U M B I A

Wisconsin River

94 **90**

Portage

C O U N T Y

Fox–Wisconsin
River Canal

22

90

Lake Wisconsin

M I N N E S O T A

MICHIGAN

60

WISCONSIN

Black R.
•Black River Falls

Area of Detail

Lake Michigan

Sauk City

Mississippi River

Wisconsin R.

★
Madison

Milwaukee•

12

Waunakee

19

I O W A

Chicago•

ILLINOIS

© 2002 Jeffrey L. Ward

YEARNING FOR THE LAND

PRELUDE

Once you have lived on the land, been a partner with
its moods, secrets, and seasons, you cannot leave. The
living land remembers, touching you in unguarded
moments, saying, "I am here. You are part of me."

BEN LOGAN, *The Land Remembers*

[1]

February is *dreich*—cold, damp, and blustery—in the Lammermuir Hills and the coastal lowlands of East Lothian, Scotland,
lending the land a gray skeletal starkness during the scarce daylight hours. I'm chilled to the bone. The rawness pervades everything, inside and out. From my promontory on Doon Hill, the
northeastern face of the Lammermuirs, the inland sweep of the
coastal plain lays a mile off and 500 feet below me. Dunbar sits at
the nexus.

Oliver Cromwell, like all southern invaders of Scotland, knew
the strategic importance of the place. The bleak, rolling moors
atop the 1,400-foot-high shoulders of the Lammermuirs had
blocked invading armies for centuries, forcing their advance up
the coast to Dunbar, despite the Dunglass and Pease Deans that
dissected the plain only miles away near the small village of
Cockburnspath. There, a handful of soldiers could stymie an army
trying to cross the deep, steep-faced rocky ravines. But the Scots
were too busy arguing religion during the spring of 1650 to
seize the advantage, allowing the English lord commander's New
Model Army of 16,000 soldiers uncontested entry into the coun-

try's heartland. Preliminary skirmishes ensued from Edinburgh eastward into East Lothian as the Presbyterian Scots mobilized an army of 27,000 troops led by Lord Leslie and a committee of military officers and Covenant presbyters.

By late summer, Cromwell's fighting force had dwindled to less than 12,000. Months in the field, bad food, dysentery and other diseases, and battle casualties had taken a heavy toll. In response, he withdrew to Dunbar to use the crude local harbors for resupply and reinforcement. He also hoped to draw the Scots out into the open for a climactic confrontation. Leslie repositioned his main force of perhaps 22,000 Scots on the high ground where I stand. Like today, conditions then were deplorable—howling wind driving recurrent rain. But the hill offered a commanding view of Dunbar and its surrounding fields. Only a fool would attack up its face. Leslie also blocked the invaders' retreat down the coast by controlling the narrow throat of the coastal plain at Cockburnspath. Cromwell was trapped and his decimated army evacuating to England, the Scots thought. The great confrontation and a great Scottish victory were at hand.

On September 1, 1650, Cromwell occupied the Duke of Roxburghe's Broxmouth Estate just outside Dunbar, gazing up at the superior Scottish force and its apparent strategic advantage. He knew the Scots couldn't stay atop the hill for long: too exposed to the harsh weather, too hard to supply. Leslie knew it too. Perhaps that's why a fortification with three concentric rings of ramparts and palisades had been built about 2,500 years ago on the flat ground of Broxmouth, rather than atop the adjacent hill. The Scots had come to fight, not to sit by and await the next English move. Cromwell's field commanders thought the situation desperate and made plans for retreat. Even the lord commander dashed off an incoherent letter to his council of state warning of possible defeat.

The next morning, Leslie's massive army descended the

heights, abandoning their superior position in preparation for the battle, confident in their righteous cause and command of the situation. Unknowingly, the Scots repeated the same strategic error they made in 1296 during another disastrous Battle of Dunbar fought on the same ground against the same enemy. Cromwell studied their deliberate movements and careful placement all day. Discerning their strategy, he told his commanders, "The Lord hath delivered them into my hand." That night—"a drakie nycht full of wind and weit"—he repositioned his troops and guns, praying that the Scots wouldn't attack before dawn as they had twice before that summer. If they did again, his unsettled and vulnerable army would be crushed. The lord commander personally directed the movements, riding a "little Scots nag" in and out of the torchlight, from one emplacement to the next, unaware that he had anxiously bitten through his lip. Blood dripped down his chin. The Scots were oblivious to the commotion, blinded by their belief that the English posed no threat, even though the two armies were only one hundred yards apart in places.

At dawn, Cromwell attacked. "Now let God arise and His enemies shall be scattered," he told his troops. The Scots were caught off guard and unprepared. Cromwell tactfully used artillery and swift flanking troop movements to trap the Covenanters' cavalry and foot soldiers on a narrow lip of flat ground between the base of the hill and Brock Burn, a steep-sided gully that separated the hill from the coastal plain. The Scots regrouped and counterattacked. Sections of the English line faltered. The lord commander called his reserves to battle, unleashing the full fury of his forces. Panic engulfed the Covenanters. They broke and ran. The slaughter ended two hours later, redirecting the path of Western history. Thirty of the English lay dead amid the 3,000 dead and 10,000 captured Scots. The union was preserved and the place of the Kirk kept separate from state, setting important precedents for later revolutions.

Just as it did that day, the wind today agitates the surf in the Firth of Forth, carrying heavy, moisture-laden clouds from the North Sea ominously overhead. Storms like this often stay for days here, although some sweep through, leaving in their wake dazzling skies of electric blue and gentle winds that carry the sweet, fecund smell of fermenting hay, moist sheep manure, and bare earth. Through the mist swirling about me this morning, evidence of the landscape's physical past stands as clear as the legacy of its cultural past.

To my west, Traprain Law, a weathered igneous intrusion rich in local history and lore, looms 650 feet above the glaciated plain. The Bass Rock, another volcanic remnant famous for its physical presence and fascinating history, squats to the north off-shore in the Firth. Millennia ago, volcanic activity laid down layers of igneous rock that appear in places where the later deposits of sedimentary rock and glacial till have been eroded—in the deans and deep ravines, and at the sea's lap in fantastic formations.

At Siccar Point, visible to my southeast, this geological complexity triggered one of the great epiphanies in modern science. In 1788, Sir James Hutton, Sir James Hall, and Professor John Playfair set sail in a small skiff from the beach on Hall's Dunglass Estate. As Playfair recorded, they set out for Siccar Point, several miles to the south, past Cove Harbor and Pease Bay, skirting the rocky shoreline in search of the termination of the secondary rock strata. What they saw that day crystallized Hutton's thinking. A lifetime before Darwin published *On the Origin of Species,* Hutton proposed that forces millions upon millions of years old formed the earth, contrary to the creationist dogma put forth by people like Archbishop Ussher, who calculated the date of creation as March 23, 4004 B.C. Playfair continued,

On landing at this point, we found that we actually trode on the primeval rock which forms alternately the base and the summit of the present land. . . . Dr. Hutton was so highly pleased with appearances which set in so clear a light the different formations of the parts which compose the exterior crust of the earth. . . . What clearer evidence could we have had of the different formation of these rocks, had we actually seen them emerging from the bosom of the deep? We felt ourselves necessarily carried back to the time when the schistus on which we stood was yet at the bottom of the sea, and when the sandstone before us was only beginning to be deposited in the shape of sand or mud, from the waters of a superincumbent ocean. An epocha still more remote presented itself, when even the most ancient of these rocks, instead of standing upright in vertical beds, lay in horizontal planes at the bottom of the sea, and was not yet disturbed by the immeasurable force which has burst asunder the solid pavement of the globe. Revolutions still more remote appeared in the distance of this extraordinary perspective. The mind seemed to grow giddy by looking so far into the abyss of time. . . .

Dreich conditions bring life to the long legacy of this landscape, highlighting its formative forces as if we were meant to see the land in this vague light. The coastal *crags,* the ruins of ancient castles, the *doocots,* the deans, and the *standing stones* tell their stories most clearly now. So do the *dykes* discolored with lichen and the dense hawthorn hedgerows that line the ancient lanes and enclose the turnip, barley, and potato fields and the pastures of sheep. In the Lammermuirs, curious shallow ruts with adjacent rounded ridges still fill a few fields. These remnants of the traditional *run-rig* farming practices that reach back twenty generations remain in the hills, spared destruction caused by the constant deep plowing on the more fertile farmland along the coastal plain. The long, low, parallel mounds date to the feudal period when most Scots worked the land in common for their *laird.* Today some 1,500 people own about 75 percent of all privately owned rural land in Scotland, a lingering legacy of that past. Perhaps the promise that common people could own land was more fully realized in what was considered by nonnatives to be the vacant, virgin wilderness of the New World.

The Scots have been gradually reforming their land laws based on historical precedence, current conditions, and future prospects, since the rise of feudalism, reflecting their long-running struggle to realign their relationship with the land. Change has been slow. Often a land law is more easily changed than its effects, and some reforms are as much symbolic as substantial, doing little to address the real issue—the concentration of ownership. That might be beyond legislative remedy. Current efforts seek to codify the traditional right of ramblers to roam the countryside, whether crossing public or private land. This pits the rights of landowners against those of the general public, a carryover of the feudal struggle between lairds and tenants. Other reforms will eliminate the last vestiges of feudal land laws, remnants that for decades have been merely faint reflections of their former importance. No controversy here. However, the plan to empower crofters to collectively acquire private property, perhaps with the use of public funds, raises a storm of contention as strong as the gales that pummel the desolate western shores where many crofters live. The question of crofters' rights touches sensitive issues throughout Scotland for historical reasons arising in the Clearances, though little land and few people are directly affected.

Yet neither the Scots nor their landscape are frozen in time. The imprints of East Lothian's past lie embedded in a changing world. I write these thoughts on a laptop computer energized by electricity generated at the Torness Point nuclear power plant that dominates this stretch of dramatic coastline. With the press of a key the Internet instantly transfers them to New York, linking my workplace in the 130-year-old schoolhouse I now let in

Cockburnspath to the New World. Below my second-floor aerie stands a *mercat cross* believed to have been erected in 1503 in the square of this circa 1,000-year-old village. The rippled-glass window distorts my view back into time.

I've come from my New World suburban home in the Midwest to this Old World rural landscape thirty miles east of Edinburgh in search of answers to deep-rooted questions about the land and its meaning. Like most Americans, I've moved several times in search of better circumstance, taking for granted the phenomenal opportunity to buy and sell land. I take the land for granted, too. It's mostly just property to me—a commodity, a thing to which I have little historical connection. I know little of its formative forces, physical or social, and have little real contact with it. I garden a bit and care for my lawn, but beyond that we share little intimacy. I live in a vast sea of suburbia and I like it. Yet I also yearn for a more meaningful connection to my home and a deeper understanding of its past. Have I lost something in my freedom of landownership and mobility, some psychological benefit from that connection? Can such a connection enrich in the same subtle, subconscious way that knowledge of one's lineage enriches?

I've asked friends to tell me the story of their landscape home and in response I frequently get a puzzled look followed by a question: What do you mean? Tell me about the place where you live, I reply. How it came to be, what forces most shaped it, how long you've lived there, and what it means to you. They grope for thoughts and words. Finally I hear a description of the community's current land use and a smattering of its recent development story and earlier settlement history.

They speak as if the history of place began only with their personal experience or included only some myopic view of the past. They speak from the *head* mostly of property values and financial security, of school quality, neighborhood charm, safety, and location convenience, of personal comfort and stability. These are important to me, too. Many have lived in their homes less than twenty years and few adults or adolescents expect to live there much longer. Like me, they hesitate to call it "home." Instead they refer to it as their "current" home as if shy to really put down roots for fear that a move is in the offing. The past and the future lay in other places. Certainly some people know much more, but from most I learn little else.

What does their *heart* say? Isn't there more to the story of place than these immediate, utilitarian concerns: a sense of continuity between the past, present, and future, whether one lives in a high-rise condo or a suburban tract home, or on a farm or a rural estate? In contrast, if I put the same question to my adopted neighbors in Cockburnspath, will I more often hear with little prompting the long history and rich folklore of this place? The question may make more sense to Scots than to Americans because it might address a more common concern in their culture—landscape.

By landscape I mean not just the appearance of our surroundings. The landscape embodies far more than scenery. To see it as simply scenery implies a separation between the viewer and the view. In this sense the landscape is merely a two-dimensional object of our gaze, little different from an Albert Bierstadt or Thomas Cole painting. This perspective strikes me as distant, lifeless, and limited.

Another common definition focuses on physical character—topography, vegetation, and human-built forms. In this sense the landscape has three dimensions, an architectural space defined by attributes like scale, proportion, color, and texture. I find this definition too analytical, too cold, too impersonal. The landscape is alive. It's much more than an abstraction.

Landscape also includes people. Our activity animates and enlivens it, transforming space into place known through personal experience. Yet place doesn't fully capture my meaning. Knowledge of the historical events and forces that created the place, together with our actions and experience, inform our sense of landscape. Myth, legend, fact, and folklore communicate its physical and cultural legacy.

[2]

In 1677 thirty-two-year-old John "the Scot" Simpson first set foot in the New World. He sought a new life with land and opportunity around Aquia Creek, a small, meandering tributary of the Potomac River in the fledgling Virginia colony. Today the area lies in Stafford County, downstream of Washington, D.C. I'm the tenth generation to follow.

Little for certain is known of John the Scot, for records are scant and they mention several others who shared his name. This particular John Simpson may have been short and stocky with blue eyes, a full head of brown hair, a prominent nose, and a beard covering a cleft chin. He likely came alone but would be tenderhearted toward the New World family he would soon father. Records suggest he could read and write. Honest and hardworking with a dignified, sober demeanor, he may have been recruited in East Lothian on behalf of George Brent, one of the colony's most prominent land speculators, to serve as his indentured administrative assistant. During that servitude, John the Scot apparently was permitted to make land deals on his own, perhaps using a 50-acre headright grant as the starting point. In 1678 it appears he and a partner acquired a 627-acre tract adjacent to one of Brent's extensive holdings. Regardless, my ancestors owned considerable land in Fairfax County, Virginia, during the 1700s. A century later, the family had sold those holdings, severing my lineage of landownership and a lasting presence in the Tidewater. Descendants dispersed throughout the East and Midwest and moved to cities. We've continued to move ever since, each generation seeking its place.

Those Scottish roots are long gone. I've never spoken with a Scottish burr and I have no apparent Scottish mannerisms. Yet I carry with me remnants of that Anglo-European legacy, as do most Americans, whether of European descent or not, whether urban or suburban, eastern or western. So does our landscape. We carry with us their values and attitudes toward the land, sans the bonds of history that tethered the Old World to its millennia-old settlement past. Those values have governed to a great extent how we've manipulated the land—how we've husbanded it— since settlement. They remain remarkably unchanged in America since John the Scot's day. As a result, I think many Americans live as if temporary occupants of the land, transients who never set down roots or form a connection to community. We live as if perpetual newcomers, never acquiring a historical knowledge of our locale. This disconnection affects our stewardship attitudes and behavior just as renters likely invest less care in their homes than owners. I suspect the key for me to find meaning in the land and reconnect with place and people rests with my recognition of and response to these values. Can I stop acting as if an alien from a distant place and abandon my five-hundred-year-old colonial attitudes? Can I become native to the land and learn to know it intimately? Can I behave as if it were my permanent home?

I yearn to be native to a place, to know the landscape in which I live, to sense its changing moods and rhythms, and to pattern my life in response. I long to feel past currents flow into the present, carrying me into the future. Not long ago, people lived intimately with the land, setting roots deep in place and patterning their lives in response. Certainly some people wandered, but most people spent a lifetime in a place and depended upon their knowledge of it for physical and psychological sustenance. Today few of us do. In the span of a few generations, we've lost the linkage to the land enjoyed by our ancestors.

This linkage can occur in any setting, not just in rural ones, provided one has lived in a place long enough to become "a partner with its moods, secrets, and seasons." However, the story of

America since its settlement by westerners has been the story of a people on the move: first westward across the continent, then from farm to factory, and most recently from city to suburb. Americans move on average about every seven years, not necessarily from one city to another, but at least from one residence to another. Few of us have the opportunity or the inclination to put down deep landscape roots since we move so frequently. And technology increasingly clothes our daily life for comfort and convenience, further shielding us from truly seeing the landscape in which we live. In many ways, that same technology hinders our sense of community as it often inhibits direct human interaction. Did we lose something of great importance when our linkage to the land was severed? Perhaps those few of us who somehow manage to live in the place of our parents and grandparents know that "the land remembers," and enjoy an abiding connection to place and commitment to community. Perhaps those fortunate few still derive a deep sense of continuity with their home that is much different from that felt by the rest of us, regardless of whether our home is set in an urban, suburban, rural, or wild world.

[3]

In the cold and damp of another February long ago, young John Muir's family left their comfortable life in Dunbar, Scotland, and immigrated to the relative isolation in the forest and prairie wilderness of Marquette County, Wisconsin. As an adult, John Muir would become one of America's most influential nature writers and environmental philosophers, championing the creation of the national park system and our current preservation ideals.

The decision to emigrate was most likely made by John's father, Daniel, in late 1848, though he had dreamed of settling in the New World for most of his life. By midwinter 1849, family preparations for the move were under way. Daniel announced the

actual day of departure to the children the night before. The next
morning he gathered John and a brother and sister and set off for
Glasgow to board a sailing ship. Daniel hoped the voyage would
deliver him to a new life in which he could practice and preach
his faith free of constraints in a fertile place where common people could actually own land. Mrs. Muir and John's remaining siblings would follow that fall once Daniel had built a proper house
and harvested the first crops.

During the thirty-eight-day voyage to New York City, the
seventy-two Scots aboard the *Warren* left behind their centuries-
old landscape legacy in exchange for the chance to begin a new
history. The immigrants were a cross section of those fleeing the
economic and social upheavals in Scotland as industrialization
reshaped the urban and rural countryside: hopeful newlyweds
seeking homes in the New World, young laborers and servants
seeking better prospects, and middle-aged tradesmen and farmers with their families seeking a fresh start. Few were older than
forty. The Muirs were swept into this flood of people, evicted
from the land by the "Clearances" and displaced by the "Enclosures" and agricultural "improvements," who poured into Glasgow on their way west. The *Warren* sailed in the armada of ships
from Liverpool filled with Scots and Irish fleeing the potato
famine and proper Englishmen acting as emissaries seeking land
for the groups that would soon follow. The Muirs joined the
uprooted from all across the Old World who sought gold in California or work logging the northern pine forests, laying railroad
track, or digging canals.

For many travelers, though, a yearning for land lay at the heart
of their leap across space and forward in time from the Old
World to the New. Come to America where fruitful land is plentiful, cheap, and easily got, the ads proclaimed throughout the
Old World. Immigration to America was big business by the
mid-1800s. Many people followed family or friends. Word from

those who went before them surely told of hardship, deceit, and failure, sober warnings to counterbalance the promotional hype. But they also spoke of opportunity, success, and land. What concept of land was left behind? What sense of connection and continuity was lost and what was gained in their stead? I've come to Dunbar to seek an answer, for part of it must rest here, today, and in the past of this fascinating place.

Daniel was not a farmer and perhaps knew less of the land than farmers did. He owned a successful dry goods store inherited from his first wife in the coastal community of about 3,000 people. Yet like so many commoners in the Old World who had been denied land ownership for generations, he sought property. Daniel was also a religious zealot who sought rich soil for God's work. He found his Eden on the sand hills and marshy bottoms of Marquette County.

Just days after he arrived that spring in the newly formed state of Wisconsin, Daniel did what would have been unthinkable in his prior Old World home—he bought land. For a pittance, and with few constraints compared with his homeland, he purchased 160 acres: the east half of the northeast quarter and the east half of the southeast quarter of Section 14, Township 14 North, Range 9 East. He bought and sold land repeatedly in the years to come, with remarkably little wonder or concern, and moved on in search of more fertile opportunities after he had depleted those at his current location, as did millions of Americans like my ancestors. Some of the answers to my questions lie there, so I'll follow the Muirs to their Fountain Lake and Hickory Hill Farms in Marquette County, fifty miles north of Madison.

I'll trespass as I wander the Wisconsin forests, fields, bogs, and knobs of John Muir's boyhood farms in search of answers to my questions. I'll trespass, too, in the close, crowded streets and the open, rolling Scottish countryside beyond the sharp edge of his Dunbar home. Why is the land so? What does it mean?

What is our place on it and our responsibility toward it? My trespass is more psychological than legal. Of course someone now owns the land, a prerequisite for trespass. Without ownership, trespass would be nonsensical. Yet the practical meaning differs in Scotland. Here, people still enjoy substantial freedom to wander the land, whether public or private. In America, "No Trespassing" signs confront walkers wherever they leave the public right-of-way.

Aren't we all trespassers on the land, though, merely temporary occupants of that which we can't really possess? Don't the philosophical underpinnings of ownership—the concepts of occupancy and improvement rooted in the new ideas of the Enlightenment and perhaps deep in the origins of English common law—miss some fundamental truth found in the prior concepts of property that they replaced? Once possession of the land meant mostly the right to use the land and take what it produced, rather than title to the land itself. Possession was often shared communally and carried with it responsibilities toward the land and village. Now we think we can actually own the land with absolute title, free from communal responsibilities. There's the rub.

We abstract the wondrous diversity and complexity of the land into maps and deeds when we survey and parcel it into private property often based on an imaginary grid so we can buy and sell it efficiently as we move about. But these things "bound" us, not the land. I've lost a connection to the very land I consider my own. That process of abstraction, description, and exchange, and my frequent movement, shape the land and my behavior, environmental and social, far more than I previously realized.

Muir's Fountain Lake Farm has been broken up and sold off, though most remains farmland. The "home eighty" was designated a national historic landmark in 1990. Erik Brynildson, a crusading landscape architect and restoration ecologist, owns some of this property and lives in a home atop the ruins of the former Muir house. He played an important role in the process that led to the designation of the landmark and now works to restore his property to the character it had when John Muir first gazed in wonder at the land and the small, spring-fed glacial lake it bordered. John Muir Memorial County Park now protects the land around the lake, including the southern portion of the former Muir farm. In 1864 Muir began a lifelong quest to protect the marshy meadow below the home site, foreshadowing his later work protecting Yosemite National Park and creating the national park system. Yet John Muir Memorial County Park wouldn't be established for nearly a century. Local politics has colored its being since inception, just as it has John Muir Country Park in Dunbar. Bessie Eggleston owns another portion of the Fountain Lake Farm. The land has been in her family since they acquired it from Muir's brother-in-law about 135 years ago. Economic pressures to subdivide increasingly threatened her cropland, just as they do much of rural America. "Muir Estates"—a pleasant residential trailer park or large-lot "community"—may well be the next use of the property, despite Bessie's wishes. Homes are often the last crop grown on a farm, Harvard historian John Stilgoe has noted.

Maurice (Morrie) and Mary Kearns now own the particular piece of glacial handiwork that was for a short time the Muir Hickory Hill Farm. The property has been in the Kearns family since his grandfather Thomas bought it in 1873. Morrie and Mary are atypical Americans. They've retained a direct lineage on a single piece of land far longer than most of us. Morrie will guide me across his fields, showing me his property and explaining his connection to the land.

Other Marquette County residents will walk with me about their property and tell me of the land and their feelings toward it. Fran Sprain will tell me of her family legacy that dates to their arrival in nearby Russell Flats in 1848. She sees the many ghosts embodied in the history of the place perhaps more clearly than any other resident. Ken Soda sees these ghosts too. His 140-year-old farm is a model of modern ingenuity and technical prowess. Yet he retains a forty-acre woodlot of white pines in part to "listen to the wind" and another stand in which he's built a medicine wheel to focus the spiritual power of the place. The spirit of the past lives in the land for Fran and Ken, though they function quite comfortably in our contemporary world. Past, present, and future fuse seamlessly for them.

Today the longtime residents of Marquette County and the recently arrived retirees, hobby farmers, and recreational property owners fight over such land-use issues as the preservation of farms, woodlands, wetlands, and riparian corridors from the spread of low-density suburban sprawl. Like most Americans, they struggle to balance individual property rights and responsibilities against those of the community. Do they seek to connect or reconnect to a landscape legacy that our society spent generations ignoring or destroying?

I'll wander about with Ho-Chunk (Winnebago) people too, looking from a different perspective at their ancestral land along the Fox River adjacent to the Muir Fountain Lake Farm. This land was neither virgin nor vacant when the Muirs arrived, for the Ho-Chunks had inhabited it for centuries. Our concepts of "wilderness," "permanence," and "property" made little sense to the land's original residents. What sense of disconnection have they suffered?

By coercion, the remaining 6,000 or so Ho-Chunk people in Wisconsin now live mostly a Western-style life not far from the Fox River. There, they use the profits generated from their hotels, gift shops, convenience stores, and gambling/gaming casinos to purchase property on which to reestablish a homeland and reinvigorate their culture. Ironically, the profits from casinos that cater to white suburbanites fund the Ho-Chunks' purchase of farms from retiring whites. They use ground-penetrating radar, global positioning satellite data, and a geographic information system—all the latest computer technology—to identify and assess potential acquisitions, and then buy them on the open market just as the Muirs once bought land. The Ho-Chunks work the discarded farms to build residential subdivisions and to restore bison and elk herds, prairies, and wetlands, while they also raise cash crops and livestock and strive to reeducate a new generation in the traditional stewardship values once on the verge of extinction along with their traditional way of life. At their annual autumn powwow, I'll try to learn how they merge their traditional values with those forced upon them by the white world. Do their traditional values have relevance for me, perhaps like those of the Scots?

In contrast, will the Scots I'll walk and talk with struggle to realize the promise of landownership and to disconnect from those nagging aspects of their landscape past that all too often constrain them? I'll walk the grounds of the Tyninghame Estate with the thirteenth Earl of Haddington and explore with him the role of the great estates, past and present, in shaping the Scottish landscape. His family acquired Tyninghame in 1628. Inheritance taxes forced him to sell the fabulous estate house and gardens in 1986. Now the earl's family lives in a wing of a sprawling mansion nestled in the heart of their 8,000-acre Mellerstain Estate, while tourists roam the rest of the residence. Do estates like these have relevance today, or should they be relegated to history books like the feudal system from which they emerged? I'll go to Floors Castle to meet the tenth Duke of Roxburghe, whose family until the 1960s owned the Broxmouth Estate where Cromwell camped. Why was it sold and what meaning does it hold for him today? What does the land mean to these descendants of feudal aristocratic lairds? How have their ancestral holdings changed over time, and what forces—economic, legal, political, social—have triggered those changes?

I'll walk the Broxmouth Estate with Graham White, an author and environmental activist living in its gardener's cottage. What does the land mean to him? How does he see the estate, now on the verge of potential redevelopment by an offshore investment company that recently acquired it? I'll learn how the balance between public interests and private rights reflected in land-use planning differs in the Old World of East Lothian from that in the New World of Marquette County, resulting in far different land development outcomes. The story of estates like Tyninghame and Broxmouth illustrate these differences, as do the management of growth around Dunbar and the creation of John Muir Country Park.

I'll visit the Dunglass Estate to chat with Frank Usher about these forces. His grandfather bought the estate from the Halls in 1919. Do the many nouveaux riches who've recently acquired estates, like the Ushers, feel and act the same toward the land as the ancestral aristocracy from whom they often purchased their property? Frank dynamited the famed Dunglass mansion in 1958 and built a much less extravagant modern house on its site, and he codeveloped a large caravan park (trailer park) on what before was a fabulous beachfront on his property. He also built a tennis court right next to the medieval Dunglass Collegiate Church, just several hundred yards from his new house. Yet in 1992 he received an award from the Royal Highland and Agricultural Society of Scotland for his efforts at developing woodlands. Since the Ushers purchased the circa 800-year-old estate, they've gradually sold off one-third of the acreage and many of the cottages. It is doubtful that the rest will remain intact beyond Frank's lifetime. What meaning does the land hold for him?

Once a year, the Dunglass parish of the Presbyterian Church of

Scotland—the Kirk—holds service in the ruin of the collegiate church. Since the Scottish Protestant Reformation in the latter half of the 1500s, the Kirk has profoundly affected the Scottish people and their politics. I'll attend that service to see how the national religion has shaped their feelings for the land and their sense of community.

I'll talk with the Hoods, a family who has tenanted land from the Dunglass Estate for about 250 years, and tenant-farmed in the area for over 500 years. What are their attitudes toward the land? Are those attitudes the same as their laird's? Ben Tindall, the son of East Lothian's pioneering planning director a generation ago, now owns Cove Harbor, once a part of the Dunglass Estate, just below the Hoods' farm. Ben is a prominent Edinburgh architect and retreats on weekends to the harbormaster's old cottage, which is lit by candles and oil lamps and warmed by a coal fire because the decrepit shack has no gas or electricity. What brings Ben here? How do the land and sea affect him? Dozens of fishing boats once anchored in Cove, supporting a lively village on the cliffs above. Today only two fishing boats dock there, and the fishing community has nearly vanished, like the seasonal shoals of herring that for centuries brought life to the tiny harbor towns along this coast. Gordon Easingwood runs one of the few remaining lobster boats working out of Dunbar harbor. Might he enjoy a relationship with the sea and connection to place that offers insights for those of us on land?

Despite the profound historical differences in land parceling, ownership, and tenure, the people here struggle with many of the same land-use issues as their counterparts in Marquette County: the balance of private rights versus public responsibility; the protection of woodlands, coastline, deans, and ravines; and the preservation of a way of life in the face of external development pressures. What lessons are to be learned here? Will the Scotland I'll come to know be the same as the land I'll return to? Despite shared roots, does the Old World remain just that: a world shaped by old forces never felt in the New? Will this be evident in the land and the people?

I hope to learn why most Americans like me know so little about our landscape and act so coldly toward it. By comparison, do the Scots know more about their landscape history and lore, and possess a stronger connection to the land and to community, because they live in a landscape shaped so strongly by their feudal heritage? Do the Ho-Chunks retain this connection too?

In both cultures, sense of place is embedded within their language much more than in American English. In Scotland, the names of fields and farms, homes and villages, and many other words have commonly known meanings related to place. Words with literal descriptions of a place, an event, or some physical characteristic form the core of the Ho-Chunk language even more. Their language tells the story of the landscape and their relationship to it in almost every phrase. The history of people and place permeates common speech. American English has little of this quality. Few words have such meanings. Our language is relatively placeless, as is our culture.

What does the land mean to Americans, Scots, and Ho-Chunks? What significance should we attach to these differences? And what does the historical legacy of each landscape mean for its future? *Yearning for the Land* describes my search for the importance of place as I recall John Muir's journey from his Old World home in Scotland to his New World home in Wisconsin. Like his, my experience will be a journey in both a physical sense, as I retrace his path, and a psychological sense, as I explore the different perceptions and meanings of the land in the Old World and New.

LOOMINGS

One night, when David and I were at grandfather's
fireside solemnly learning our lessons as usual,
my father came in with news, the most wonderful,
most glorious, that wild boys ever heard. "Bairns,"
he said, "you needna learn your lessons the nicht,
for we're gan to America the morn!"

JOHN MUIR, *The Story of My Boyhood and Youth*

[4]

Did that February morning leave John and his brother David
time for one last look at the remains of ancient Dunbar Castle
and the two small fishing harbors it symbolically guarded at the
foot of the *brae,* the rise that partitioned the town into its coastal
community along the rugged shore and its town center above.
For nearly a thousand years, Dunbar had been the southern gateway into Scotland, and the castle one of the country's most
important medieval strongholds until it was destroyed in 1567
after Mary Queen of Scots fled its safety for the final time. Oliver
Cromwell contributed £300 to improve the storm-damaged "old"
harbor several years after his victory in 1650. The "new" harbor,
named "Victoria" in honor of the new queen, was built in the early
1840s, its sea entrance blasted through the remnants of the castle
left by the lord commander and the hand of God. John probably
attended its gala christening as a toddler. Did he and David dash
down to the rocks and ruins, now indistinguishable after centuries of pounding surf, wind, and cannon fire, where they so often

played William Wallace and Robert the Bruce, who first fought each other, then fought the English for Scottish independence, on some of that same ground? Could they see Doon Hill, where they so often reenacted Cromwell's crushing defeat of the Scots, standing sentinel a mile off over the fields outside Dunbar?

The way to the train was just a few blocks south on High Street, past the homes of family and friends on the upper floors of the stone and harl-clad buildings standing shoulder to shoulder; past the small ground-floor shops and stores whose windows lined the street, watching the villagers walk by; past the everyday places of their lives. Did friends emerge from each crowded *close* to join in an entourage to the station so near that all could easily walk alongside the wagonload of possessions packed for the journey?

Imagine Anne's emotions as she watched her family ripped apart, her handsome husband, Daniel, taking sons John (nearly age eleven) and David (age eight) and their older sister Sarah (age thirteen) to somewhere in the wilds of North America. Anne would remain behind with her young twins, Mary and Annie (age two), Dan (age five), and Maggie (age fifteen), to endure the wait until summoned in the autumn. The parents planned to reunite in the New World then, after a permanent home was built and fields planted. Anne likely had little say in the matter, as was the place of the dutiful wife in Victorian Scottish society. Tall and quiet, she had a stern face that belied her gentle disposition and bubbling humor. Nature and gardening were her lifelong passions, cross-stitching, drawing, painting, and writing playful poetry her adolescent pleasures. Despite the life imposed on her by Daniel and Scottish society, Anne lived in "tranquil independence" of the circumstances, neither aloof, passive, nor unaffected, just secure in her own being and able to make her own happiness. John was later fond of saying, "I am always happy at the center," even during turbulent times. Perhaps he acquired that wonderful gift from his mother.

Daniel's simple plan outraged Anne's prosperous parents, David and Margaret Gilrye, who lived across the street in a three-story stone building with "Gilrye Place" chiseled in the tablet above the door. The building and the flats around the courtyard behind housed David's flesher (butcher) business as well as an extended family of relatives, store workers, servants, and tenants. The stone structure reflected David's character—solid, stable, and caring. He had served on the town council and was an elder in the Kirk. Now Anne's children filled his retirement life. David and Margaret always felt that Anne married beneath her station; after all, the Gilryes were descended from a Highland hero, while Daniel Muir had no lineage. They also found his form of religious fanaticism offensive. Their objections to the marriage went unheeded, though, as did their objections to the move, although they compelled Daniel to leave Anne and some of the children initially behind until completion of a comfortable house.

Young John and David were thrilled with the prospects. "No more grammar, but boundless woods full of mysterious good things; trees full of sugar, growing in ground full of gold; hawks, eagles, pigeons, filling the sky; millions of birds' nests, and no gamekeepers to stop us in all the wild, happy land," wrote John. "We were utterly, blindly glorious. . . . To my schoolmates, met that night on the street, I shouted the glorious news, 'I'm gan to Amaraka the morn!' None could believe it. I said, 'Weel, just you see if I am at the skule the morn!' " Grandfather Gilyre knew better. With eyes downcast toward the floor, he spoke to the boys in a low, trembling voice, "Ah, poor laddies, poor laddies, you'll find something else ower the sea forbye gold and sugar, birds' nests and freedom fra lessons and schools. You'll find plenty hard, hard work." Wisdom wasted on the young, John recalled when a grown man. "Nothing he could say could cloud our joy or abate the fire of youthful, hopeful, fearless adventure."

Was Daniel Muir blinded by the same emotions? How did he plan to provide for his family in the wilderness? Presumably farming; yet he only knew farming secondhand through his customers and from his memories as an orphaned child reared by relatives on the unrelenting drudgery of their poor tenant farms outside the tiny village of Crawfordjohn in Lanarkshire. Like much of Scotland, it was a hard land of harsh weather and steep, rocky moorland covered by a thin layer of starved soil in which even the heather struggled to survive. Sheep and people fared no better. Scotland "consists of two things, stone and water," observed Samuel Johnson in the late 1700s. "There is, indeed, a little earth above the stone in some places, but a very little; and the stone is always appearing. It is like a man in rags; the naked skin is still peeping out." Daniel knew this firsthand. The sentiment caught his son John's eye many years later in a much different land. John copied the passage onto the endpapers of his personal volume of James Boswell's *Life of Samuel Johnson*.

Hard work, hard conditions, and hard times could make the Scots who scratched subsistence in Lanarkshire as hard and dour as the land. It could also make them revel in lighthearted dance, song, and story, and find joy in the simple pleasures of family and friends. And it could fill them with wanderlust to escape in search of a job in a big city or better land free from feudal oppression. America was the destination of choice for many. There, they heard tell, a commoner could get lots of fine land for a song, free of leases and lairds, and rise according to one's own abilities. Hector St. John de Crèvecœur documented the dream in his famous *Letters from an American Farmer* (1782). He described Scottish emigrants who fled the "high, sterile, bleak lands of Scotland, where every thing is barren and cold," lands of the "north of Britain, of the Orkneys, and the Hebride Islands . . . unfit for the habitation of men," lands that "appear to be calculated only for great sheep pastures." Crèvecœur highlighted one "simple Scotchman" he called "Andrew the Hebridean," who disembarked at Philadelphia in 1774 to pursue his dreams of opportunity. Like many of his countrymen, Andrew arrived pale and emaciated and rose in several years from "indigence to ease; from oppression to freedom; from obscurity and contumely to some degree of consequence," as he acquired a sizable farm property. The conditions that cast those emigrants from their Scottish homeland intensified over the ensuing forty years, and stories like that of Andrew the Hebridean became part of the Scottish mythos. Perhaps those effects made the Scots ripe for the Calvinism that swept the country in the 1560s. Life in Lanarkshire likely made Daniel as hard as the land and eager to leave it.

His conversion came at age fourteen in 1818. His escape came at age twenty-one, when he simply ran away one morning with only his Bible, a fiddle, and a few shillings. But in the teeming streets of industrial Glasgow—"that great bottleneck of wretched humanity"—he found no job to earn passage-fare to America. When his last ha'penny was spent, he enlisted in the British army in desperation. He was posted to Dunbar as a recruiting sergeant four years later, and promptly married the heiress of a flourishing grain and feed store.

She proved inept at business, running the store toward bankruptcy, so Daniel left the army to help manage it. Their partnership ended with her sudden death. Daniel inherited the store and rapidly rebuilt it into a thriving enterprise that occupied a large, well-situated building on High Street. By the 1840s, remarried with a large family, Daniel was a prominent person in the community. His success afforded the family servants and a comfortable flat above the store. He served on the town council and had donated money to the Ebenezer Erskine Secession Church, a fundamentalist sect that had splintered from the Kirk. Even it soon became too staid to satisfy his growing liturgical passion and his rejection of election and patronage.

His passion was a product of the times. The Kirk suffered a long-standing evangelical strain that created tension between the mainline Calvinists and those with a more impassioned liturgy. This tension prompted so many sects to secede from the mother church during the preceding hundred years that "hiving off" became a part of Scottish theology. The same predilection affected political affairs, too. Daniel's faith happened to form in the early to mid-1800s, a time when a rash of revivals swept Protestantism in both the Old World and New, leading him from one sect that had hived off to another.

Daniel sold his building to Dr. John Lorn, a local physician, several weeks before departure. Among the possessions he kept to take on the long journey to the New World was a big ironbound box that weighed about 400 pounds, for it contained an old-fashioned beam scales, complete with a full set of cast-iron counterweights, in pairs, ranging from 56 pounds each to a pound each. Did he consider possibly opening another grain and feed store? If not, why haul a heavy merchant's scale to a wilderness farm half a world away? His plans were far from settled. He'd not even found a final destination in North America. Perhaps, he thought, they'd go somewhere in Canada where members of his faith were establishing colonies in Ontario and other eastern provinces. Beyond that, he knew nothing of the place. His geographical knowledge of the New World was as shallow as his knowledge of farming. These were minor details to him. God, he believed, would lead him safely to the right place.

What forces drove Daniel to rip apart his family and set off for an unknown life in a wild land far removed, dependent on the possessions they carried and their savings to support them until he'd successfully begun a new agrarian life? Was he so blinded by his religious zeal that all other practical concerns became inconsequential? Certainly the quest for fertile new ground to practice his fundamentalist Disciples of Christ faith drove him westward, as it did other followers of the faith's Scottish-born founders Thomas Campbell and his son Alexander, and their American partner Barton Stone.

The faith flourished on the frontier farms of the American Midwest during the wave of revivals in the early 1800s. Its religious individualism and literal adherence to the New Testament free from frills and clerical interference appealed to the isolated, independent-minded pioneers fighting the physical and moral war to tame the raw land. Alexander brought the word back to Scotland in the early 1840s, where his mesmerizing preaching attracted scores of converts to the fold. Perhaps the faith appealed to the Scots for the same reasons it appealed to the Midwest pioneers.

It apparently did to Daniel. His faith was austere, stripped of embellishments; its practice was regimented, perhaps reflecting his military training. He patterned his personal life accordingly, abandoning his youthful joys in song, dance, story, and poetry. He imposed the same behaviors on the household and forced the children to memorize and perfectly recite the Bible line by line, verse by verse, or endure a beating. The Muir home in the New World would be harsh and preoccupied with work and worship; nonetheless, it would be filled with love and, beneath the dour facade, those youthful joys. Anne would see to it, especially during Daniel's frequent outings to preach.

America's beckoning call as an Eden—an unspoiled virgin paradise—probably fed Daniel's quest for the proper religious environment. It also beckoned to his passionate desire for a democratic-like say in his religious, political, and social affairs. Perhaps he chafed at the lingering feudal yoke in East Lothian, feeling that the rigid caste system based on aristocratic privilege and landownership had stifled him, even though he had prospered and improved his station.

And he must have been drawn by the opportunity to own land in America and enjoy the freedoms and possibilities that that offered, like those enjoyed by Andrew the Hebridean. Crèvecœur again captured the sentiment, "The instant I enter on my own land, the bright idea of property, of exclusive right, of independence exalt my mind. Precious soil, I say to myself, by what singular custom of law is it that thou wast made to constitute the riches of the freeholder?" What should we be, he continued, "without the distinct possession of that soil? It feeds, it clothes us, from it we draw even a great exuberancy [*sic*], our best meat, our richest drink, the very honey of our bees comes from this privileged spot. No wonder we should thus cherish its possession," he concluded, "no wonder that so many Europeans who have never been able to say that such portion of land was theirs, cross the Atlantic to realize that happiness." He felt landownership established "all our rights; on it is founded our rank, our freedom, our power as citizens, our importance as inhabitants of such a district." That was certainly true in the Old World. The problem in the Old was that too few people enjoyed those benefits, and those who did traditionally kept tight control on access to them by limiting opportunities for others to gain clear title to land. Landownership was the basis for power and privilege in both the Old World and New. The difference in the New was opportunity—only there could common people acquire land and share in those benefits.

Poor business prospects might have driven Daniel away as well. Business in Dunbar was bleak at the time, as it was throughout much of the British Isles. The "Hungry Forties" resulting from the potato crop failures of 1846–47 cast a pale over the land and the people. Dunbar suffered in the tragedy, despite the local fishing economy. The potato was a principal crop in the fields and a staple on the family table, then as today. Poverty was commonplace, prompting John to later write about all the bent, gnarled poor people he saw about town. Emigration peaked at this time as hordes fled the human and economic privations. Daniel's business surely suffered and his future prospects declined. He likely had little patience for these limitations as he had quite an appetite for wealth, more to fund his religious causes than for personal aggrandizement.

Perhaps in some subtle way his emigration was also an extreme form of hiving off. Could the Scots' tendency to split from the mainstream in religion and politics share some behavioral basis with their historical mobility? Emigration and migration were commonplace in Scotland, whether one was evicted or left for military service, or left voluntarily or in a desperate search for opportunity. The Scots had been a people on the move for several hundred years. Millions would immigrate to Australia, Europe and Scandinavia, and North America. Many others moved internally. They were an unsettled people in some ways, always searching for better circumstance at home or abroad, whether in religious, economic, political, or personal affairs. They were open to new ideas and intolerant of the old. They were willing to run counter to the norm and focused abroad, while at the same time they were devoted to tradition and deeply rooted to the homeland.

All these forces—the quest for religious fulfillment and personal freedom, the opportunity to own land and improve one's station, a quest for better business prospects and greater wealth, and the willingness to strike out for what one believed—I suspect drove Daniel westward, as they did millions of other Scots and Europeans.

That was the extent of Daniel's plan and the tentative beginning to the family's move. The wind must have blown the cold and damp through one's clothes that morning, as it did most winter mornings, when they walked to the new station, perhaps for a 7:45 train, perhaps on their first train ride. The railroad had only been opened in June 1846, the first line connecting Edinburgh to Berwick-upon-Tweed, the main route to London. Trains were still quite novel. In the mid-1840s, four classes of travel were common: first class seated passengers in the comfort of an enclosed carriage with cushioned seats and glazed windows; second class sacrificed the upholstery and the glazed windows, so the compartment was drafty; third class had no roof; and third-class "stand-ups" had neither seats nor a roof, popular in fair weather but quite scandalous in winter. Fares for the one-hour, fifteen-minute journey from Dunbar to Edinburgh were expensive at the time, being around 6s., 4s., 3s., or 2s. 5d. for first through stand-up class, respectively. Once at the station in Edinburgh, the Muirs likely changed quickly to a connecting train for the forty-seven-mile, two-hour, fifteen-minute trip to Glasgow, which cost about 8s., 6s., 4s., or 2s. 6d. more. Much to the railroads' consternation, most passengers chose the lesser classes even if they could afford first class. Comfort at that price was too much to pay for most frugal, hearty Scots, well-to-do or working class.

The Muirs loaded their luggage, said their goodbyes, boarded, and were off for the New World amid the smoke and steam, as simple as that. Anne and the grandparents were left behind, standing alone with their thoughts on the platform, watching the train disappear as it made the long left-hand bend westward out of town. Emigrants now, Daniel, John, David, and Sarah joined the uprooted and rode off in search of opportunity.

Anne and the remaining children would join the others in Marquette County early that November, as the last crops stood in the new fields and the glorious hardwood foliage blazed with the fiery colors of autumn: gold, orange, red. Grandmother Gilrye would die in 1851; grandfather would follow her two years later. Only John would ever return to Dunbar, forty-four years later, for a brief visit. On arrival in Edinburgh, he wrote his wife back in America, "I am a Scotchman and at home again." The next day he took the train to Dunbar, riding the same route that had carried him away so long before. Enraptured revisiting the places of his childhood memories, he wrote that the waves of the once familiar surf "made a grand show, breaking in sheets and sheaves of foam and granted songs—the same old songs they sang to me in my childhood, and I seemed a boy again, and all the long eventful years in America were forgotten while I was filled with that glorious ocean psalm."

[5]

Uncertainty clouds the sky this particular February morning as I board a sleek, dark blue electric train that runs along the route now. An ominous cloud bank looms over the Lammermuirs like a wave waiting to crash. The continental high that has dominated the weather the past week, bringing spectacular blue skies that dry the damp fields, struggles to hold off a North Atlantic low. The victor will determine if the sun remains or another dreich day replaces it. Dunbar to Edinburgh takes only twenty-five minutes. The Glasgow leg adds another forty-eight minutes, after the connection at Waverley Station. The trip costs about £5 for coach, with cushioned seats, glazed windows, and a roof nonetheless.

The broad tidal flat of the River Tyne and the Biel Water appears just after the train pulls away from the platform, between Belhaven and West Barns a mile west of the station. Doon Hill, ever present, lurks inland to the south, watching my progress westward. The estuary now serves as the John Muir Country Park, mostly a salt marsh of meadow grass and sand dunes with piney woods marking its northwest boundary along the Tyninghame Estate. John knew this shoreline intimately from his many rambles exploring the rocky outcrops and sandy stretches around Dunbar. He knew the wondrous assortment of birds and sea creations it nourished, too, having been fascinated with local lore and naturalists like Alexander Wilson and John James Audubon. "When I was a boy in Scotland," he recalled, "I was fond of everything that was wild, and all my life I've been growing fonder and fonder of wild places and creatures." "Fortunately," he continued, around my native town of Dunbar, by the stormy North Sea, there was no lack of wildness, though most of the land lay in smooth cultivation. . . . I loved to wander in the fields to hear the birds sing, and along the seashore to gaze and wonder at the shells and seaweeds, eels and crabs in the pools among the rocks when the tide was low; and best of all to watch the waves in awful storms thundering on the black headlands and the craggy ruins of the old Dunbar Castle when the sea and sky, the waves and the clouds, were mingled together as one.

The dome-shaped hulk of the Bass Rock stands through the morning mist omnipresent in the Firth. Some calm spring day, John must have taken a small skiff out to the curious island to see it teeming with nesting seabirds, seemingly millions of guillemot, razorbill, cormorant, puffin, tern, eider, and especially the gannet, which takes its Latin name—*Sula bassana*—from the rock. For centuries the island provided sanctuary for various people: a retreat for Saint Baldred in the sixth century; a fortress for successive conquerors; a prison for bothersome Covenanters; and in the early 1690s, the last bastion for a few desperate supporters of a Stuart monarchy already deposed everywhere on land in the latest glorious revolution. Now it's a protected bird sanctuary, much to John's probable approval.

The Firth coastline bows northward from the park, broadening the plain by several more miles. Land and sea collide abruptly in East Lothian. Cliffs form the edge with open, fertile farmland right to the face, unlike coastal zones where expansive wetlands and back bays emit a pungent smell foretelling the change from land to sea miles away. The large lush fields drape over the layers of sandstone beneath the coastal plain. The land lies in gentle folds, dissected by sharp gullies cut when glaciers discharged torrents of meltwater 14,000 to 20,000 years ago. The first rolling hills of the Lammermuirs gather to the south like an approaching ocean swell, still patterned with a patchwork of snow. Tractors turn dark patches of reddish brown soil in preparation for the next crop of barley, potatoes, or oilseed rape. Round bales of recently harvested hay, some wrapped in black plastic, stand end to end in long rows, like giant fallen columns, on the field margins. A few fields still have sprouts to harvest. Sheep feed on turnips in others, while lambing has begun for ewes inseminated a bit early. A sprinkle of yellow flowers brighten the prickly gorse and the first blooms of white snowdrops lighten the forest floors, though new leaves have yet to appear on the hedgerows and deciduous windrows.

The train speeds westward toward Edinburgh, cutting quietly through the picturesque rural landscape. A patchwork of fields stitched together by hedgerows and dykes form its basic fabric. Inset sit small villages of red pantile-roofed cottages huddled tightly together. Long rows of low attached cottages that once housed farmworkers lay scattered along narrow lanes lined with hedgerows and dykes that connect village to village. Fields spread outward from widely spaced *farm steadings,* many of which were rebuilt by prosperous nineteenth-century landowners or tenants. Their stately homes stand near the giant barns built in the form of a quadrangle, resembling a monastic cloister, complete with an arched entryway and a prominent smokestack. The imposing complexes were built to house the new steam-powered machines, proudly proclaiming the arrival of the industrial age and the owner's prosperity. These farms nest within a second pattern of even wider-spaced estates—the grand ancestral estates of the landed aristocrats, often set apart from their surrounding tenants by high stone walls and colonnades of trees lining the perimeter.

The stone walls, stone cottages, stone farm buildings, and grand stone homes lend the landscape sweeping past my window a palpable sense of permanence in sharp contrast to the temporary feel of the wood-framed constructions prevalent in America.

So do the occasional castle ruins, the standing stones, and the doocots. This is an organic landscape formed from ancient forces, not from the relatively recent ideas of economic, environmental, and social expediency seen in the ubiquitous use of the grid in the layout of American cities and countryside. Most villages have grown without plan, their cluster of small cottages standing shoulder to shoulder along narrow closes and *wynds* running outward from a main street or square. Outlying fields display only the slightest hint of a general pattern or alignment. No abstract geometry dictates spatial organization here. But the land is not randomly organized. The patterns are subtle and derived from feudal forces rather than blatant actions that bespeak technological dominance.

I see other not-so-quaint scenes as I pass swiftly by. New detached and semidetached harl-clad homes have been built at the edge of some villages. An occasional caravan park appears, too. And power lines march across the fields.

What don't I see? I don't see many subdivisions of suburban sprawl, even though I'm only twenty-five minutes by train from Edinburgh. Here, many new residents live in homes recently built on vacant lots within town boundaries, or in old buildings recycled into new uses. This approach reduces the need for new homes built on vacant land outside the town. I see none of the large-lot housing that lines many rural roads at the urban fringe around American cities. I see no billboards along roads and rail lines. I see much less strip commercial development and far fewer convenience stores at highway interchanges, and I see a highway network dominated by rural roads rather than by multilane highways and limited-access freeways. I see no traffic lights; roundabouts replace them here. More of these signs of our contemporary Western auto-oriented consumer landscape can be found at the immediate fringe of Edinburgh, where "power centers" composed of "big box" retail superstores line parts of the

city's perimeter. But few of these are found here, not far beyond
that perimeter. Scottish cities and towns are more tightly knit
than most American cities, which gradually unravel into the surrounding rural fabric. The hem between town and country is less
frayed here. A "greenbelt" limits development in a swath several
miles wide around Edinburgh, preserving a clear, crisp edge
between city and countryside. Planning holds the line more
tightly around smaller towns, too, maintaining the landscape's
physical and aesthetic character. John Muir would recognize the
area around Dunbar today.

Ten miles further on, between the towns of East Linton and
Haddington, Traprain Law stands to the south, a silent record
of other forces. A massive laccolith, the humpbacked hill was
formed during a period of volcanic activity in the area 320 million years ago, when molten magna was forced upward, warping
around it the layers of surface rock as it swelled beneath the
smooth skin of the coastal plain. The outer rock layers that covered the intrusion have since been eroded or were scraped away
by glaciers, leaving the plug exposed in a "crag and tail" form
pointed in the direction of the most recent glacier's path as the
hard mass deflected the ice sheet around its flanks.

Traprain visually dominates the surrounding plain and the
River Tyne valley that opens the land like a giant wound just to
the north. The view from the top is stunning—a fifty-mile-wide
panorama of the Firth of Forth and its adjacent plain, from
Arthur's Seat in Edinburgh and the Pentland Hills beyond to
Doon Hill outside Dunbar. The tapestry of fields, hedgerows,
and dykes lay like a carpet below you. In the past, the Law also
dominated the surrounding landscape militarily. Human use of
the hilltop dates back to Neolithic times (circa 4000 B.C.), when
communities sought to command the area from atop its preci-
pice. Since the Bronze Age (circa 2000 B.C.), the Law has served
as a fortress and an important ceremonial site. The powerful

Votadini people ruled the region from the massif for centuries early in the first millennium, before relocating to what is now Edinburgh. Making the steep climb to the top, it's easy to imagine them making the same climb two thousand years ago. The way to the summit leaves from a small car park partway up on the north side, ascending through ancient ramparts. The rugged climb past large boulders strewn about the thick tufts of grass feels right for the February rawness and drama of the setting. Land and history are in harmony. Here, powerful physical forces and long human occupancy have combined to produce a landscape that evokes its rich legacy.

Legend also forms a part of that legacy. Local tradition has long associated fairy lore with it. And if the old monkish chroniclers are right, the city of Glasgow owes its existence to the Law. According to one tale, in the early sixth century a powerful Pict king named Loth (from which "Lothian" is derived) ruled over all he could see from the fortified settlement atop the Law. King Loth was half pagan and half Christian, as Christianity had only recently arrived in Dalriada (Scotland) and he wasn't sure the Christian god was more powerful than his pagan gods. Events involving his headstrong Christian daughter, Princess Thenew, would challenge his faith.

As was the custom, the king and queen selected a husband for their only child; the suitor being an arrogant, conscienceless, overbearing young pagan prince from Galloway named Owen Ap (presumably he had other redeeming qualities). Princess Thenew detested the prince on first glance and refused to be betrothed. This was intolerable. The king had no choice but to banish his beloved daughter from the kingdom for her disobedience. The princess fled south into the Lammermuir Hills, where she became a shepherdess and soon discovered the tranquil lifestyle to her liking, much to her surprise.

Meanwhile the king tried to placate the rejected and enraged prince with lavish entertainment and feasts. These only made his anger worse. On learning that the princess was actually enjoying her banishment, the paranoid prince bid King Loth an amicable goodbye, ostensibly to return to Galloway, then sent his servants to scour the hills in search of her. She was soon found and he rode off to confront her. Princess Thenew greeted Prince Ap with cold politeness, whereupon he raped and beat her mercilessly while his laughing servants blocked her escape. Her tormentors then left her for dead, alone in the hills and unable to return home. The battered princess summoned the last of her strength to pray for peace, comfort, and courage. Miraculously, with the help of an old shepherd who took her in and cared for her, she survived. So did the new life within her.

When word of these events reached the king, he wept sorrowfully for his beloved child. But the tragic events left him in a quandary: custom called for her death since she was pregnant without his consent, regardless of the circumstances. To make an exception might undermine his reign. Consequently, he ordered his servants to hunt down and kill the prince, and bring back his daughter to face her fate. The prince escaped; unfortunately the princess was found. The king ordered her bound to a stake and stoned to death. This caused him great anguish, for he did genuinely love her. So did his subjects. No one would lift a stone against her. Now what to do? After several days of soul-searching, he ordered her cast over the cliff edge. Let the gods decide her fate.

Amid the wails of the people, two trusted servants took her ceremoniously to the edge and did the dreadful deed. Much to everyone's amazement, her voluminous dress opened as she fell, catching in the branches of a tree and breaking her fall. It was a miracle, the people felt. They dropped to their knees in prayerful rejoicing. Her god must have heard her prayers, and those of the people.

This left King Loth in an even bigger quandary. Was this the work of her Christian god or a message from his pagan gods? After several more days of agonizing, he decreed that the princess be bound in a small coracle made of animal hide and set adrift in the Firth. Leave her in the hands of Lamannan, the pagan god of the sea, he concluded. The people wept as the tide carried her away. And once again fate or faith intervened.

Her coracle floated not out to sea but fifty miles upriver to be rescued by monks near the village of Culross. There, they cared for her in the monastery and she gave birth in 518 to a son she named Kentigern, meaning "chief lord." The boy was raised in the monastic way of life, becoming much beloved and respected for his scholarship. As a young man, Kentigern was sent westward to found his own monastery. This he did near the banks of the River Clyde. A village soon grew around the monastery, becoming the city of Glasgow. Despite trials and tribulations, Kentigern rose over time to be the Bishop of Cumbria and his lifetime of good deeds was recognized when he was sanctified as Saint Mungo, Glasgow's patron saint. He died in 603 and was buried in Glasgow Cathedral. Princess Thenew was also canonized as Saint Enoch. Today various places in Glasgow share the name of Saint Mungo or Saint Enoch.

Like many Scottish place names, the etymological origins of Traprain tell a tantalizing story that captures its physical and cultural history. *Tra* derives from the common Brittonic word *tref,* meaning settlement or village. The meaning of *prain,* a derivative of *pren,* is less clear. In one interpretation, it means a tree or trees, though not necessarily associated with a forest as a landscape feature useful for place identification. The tree could be a pole or an individual tree used as a ritual object by the local community. Traprain then stems from *tref-pren,* or "farming settlement at tree" (or trees). Perhaps a single tree or a small grove once stood curiously atop the Law, leading ancient people like the Votadini to create a legend about the mysterious presence and name the place in response. By then East Lothian and the Lammermuirs had already been stripped of forest and were intensively farmed. And Lammermuir translates in Celtic to *Lombor Mor,* meaning "great bare plateau" and by English speakers as *Lambra Mor,* or "moor of lambs." Or perhaps an ancient people erected a pole atop the summit for some ceremonial purpose, serving a community function like the mercat cross common in medieval villages like Cockburnspath.

Prain is alternatively defined as a spear or palace, which relates to another name given the Law, *Dumpender.* In *The Lay of the Last Mistrel,* Sir Walter Scott described the far-off beacon fires visible from Edinburgh, warnings set on distant promontories like Dumpender (Traprain),

> Till high Dunedin the blazes saw,
> From Soltra and Dumpender Law;
> And Lothian heard the Regent's order,
> That all should bowne them for the Border.

Dumpender derives from the Cumbric *Din Pelydr* and earlier *Mons Dunpelder.* Pelydr is the plural form of *paladr,* meaning "shaft." *Dun* (or *dum* when followed by a palatal) is an oft-used Gaelic and Brittonic prefix in Scottish place names, meaning a hill or mound, sometimes a fortress or castle. Hence Dumpender becomes a hill fort of spear shafts, a possible description of the Iron Age (circa 500 B.C.) palisade-stockade battlements built on the Law and common throughout East Lothian. Clouded and complicated, the origins of the place name, like the land itself, contain layers of meaning left by the many people who have occupied the Law and the landscape it commands.

Traprain recedes behind me. Arthur's Seat and Edinburgh draw me ahead. This landscape—west of Traprain—would be less

familiar to John since he probably saw it only from the heights of
Doon Hill. Twenty minutes after his departure, he left his old
world forever behind and began a new life. "Wildness was ever
sounding in our ears," he wrote, "and Nature saw to it that
besides school lessons and church lessons some of her own lessons
should be learned, perhaps with a view to the time when we
should be called to wander in wildness to our heart's content. . . .
Kings may be blessed," he continued, but "we were glorious, we
were free. . . . These were my first excursions—the beginnings of
lifelong wanderings."

[6]

My train glides into Waverley Station right on time. Brilliant
sunshine and a glorious blue sky show the high has temporarily
had its way with the low. The approach to the station sweeps in a
left-hand curve around the royal palace and grounds of Holyrood
and, behind, the base of Arthur's Seat, another massive volcanic
remnant with an 825-foot-high peak. Like a voyeur, I catch only
tantalizing glimpses of the royal lifestyle and the fabled earth
form. Their fascinating histories lie screened by great cultural
and geophysical gulfs. Four-story blocks of apartments, new and
old, also screen the view, making it all the more provocative. We
suddenly plunge into darkness as the train enters a long tunnel
just beyond; the station waits on the other side. It is doubtful
that the two adjacent Edinburgh stations in 1849 had the hustle
and bustle of Waverley today, but the commotion still must have
made quite an impression on John, David, and Sarah.

Waverley Station sits in a narrow valley between two roughly
parallel ridges that run east to west, as if the tracks cleaved Edinburgh's town center into two distinct halves—crowded, chaotic
"Old Town" atop the southern ridge, and formal "New Town"
atop the northern ridge. The Old Town streets are narrow and

lined with tall stone buildings containing small stores at curb-side, with businesses and flats above. The New Town streets are straight and symmetrical, broad and grand, lined with block after block of neoclassical Georgian town houses that now contain prosperous business and professional offices. The Old Town remains medieval and organic, formed when the burgh huddled within the protective shelter of an enclosing wall, forcing growth up rather than out. The New Town stands orderly and dignified, the brainchild of the Enlightenment. The "Royal Mile" runs down the crest of the ridge in the Old Town, from Edinburgh Castle at its peak to Holyrood Palace at its base behind me. St. Giles (the mother church of the Kirk), the old and new Parliaments, and the University of Edinburgh sit intermingled with endless pubs and specialty shops that line the tight streets. George Street forms the spine of the New Town, running along its crown, with Princes Street and Queen Street aligned in parallel along its shoulders. The layout is a showpiece of squares, circles, crescents, parks, and terraces, with an occasional statue or architectural set piece interspersed. Despite 250 years of growth and development since the New Town was planned, the city center's character remains largely intact, with remarkably few sterile modernist or gaudy postmodernist high-rises to diminish the effect.

The core's split physical character seems an appropriate reflection of the dual legacies that shape the Lothian landscape—the lasting effects of feudalism and the new ideas of the Enlightenment and the Industrial Revolution. The Muirs would recognize the place today and likely sense the tensions between its two formative legacies, tensions between the constraints of the past and the promises of the future. In many ways, those tensions triggered Daniel's flight from Dunbar that day.

The dozens of donated park benches that line the promenade just below Princes Street, along the upper edge of the public gardens, afford perhaps the best setting to sense those tensions. My favorite bench sits at the base of the Sir Walter Scott Monument, appropriately, since Scott's romantic writings around the time that the New Town was built were so influential in redefining the Scots' sense of self and landscape. The rustic teak bench is a bit weathered and worn with a flaking finish, but I like the donors' inscription: "Rest awhile with the Reidfords of Corskie." Thank you, I shall. The message makes a pleasant change from the "In loving memory of . . ." inscriptions found on most of the other benches.

From the Reidford bench on a brilliant February day like today, the huge stone crown atop St. Giles glows above the building mass of the Old Town, as if God was highlighting the place of the Kirk in shaping Scottish society since the Reformation. The low sun angle also irradiates the deep earth tones of the rocky cliff face beneath the castle, calling attention to the nation's feudal past. The castle's commanding presence provided a constant reminder of the dominant feudal social order for all huddled beneath. So did Holyrood Palace. Yet as the long, narrow *toft* lots of the medieval burgh were built over, people of all classes mixed cheek by jowl and all aspects of life played out in the Old Town market streets and the tight closes. Dirty, messy, with stifling density and a surging population, by the eighteenth century the Old Town was both alive and outdated in the face of changing economic, political, religious, and social structures. A new physical structure was needed to accommodate these.

The refined architectural order of the New Town was the response, a showcase of the new thinking. On the surface, it appeared to reject the Old Town's outdated feudal forms and embrace the new thinking of the Enlightenment, the Reformation, and the Industrial Revolution. However, beneath the elegant facade, the built form reflected and reinforced a heightened sense of class consciousness, separating the classes horizontally and vertically. The new order segregated rich and poor, powerful and powerless, much more than the disorder of the Old Town.

Yellow, white, pink, and purple crocuses dot the park's south-facing grassy slope beside the promenade. Above and behind me, on the north side of Princes Street, large buildings long ago replaced the original eighteenth-century buildings, to accommodate the need for more retail space and a reordered retail environment as Edinburgh prospered during the industrial age. Today another change in the commercial and cultural fabric is under way, triggered by the preferences of the current shoppers and tourists that crowd the broad sidewalk along the city's commercial heart. A quickened pace of economic and social change in Edinburgh poses new challenges for the city's aging urban form. The grand department stores of the Victorian and Edwardian eras now compete with multinational chains like the Gap, Levi's, and Disney. Specialty stores are gradually replacing the giant general stores that dominated the retail landscape when people traveled by ships and trains rather than cars and planes. Both types of stores are based on global commerce, but the speed differs dramatically.

To date, the striking physical character of the core remains remarkably true to the centuries-old New Town plan. Great care has been taken to ensure that most renovations and new construction are compatible with the historic character of the district, and construction on the park side of Princes Street has been tightly controlled to maintain the dramatic view of the Old Town across the valley. However, more and more businesses find such controls too limiting to meet their changing needs, and relocate outside the core in search of more functional and efficient space. If the trend continues, the historic core may well become a tourist-oriented district with little relevance to local residents.

I dash the fifty yards across the cold, open-air station, past the newsstands, bookshops, and the giant overhead arrival/departure screen to catch the next shuttle to Glasgow, even though one leaves every fifteen minutes. The shuttle only has several carriages. In contrast, my train from Dunbar to Edinburgh originated at London King's Cross Station and contained nine carriages, including a dining car and first-class accommodations catering to long-distance travelers. I'm off again in a matter of moments, heading westward through the valley that slices Edinburgh in two, past the public gardens and Princes Street to my right and the sheer wall of buildings that form the edge of the Old Town to my left.

As it was for John Muir, this is my first trip to Glasgow. I'm eager to see Broomielaw Quay, from which he and thousands of other emigrants set sail for distant lands, a place whose story tells so much of "modern" Scotland's tale of tradition and folklore, of outreach to foreign lands, of political struggle with England, of power and oppression, of innovation and industrialization, and of recent revitalization. Broomielaw reflects one of the core aspects of Scottish history and culture: this is a land that faces the sea; a place where most people live within fifty miles of the ocean; a country continuously shaped by forces beyond its borders; an islandlike nation.

Broomielaw—meaning broom- or gorse-covered slope—has been used for access to the river since the area's earliest settlement. It was close to St. Mungo's monastery, later Glasgow Cathedral, and the center of the growing burgh. Perhaps its gradual slope down to the water's edge made it a convenient place to beach boats at the head of the tidal estuary. The Clyde was shallow and narrow there, more of a large stream than a navigable river. By the 1600s, this forced the development of docks at Port Glasgow and Greenock miles downriver, where the Clyde widened and deepened enough to accommodate the deep-draft ocean-going vessels of international trade and mass emigration.

England didn't relish the competition from its independent-minded northern neighbor; so for this and other political reasons, it passed repressive legislation (the Navigation Acts of the mid-1600s) limiting the Scots' access to the riches of the New World. The reversal of these restrictions became one of the most important enticements to the Scots to approve the Act of Union in 1707, which formally "married" the two nations after a contentious century-long courtship. The repeal actually constituted a thinly veiled form of economic blackmail, albeit supposedly to both nations' benefit by creating a larger free-trade market. Article IV of the act, titled "Freedom and Intercourse of Trade and Navigation," provided for Scottish shipping to enjoy duty-free entry to English domestic and colonial markets, and Article V recognized all Scottish-owned vessels as ships of Great Britain, granting them the protection of the Royal Navy. The benefits of the new privileges accrued slowly, accompanied initially by damaging competition for such sensitive Scottish industries as the woolen trade and brewing. Nor did the act end all English meddling in Scottish economic affairs, maritime, industrial, or agricultural. Policies set in Westminster in response to British wants and wishes often affected the Scottish economy differently than the English economy, since the two were at different developmental stages. But by mid-century the benefits began to transform Broomielaw, Glasgow, and much of Scotland.

Tobacco and sugar fueled the change. Aggressive Scottish merchants raised smuggling and fraud to new heights in the first decades after the union, undercutting English competitors' prices on the American and Caribbean products. They also instituted innovative (legal) business practices to cut costs and better control supply. London and Liverpool retaliated with legislation and increased customs policing. By the mid-1700s, as smuggling dwindled, a handful of Glaswegian merchants dominated the immensely profitable market, importing leaf and cane from the colonies and reexporting it throughout Europe. Clothed in scarlet cloaks and black suits, the "tobacco lords" met in front of the Tontine Hotel at Glasgow Cross to conduct business. There, the "four apostles of Glasgow's prosperity"—William Cunningham, John Glassford, James Ritchie, and Alexander Spiers—engineered a widespread economic boom for the city. Banking and many other businesses followed on tobacco's coattails. The urgent need to move the Clyde harbors closer to the city core underpinned that boom.

John Smeaton's report in the 1750s provided the answer: dredge the river to make a deep-water channel to Broomielaw. Work quickly began on the massive project. Additional deepening and widening would occur intermittently over the next hundred years to accommodate the gradual increase in ship size. Good thing that the dredging and the diversification of the local economy came hand in hand, for the tobacco market collapsed when the upstart colonies revolted. Cotton textiles replaced tobacco as the port's major commodity and the city's economic engine, and remained dominant until the 1860s, when another war in the New World would again change Glasgow markets and Broomielaw. And once again innovation and industrialization would prepare the city for a smooth transition to its next economic incarnation.

The Muirs arrived in Glasgow at Queen Street Station in the midst of this transformation. Power was the key. Steam-powered mills had transformed the Glaswegian textile industry in the late 1700s, propelling it from secondary status to prominence. Sixty mills employed 25,000 workers by the industry's peak in 1860 as Scottish linens were shipped worldwide from Broomielaw. Yet even during the textile industry's ascendancy, other technological innovations were combining to transform the port and city once again.

This time the raw materials were local. A deposit of blackband ironstone was discovered east of Glasgow in 1801, which became a prime ingredient in iron production after the invention of the hot-blast furnace twenty-seven years later. Coal-fired steam power and iron remade industrial Glasgow in a generation. Poor roadways and canals were replaced by railroads in the mid-1800s, enabling the efficient movement of both raw materials and finished product. Over one hundred ironworks were producing 400,000 tons of pig iron by 1840, much of which was exported, requiring bigger ships and the continued development of Broomielaw. Ships were soon transformed as well. Henry Bell launched his newfangled steamship *Comet* in the Clyde in 1812. The first iron-hulled ship followed in 1835. By the 1840s, fourteen shipyards employed 14,000 men. Glasgow's prominence in shipbuilding was established. The iron industry and shipbuilding transformed Glasgow physically and socially, dominating city life for the next century, just as the American Civil War cut off cotton imports.

People continued to be a major export as well, reaching a peak around 1850 due to the potato famine and the profound social upheavals related to industrialization on the farms and in the factories. The Glasgow of Daniel's first "escape" in 1825 was a dirty industrial town built on the backs of common workers. The Glasgow of his second "escape" in 1849 was probably worse.

[7]

The *Warren* was one of eight vessels to enter the busy Broomielaw harbor on January 30, 1849. She was a modest-sized 415-ton "ship"—three masts, square-rigged—built in Portland, Maine, four years earlier and registered at New York in August 1847. Woodhull & Minturn, a prominent New York shipping company based on South Street, owned her and ran her in their "Old Line" packet service established between New York and Glasgow in 1845. Packet lines carried cargo and passengers between two ports on a regular schedule, a relatively recent innovation in maritime commerce. The new form of shipping required significant capital and business acumen, hence packet lines often marked a major improvement in professionalism over the unruly practices of prior forms of transoceanic trade. Old Line packets set sail from each port for the monthlong voyage on the first and fifteenth days of the month, conditions permitting. On this voyage the *Warren* carried 700 barrels of flour; 3,643 bags and 775 quarters of Indian corn; 228 bales of cotton; 252 boxes and 56 casks of cheese; 300 bags of peas; 100 boxes of bacon; 50 barrels of pork and 27 hogsheads of salted pork; 50 bales of pigs' hair; 50 kegs and 50 barrels of lard; 50 tierce of beef; 50 barrels of rosin; 3 bales of general merchandise; and 2 boxes of cheese, 2 barrels of apples, and 2 pairs of Indian rubber shoes consigned to Job G. Lawton, the ship's captain.

The *Warren* was unloaded, repaired, and refitted in two weeks. Reloading began on February 13 at berth 16 on the northside quay. Her return cargoes valued at just under £3,000 were the principal products of Glasgow's dominant industries: 400 tons of pig iron; 20 barrels of beer; 34 barrels and 1 firkin of ale; 304 casks, 7 bales, and 20 boxes of cold cottons; 1,441 yards of woolens and cottons; 2,800 pounds of cotton thread; 6,600 yards of pin linens; and unlisted quantities of sewed collars, dressed calfskins, woolen carpeting, soda ash, and bleaching powder.

The Muirs probably arrived at the Queen Street Station a bit bewildered in midafternoon. Daniel likely hired a wagon at the busy West George Street entrance to send their load of luggage to the quay. I suspect the awestruck family then walked south a block, through the throngs of travelers, businessmen, and shoppers, past George Square—the heart of the city, which sits diagonally across the street from the station—on their way one block west to Buchanan Street to pick up their tickets at number 182, the office of the ship's Glasgow agent, Thomas Pickersgill & Co. It's doubtful that Daniel arrived in Glasgow without having made prior travel arrangements. Packets like the *Warren* were booked with passengers and cargo well in advance. This facilitated their relatively quick turnaround time in port and limited the need for flashy advertisements in local newspapers to attract last-minute travelers; indeed, no ads for the voyage appeared in them. With tickets and travel documents in hand, the family then headed for the wharf, just a few short blocks southwest from the Pickersgill office.

The harbor teemed with life. Dozens of sailing vessels of various types—ships, schooners, brigs, barques, and steamers—were loading for distant ports: the 148-ton *Packet* for Antigua; the 316-ton *Amiga* for Valparaiso; the 548-ton *Victory* for Sydney; the 228-ton *Diana* for St. Thomas; and the 470-ton *Princess* bound for Boston. Others were headed for Rotterdam, Malta, Montreal, Singapore, and Ceylon. Dozens more smaller vessels were destined for "coastwise" ports of the British Isles. The water must have been thick and rank and the air filled with the sour stench of brine, sewage, and salty timber. Lingering smells of rotten cargo and mildew emitted from the holds likely assaulted the senses too, testimony to the ships' previous voyages. Carriages carrying merchants and the well-to-do and wagons carrying cargo and luggage clattered along the broad cobblestone street adjacent to the northside quay. Porters and stevedores hurried with their loads around the tangle of heavy lines that tied the ships to the black, bulbous-shaped bollards. And hundreds of emigrants, urban and rural, rich and poor, moved among the mess toward their ships and their dreams.

The *Warren* sailed from Broomielaw on February 24 with seventy-two hopeful passengers and a crew of thirteen, pausing the next day at Greenock thirty miles downriver to take on another crew member and more cargo: 50 tons of pig iron, 75 hundredweight of copper, and 15 boxes and 1 bale of calfskins. The shallowness of the Clyde upriver from Greenock likely meant the last of the cargo couldn't be loaded until the *Warren* made deeper water. This last load probably accompanied the ship from Broomielaw in "lighters." Foul weather must have accompanied the ship as well as she sat at Greenock for a week, her crew and anxious passengers eager to get under way while settling into shipboard life. On March 3, the *Warren* finally set sail for New York, the immigrants' gateway to the New World.

What were Daniel's and the children's jumbled emotions as they made their way through the tumult and boarded: fear, nervous excitement, or relief? Was it a sad or joyous occasion? How did they feel as the lines were cast off and the *Warren* eased away from the quay that day? Had those feelings changed as her sails first caught the wind at Greenock and she slipped silently down the Clyde, making the sharp turn to port to head south through the narrow strait between the Isle of Bute, to starboard, and the Great Cumbrae Island, to port, thence into the broad mouth of the Firth, before finally losing sight of Scotland as the Isle of Arran disappeared behind them? This was likely their first time aboard a ship. They probably had a tiny cabin crowded with four bunk beds and their luggage on the first level below deck. A square transom window might have provided light and fresh air. Shipboard life for the Muirs was relatively pleasant, unlike that on the infamous immigrant ships that crammed several hundred terrorized people in the dark, airless steerage holds, often locked below for weeks during rough seas. The *Warren*'s dank holds, each less than six feet high and squeezed between the giant beams and curving hull, carried its pig iron and cotton cargo, not a human cargo confined to inhuman conditions. Muir recalled, "[We] joyfully sailed away from beloved Scotland, flying to our fortunes on the wings of the winds, care-free as thistle seeds." Was it so easy for Daniel? John continued,

We could not then know what we were leaving, what we were to encounter in the New World, nor what our gains were likely to be. We were too young and full of hope for fear or regret, but not too young to look forward with eager enthusiasm to the wonderful schoolless bookless American wilderness. Even the natural heart-pain of parting from grandfather and grandmother Gilrye, who loved us so well, and from mother and sisters and brother was quickly quenched in young joy.

Today Broomielaw is a ghost of its former self in its heyday. No ships load and unload here. That once again takes place well downriver. The smokestack industries of the 1800s and 1900s— iron, textiles, and shipbuilding—no longer dominate the local economy and culture to such a degree. Glasgow and Broomielaw are reinventing themselves once more. The northside quay I stroll along has been transformed into a river walk paved with cobblestones. A dozen black bollards, some period lights, and a few pilings remain too. Otherwise the past is completely lost. The promenade probably looked fine in plan, though the reality disappoints. Only an occasional pleasure craft plies the river now. Even at noon on this sunny, comfortable day, I'm nearly alone on the walk. There's noplace to go and no reason to come, nothing to see and nothing to do. The new vibrancy of Glasgow awaits several blocks away, around George Square, Buchanan Street, and St. Enoch Square. Nor does the river walk offer "green relief" as an attractive garden from the urban scene nearby, as does the Charles River Esplanade in Boston. Yet like the Charles River, the Clyde appears nearly stagnant, lifeless, and black—the viscous fluid found in dirty tidal rivers that flow through many industrial cities. A gambling casino sits at the foot of the quay, just below the elegant stone arches of the Jamaica Bridge that have marked the upper end of Broomielaw and the river's navigability for large vessels for about two hundred years. But Broomie-law is no longer a destination for people or ships; now it's only an out-of-the-way afterthought.

[8]

Something must have happened on the *Warren* between Glasgow and New York, something that happened on most ships carrying immigrants. It must have happened to Daniel Muir, age forty-five, occupation: trader, as recorded on the ship's official manifest. It must have happened as well to John Bird, twenty-two, blacksmith; to John Cunningham, twenty-two, farmer; to Janet Gibson, thirty, housewife; to John Green, twenty-five, optician; to Richard Hood, twenty-five, miller; to Robert Johnson, twenty-three, tailor; to Thomas Moss, forty, weaver; to Margaret O'Neill, seventeen, servant; to William Robertson, twenty-five, cotton spinner; to John Thompson, forty, miner; and to George and Joan Walker, twenty-nine and thirty-three, laborer and house-wife. Sometime during that voyage, they must have discarded their old attachments to the land as if jettisoning useless baggage overboard, and begun to adopt a new set in their stead. Gone was their linkage to the land and community formed over genera-tions. Long-learned patterns of farm, village, and parish life were left behind. Those links were severed as the *Warren* made to sea; they weren't transferable. Perhaps new links could be formed in the new land, but they could never be the same as those left behind. Gone was a landscape home alive with history. Over the side went Cromwell and Hutton, Loth and Thenew, dykes, deans, castles, and crags. Lost were centuries-old family roots and the places in which those roots were set—hills and cliffs, rivers and bays, forests, fields, and farms, houses, and villages—places with names, places with a past. Lost too was the magic and mystery of a place embedded in lore, poetry, story, and song. The intimate connection to the land that permeated their Old World culture could not be reconstructed in the New World. Time and circumstances precluded it.

Gone was the sense that the land had always belonged to someone, usually a "superior." It had been that way for as long as anyone could remember. All land was owned, none was vacant and free for the taking. Gone as well were the Old World constraints on ownership. No more lairds. No more feudal dues. No more dependence on the nobility to govern one's affairs. Those too were cast overboard. Now the emigrants would own land. Now they would be independent and self-reliant. Ironically, those who had been deprived of that opportunity for centuries and been subjugated by those who controlled it would now deprive the native population they would displace of the opportunity to freely inhabit the land. And gone was a sense that all the land was settled. "Wildness" might have existed in the Old World, but not "wilderness." People had "occupied" and "improved" the Old World since before written history. The New World had vast areas where that was not the case, they thought. For the uprooted adults and adolescents aboard the *Warren,* people who set to sea in search of opportunity, the landless weeks afloat separated the Old World from the New both geographically and psychologically.

To John and David, the voyage wasn't so profound. "That long voyage had not a dull moment for us boys," John later wrote. "Father and sister Sarah, with most of the old folk, stayed below in rough weather, groaning in the miseries of seasickness, many of the passengers wishing they had never ventured in 'the auld rockin' creel,' as they called our bluff-bowed, wave-beating ship." Sarah, in fact, never left her bunk the entire voyage as the ship encountered storm after storm during its early spring crossing. Memory of the experience would make her nauseated all her life.

In moderate weather, passengers met on deck to share stories of home and plans for the future, to pass the hours of mind-numbing monotony and mounting anxiety. Day after day they had nothing to do but sit and wait in their tiny cabins or on the deck crowded with people amid the tangle of ropes and rigging, helpless to affect their fate. A ship about 100 feet long and 25 feet wide with several decks and towering masts might have looked grand at Broomielaw, but after weeks at sea with eighty-six people aboard, seemingly adrift, forever rising, falling, rolling over rough swells in an endless void where sky and water often fused to form an indistinguishable dark gray mass, the *Warren* became tiny indeed. Conversation buoyed spirits and lessened the overwhelming sense of confinement. In the evenings they sang songs for entertainment, "The Youthful Sailor Frank and Bold" and "Oh, Why Left I My Hame, Why Did I Cross the Deep." After several weeks, though, it must have all been said and sung and the initial novelty well worn. What fresh enthusiasm and excitement they brought aboard must have become as damp, stale, and putrid as the food, water, and smell.

Fortunately, John and David enjoyed a strong stomach for life at sea. "No matter how much the old tub tossed about and battered the waves," John recalled, "we were on deck every day, not in the least seasick, watching the sailors at their rope-hauling and climbing work; joining in their songs, learning the names of the ropes and sails and helping them as far as they would let us; playing games with other boys in calm weather when the deck was dry, and in stormy weather rejoicing in sympathy with the curly-topped waves."

Daniel had other concerns. A decision on their final destination couldn't be avoided much longer. Word of Canada among the passengers told of an endless forest so dense one would have to work a lifetime to clear a small field. The American "West"— new lands in Michigan and Wisconsin then opening to the latest wave of white immigrants from the teeming eastern port cities, pioneers following Horace Greeley's charge to "go west, young man, and grow up with the country"—sounded more promising: fertile soil, well-watered, with scattered "oak openings" within the forest that enabled a fine crop to be planted the first year. Central Wisconsin seemed ideal. There, the word went, work on a canal was under way to link the Fox River to the Wisconsin River. This would connect the region to the Gulf of Mexico and southern ports via the Mississippi River, and connect it to Canada and Atlantic ports via the Great Lakes, the St. Lawrence River, and the Erie Canal. The region would surely boom, they felt, as its farm products flooded those markets. It was perfect. The land was cheap and ripe, and Scottish settlers were already being welcomed. In fact, Daniel heard from other Disciples of Christ members he met on board that the sect had just established several small settlements in Wisconsin. God did seem to be directing him to the right place.

"As we neared the shore of the great new land," John recalled, "with what eager wonder we watched the whales and dolphins and porpoises and seabirds, and made the good-natured sailors teach us their names and tell us stories about them!" The entrance to safe harbor at New York was a bit tricky. The *Warren* likely passed through the six-mile-wide Gedney Channel between Sandy Hook to the south and a series of sandy shallows to the north. Then it turned to starboard, rounding the Southwest Spit, and headed northward up the main shipping channel to the two-mile-wide Narrows between Staten Island and the Brooklyn end of Long Island. At one place the Narrows squeezed to three-quarters of a mile wide, forming a bottleneck through which passed much of the nation's commerce. Once ships cleared quarantine inspection there and the seriously sick were removed, they proceeded directly for dock through the deepwater channel running between shallow flats on either side of the four-mile-wide Upper Bay.

The "Maritime Journal" in the *New-York Daily Tribune* listed twenty-eight ships, schooners, barks, and brigs that made port on Tuesday, April 10, 1849. Most came from U.S. or Caribbean ports carrying sugar, molasses, or cotton. Woodhull & Minturn had two ships arrive from Glasgow that day. The *Hyndford,* piloted by Captain Stevenson, made the crossing in thirty-one days, carrying general merchandise and 134 souls in the steerage. The *Warren* was the other. She docked without fanfare or formalities at Pier 17, East River, at the foot of Pine Street one block north of Wall Street. The Muirs had arrived. What were their feelings?

If wharf life was hectic in Glasgow, it was frantic in New York. Passengers were simply disgorged at dockside. No paperwork, no passports, the Muirs just walked off the ship, collected their luggage, and left. Agents and hucksters of all types awaited them. It was a feeding frenzy for those who preyed on the bewildered 200,000 immigrants who arrived in the harbor that year. Daniel had much to do: keep the children safely in tow; make reliable arrangements for the luggage; and find accommodations while he booked the next leg of their journey. Could he sort the truth from all the fiction and find good value among all the cons?

Even newspapers had difficulty differentiating one from the other in article after article claiming to report the actual happenings in California from firsthand observation. Events there dominated the news in New York, just as they filled the Glaswegian papers. The center column article on the front page of the Wednesday *Tribune,* titled "A Letter from California" sent from "Sutters, Upper California, November 4, 1848," was typical. It began, "The following extract from a letter received yesterday by Arnold Buffum, 112 Broadway, from his son, Lieut. Edward Gould Buffum, now two years resident in California, though not of recent date, furnishes an additional confirmation of the reports heretofore received, of the richness of gold placers in California."

Booking information for passage to California dominated the ads for ships, trains, and canal boats. And advice columns and sales ads for supplies needed for those trips filled the merchandise section. Daniel, though, quickly booked passage on a Hudson River steamer to Albany, the first leg of their journey to their next destination, Buffalo. After a day or two in New York, the family continued its westward move.

Why Buffalo? Presumably Daniel chose it so he could stay briefly with William Gray, whom he likely knew from Dunbar. William organized the Dunbar group in which Daniel found his long-sought spiritual home—the Disciples of Christ—shortly before immigrating to America. His brother Philip led the Edinburgh chapter. Surely William would have the latest information on the sect's new colonies being established in the New World. He'd also be able to offer trustworthy advice for the travelers. Philip would soon follow his brother and other members of their Scottish flock, settling in 1850 on the south side of Fountain Lake, a mile from the Muirs' new Wisconsin farm.

The lush scenery along the Hudson River valley in early spring must have been spectacular and the trip far more relaxing and leisurely than the ocean voyage. This was the glorious landscape, at once rugged, romantic, and pastoral, captured in immensely popular paintings by Thomas Cole, Frederic Church, and other artists in the "Hudson River School." Many of their canvases depicted the settlement of the "wilderness" as an allegorical story in which pioneers brought the "light" of civilization and God's blessing to what they considered to be a dark, ominous wasteland, a paradise in the rough. Daniel intended to do much the same thing.

To get from Albany to Buffalo, Daniel probably planned to take an Erie Canal packet, as did many westward-moving settlers. But the canal didn't officially open that spring until the first of May, due to unusually late ice in the waterway. He still might have found passage on a packet that began service early, since the boats were all privately operated and not necessarily bound by the official opening date. However, I suspect the family simply took one of the faster and affordable trains that paralleled the canal, even though rail service in the region wouldn't be standardized and integrated until formation of the New York Central line in 1853. A canal boat usually made the 350-plus-mile trip in three or four days. By train, they could probably make it in a day. The several days saved might be significant for pioneers in a rush to get settled. What differences between the New World and Old would they have seen in people and places on that trip, in contrast to their train ride across Scotland just weeks earlier? Would they have detected differences in class consciousness or ethnic diversity? Would they have sensed a different spirit in the air, an energy and optimism free from the lingering constraints of feudalism? Would they have seen a new landscape recently reconfigured to accommodate "the plow and the cow," a place stripped of history, a land of dynamic change?

The Muirs apparently paused no longer in Buffalo than in New York: just a day or two; just long enough to learn from a local grain dealer that most of his wheat came from Wisconsin; just long enough to hear William Gray recommend Wisconsin; and just long enough to book passage there on a lake steamer filled with Yankees and Europeans heading west. Powerful forces drove Daniel westward, compelling him to continue until a new home was found. Few people like to be uprooted and unsettled, especially those seeking land. Daniel was landless and disconnected while in motion. The desperate hope of getting settled, wherever, with fields set before the spring planting season ended, must have carried him forward. Momentum and the flood of immigrants passing through those important gateways swept him along as well. Daniel was on a mission and much work still remained.

Milwaukee was the next milestone. Five days aboard the steamer from Buffalo left the Muirs again at wharfside with no contacts or set plans in a bustling but crude town whose explosive growth in the 1840s mirrored that of each region in the nation's interior when the wave of settlement reached it. In 1840 Milwaukee was a village of 1,720 people; a decade later it had grown over tenfold to more than 20,000 people. The territory, then state (1848), grew at the same phenomenal rate: from 11,000 when the territory was organized in 1836, to 31,000 in 1840, to 305,000 in 1850. Both the city and the state would more than double in size again in the next decade. Steam power made the newly opened region more accessible just as a surge of European immigrants reached eastern ports, their presence in the New World in part triggered by the effects of steam power on life in the Old. Wisconsin replaced Ohio as the preferred destination for pioneers seeking cheap, fertile land. Its availability brought them in droves to Milwaukee, as it did the Muirs, amid a speculative frenzy that defied description.

The amount of land changing hands in America staggered the mind, in many years exceeding the total land area of some European countries. In the boom years of 1835–37, for example, the government's General Land Office sold 38 million acres from the public domain, twice the land area of Scotland. Large-scale land speculators rather than pioneers bought much of the land initially, but it was usually soon resold to settlers. Millions more acres were bought from and sold by individuals. In the dozen or so years since Wisconsin's southern section was surveyed and officially opened for settlement, the General Land Office sold perhaps 5 million acres there. Millions more remained of the state's 36-million-acre total area, so Daniel still had much to choose from. And the seemingly limitless supply offset the seemingly limitless demand, holding the cost of raw land around the $1.25 per acre minimum sales price offered by the General Land Office.

Like St. Louis and St. Joseph, Milwaukee was a uniquely American type of city when the Muirs arrived—a pioneer boomtown never seen in the Old World. Land, opportunity, and optimism were its currencies. And like all boomtowns, its currencies would soon be spent and the wave of pioneers would move further west, leaving to the residents remaining behind the job of building a sustainable future for the city. At the moment, though, Milwaukee was one of America's important developmental doorways. It differed from Buffalo, although both were important lake ports and pioneer portals, in the same way that New York differed from Glasgow: Glasgow and Buffalo were starting points, places of departure, somehow a part of the familiar and a piece of the past. New York and Milwaukee were points of arrival, new and unfamiliar places focused on the future.

Once again Daniel moved on quickly. For thirty dollars he hired a farmer just in from Fort Winnebago with a load of wheat to haul the family seventy-five miles northwest to Kingston, a tiny hamlet ten miles east of Marquette County. This was the region recommended by William Gray. The nearby Fox River marked the northwestern edge of the land then open to settlement in this part of the new state. "Wilderness" lay beyond—land not yet surveyed and parceled, land not yet ready for conversion to property. In the patchwork of forest and new fields not far outside Milwaukee, the Muirs first found release from the most troubling constraints of their Dunbar world. Daniel found in the unspoiled Eden of vacant land a release from his religious and feudal bondage. John and David found in the frontier "wilderness" the freedom to explore their fantasies. And Sarah perhaps found a release from the Victorian culture that stifled her mother's life.

Their wagon was overloaded, piled high with far too much luggage brought from Dunbar, including old iron wedges, carpenter's tools, and the beam scales. To this haul, John recalled, his father added in Buffalo a big cast-iron stove, pots and pans, provisions enough for a long siege, and a scythe and cumbersome cradle for cutting wheat, as if basic necessities couldn't be bought in Wisconsin. The stout team of horses strained under the weight, their hooves sinking in the mud and ruts of "roads" barely cleared of stumps and fallen timber. The family probably walked alongside to lighten the load. The spring thaw and torrential rains must have transformed parts of their path through the prairies and oak openings into quagmires that caught each stride and caked the wagon wheels. The weeklong journey crossed some of the state's most fertile land, but they passed few farms along the way. The area was so recently opened that much vacant land remained and many settlers like the Muirs naively sought land northward with more immediate access to surface water and more timber, thinking the woodland indicated better soil. As John later recalled, all this prompted the poor farmer they hired to declare that "never, never again would he be tempted to try to haul such a cruel, heart-breaking, wagon-breaking, horse-killing load, no, not for a hundred dollars."

Daniel booked a room at the new Kingston Inn, which over-looked the Grand River and an adjacent sawmill, then sought advice on finding a parcel to buy. A local land agent referred him to a nearby bighearted Scottish farmer named Alexander "Sandy" Gray, who was well known for his knowledge of the section lines and soils, and his willingness to help both neighbors and new arrivals. The Grays (no relationship to William and Philip) had originally emigrated from Aberdeenshire to Glengarry, Ontario. Sandy, his brother George, and sister Elizabeth then made their way one by one to Marquette County in the 1840s, where their farms sat scattered within a mile of one another along the county-line road. Sandy prospered. He owned at least 360 acres, a team of oxen, and one of only two teams of horses in the area. His home farm was a "quarter section"—160 acres—of which half (a "half-quarter") sat along the road just inside

Marquette County; the other half-quarter sat across the road in Columbia County.

As soon as Daniel settled the children in at the inn, he got a horse and rode off to find his friendly countryman. In no time John and David were dashing about the village, weeks of pent-up energy and exuberance flooding forth. Daniel soon returned with Sandy, who was driving a big wagon drawn by white oxen, and the family was quickly off again, on its way to the home of Sandy and Jane Gray. That night the two men and the two boys slept in the haymow while the two women slept in the one tiny bedroom of the whitewashed farmhouse. The men left the next morning to look at land, the boys continued their wilderness frolic, and Jane began Sarah's introduction to pioneer farm life. Sandy and Daniel returned by nightfall having selected a property of two adjacent half-quarters six miles to the northwest, one abutting a spring-fed glacial lake several hundred yards from the Fox River. Oak and hickory woodlands, oak openings, prairie, and marshy bot-tomland covered the gently rolling property—a place sculpted during the same glacial period that shaped the Muirs' Scottish homeland.

Daniel, Sandy and his hired hand, and some neighbors began work on a temporary house there the next day. The crude one-story shanty with a single window was quickly assembled once the rough-hewn boards for the bur oak walls and the white oak roof and puncheon floor were readied. In late October, a fine two-and-a-half-story house of eight rooms and a wide front hall-way replaced the shanty. "A palace of a house," thought the car-penters who helped build it with white pine imported from the north. Yet like Daniel's ofttimes dour attitude toward life, the house was devoid of decoration. That, nature's garden outside would have to provide, aided by some lilacs planted by Sarah, with Daniel's help, near the door to welcome the remainder of the family several days later. The home sat slightly east of the shanty on a small knoll facing southwest into the setting sun, looking across an open meadow toward the shimmering lake that touched the property's southern part. Oak, hickory, and tamarack framed the gorgeous view. Since the lake was then unnamed, Daniel called it "Fountain Lake" for the springs that bubbled forth in the meadow below the brow on which they built the house. Neighbors would know the lake as "Muir Lake" until 1865, when James Whitehead bought the parcel that contained the meadow and lake frontage. He soon sold it to William and John Ennis, and the lake assumed their name—"Ennis Lake"—as it remains today. Of his arrival at his New World home John later wrote,

> This sudden plash into pure wildness—baptism in Nature's warm heart—how utterly happy it made us! Nature streaming into us, wooingly teaching her wonderful glowing lessons, so unlike the dismal grammar ashes and cinders so long thrashed into us. Here without knowing it we were still at school; every wild lesson a love lesson, not whipped but charmed into us.

That day in May, Daniel Muir bought two 80-acre parcels, each one-half mile long by one-quarter mile wide, oriented north to south. His mile-long-by-quarter-mile-wide swath of paradise cost him only $200. He bought the property from the Fox and Wisconsin River Improvement Company, the private enterprise struggling to complete the much anticipated canal that initially attracted him to the area. The proposed canal would follow the portage path used for centuries by Indians to carry their canoes about a mile from the Fox River to the Wisconsin River. When French explorers and traders—*voyageurs* and *coureurs de bois*—first entered the area in the 1630s, they established a trading post called Le Portage at the "carrying place." Louis Joliet and Father

Marquette portaged there on their famous descent of the Mississippi River in 1673. The English gained control of the trading
post in the mid-1700s, following their victory in the French and
Indian War, and replaced the cooperative trading practices with
the Indians with a more aggressive approach. By the War of
1812, they'd militarized the post to defend the region from the
Americans. U.S. victory brought John Jacob Astor's even more
aggressive American Fur Company to the territory, hell-bent on
competing with the British fur-trading colossus, the Hudson
Bay Company. Greater white settlement and resource exploita-
tion interests followed too. Indian uprisings and violent white
reprisals ensued, leading to construction of Fort Winnebago
nearby in the late 1820s, to secure white interests. It wasn't
needed for long. Those interests quickly overwhelmed Indian
resistance. By 1838 the United States evicted the native peoples
and cleared the territory for white occupancy. When the Muirs
arrived in 1849, the fort had been abandoned by the military and
Le Portage had been renamed Portage.

The government had granted the Fox and Wisconsin River
Improvement Company large tracts of land to sell, with the revenues to be used to finance the construction of the canal. This
was a common way of funding the development of needed public
infrastructure like roads, railroads, and canals. It was also a way
for political and business insiders and speculators to get rich.
Despite the abuses, the process was successful as often as not,
though for the Fox–Wisconsin Canal it was a debacle.

The next May (1850), Daniel doubled the size of the farm
when he added an additional 160 acres—the northwest quarter
of Section 13, Township 14 North, Range 9 East—bought
directly from the state of Wisconsin, again for $1.25 per acre.
The new acquisition abutted the eastern side of the farm's upper
half, forming a flag-shaped property with the bulk on better-
drained prairie land northeast of the lake and meadows.

How quickly it was all done: the land found and purchased, a house built, work under way to clear fields and plant crops, and a new life begun. The merchant and his family from a thousand-year-old fishing and farming village made the leap forward in time and space from the Old World to the New. Marquette County in total had only half the inhabitants of Dunbar, and the Fountain Lake Farm had no white neighbors and no "roads" within miles. A few Ho-Chunk Indians, the area's native inhabitants, still frequented the place, although the Ho-Chunk people had been evicted when whites "organized" the territory, transforming it from "wilderness" into property. Shortly after his arrival at his new home, John found a small mound overlooking the lake at the south end of the farm. On its edge was a row of grass-thatched Indian graves. Other graves were soon found on lower ground. "We ploughed them down," he later remembered regretfully, "turning the old bones they covered into corn and wheat." While many immigrants reveled in the rich landscape legacies of their homeland, they set about destroying or ignoring the rich landscape legacy of their new home. The New World was about the future, not the past. Perhaps it remains so today.

The New World

Oh, that glorious Wisconsin wilderness! Everything
new and pure in the very prime of the spring when
Nature's pulses were beating highest and mysteriously
keeping time with our own! Young hearts, young
leaves, flowers, animals, the winds and the streams and
the sparkling lake, all widely, gladly rejoicing together!

JOHN MUIR, *The Story of My Boyhood and Youth*

[9]

Fountain Lake glistens in the late afternoon sun, as if freshly
scrubbed for my first visit. A line of thunderstorms just moved
through the area. The sky remains a mess of massive clouds with
scattered breaks of brilliant blue and bright sunshine. Tomorrow
promises to be glorious as the storm front moves further off and
a Canadian high settles in for a few days, although at the moment the threat of a shower lingers. Such storms were new to the
Muirs. "So unlike any seen in Scotland," John wrote. "Gazing
awe-stricken," he continued, "we watched the upbuilding of the
sublime cloud-mountains—glowing, sun-beaten pearl and ala-
baster cumuli, glorious in beauty and majesty and looking so
firm and lasting that birds, we thought, might build their nests
amid their downy bosses."

The black-browed storm-clouds marching in awful grandeur
across the landscape, trailing broad gray sheets of hail and rain
like vast cataracts, and ever and anon flashing down vivid

zigzag lightning followed by terrible crashing thunder . . . for oftentimes the whole sky blazed. After sultry storm days, many of the nights were darkened by smooth black apparently structureless cloud-mantles which at short intervals were illumined with startling suddenness to a fiery glow by quick, quivering lightning-flashes, revealing the landscape in almost noonday brightness, to be instantly quenched in solid blackness.

Despite the recent rain, the land looks little affected. The water lies unnoticed in the fens, sedge meadows, and wet prairies around the thirty-acre lake. The sandy soils of the surrounding oak openings and old fields have soaked up the rest like a sponge. I park by the small boat ramp on the west lip of the dogleg-shaped lake and walk out on the little wooden pier to look eastward across the narrow neck toward the meadow and the small rise above on which the Muirs lived 150 years ago. They're hidden, though, by the curvature of the lake and by the passage of time.

Fountain Lake Farm fascinated John: the lake rimmed with white water lilies, the flowery glacial meadow from which flowed twenty or thirty springs that fed it, and the surrounding "low finely-modeled hills dotted with oak and hickory, and meadows full of grasses and sedges and many beautiful orchids and ferns," as he recalled. It teemed with life, sound, and song, day and night, color and fragrance, all changing with the seasons.

His beloved birds filled the sky—jays, thrushes, orioles, scarlet tanagers, redwing blackbirds, bluebirds, robins, song sparrows, kingbirds, hen hawks, nighthawks, nuthatches, meadowlarks, bobolinks, bobwhites, whippoorwills, warblers, woodpeckers, jack snipes, swans, geese, pigeons, partridges, prairie chickens, chickadees, owls, and glorious sandhill cranes.

The fields and forests were filled with mice, chipmunks,

squirrels, gophers, foxes, rabbits, raccoons, badgers, woodchucks, muskrats, and black bears. Swarms of insects in the meadows bedazzled (and at times bedeviled) him, too: black water bugs and skaters, dragonflies, wasps, and wild bees, butterflies, beetles, moths, and mosquitoes. He remembered that "when we first saw Fountain Lake Meadow, on a sultry evening, sprinkled with millions of lightning-bugs throbbing with light, the effect was so strange and beautiful that it seemed far too marvelous to be real." The lake harbored pickerel, sunfish, black bass, perch, shiners, pumpkinseeds, ducks, loons, bullfrogs, snapping turtles, and snakes.

The land bloomed with lilies, orchids, pasqueflowers, lady's slippers, calopogon, pogonia, spiranthes, Turk's-turbin, butterfly weed, asters, goldenrods, sunflowers, daisies, liatris, meadow ferns like osmundas and ostrich fern, strawberries, dewberries, cranberries, huckleberries, wild apples, hazelnuts, and hickory nuts. The plentitude of life astounded him. Fountain Lake Farm was truly an unspoiled garden. "First," he said, around the lake "there is a zone of green, shining rushes, and just beyond the rushes a zone of white and orange water-lilies fifty or sixty feet wide forming a magnificent border. On bright days, when the lake was rippled by a breeze, the lilies and sun-spangles danced together in radiant beauty, and it became difficult to discriminate between them." The collar of green rushes and glorious white water lilies is gone now, as are some of the plant and animal species he found, but the basic landscape fabric of Fountain Lake remains, a microcosm of the general area.

It's a more complicated physical fabric than that around Dunbar. Although both originated from fire and ice, the results differ dramatically. Volcanic fire from several hundred million years ago shaped the geomorphology of East Lothian, leaving many of the imposing surface features that still dominate the landscape, though the direct effects of the volcanic past on the plants, animals, and people of John Muir's day were diminished by the passage of time and other physical forces. Wildfire dominated the Marquette County landscape as recently as the arrival of whites. The frequent fires, often ignited by lightning strikes, dictated the distribution of plant communities and the dependent wildlife that John so admired. Its effects were immediate and tangible to him. So were the glacial effects.

About twenty thousand years ago, a massive ice sheet hundreds of feet thick scoured both his boyhood homes. In East Lothian it left the crag and tail form of Traprain Law and smoothed many surface features, while its meltwater ripped some of the sharp cuts in the coastal plain through which ran rivers and burns. And atop the sandstone bedrock it left a layer of unconsolidated rock fragments called glacial till or drift, the parent material from which the fertile soils formed. I suspect those effects also seemed distant to the people of John's day, overlooked because of their subtlety and hidden by centuries of settlement. In contrast, glaciation formed a more complicated landscape in Marquette County as the ice sheet advanced and retreated across the area, its terminus just miles away. The landscape it left at the margin was a diverse mosaic of small rounded knobs and knolls interspersed among sinuous riparian corridors, broad wetlands, lakes, and small "kettle" holes. This complexity affected the distribution of soil types, plants, animals, and people. To John, the glacier must have seemed recent and its effects immediate, little ameliorated by the passage of time or the presence of people.

The highest hill near Muir's New World home was Observatory Hill, the "great cloud-capped mountain of our child's imagination," John called it, about two miles from the farm. A dense cedar forest grew atop the 300-foot-high rhyolite knoll. The southeastern lip was a bare outcrop of the rounded pinkish rock, polished smooth and etched with striations by the glacier. It's a pleasant place to sit, providing the area's best panoramic view.

John liked to come here on the few days a year he could escape the farm. He must have marveled at the differences between the landscape he saw that first spring and that seen from Doon Hill. Here he looked across a savanna-like expanse of rolling hills and prairies covered with widely scattered trees. Here he saw broad, open marshes and lowlands stretching for miles to the east and south. To the west and north he saw more hills and prairies than in the other directions, with marshes and lowlands and a few forested spots interspersed. Above all, he saw little sign of human disturbance in any direction.

Oak openings covered most upland. James Fenimore Cooper once described them as scattered growths of oak, in particular bur oak, standing in a parklike "air of negligence that one is apt to see in grounds where art is made to assume the character of nature . . . and the spaces between [the trees], always of singular beauty, have obtained the name 'openings.' " Fires every few years, caused by the lightning strikes that Muir marveled at, maintained the openings by killing off other fire-sensitive species. On moister north-facing slopes where the effects of periodic fires were dampened, a closed canopy wood of oak and hickory developed. The wet lowland landscape was typically open, too, shaded by occasional stands of tamarack. The wetlands disrupted the frequent fires, not allowing them to burn the land as completely as occurred just fifty miles south where the absence of wetlands allowed fires to sweep across vast areas, giving rise in combination with other physical differences to more prairies.

Unlike Observatory Hill, most hills in Marquette County were small and low, some forming linear ridges running east–west aligned by glacial forces. This was a scrabbled, hummocky landscape of great variation. In contrast, the East Lothian landscape was one of grand panoramas of sensuously rolling fields when seen from features like Doon Hill or Traprain Law. From the surface, it was a simple landscape of subtle differences dominated by the pinnacles standing in isolation above the coastal plain, a middle landscape between the sea and the Lammermuir Hills. It was a land on which layer upon layer of cultural history was visible in John's day—a settled land for thousands of years. Not so in the New World. Pioneers ignored the existing cultural layer of the Indians, in effect regarding the land as a blank slate devoid of human imprint.

White settlement suddenly changed that slate. In just several seasons, the army of settlers remade the place as they waged war against the land in a quest to reconfigure it to their liking. Right before John's eyes, the Wisconsin "wilderness" was transformed seemingly overnight into cultivated property. The human industry that that required defies description. Such swift and profound change had never occurred in the landscape visible from Doon Hill.

Within five years of the Muirs' arrival, virtually all the sections in the county were purchased and much of the land was cleared and cropped. Scots abounded around Fountain Lake and were joined "only here and there [by] Yankee families from adjacent states," John said. The pioneers came "drifting indefinitely westward in covered wagons, seeking their fortunes like winged seeds; all alike striking root and gripping the glacial drift soil as naturally as oak and hickory trees. . . . Few of [the Scots] had owned land in the old country," John recalled. "Here their craving land-hunger was satisfied." The pioneers were happy and hopeful, he continued, "establishing homes and making wider and wider fields in the hospitable wilderness."

The axe and plough were kept very busy; cattle, horses, sheep, and pigs multiplied; barns and corn-cribs were filled up, and man and beast were well fed; a schoolhouse was built, which was used also for a church; and in a very short time the new country began to look like an old one. . . . No other wild country I have ever known extended a kinder welcome to poor immigrants. On the arrival in the spring, a log house could be built, a few acres ploughed, the virgin sod planted with corn, potatoes, etc., and enough raised to keep a family comfortably the very first year; and wild hay for cows and oxen grew in abundance on the numerous meadows.

A new cultural layer was imposed on the landscape, one that altered the existing condition far more than had the Indian layer it obscured. The forest cover was cleared and an orderly pattern of fields and pastures appeared in a few years, aligned according to the distinct geometry of the national land survey system established by the Land Ordinance of 1785. No single policy or program has more influenced the Marquette County landscape, or that of America. The Land Ordinance both reflected and defined the most fundamental differences between the Old World and New.

The need for a uniform system to survey, parcel, and disperse a vast land area was one of the paramount issues that confronted the Continental Congress as it struggled to create a new nation in the aftermath of victory over the British in the Revolutionary War. With the stroke of a pen at the signing of the Treaty of Paris in 1783, America more than doubled in size as it received claim to over 400,000 square miles of land outside the original colonies: land largely unoccupied by Euro-Americans; land zealously coveted by many in the new nation and many abroad. America was now nearly 900,000 square miles, one of the world's largest nations. But it was a nation divided physically and psychologically into two halves by the Appalachian Mountains—old and new, east and west, coastal and interior.

Acquisition of the new land created extraordinary opportunities and posed extraordinary problems. While the treaty transferred claim, it left unanswered how the land was to be stitched into the national fabric along the Atlantic coast. Practical questions included: Who would hold initial claim to the land, the states or the federal government? For what purpose would the land be used? Would it be sold, given away, or leased to individuals or companies, or would it be held in common? How would this massive undertaking be accomplished? And what would be the predominant form of settlement and development? Politically, how would the new land be governed and what would be its relationship to the original states? How was the lengthy and remote border to be secured from foreign encroachment? And how were the existing inhabitants to be treated, especially the Indians? The answers to those momentous questions laid the foundation of our national landscape. The organization of the Northwest Territory (1787) answered many of the political questions. The Land Ordinance answered most of the practical ones. The ordinance stamped the American landscape west of the Appalachian Mountains with its most distinctive characteristic—the national grid. Ultimately the grid covered 69 percent of continental America (excluding Alaska), the most extensive area in the world surveyed with a uniform system.

Officially titled "An Ordinance for Ascertaining the Mode of Disposing of Lands in the Western Territory," the Land Ordinance derived from a report drafted a year earlier by Thomas Jefferson as the chairperson of a committee composed of two representatives from the New England states and two from the southern states. The bill that emerged was a political compromise of northern and southern settlement conventions and customs, as well as a compromise between traditional survey practices and those of the Enlightenment. It seemed to establish a practical land survey and distribution system with straightforward rules and procedures. It began the systematic division of the landscape into the checkerboard of one-square-mile parcels that today blankets the country. Each square-mile section contained

640 acres, a size that was later found could be conveniently
subdivided into smaller parcels of 320 acres (a half section), 160
acres (a quarter section), or 80 acres (a half-quarter section). A
township, as traditionally sized in New England, was an aggre-
gate of thirty-six sections, amounting to six miles square. All
section and township boundaries were oriented north–south/
east–west along lines of longitude and latitude. Prior to the
opening of an area, base survey lines would be set and the region
surveyed into townships and sections. Half of the townships then
would be sold to large land companies and speculators, the other
half sold by sections to individual white males over twenty-one
years of age. One section in each township would be set aside to
support public education and four others for the exchange of land
warrants given in payment for military service during the Revolution. Sale would be by auction at a minimum price of $1.00
per acre plus survey costs of $1.00 per section.

However, the ordinance didn't resolve all the land distribution
issues that confronted and confounded the young nation. Land
distribution remained complicated by technical snags for decades.
Preemption, special exemptions, and preferential treatment tangled the process. Trial and error in its implementation gradually
refined its operation. Over the next century, Congress revised the
grid again and again in reaction to procedural problems, politics,
and economics. The minimum parcel size, sale price, terms of
payment, and response to preemption were repeatedly adjusted.
But the basic approach remained steadfast across the continent
and across time.

Despite its many faults, a number of landmark precedents
underpinned that approach. The Land Ordinance established
that the new western lands—the public domain—belonged to
the American people, not to the states, after the claims of the
native peoples had been obtained. It established that the public
domain was not a permanent or an irrevocable possession of the

federal government. Instead prompt dispersal of land into private ownership would be the national policy and priority. Dispersal meant fee simple sale, not the long-term lease or the holding of land in a national commons. The ordinance affirmed and reinforced the national preference for autonomous private property rights and universal ownership. It rejected alternative landownership patterns based on tradition and geography and broke any ties to the nation's European feudal roots. Land would be bought and sold. Ownership would be decentralized and dispersed to the common citizen under government rather than private control, although historically the ordinance resulted in the initial acquisition of land as much by wealthy speculators and big business as by the yeoman. From the beginning, this dispersal tolerated widespread abuse of policies and procedures and granted endless exemptions, preferential priorities, and special privileges.

At its core, the Land Ordinance reflected traditional Euro-American, Judeo-Christian landscape values: values that regarded land as an abstract commodity, as property; values that regarded people as separate from and superior to the land they sought to reshape into an earthly paradise; values that considered the land from rational, utilitarian perspectives, absent any historical or folklore contexts; and values that portrayed the "wilderness" as a moral wasteland and physical threat, making its "conquest" and the imposition of "civilization" an imperative. America was limitless, endlessly abundant, fertile, and resilient, they thought. To Old World pioneers like Daniel Muir and the westward-moving Yankees he joined, it certainly seemed that way in the mid-1800s. To many Americans today, it might still seem that way as we struggle to cast aside these deep-rooted values and adopt new ones that better reflect the limits of our modern world.

Like Jefferson's ideals, the national grid was rational, efficient, and systematic, a reflection of the Enlightenment that glorified democracy, capitalism, classicism, Protestantism, and science.

Each section of land was treated the same as the next, and each citizen (as then defined) had the opportunity to acquire one in theory, if not practice. Egalitarian. Orderly. Pragmatic. The grid dispersed people across the landscape to promote Jefferson's cherished rural society. It made a national landscape as it obfuscated local and regional differences. As J. B. Jackson, a pioneering commentator on the American landscape, observed, adoption of the grid marked a profound shift in social philosophy: its free-title landownership promoted a sense of individualism and isolation, and as the land was reordered to fit its abstract geometry, it deprived people of community support, sacred spaces, and custom. People believed in the grid. They identified with it. The grid indelibly etched the land and the American psyche as it governed the dispersal of 1.3 billion acres of the public domain. "Squareness" was good. A "square deal" was a good deal; to be a "four-square man" was to be solid, honest, and hardworking. The grid defined America physically and psychologically.

The nomenclature of land had changed, as Daniel learned when he purchased his properties. The new shorthand of exchange first redefined the environment as "wilderness," then transformed it into "land" and "property" when it was surveyed and parceled to make it a commodity for human purposes. The endless wonder of nature was abstracted into two-dimensional maps and partitioned with imaginary lines in an effort to bound it, though I suspect the lines bound the people, not the land. Daniel and most pioneers fell prey to this process. John didn't.

Standing on the promontory of Observatory Hill, I see a landscape that differs both from the one John first beheld and from that formed by the extraordinary change he witnessed in the subsequent few years. More forest cover exists now than when he gazed across the rolling hills and broad lowlands, obscuring the initial patterns created by the grid. Many fields once cropped or pastured on marginal-quality soils have been abandoned for economic reasons, permitting succession to revert the cleared land to thick stands of trees and understory vegetation. This reforestation has yielded a new landscape aesthetic—more closed and more "wild" in appearance—aided by the suppression of wildfires that had before maintained the oak openings and meadows. A new mix of plant species, some native, many exotics, has supplanted what existed before settlement. Large pine plantations planted in the 1900s for conservation purposes are common. Were John standing with me today, he'd recognize less in the landscape we see here than in the landscape we'd see were we standing on Doon Hill looking across East Lothian. The Old World around Dunbar certainly has changed since John left, but not sufficiently to obscure the old layers. In contrast, white settlement has added two new cultural layers to his New World home from the time he first stood atop the hill, layers that nearly erased the prior conditions: the first as pioneers initially cut farms into the indigenous landscape, and the second when those farms assumed a revised form this century.

That second layer is the one I now see from Observatory Hill and as I drive the chip-sealed and paved roads around what was Fountain Lake Farm. Dairy farms dominate. Black-and-white-mottled cows graze the pastures on the drained bottomlands and the rolling hills. I also see black beef cattle, sheep, and swine. Red-painted wooden barns with crisp white trim stand surrounded by fields of wheat, corn, oats, and alfalfa. Some farms resemble a Norman Rockwell painting, others don't. Some are still small-scale family operations, others larger and more corporate-looking, often with extensive center pivot spray irrigation. Some scenery is charming and pastoral, neat and tidy. Other places like wetlands and marshes look disheveled with the scruffy appearance of abandonment and succession. Vacation homes surround the many lakes. Mobile homes and houses set on large lots line many back roads.

The area remains rural, though not for much longer. It sits about ten miles from Montello to the northeast, the county seat and largest city, with a population of 1,500 residents. Portage is larger—more the size of Dunbar—and lies about fifteen miles to the southwest, just over the county line in Columbia County. More importantly, major cities like Madison, Milwaukee, and Chicago are now within commuting distance, made possible by interstate highways.

As a result, an invasion of commuter homes, retirement homes, "hobby" farms, and vacation cottages threatens this "traditional" landscape. Current land cover shows little hint of the confrontation. The one-third of the land that's arable remains farm fields and pasture. Forest, mostly second-growth pine plantations on the knobs and knolls, and open wetlands (called waste land locally), each constitute a bit less. Scattered large-lot housing forms the remainder, with just a fraction of strip commercial development. Fewer than 1,000 people live in the vicinity. Neighbors remain shouting distance away, as they were in John Muir's day.

Yet change is there. The signs are all around. Building placards announcing the latest subdivision of five-acre lots sprout among the fields along country lanes, especially those near major highways. Interchanges have sales lots for premanufactured homes— mobile homes—catering to the changing residential mix. And new log homes set well back from the road appear, often surrounded by a cornfield, where before only the crop was grown. It's a well-known story told of many rural regions. The economics of farming here have changed in the past fifty years, resulting in a loss of competitiveness with other regions due to high input costs needed to match yields on better-suited soils. Farming has changed too: less labor-intensive, more mechanized, specialized, and corporate. More environmental regulations and governmental programs complicate the operation. With poor profitability, fewer children wish to inherit the burden. Combine this with social changes in nearby urban centers and good highway access and the result is a growing number of city dwellers seeking acreage in the country, bidding up property values, creating an attractive alternative for retiring farmers or those simply selling off lots along their road frontage. The lakes have been ringed with seasonal cottages for years, and the many water bodies and wetlands have long been popular with boating, fishing, and hunting enthusiasts. But more and more they come now—commuters, retirees, recreational visitors—and more and more they buy property.

What don't I see? I see no hierarchy of property ownership in the landscape as I did in East Lothian. Some homes are grander than others, but the difference isn't a function of longtime land-ownership patterns. I see few clusters of homes. Most homes sit widely spaced on large individual properties. I see few brick or stone structures. Most buildings are wood, constructed using the balloon-framing technique pioneered in the Chicago area in the 1830s to enable strong, flexible, and efficient construction of structures on the plains and prairies that utilized a minimum of the scarce material. Despite this consistency of form, I see little architectural harmony among buildings. And I see little sign of land-use regulation. Mobile homes and other building types appear mixed without rhyme or reason, and people appear free to develop their property as they see fit. I see few buildings or man-made artifacts older than 100 years, none more than 170 years old. I see no dykes or hedgerows lining fields and roadways. Fences are wire, not stone, lending the land parceling a more temporary, less permanent feel than that in East Lothian. What do I see: "No Trespassing—No Hunting" signs, a more dense network of high-speed roads (although no local passenger rail service), and much more public land, most held in nature preserves and wildlife areas.

[1 0]

Grandfather Gilrye was right. The laddies found plenty of hard, hard work. With no school, little social contact, and little leisure,

everyone in the family set about the herculean effort of crafting
a European-style farm of row crops and livestock where none
existed before. Each person had duties; some were shared. Although Daniel would hire farmhands to help, he relied most heavily on the older children—John, Sarah, Maggie, and David—to
do the work. John wrote, "We were called in the morning at four
o'clock and seldom got to bed before nine, making a broiling,
seething day seventeen hours long loaded with heavy work. . . ."
Farming here meant first clearing the land of timber and scrub
and chopping out stumps, then turning the soil, removing rocks,
and draining the new fields. It meant building a barn and a
corncrib. It meant fencing fields and pastures. It meant displacing any plants, animals, and humans seen as competitors for the
land and its resources. It meant transforming the environment to
meet their wants and wishes, rather than reforming those wants
and wishes to match the existing conditions. The pioneers came
with a vision but not with insight and sensitivity, notes Wes
Jackson, a leading agricultural and environmental expert.

They knew the dilemma. John overheard his father discussing
it with George Mair, a Scottish neighbor. "Mr. Mair remarked one
day that it was pitiful to see how the unfortunate Indians, children of Nature, living on the natural products of the soil, hunting, fishing, and even cultivating small corn-fields on the most
fertile spots, were now being robbed of their lands and pushed
ruthlessly back into narrower and narrower limits by alien races
who were cutting off their means of livelihood." Daniel replied
that "surely it could never have been the intention of God to allow
Indians to rove and hunt over so fertile a country and hold it
forever in unproductive wildness, while Scotch and Irish and
English farmers could put it to so much better use. Where an
Indian required thousands of acres for his family, these acres in the
hands of industrious, God-fearing farmers would support ten or a
hundred times more people in a far worthier manner. . . ."

Mr. Mair responded that "such farming as our first immigrants were practising was in many ways rude and full of the mistakes of ignorance, yet, rude as it was, and ill-tilled as were most of our Wisconsin farms by unskilled, inexperienced settlers who had been merchants and mechanics and servants in the old countries, how should we like to have specially trained and educated farmers drive us out of our homes and farms, such as they were, making use of the same argument, that God could never have intended such ignorant, unprofitable, devastating farmers as we were to occupy land upon which scientific farmers could raise five or ten times as much on each acre as we did?"

John sympathized with Mr. Mair's position, although at the time unable to affect the situation. What could he or anyone do? It was too late and the differences too deep to mediate. He felt that at this stage of the struggle between the white pioneer and the Indian for the rightful possession of the land, it had become "only an example of the rule of might with but little or no thought for the right or welfare of the other fellow if he were the weaker; that 'they should take who had the power, and they should keep who can,' " as Wordsworth once described the thinking of maundering Highlanders.

In the Old World, farming also meant hard work, but for as long as anyone could remember, it continued to farm land that had been farmed before. There it meant mostly maintaining the farm, its seasonal rhythms and traditions. Here it meant "breaking" new land, imposing new patterns, discovering new rhythms.

In the spring they began plowing as soon as the ground was frost-free. They planted corn and potatoes and sowed spring wheat while the nesting birds sang and a profusion of fragrant flowers covered the marshes and meadows and unfelled forests. Lambing and calving joined the rebirth. New growth on the remaining oaks formed a beautiful purple mass as if every young leaf was a petal. Wondrous, seemingly endless flights of passenger pigeons filled the skies, streaming up from the south. Flocks of geese and cranes soared elegantly overhead on whistling wings, their guttural calls carried onward by gentle winds.

Summer work was heavier, especially corn hoeing and harvesting the first few years, until cultivators and special plows were acquired. Chores began before breakfast and continued around meal breaks all day: feeding the animals, sharpening scythes, chopping wood, and carrying water up the hill to the house from the springs in the meadow below. Then it was off to the harvest or hayfields for mowing or cradling, the most exhausting of all the farmwork. "In the harvest dog-days and dog-nights and dog-mornings," John wrote, "when we arose from our clammy beds, our cotton shirts clung to our backs as wet with sweat as the bathing-suits of swimmers, and remained so all the long, sweltering days." The noon dinner and household chores lasted an hour, before they returned to the fields until dark; then supper, more chores, family worship, and bed.

Most of the hardest farmwork fell to John, as the eldest boy, especially since his father's interest in the farm quickly waned and his interest in preaching rose. Daniel left it to John to split rails of the knotty oak timber with ax and mallet for long lines of zigzag fences. And he was put to the plow the second spring even though his head barely cleared the handles. He did most of the plowing from then on, quickly becoming a good ploughman. No man could draw a straighter furrow, he boasted. Rocks, roots, and tree stumps made the backbreaking work torturous for the first few years as the fields were gradually set. Stumps eventually had to be removed rather than avoided, to make way for the McCormick reaper. "Because I proved to be the best chopper and stump-digger I had nearly all of it to myself," John claimed. "It was dull, hard work leaning over on my knees all day, chopping out those tough oak and hickory stumps, deep down below the crowns of the big roots."

Autumn plowing for winter wheat was easier. He would walk barefoot in the furrows, enjoying the musky smells of turned earth and desiccation, his eyes dazzled by the colorful sight of the golden foliage and harvest, and his feet reveling in the feel of the fertile soil. Pumpkins, watermelons, and muskmelons, rich and sweet, crisp and sumptuous, were nature's most generous gifts, thought the boys.

The harsh winters of biting cold and mealy, frosty snow offered no respite from the work. They still had to feed the horses and cattle, sharpen axes, chop wood, carry water, and repair fences. During heavy rains or snows, John recalled, they "worked in the barn, shelling corn, fanning wheat, thrashing with the flail, making ax-handles or ox-yokes, mending things, or sprouting and sorting potatoes in the cellar." But the frozen Wisconsin winter also offered rich rewards. Fountain Lake sang a loud chorus of roars and rumbles as its ice cracked, shrank, and expanded. Ice storms periodically encased every branch, twig, and trunk in a glistening crystalline cocoon. At night the spectacular starry heavens dazzled most wondrously in the clear, cold air, made even more glorious by the occasional aurora borealis. The milky, flowing eddies of long white or pale yellow currents, called "Merry Dancers" in Scotland, streamed with "startling tremulous motion to the zenith," John said. During their third or fourth winter, the aurora was an extraordinary color. "The whole sky was draped in graceful purple and crimson folds glorious beyond description," John remembered. "Father called us out into the yard in front of the house where we had a wide view, crying, 'Come! Come, mother! Come bairns! and see the glory of God.' "

At first they grew wheat, corn, and potatoes, especially wheat. Like many immigrants, they learned on the job. Wheat yields dropped from twenty-some bushels per acre on the better fields to just five or six bushels per acre in several years as the soils were quickly exhausted. So they switched to corn, only to find the same results, until they discovered the use of English clover. The enriching clover could be grown on even the most exhausted fields, plowed under, and corn or wheat replanted to yield good harvests again. Farming practices gradually changed. More corn and clover were planted with the crop fed to cattle and hogs. The corn was at first cut, shocked, and husked in the autumn, at times enjoyably amid the balmy warmth of "Indian summer" days. This brief pleasure was lost, though, when an overnight guest convinced Daniel that it was better to let the corn stand and husk it when time permitted over the winter. The cows could then be turned out into the fields to eat the residual leaves and trample the remaining stalks into the ground so they could be plowed under in the spring. Each family member took two rows at a time and husked them into a basket. They poured the corn onto the frozen ground in piles of fifteen to twenty basketfuls to be later loaded in a wagon and hauled to the crib. "This was cold, painful work," John recalled, "the temperature being oftentimes far below zero and the ground covered with dry, frosty snow, giving rise to miserable crops of chilblains and frosted fingers—a sad change from the merry Indian-summer husking, when the big yellow pumpkins covered the cleared fields: golden corn, golden pumpkins, gathered in the hazy golden weather."

It wasn't enough for Daniel Muir. Never content, always searching, like so many pioneers, he bought more property several miles to the southeast, adjacent to Sandy Gray's. In January 1855, Daniel bought 320 acres for $1,600: the east half of the northeast quarter and the east half of the southeast quarter of Section 29, Township 14 North, Range 10 East; and the west half of the southwest quarter and the west half of the northwest quarter of Section 28, Township 14 North, Range 10 East. The prior owners had apparently acquired the property in 1848, perhaps in speculation, and never developed it. As the state was settled over the ensuing seven years, the value of their land escalated fourfold from the $1.25 per acre government base price.

John was furious, thinking it too much, like gluttony. Better, he thought, for people to live on and work smaller parcels with greater care. Better for people to enjoy life rather than be a slave to overindustry. He'd also be responsible for most of the back-breaking and often hazardous work. "After eight years of this dreary work of clearing the Fountain Lake farm," he wrote, "fencing it and getting it in perfect order, building a frame house and the necessary out-buildings for the cattle and horses—after all this had been victoriously accomplished, and we had made out to escape with life—father bought a half-section of wild land about four or five miles to the eastward and began all over again to clear and fence and break up other fields for a new farm, doubling all the stunting, heartbreaking chopping, grubbing, stump-digging, rail-splitting, fence-building, barn-building, house-building, and so forth." The new farm was named Hickory Hill for the many fine hickory trees on the property and its long gentle slope ascending from Grouse Road that now runs along its southern edge.

John walked back and forth between Fountain Lake and Hickory Hill, like a daily commuter, to prepare the new property. The family made the move after two growing seasons, when the fields were initially set and the needed temporary buildings built. A two-story frame house and a full-size barn were added in 1857 on a small knoll in the middle of the property. The house faced south with a grand view across the valley. The new farm had better soil, virtually all of which was arable, but it lacked ready access to surface water. That meant a well had to be dug. Of course, the task fell to John. Day after day for months, Daniel lowered his son in a bucket to the bottom of the hole three feet in diameter to chip the ninety-foot-deep well out of the sandstone bedrock with hammer and chisel. The effort nearly killed him once and affected his health the remainder of his life.

What to do with the beloved Fountain Lake Farm? Daniel could keep it and try to farm it with hired hands; or perhaps like a laird he could lease it to a tenant, as was common in the Old World; or he could sell it. He decided to sell. The farm was gradually split up and cast away as the Muirs cut their roots there and reset them at Hickory Hill. The initial sales kept the land in the family. In October 1856, Daniel sold David Galloway, his daughter Sarah's fiancé, 120 acres of the original Fountain Lake property for $2,000. The two also made an arrangement for David to work Daniel's remaining 200 acres. David was a Scot from Fifeshire, which sat opposite East Lothian across the Firth. He was also a Disciple of Christ. His father was a tenant farmer who decided to make the leap from the Old World to the New when his farm lease was about to expire. David's parents and his seven sisters, some with their families, made the crossing in 1855.

In return for selling his son-in-law-to-be the heart of Fountain Lake Farm, Daniel paid David $1,200 for the 80-acre parcel abutting Hickory Hill that David had acquired just months before. Hickory Hill Farm was now 400 acres for John and his siblings and the hired hands to work. Sarah and David were married in December and set up residence in the former Fountain Lake Muir house.

Yet the new Hickory Hill roots were soon cut as the other children came of age and moved away. John left next, at first temporarily in 1860, though never to return as more than a guest. Maggie married a nearby farmer named John Reid and moved off that year as well; the wedding was held in the Hickory Hill house. The next year, David joined John, who lived in Madison while studying at the University of Wisconsin. Dan soon announced that he too preferred to go to college, rather than farm. So, the remaining family—Daniel, Anne, Dan, and his three sisters (the twins and Joanna, who was born at Fountain Lake in 1850)—moved to Portage to enable the children to attend school. This allowed Maggie and her husband to move into Hickory Hill, having lost their farm due to financial difficulties.

In late summer 1862, Daniel gave away three parcels as he continued to transfer ownership of his property to his children. Son David got the northern half and daughter Maggie the southern half of the quarter section at Fountain Lake bought in 1850. Son John got 80 acres of Hickory Hill. Despite some internal shuffling of titles, these lands didn't stay in the family for long. Nor did Daniel's children stay in place. David promptly sold his 80 acres days later for $400 and soon started a thirty-year career as a haberdasher in Portage. The Reids sold Maggie's half-quarter for $360 the next year to the Galloways, who sold it months later to buyers outside the family. John quickly sold his half-quarter to his brother-in-law John Reid for $620, who sold it for $1,000 to a person outside the family three years later. In the spring of 1863, Dan fled to Canada to avoid the draft, never to live again in Marquette County. He eventually became a successful medical doctor in Racine, Wisconsin. John followed him to the wilds of Canada the next year, like other young men a century later fleeing on moral principle a war they couldn't support.

With the Portage home rapidly emptying, the remaining five Muirs moved back to Hickory Hill Farm in late 1864. Daniel sold the last 40 acres of the first Fountain Lake purchase to Sarah and David Galloway for $100 in autumn 1865. Daniel was now free and clear of Fountain Lake, his original piece of paradise. Sarah and David subsequently sold the "home eighty" of Fountain Lake to James Whitehead in October for $825 and moved to Portage to escape the endless, debilitating farm work, although they still owned the northern 80 acres. A year later they sold that parcel too, to John Ennis for $500. The southern parcel promptly changed hands again and the lake was renamed Ennis Lake after the property's new owners. With this transaction the former Muir Fountain Lake Farm was no more—all the property had passed to people outside the family and the lake had lost the name given it by the Muirs.

The 320 acres of Hickory Hill was all that remained for the five Muirs living there. By the end of the decade the household dwindled further as the three youngest daughters left the nest to teach school in the area. Hickory Hill was quiet, too quiet for Daniel. His family workforce had left and he was apparently well off enough to support his religious causes out of pocket. He had no reason to farm and no interest in farming. More than ever, his calling lay elsewhere.

By 1872 his mind was made up. His eyes were always cast heavenward and his heart filled with the Lord. The farm and the land never meant much to him. They were merely vehicles for him to obtain the wealth he wanted to do God's work. Daniel decided to sell the farm, despite Anne's pleadings to keep the home. Hickory Hill sold in three parcels in March for a total of $1,300 (though an additional payment may have been made later for at least one parcel). Anne and Daniel moved back to Portage. John thought the sale was a "diseased act," he wrote his sister Sarah, "but father is a comet whose course only heaven knows." Anne later wrote, "I do not allow myself to think often of our dear old home. It seemed hard to leave the place that we had built[,] planned and planted." "Time," she concluded, "brings changes." The next year it did again.

Daniel abandoned his dutiful wife and his extended family living around Portage to go proselytizing in Hamilton, a Canadian port city on Lake Ontario. He returned to Wisconsin briefly and tried for years unsuccessfully to persuade the family to join him up north. Anne had had enough and wouldn't budge. She died in Portage in 1896, her life on Fountain Lake and Hickory Hill distant memories in time, though nearby in place. Her life in Dunbar was even further distant in time and place, shrouded in the mist, obscured in the same way the dense droplets of *haar*—the soupy sea mist that frequently engulfs the Scottish shore—diffuse detail into vague gray forms as if apparitions without shape and substance.

As is well known, John found fame in the Sierra Nevada range of Yosemite. He married successfully and the devoted couple raised a family on her father's fruit farm in Martinez, California (outside San Francisco). John managed the profitable property and eventually inherited it on his father-in-law's death. John's prosperity, lifelong generosity, and constant caring served as magnets attracting his siblings. Eventually sister Sarah, widowed in 1884, moved to California. So did sister Maggie and her husband, brother David, and sister Annie (who would return to Portage after an extended stay). Brother Dan remained in Racine; sister Mary moved to Nebraska, and sister Joanna moved to Kansas City, with whom father Daniel was living when he died in 1885. With Annie's death in Portage in 1903, the Muir family roots in Marquette County were completely severed. "As a family," John wrote, "we are pretty firmly united and you know that no one tree of a close clump can very well fall. In my walks through the forests of humanity I find no family clump more interwoven in root and branch than our own." Like most American families for much of the nation's history, the Muirs moved repeatedly, usually westward. The family linkage to their land at Fountain Lake and Hickory Hill was lost in a generation as Daniel and Anne's children followed in their parents' footsteps and set off in search of their own lives.

John wandered far from his first home in Dunbar before finally settling as an adult near San Francisco. Once there he continued to travel widely, touring Alaska, Europe, and South America. Yet he retained vivid memories of and affection for each of his two Wisconsin homes, as well as his Scottish home. John loved the landscape, not as a source of power or some utilitarian commodity, or as a vehicle for profit as did Daniel, but simply as a source of childlike wonder and unadulterated joy. Landscape profoundly affected John his entire life. He was acutely sensitive and responsive to it. He was the rare person who apparently needed to set down roots deep in a place and form a strong sense of connection to the land and community. I think this enabled him to always be at home wherever he roamed. John was never really uprooted, nor could he be, for he carried within him a love of place and a passion to truly know the land. Like the wonderful lesson his mother offered him on finding personal contentment, this is a wonderful lesson he offers me.

{ 1 1 }

I've returned to Fountain Lake for a look around John Muir Memorial County Park and the adjacent John Muir National Historic Landmark. Unfortunately, unsettled weather has returned too. The swirling wind snatches at the sun through fleeting gaps in the heavy overcast. A light drizzle drops from gray cotton clouds. It's the familiar dreich day of Scotland, except for the more mild temperature. I think John and his disciples have left me another lesson here, one to discover as I walk about the lake and recall his family's settlement story. The lesson has at its core the century-long efforts to protect this landscape. It's a lesson about the importance of preserving our special places. They're the lampposts to our landscape legacy. They illuminate our past and help link us to it. They tether us like a lifeline to our home as we wander far afield, and they guide us back like a beacon in the night. John would relish the park and the landmark, for they preserve some of his most cherished places—Fountain Lake and the meadow below the first Muir home site in the New

World. He'd also commend their conservation philosophies and practices, although I suspect he'd want to kibitz on their details.

I park my car on the brow of the knoll overlooking Ennis Lake, just past the lilacs planted 150 years ago by Sarah near the door of their Fountain Lake farmhouse. The lilacs welcome me today, as they did Anne on her arrival that November. Erik Brynildson welcomes me as well. He now owns some seventeen acres of the landmark, including the former Muir homestead. He's remodeling the fifty-five-year-old house that he believes sits on the exact site of the Muir house. His home is the third here.

The Muir house was abandoned in the late 1800s, and by the early 1900s it had become a makeshift getaway for local men who gathered for evenings of comradeship—drinking, smoking, maybe some gambling—before a stoked fire. One night after they left, the dilapidated house burned down. A prominent local farmer and Muir devotee named Archie Schmitz acquired the property years later. Right after World War II, he built a simple frame house for his retirement atop the ruins, using a horse-drawn trawl at the start of construction to scoop out the former cellar. By the 1980s, that house had also fallen into disrepair. Erik moved in when he acquired the property in the mid-eighties and began the gradual renovation, keeping changes within the footprint of the original Muir farmhouse. The new house will be taller and more comfortable, and will include a library for his extensive archive of Muir materials. The house now encases the old, adding another layer of history to the site. I like the fact that the property will be occupied and cared for, once again providing enjoyment for an appreciative owner, its charms once again able to enchant another generation just as they enchanted John Muir.

Erik is perhaps the perfect owner for the property: devoted to the land and the Muir legacy, both its history and its philosophy. He might even share some traits with John. Erik is a bit scruffy-looking, his sandy brown hair with a tint of steely gray a bit untamed. John often appeared unkempt too. He was a gaunt five feet ten, as described on his passport application in 1903, with a medium forehead, a long thin face, gray eyes, Roman nose, ordinary mouth, prominent chin, long gray beard and gray hair, and a fair complexion. Erik is much bigger than John, a powerful six-foot-tall man with a round face who could envelop John like a bear. Today he's dressed in blue jeans and a buff-colored cotton T-shirt to work around the house. Erik strikes me as having an edge to his personality as if he is impatient with incompetence and needless bureaucracy. He's passionate in his beliefs, a practical idealist, friendly and warm. Erik is a doer, I think, a person of action once he's done his homework and is ready to begin. He's well prepared, well reasoned, and hardworking, a person who knows his mind and is a bit bothered by those who waste his time. I think John was all of these things as well. The two would surely argue, but get along splendidly in the process.

Erik came of age during of the Vietnam era. Perhaps his passion and idealism arose then. He was a conscientious objector during the war and instead of fleeing to Canada did draft counseling in lieu of military service. Now he fights to restore landscapes, especially his Fountain Lake homestead. His love of the land and heartiness must have come from growing up amid the forests and lakes of northern Michigan, the son of a fisheries biologist who studied with Aldo Leopold and hunted a bit with the great conservationist shortly before Leopold's death. Both Erik's parents grew up on Wisconsin farms, his mother near Spring Green and his father west of Black River Falls. The family moved back to Wisconsin when his father left the U.S. Fish and Wildlife Service for a position with the state Conservation Department in Madison. Erik went to high school there and continued on at the University of Wisconsin where he completed degrees in wildlife ecology and landscape architecture, interspersed with a seven-year stint as a park superintendent. Now he has his own consulting practice, working with public and private clients across the country to restore native plant communities within historical and cultural contexts, just as he does on his portion of the Muir landmark.

We stand on the brow of the knoll, between piles of construction materials, looking at the sedge meadow below and lake beyond—the same view that Muir depicted with pen and ink in words and sketches later included in some of the books he wrote and illustrated. John was a good amateur artist and made realistic drawings that accurately reflected the view. The view has changed since then, Erik says.

When he began work on the property in 1986, a dense line of silver maples just below the brow blocked the view. These he cut and burned to reopen the vista and reestablish the cooling flow of fresh air circulating across the knoll. The land around the lake had changed appearance as well, becoming more enclosed by dense stands of trees and shrubs. With no more wildfires to periodically burn the sedge meadow and oak openings, species like dogwood and willow encroached. What before was an open meadow and a surrounding parklike landscape of majestically shaped bur oaks, white oaks, and shagbark hickories became a dense thicket. Today the meadow and oak openings have the messy look of most disturbed landscapes undergoing succession—untidy and out of control. Nature is reconfiguring itself. In Muir's day, the landscape possessed a romantic, pastoral character, hardly wild or unruly. The oak openings had only twenty or so "open-grown" trees per acre, and little shrub understory. The wide spacing enabled branches to spread horizontally, unaffected by nearby competition for solar access. The contorted branching patterns of the trees Erik and I see reflect the conditions in which these trees grew. A drop in the water table and a drying up of some of the springs due to heavy cropping and pasturing probably contributed to the changes as well. Erik burns what he can to replicate the natural disturbance regime and kill off the invaders. But he owns only a portion of the land. The state owns most of it. And controlled burns can be a costly and politically sensitive matter. The "wilderness" about the lake that John reveled in looked much less wild than the abandoned fields undergoing succession there today.

We walk around to the north side of the property during a break in the clouds and a brief period of sunshine. The house sits about a quarter mile in from Gillette Drive, which separates the Muir's lower half-quarter from the upper half-quarter. Daniel centered the house here, and at Hickory Hill, following the common siting practice among Scottish pioneers. Prairie flowers once again bloom in the field between the Fountain Lake farmhouse and Gillette Drive, as they did when the Muirs arrived. Erik planted the prairie in the spring of 1988, after he clearcut the "dog-haired thick" red pine plantation planted decades before. Erik had no more use for the pines than the Muirs had for the prairie.

That first spring Daniel used a giant "breaking" plow to rip apart the thick prairie turf, tearing the tangle of deep roots in preparation for planting wheat in the light (sandy) soil. It can be a surprisingly fragile soil with much of its nutrient richness stored in the plant mass. Break the turf and cut the tangle of roots anchoring the soil in place and you can easily lose much of the fertility. On one Muir field this caused a "sand blow" as the wind carried off the topsoil. The Muirs cropped most of the land on the home eighty—now the national historic landmark. Perhaps they left the meadow untouched because it was too wet to crop without being drained and the task of draining it was too demanding to be done immediately. Unfortunately, yields on the "thin" soils they did crop quickly declined, as happened throughout the area. The conversion to corn had little benefit as the sensitive soils were simply exhausted by intensive use. Pasturing for cattle followed, with crops grown in lesser amounts mostly to feed the stock. Daniel was learning to better care for his paradise, but it was too little too late. The decline in productivity must have played a big part in his decision to move on. Like many pioneers, instead of restoring the land, he left it to another, like an abandoned child, and bought new to begin again. Daniel was not of a mind to stay put and return the land to a sustainable use. Land was too cheap and too readily available. He had no connection to it, no roots yet set down.

Erik now works on his property to undo the damage left by Daniel and the subsequent owners of Fountain Lake Farm. He owns the northeast corner of the lower half-quarter and intends to be the last person to privately own it. He thinks it too important a place historically and too significant a place ecologically to remain in private hands. He hopes the National Park Service will acquire the parcel. Marquette County owns the remainder of the national historic landmark, which is managed by the Wisconsin Department of Natural Resources with much the same goal as Erik's. The state also co-manages John Muir Memorial County Park with Marquette County. The origin of the park and the landmark began a century earlier with the effort of the man who pioneered the preservation of land for public purposes—John Muir. It was here that his interests in and efforts at landscape preservation began, long before he heard of national parks.

Just before John fled the draft in 1864, escaping into the Canadian wilderness around Georgian Bay, he planned to attend medical school at the University of Michigan. He probably knew he'd no longer live on the family properties. He also saw the family splitting up as siblings matured and moved away. He watched the farms gradually being broken up as well. And he might have sensed Sarah and David Galloway's dislike of the drudgery on their Fountain Lake Farm and feared they might sell it. These changes meant that his cherished sedge meadow might be lost to the ravages of farming practices, whether those of his brother-in-law or a potential new owner. In response, he told David, "Sell me the forty acres of lake meadow, and keep it fenced, and never allow cattle or hogs to break into it, and I will gladly pay you whatever you say. I want to keep it untrampled for the sake of its ferns and flowers." David refused the offer, thinking it impractical because a zigzag fence, the type John had split wood for and helped build around the farm, wasn't strong enough to keep cattle out. John's fears proved well founded. David soon sold that part of the farm, and stock was soon set to pasture on the meadow by the Ennis brothers.

John persisted. While living in Yosemite in 1871 and beginning his rise to later fame as the leading voice for wilderness preservation, he wrote David, "If you think that the cattle and hogs can be kept off by ordinary care and fencing, I wish you would offer Ennis from two and a half to ten dollars as you can agree, but if you think that the stock cannot be fenced off out I do not care to have the land at all." Again the offer failed. An agreeable purchase price could not be reached and David still doubted fencing would work. Yet, that wasn't the end of it. John tried at least once more in the decades to come to acquire and preserve the meadow property. The nation's most famous preservationist of the nineteenth century, a leading voice for the formation of the national park system and the preservation of places like Yosemite, couldn't protect his beloved childhood meadow, the place where many of his preservation ideals originated. That would fall to America's most famous conservationist of the twentieth century.

Aldo Leopold lived the latter half of his life only miles from Ennis (Fountain) Lake. He taught wildlife management and land conservation at the University of Wisconsin in the 1930s and 1940s and worked weekends and holidays restoring an abandoned farm ravaged by the same shortsighted practices initially applied by Daniel Muir and the later owners of the nearby Fountain Lake Farm. It was in the cottage on his abandoned farm—formerly the farm's chicken coop—that Leopold wrote perhaps the bible of twentieth-century land conservation, *A Sand County Almanac.* On April 14, 1948, Leopold wrote Ernest Swift, the director of the Wisconsin Conservation Department,

> [I have just been reminded] of a project that has been on my mind for a long time: the acquisition of at least one of the two boyhood farms of John Muir as a state park. . . . Before deciding either way on this proposal . . . [people] should read Muir's book *The Story of My Boyhood and Youth . . .* it is necessary background.
>
> One reason I have hesitated to recommend this project in the past has been that the Muir farm is undoubtedly badly depleted floristically and otherwise, and hence any possible restoration at this time might be a pretty drab affair compared to the original farm described in Muir's book. It now occurs to me, however, that this area might fall half way between a state park in the ordinary sense and a "natural area," the objective being to restore the flora to something approaching the original. . . .
>
> In more general terms, such a state park should be something more than a mere stopping place for tourists lacking something to do. It might be made a public educational institution in the ecological and intellectual history of Wisconsin. . . .

It was a novel concept, well ahead of its time, just as Muir's initial desire to protect the meadow foreshadowed the national park system and other programs that preserve natural areas. Yellowstone, the world's first national park, was established in 1872; Yosemite would follow next in 1890. By 1900 the practice

of protecting portions of the public domain from intensive development, setting them aside for recreational and environmental preservation purposes, was well established, although many
philosophical and management nuances remain controversial
even today. Tragically, Aldo Leopold died fighting a wildfire on a
neighbor's property just days after mailing the letter. The proposal was forgotten. From then on the effort would rest in the
hands of relatively unknown local people, appropriately, as Muir's
and Leopold's lasting legacies are best seen in their influence on
common people worldwide.

A local businessman and amateur archaeologist named Syl-
vester Adrian took up the cause. After World War II, Adrian
operated a little tavern and resort called "Indian Echoes" on
Route 22, about ten miles northeast of the site. He had little
education but a deep interest in Indian history and John Muir.
Beginning in the late 1940s, he spearheaded an effort to persuade
Marquette County to preserve the land around Ennis Lake and
make it a park. At the time the county didn't have any parks
(fifty years later, it still has only one—John Muir Memorial
County Park). Adrian organized local groups, wrote letters, and
lobbied local officials, to little avail. Fortunately, the farmland
around Ennis Lake escaped the subdivision and recreational development that occurred on other nearby lakes. Most of the property
owners around the lake, some of whom had been on the same
land since the Muirs were their neighbors, continued to farm. At
this time, too, Archie Schmitz owned the Muir homestead property, where he built his retirement home atop the ruins of the
Muir home. Archie recognized the site's historical significance
and wasn't about to subdivide the land.

In 1955 Adrian convinced Audley Cuff to donate some of his
land around the lake to the county for a park. County efforts to
enlist state support failed, as the size of the proposed park fell
well below the state's 2,000-acre minimum. Cuff's offer was re-

jected. Two years later, however, after about a decade of lobbying, Adrian's campaign succeeded. The county accepted Cuff's 41.5-acre donation and dedicated the park. Yet the park contained none of the former Muir property, including the meadow, and the park was intended for general-purpose recreation, not preservation as Muir and Leopold had advocated.

Adrian and others persisted. In 1965 the county authorized Adrian to negotiate on its behalf for the purchase of the former Muir property. Two years later the deal was closed. A hundred years after Muir began the effort, his meadow was finally protected. With two federal grants from the Land and Water Conservation Fund, the county finally acquired some 62 acres—the bulk of the Muir home eighty, including the meadow and lake frontage (Archie Schmitz still owned the remainder of the 80 acres). The county also bought 12 acres of land abutting the south shore of the lake so the park would have access around the lake. Gradually the pieces of the current park and landmark were put in place.

The state of Wisconsin finally became involved in the early 1970s, twenty-five years after Aldo Leopold made the proposal. In 1972 the Department of Natural Resources established Muir Park State Natural Area and entered into a cooperative agreement with the county to oversee the park's natural areas. In effect, the county manages the original 41-acre park for recreation while the state manages the remainder to "maintain the fen, prairie and sedge meadow communities by controlling woody encroachment and exotics, and to restore prairie and oak opening communities. Additional land will be left in old field habitat. The communities will be managed to simulate presettlement conditions using prescribed burning and brushing as the primary management tools." John Muir's wish had been realized at long last, though the story has one more part—the part that brought me to Erik's home today.

Muir's transcendentalist-like philosophy regarding the human relationship with nature first brought Erik here in the 1960s, as he searched for answers to personal questions, doubts, and longings while on walks around the lake. Muir once wrote,

> The World, we are told, was made especially for man—a presumption not supported by all the facts. A numerous class of men are painfully astonished whenever they find anything, living or dead, in all God's universe, which they cannot eat or render in some way what they call useful to themselves. . . . Why should man value himself as more than a small part of the one great unit of creation? And what creature of all that the Lord has taken the pains to make is not essential to the completeness of that unit—the cosmos? The universe would be incomplete without man; but it would also be incomplete without the smallest transmicroscopic creature that dwells beyond our conceitful eyes and knowledge.

That common conceit, evident in college courses, alienated Erik from standard curricula and sent him off on an alternate educational and life path. He found a model in Muir's words and life. "My efforts at Fountain Lake Farm began with a heartfelt fascination for the place even as a teenager," Erik told me. "It was the late 1960s and I was just out of high school with an all-too-low draft lottery number. I was often drawn by the magnetism of the landscape here and the history it holds. It became my refuge from suburban numbness, the sizzling city, and social insanities. My saunters about the lake countryside guided my thoughts and gently nudged my confusion towards clarity. As a result of this evolving relationship, I became a government-sanctioned conscientious objector, as well as an activist against the folly of war." The similarities with John Muir's life and beliefs are striking.

In 1984 Erik began work on an M.S. thesis for which he would document the site's historical significance as if for an application to designate the homestead as a national historic landmark. "The project quickly became my life," he said. His research uncovered a handful of local people who had been touched by Muir's work and writing among the many residents who had no knowledge of it. Erik tapped into the loose network of Muir devotees, supporters who assisted his research by sharing personal stories, memories, and archives. A retired university professor living in Atlanta who was a keen Muir aficionado provided important material after his relatives in Portage saw an article on Erik's research in the Portage paper. Another local resident shared with Erik old photographs of the home site. Archie Schmitz's son, Irv, became a good friend. Erik was hooked. "I sold a home in Madison in 1986 to purchase the property for a price many local people thought was certifiable insanity," he told me. "Only someone that recognized and cherished the sacredness of the place would have paid so much. I knew the family through my research and dealt directly with them. The property wasn't really for sale, but they somehow thought I should have it."

His thesis work evolved into the actual application in collaboration with several supporters, while stirring up local politicians and personalities against the proposal. "You have to realize that various levels of government, especially state agencies, could have secured the old Muir homestead for no more than meager back taxes several times in its history," Erik noted. "The Wisconsin State Historical Society declared that the site possessed 'no real historical significance'; at the same time, the Wisconsin Conservation Department decided it had 'nothing special ecologically.' " But the application went forward. National historic landmark designation was granted in 1990. "Both the saving grace and biggest obstacles are right across the street—local folks who are afraid of nature groups and the government owning more land; people who don't believe much in the philosophy of land preservation to begin with; people who adhere to a very utilitarian outlook." The same conceits that Muir noted one hundred years earlier are as persistent today among the majority of people as they were then.

Erik hopes the remaining unprotected acres of the original Muir purchase at Fountain Lake will be protected as well. Bessie Eggleston, a relative of the Ennis family, owns that land—the northern half-quarter of the purchase. Her home sits a short five-minute walk west on Gillette Drive from Erik's drive, then north a bit on Highway "F."

Bessie is nearly ninety years old, so she leases the land to a neighbor to farm. It's not a part of the park or the landmark and has great development potential. Real estate agents knock on her door all the time eager for her to sell. She has no intention to and hopes that her property will avoid subdivision. Its fate is uncertain, though, as she has no children, dwindling assets, and lapses of resolve as she ages. Like Erik, she loves the land. "There's something magical about it," she explained with a twinkle in her eye when we spoke about the past and the future in her small home. The biggest change she sees has been in the people, not the land. "When you grow up on a farm, working the soil, you appreciate the land because you depend on it for your livelihood. It means more to you," she told me in a soft voice. She thinks too few newcomers share that feeling, a loss that has weakened the sense of community, the sense of neighborhood. The land is personal to Bessie. "It's not personal to them," she said, meaning those newcomers who view the land and farming only in material terms. They often become indifferent to the land, she thinks. "People focus too much on what they can get from it," she said, rather than "enjoying it and puddling around in it."

Bessie lives alone across "F" from the former Muir fields. Her dog Bobbie provides companionship. The front window looks out at the land. Muir Park sits several hundred yards diagonally to the southeast. Her father was born in the house that stood where the commemorative marker for John Muir now stands in the park, and the farms of brothers and uncles are all about. Bessie's home is cluttered with unfinished projects—cleaning never completed, papers never put away—trivial things to someone her age, forgotten or set aside in favor of something more meaningful. The house is full of the past, the possessions and memories of a long life.

She remembers when the area was electrified when she was a young woman, and when the roads were first paved with gravel when she was still a young girl. The sharp stones meant she could no longer carry her shoes on the walk home down the dirt road from the small schoolhouse. She remembered an incident just down the road, by the curve past the creek where the tree canopy closed to form a tunnel, when a wildcat dropped suddenly from the overarching tree branches, raking its sharp claws down the flanks of a frightened horse ridden by the schoolteacher on her way to class. For weeks after, Bessie's father walked her safely past that spot each day. She remembered when an old woman, "so thin and stooped I always felt sorry for her," stopped climbing Observatory Hill to hang a lantern each night as a beacon for those making their way over the dark, unpaved, and unmarked county roads. She remembered the stern parental warnings not to swim in the part of Ennis Lake where the springs fed in. A teenage boy once drowned there, caught in the current. She remembered the family finally being able to attend the Marquette County fair, held fifteen miles north in Westfield, and the fun picnics they shared there with friends and neighbors. The fair was too far to go by horse-drawn wagon. But when they got a Ford touring car around 1920, their world expanded. Now they could also go every summer Saturday evening to Endeavor, several miles away across the Fox River, to join the throng watching the free silent movies shown outside on the wall of a store. She remembered playing in the large "dooryard" beside the house and the sour taste of wild apples picked from the windrows and hedgerows. She remembered the blowing dirt of the dust bowl and her father warning neighbors for years before to plant sheltering trees along their fields. And she remembered the many friendly Indians, especially White Eagle, who became a good friend of her father's. He often hired the kind, curious man to help around the farm. White Eagle loved to drive the horses to plow. In return, perhaps he tried to teach the family his concept of "respect" for oneself, for other people, and for all creation.

Like many in the area, Bessie's ancestors were Presbyterian Scots who arrived in Marquette County during the initial wave of white settlement in the 1840s. She would lead the effort to restore rather than demolish the wooden "Wee White Kirk" that served for several generations as the community's spiritual center. Today it still stands as handsome as ever on a rise overlooking the intersection of county roads "13" and "O": tall, black-shuttered windows accent the white clapboard siding, pitched roof, and plain box shape of elegant proportions, simple, unadorned inside and out, like the faith. Galloways lie in its graveyard. Daniel Muir, legend has it, preached from its raised platform to those seated on the plain board benches against the walls. No written records confirm it, though he did preach in many homes and schoolhouses around the area.

Places like the Wee White Kirk, John Muir Memorial County Park, and the John Muir National Historic Landmark link us with our past. They connect us to the land, even if we travel far away. Bessie told me of two women from California who returned to a reunion of parishioners at the Wee White Kirk held during the renovation effort. The women remembered the place inside where their families sat and other details of the church, despite the passage of decades. What would prompt them to travel all that way for a reunion of a place and a people from so long ago in their lives? I think Erik Brynildson and Bessie Eggleston understand why. I think they sense the importance of special places and the importance of their preservation. I think John Muir did too.

[1 2]

"Hickory Hills Estates," the marquee proclaims in bold black letters on the white construction placard announcing the newest subdivision of large-lot homes on Grouse Road. "For Sale 5-Acre Parcels. For information call . . ." A simple plat diagram of the new development shows how the fifteen individual lots will line the cul-de-sac or face directly onto Grouse Road. The 4-by-8-foot sign stands 40 feet back from the road, amid a tangle of weeds. These annuals, biennials, and herbaceous perennials—the storm troopers of old-field succession—claw at the two 2-by-10-inch posts that hold the alien sign upright. A bulldozer stands 40 feet further behind by the dirt path it scraped into the former farm field. The blade seems to be smiling at me as if pleased with its handiwork. The bulldozer is to suburban development what the tractor was to the farm being supplanted. The big Caterpillar scrapes away the farm just as the big John Deere plowed away the wilderness. Soon miniature John Deeres will mow crops of bluegrass lawns. More and more houses face the frontage on this stretch of Grouse Road, between roads "14" and "15." Fewer and fewer farms survive.

What's happening here? What does the sign symbolize? Does it mark progress? It's a nice sign—neatly made and clearly read from the road. Perhaps the developer hopes a person driving by in search of a piece of paradise will be enticed to buy one of these. I'm passing by on my way to the Hickory Hill Farm of Maurice (Morrie) and Mary Kearns, their family's piece of paradise for the past 130 years. It sits just down the road on the next section east. How have they managed to stay in place for so long while most of us have moved so frequently? What does the land mean to them? How do they feel about the changes occurring all around them?

Morrie meets me in the barnyard, his boots caked with mud and manure. The dogs bark suspiciously at me. I've come at noon so he's breaking off work for dinner. This way our visit will least disrupt his busy workday. He and Mary don't mind most of the visitors who come to see the Muir legacy. Many pilgrims come from California, Sierra Club members mostly. Fewer come now than in past years. The couple knows the Muir Hickory Hill story but seem very nonchalant about living here. I sign their guest book.

Morrie is seventy-one years old and still works the farm. He's of medium height and trim build. I think his sinewy arms could snap me in half. Morrie has a Henry Fonda–like air about him, similar to Fonda's portrayal of Tom Joad in *The Grapes of Wrath*— quiet, unassuming, unflustered, enduring. His father, Harry, was vigorous well into his nineties and lived to be one hundred. Grandfather Thomas bought the farm in April 1873 for $300 from John Mahaffey, who had bought it about a year earlier from Daniel Muir. In fact, Mahaffey may not have fully settled his purchase with Muir, so the sale of the property to Kearns might have been partly a transaction between Muir and Kearns.

Both sides of the Kearns came from Ireland—County Cork and County Ross. Morrie doesn't know what they did there, although on arrival in America around 1850 his great-grandfather worked for a short time in a New Jersey factory. The family moved westward a year or two before the outbreak of the Civil War to join relatives in Portage. At first they farmed nearby in Lewiston but found the land wasn't very good. Hickory Hill was their third farm. They grew wheat mostly. Then, like others in the area, they gradually changed crops and focused more on dairying. Morrie's grandparents raised four boys and a daughter, who at one time had four farms among them in the area. All the farms save this one are gone now, gradually sold off outside the family.

The evolution of farming practices at Hickory Hill paralleled that of farms regionwide. Wheat was the primary cash crop in central Wisconsin well into the 1800s. Feed crops—corn, hay, oats—were grown for the livestock. Each farm usually had a few horses or oxen to pull plows, wagons, and reapers, and some beef and dairy cattle, sheep, hogs, and chickens, mostly for domestic consumption. Manure from the livestock was spread on the thin soils to replenish the nutrients lost in constant cereal cropping. Improved crop rotation, plowing practices, and fertilizers, however, couldn't compensate for the poor fundamentals of depleted soils, a vast supply of superior land for wheat production westward on the plains, and rising property values. Many farmers sold out and moved westward. Those that stayed were forced to find more profitable uses for the land based on the combination of soil types, climate, markets, technology, and farming preferences. By 1900 dairying emerged as one such use on many farms, though some persisted in wheat production, others emphasized corn, and still others focused on beef cattle or other livestock. Most farms switched emphasis several times over the years. This often meant the mix changed in the amounts of crops grown and livestock raised—more of this, less of that. By the mid-1900s, many farms specialized in specific crops or a stock. Little has changed today: dairying dominates, though various crops are grown and other types of stock are managed. Each farmer finds his/her niche, often influenced by family tradition and lifestyle preferences. Change tends to be gradual, not wholesale. At Hickory Hill, wheat gave way to dairying, which gave way to beef cattle, while all along a mix of crops were grown.

Mary joins us in the open-plan "country" kitchen that serves both as an eating area and as a general-purpose family room. She begins work preparing the meal. The house is cluttered, like many farmhouses I've visited. Little furniture and few fixtures are new. Immaculate, trendy homes exist in magazines, not on active farms. Life bristles in farm homes, especially those with lots of kids around. Morrie and Mary raised eight children in the house; most still live in the area so the household is frequently filled with grandkids. Farm homes seem to be perpetual works in progress. This one has always been. The original wood-clad Muir house has been expanded several times and the exterior long since encased in brick. Pointing to a doorway, Morrie said one rainy day he took a sledgehammer to the wall that once stood there and smashed the passageway through. The dust made quite a mess, Mary remembered. Other projects are planned. Perhaps someday he might have time for them. It's the same with the other farm buildings—they're never complete, either in construction or destruction.

The farm expands and contracts too, just as it did when Daniel Muir owned it. Today Morrie farms his 270 acres plus fields on several neighbors' farms. He crops about 170 acres in corn, soybeans, oats, wheat, and alfalfa hay on the home farm. Thirty to forty-five head of beef cattle pasture on the remaining 100 acres. His land isn't great, he tells me. Most years he sells between 4,000 and 5,000 bushels of corn, from a yield of a bit over 100 bushels per acre. When it's dry during the growing season, the yield has dropped to 60 bushels per acre. He doesn't irrigate his sandy-loam soils, too expensive for a small operation like his. Nor does he specialize and grow a single cash crop like many bigger operations. Hickory Hill remains much the same type of small-scale, integrated farm as that managed by the Muirs. Morrie still grows most of the same crops as they did and still raises livestock as they did, aided now by more mechanization and better management practices. Perhaps Morrie heeds John Muir's admonition to eschew the land greed he saw in his father Daniel: better to take on only what one can manage well; better to enjoy life a bit than waste a life to overindustry in quest of mammon. John would recognize the place today. The farm remains about the same size and configuration and the fields serve much the same function, though the woodlots from his day are gone and virtually all the land is in production.

What advantages Morrie gains over his bigger, more specialized competitors—lower costs, greater flexibility to switch among several crops to better suit the market, and the ability to offset losses in one product with gains in another—he loses in the diseconomy of his small scale. Three of his sons farm near Kingston, bigger operations of 500 to 600 acres, milking eighty cows. "That's the trend today," Morrie says, "but you have to have the equipment, and dependable help." It's real tough to make the costs work if you have to buy the land and the equipment now, he tells me. He's survived because the farm was inherited. Bigger, more specialized neighbors can get 150 bushels per acre reliably year in, year out. They must, to offset their higher input costs and the vagaries in commodity prices. Morrie must simply weather the dry years and rely on the livestock to keep the farm solvent. A small insurance company he runs for local farmers earns additional income. Paperwork is done mostly during the "slack" season in the winter.

Tell me what the land means to you, I asked. "I suppose it's a living to us, I guess," he replied. "We try to take care of it so it'll still be here for the next generation." But it's an unfair question— easily asked, difficult to answer in a few hastily chosen words. How can you express what the home where your kids were born and raised, and you were born and raised, and your father was born and raised, and his father lived, means to you? I suspect the place meant more to Morrie than what he just said. He told me he had a thousand stories about the land. He shared only a few.

He's been on the farm his entire life, except for two years in the army during which he spent nineteen months in Germany.

He vaguely remembers when Grouse Road was graded and graveled in the 1930s, replacing the rutted dirt road as the major link to the outside world. However, until recently, for daily contact folks continued to use a network of footpaths that ran from farm to farm. He remembers playing behind the barn until age thirteen, when he was put to the plow—driving a tractor. He thought himself big stuff for that, he said. It was during the war so labor was dear. He remembers party-line telephones. He remembers the changes in the mix of crops and livestock over the years. He remembers the loss of the great willows down at the stream. He recalls when farms lined Grouse Road and the families each had seven or eight kids. Some farmers have retired and now lease their land, he says. Some sold out and moved away. Now the old homes and the new homes have far fewer kids. Couples can't afford the time for large families anymore, he tells me, and both parents usually work to make ends meet—there's just no time and not enough money for big families.

We walked outside so he could show me around the property. There was the cellar where John Muir made miraculous gadgets out of wood and scraps from the farm. There was the well he chipped with hammer and chisel, now capped and in need of a new pump. The old windmill no longer works. There was the barn Daniel Muir had built. Inside, the huge hand-hewn timbers, some only partly squared, loom overhead as strong as ever. The original barn sat at grade and had three bays: two for storing grain and the middle serving as a pass-through and providing space for flailing the crop. It was typical of barns in the region designed primarily to serve the needs of wheat farming in the mid- to late 1800s. By the 1900s, farms focused more on dairying, requiring a different barn design. Many farmers modified their barns instead of demolishing the outmoded three-bay threshing structures. Around 1906 Thomas Kearns did too. A twenty-man crew of neighbors helped raise the barn using giant jackscrews, then built a stone foundation beneath. The lower level sheltered the stock and the upper three bays became the haymow. A dirt ramp banked from ground level up to the barn door provided access. These remodeled barns were so common that they became known as "bank barns."

Why has the farm stayed in the family for so long, I asked. "My dad kinda liked farming and I kinda did," he replied in his low, monochromatic voice. He speaks fast, almost mumbling. "We never made very much money but we raised a family with eight children here. One of them will probably have it when we're gone, unless something happens and we have to let it go." What do you like about farming, I asked. "I don't know, it's just one of those things. We're satisfied with what we're doing. In hindsight, I suppose I would've taken a job off the farm on the side. We managed to make a living here but we didn't build up any reserve. You might say the only things we've got are our good health and the land, otherwise we have no pension."

He tells me of the farmer across the way who sold off twenty-four 5-acre lots for $30,000 to $40,000 each. The buyers then built $200,000 homes. "We never thought we'd see people pushing out here forty miles from Madison, but here they come," he says. Now he looks out his front window at their houses across the valley on the far side of Grouse Road. Hickory Hills Estates is next. No bitterness to his comments, just a hint of resignation in the face of the larger forces that led to this. Morrie has never seriously considered selling off lots, although he lopped off a small piece in the corner of the farm for his daughter and son-in-law to live on. He hasn't really needed or wanted the money yet, but he knows that day could come.

Many local officials, real estate agents, and farmers foresee a bleak future for agriculture in the area. Perhaps the larger, specialized farms will survive, but traditional small-scale farms like Hickory Hill face real problems as the marketplace seeks the new "highest" and "best" use of the land. That use may well be as a "bedroom" suburb and recreational playground for nearby cities. It's hard for many people to envision that fate for this farming community. A recent lakefront subdivision illustrates the situation.

A development company bought a 60-acre chunk from an old farmer for $340,000. Perhaps the sale financed the farmer's retirement, and he still retained the bulk of the farm. The company then went through the simple county approval process, put in a road, cleared the site, and built a 24-acre subdivision with four lakefront lots. A doctor snapped up two adjoining parcels along the lake for $380,000 and built a 4,000-square-foot log home on the combined properties. The developer spent in total about $500,000 on the project, which he promptly recouped with the sale of just the four lake lots. Revenues from the sale of the other lots constituted mostly profit, three-quarters of which were soon sold. Certainly lake frontage sells for a premium and the process is rarely that easy or that profitable. But person after person told me the same general tale. In twenty-five years they expect the county to be much different: more recreational-based with more large-lot homes and fewer full-time farms.

The economics at the moment certainly favor it: $250,000 buys a "quarter-quarter" with a nice country house away from the hassles of city and suburban life, leaving an hour's commute to Madison. Maybe the new owners farm a bit for fun or keep horses, or like to hunt, fish, or boat. Maybe they're retiring and want peace and quiet. Maybe they just want more contact with "nature." Or the $250,000 buys a five-acre lot and a comfortable home in a subdivision like Hickory Hills Estates. So they sell their homes on small lots in cramped suburbs and move out to the country. The cost is a wash. Potential buyers are plentiful; potential sellers too. As a result, house prices have nearly tripled in the past decade, bid up by the influx of city money, with no letup in sight. This drives up property tax assessments for everyone, including the many longtime residents on rural or fixed incomes, as opposed to higher city incomes. The dynamics of the land-use change are complicated and the political tussle to control it very controversial. It's a hot-button issue in the county.

How can farms survive, caught in the squeeze between poor profitability, a changing social atmosphere, an aging farm population with fewer and fewer children choosing to carry on the family business, and the potential sale value of farm property? Initially I was inclined to be romantic and nostalgic about the farming landscape and lifestyle and bemoan the change under way in Marquette County. Now I'm not so sure. Perhaps it's simply progress. Most farmers I spoke with generally accept the change, though not yet on their property. Morrie and Mary are among them. The more recent arrivals tend to be those most against it. The area's rural character attracted many of them. Now they want to protect it in the face of further change as more people like them come in search of that same character; having arrived, they now want to "pull up the drawbridge." What to do? Whose values take precedence? How do you balance private property rights against communal responsibility?

Places with controls on land use most commonly implement them with a zoning ordinance and a subdivision code derived from a land-use master plan. But zoning is a dirty word for many people in Marquette County. You might as well call it Communism. Many longtime residents, farmers, and others want no part of it: it limits their freedom to use or dispose of their property as they wish. That's why many of their families immigrated to the United States. Like the Muirs, they came for the opportunity to own land free from outside interference. That freedom is deeply rooted. The sanctity of private property rights remains little changed. It hasn't needed to change in this area, at least until now. Recent arrivals are often the strongest supporters of land-use controls. Most moved from settings where zoning is commonplace and widely accepted as a positive way to protect property values and preserve a preferred way of life. Now they want to use it for the same purposes here.

The townships and the county struggle in the awkward first phases of land-use control. The county zoning administrator, the closest position in the county to a "planning" position, has a degree in soil science, not any land-use planning-related discipline, and works mostly on permit approvals. Yet most responsibility and power still rests with the fourteen townships, each governed by an elected council. Morrie was chairman of Buffalo Township for five years, his father Harry for five years, and his grandfather Thomas for thirty years. Of the fourteen townships, only nine have zoning/land-use plans (four added them in the 1990s), and these are relatively simple, concentrating on lot size and usage restrictions. Three townships have no controls on land division or development beyond minimum lot size (30,000 square feet) set by septic tank requirements. And two townships are in the midst of the controversial process of writing them. Buffalo Township has no controls, though the debate has begun. In many parts of the county you can still subdivide your property into five-acre lots by right—basically without question. The debate grows over fundamental questions about the future: What type of community do they want to be? What type of people do they want as their neighbors and seasonal visitors? What type of economy do they favor? And what type of landscape do they envision? The actions they take or don't take now on adopting land-use controls will shape the answers to these questions. John Muir's East Lothian Old World home grapples with the same questions. However, their land-use controls differ dramatically, as do the results.

Premanufactured homes pose a particularly tough land-use dilemma in Marquette County. Mobile homes have been popular in the area for years. They're inexpensive, convenient for seasonal use, and until recently weren't specifically regulated as long as they met minimum dwelling-unit size requirements—at least 18 feet wide and containing at least 900 square feet. Consequently, they're nearly as plentiful in the area as fixed-site homes. Most of the eight hundred or so sanitary (septic tank) permits granted annually over the past half dozen years have been for manufactured housing. With rapidly escalating house prices, "double-wides" are becoming even more popular, particularly with first-time home buyers who work locally in lower-paying rural jobs. As little as $60,000 to $80,000 buys a nice double-wide, half the cost now for a small fixed-site home. Plus they're movable and much easier to set up than building a new home on-site. The problem with mobile homes for some residents and county officials is aesthetic. Trailers, even handsome double-wides, have a different appearance than fixed-site homes. Perhaps, some people claim, they also don't wear as well over time and aren't in general as well maintained. Some of the opposition might be social too. Many people attach a stigma to trailers and their occupants—suspect housing sheltering suspect people as if they were vagabonds or gypsies. East Lothian has a similar problem and similar stigmas, though the response there differs.

Marquette County struggles as well with environmental issues, best seen in the debate over its many marshes. Protection and restoration of wetlands has been an important national environmental goal for the past twenty-five years. The result: "swampbuster" provisions to stop the draining of wetlands for agriculture and "no net loss" provisions to replace wetlands destroyed by real estate development. Many recreational enthusiasts, commuters, and retirees in Marquette County favor conservation programs to protect marshes since they hunt and fish on them. Some farmers oppose the programs since they crop or pasture the rich organic soil once it is drained. John Muir's experience over a hundred years ago trying to protect his beloved meadow foreshadowed the dilemma.

Until recently the government supported and often subsidized draining wetlands to bring more land into cultivation. Unproductive waste land, according to the prevailing wisdom, though if drained it could yield plentiful crops. Thinking changed in the past generation, splitting public opinion. Government programs now pay to restore the wetlands, the same wasteland previous programs helped drain during the 1940s and 1950s to boost crop production. On one hand, some muck farmers who have drained their wetlands, cropped it, and in some cases polluted or depleted it sell use-easements to the federal government's wetland reserve program for $1,000 per acre. The farmer still owns the property but must restore the wetland. He then sells the wetland to hunting and fishing enthusiasts who pay handsomely for high-quality sporting habitat. Other farmers cringe at the idea of converting productive land back into waste land. "It looks ridiculous to me," said one farmer whose family had worked the land here since before the Muirs arrived. He seethed at the idea that the Wisconsin Department of Natural Resources was buying farmland to restore the wetlands. "What good is it compared to useful, productive farmland?" he asked. "Why waste perfectly good land and flood it with shallow water?" The one common thread among the points of view I heard was the perception of land as mostly a commodity, a thing to be bought and sold, something to be managed as an asset, whether for farming, fishing, or hunting.

Morrie and Mary see it that way too, though I suspect they also have other feelings for it. The land is a way of life for them, and Hickory Hill is their home in a sense that I cannot fully comprehend. My experience of moving repeatedly makes it difficult for me to understand the meaning of home to them. "I can't imagine living in a city," Mary said. Her voice is one of those that instantly cheer you up and make you a friend. Her personality does too. Her feelings for the land are inextricably linked to her feelings for the family. With most of her siblings and children nearby, "which is nice," she said, "I can never imagine what it would be like to see your family just a couple times a year." She'd miss the grandkids most, if she ever moved. However, nothing could replace the farm. "We always stayed home" when she was growing up on a nearby farm, she told me, "we did everything together. We went to church, we never went anywhere; people just worked. Sunday people rested." Spring is her favorite season, but she rarely has time to enjoy it. "Winter used to be good because you could rest more, but now you don't do that because you're so busy." Do the kids feel the same about the land, I wondered. "Oh, the boys, yes. They love the farm; the girls less so, but they love to visit," Mary replied. What about the new people living along Grouse Road, I asked. Do they feel the same about the land? "I don't think so," she responded, "they have to work the land to appreciate it."

I left Morrie and Mary standing with the dogs beside *their* home, not the Muir house, and drove down the hill a quarter mile to Grouse Road. I stopped at the bottom of the gravel drive to take some pictures and linger awhile. For some unknown reason I just wasn't ready to leave. Morrie and Mary would eat dinner and resume their day. Mary would resume her household chores. Morrie would put back on the mud- and manure-caked boots and go back to work with the dogs at his side. Somehow the visit wasn't what I expected and I hadn't worked out in my mind how or why. Now, nine months later in Scotland, I think I know.

I expected them to talk at length about the land and their deep emotional attachment to it that arose from the family's 130 years at Hickory Hill; instead they talked more about family. I expected them to tell me about the many special places they have around the farm, places where they go to escape and refresh;

instead they talked about the practical, workaday world. I hoped
to hear stories of Hickory Hill farm lore passed from generation
to generation; instead they spoke of farm economics and changes
in crops and stock over the years. I expected they would bristle at
the changing land use and dwindling farm community along
Grouse Road; instead they neither romanticized the past nor
eagerly embraced the future. And I expected the farm to be more
modern and somehow more intensive; instead I was struck by its
sense of tradition and informality. Morrie talked a lot about the
Amish. Now I see that the Kearns are a throwback to an earlier,
mostly lost way of life, one centered on family in a different way
than I know. Their linkage to the land and feeling for place can't
be separated from their family ties. It was certainly that way for
John Muir. Family ties and feeling for place *are* inextricably
linked, enriched by the length of residency. Each complements
and enhances the other.

[1 3]

Time is at the heart of the matter. How we conceive of it has
much to do with our ability to set down roots. Westerners, I
think, have a rather narrow and linear sense of time, especially
Americans, since as a culture we have no history when time was
considered differently. Indians do; so do many Eastern and Asian
cultures. Even our Old World origins retain remnants in their
contemporary cultures of an alternative view of time. The Scots
do. Time merely flows by like water in a stream for most Americans. It comes; it goes. What's in the past we know only through
direct experience or the historical record, and we're incapable of
foreseeing what lies ahead. History for us is the story of time.
However, if you change your concept of time slightly, your sense
of history and your ability to know the landscape and set down
roots change dramatically. Fran Sprain and Ken Soda showed

me this. For them time is also accumulative, like water pouring into a bucket rather than simply rushing downstream. History becomes alive and ever present; it becomes the story of place. And place fills with the ghosts of the past. Past, present, and future fuse to form a seamless whole.

Everywhere Fran goes in the county she bumps into the past and sees its ghosts. She recorded them in a popular column she wrote weekly for seventeen years in the *Marquette County Tribune;* not supernatural ghosts, rather the stories of people, events, and things that combine to make place. She wrote of John Muir, Harry Kearns, Observatory Hill, and the Wee White Kirk. She also wrote of Louise Kempley's turkeys and Clara Herman's chickens. She told the story of the Brakebush brothers' poultry plant and Westfield's farm dairies. She described the smallpox epidemic of 1873, the Westfield fire of 1880, the mad dog of 1908, and little settlements that came and went. She wrote of hotels, breweries, mills, stores, schools, churches, and the cast of everyday characters that make a community—hundreds of stories, some collected and republished in three paperback volumes titled *Places and Faces in Marquette County, Wisconsin.* Taken individually, the stories are quaint and full of local color and charm. Taken collectively, they're much more. Collectively, they transcend the mere recording of historical fact and personal recollection to make history and place come alive. Fran now lives in a world crowded with all these memories—all these ghosts. Past and present fused; the future foreshadowed.

Her family (the Russells) emigrated from Northern Ireland in 1848, refugees from the potato famine who came in search of land and opportunity. America won out by one in the family vote over Australia as the destination. The father was a linen weaver who also tenanted a farm that a son worked. The other sons left the land, as did so many Scots in search of their futures; too little land for too many sons. She suspects the family was originally

Highland crofters displaced during the Clearances. Her great-
aunt Nancy recalled the journey from Raleagh, near Ballyna-
hinch, County Down, begun on May 14, 1848. Fran retold her
story in a 1986 column.

The pending move reunited the Russells for the first time in
nearly twelve years, since Nancy and her sister had lived with relatives following the death of their mother. Her father and brothers had stayed on the farm. When the family gathered together
before departure, Nancy, then seventeen years old, was made
responsible for packing the clothing, including her father's thirty
white linen shirts, the bedding, and the provisions. She baked
loaves of bread at home, then had them rebaked in a commercial
oven to make them hard and dry for the six-week ship voyage.
Aboard ship, the family was permitted a fire once a day to make
tea, weather permitting. The strawberry jam Nancy brought in
her basket lasted only a week. On arrival in New York harbor, she
was so thin and weak after weeks of seasickness that the immigration inspectors tried to turn her away. Her towering father
objected, intimidating the inspectors. They relented on condition that she never become a public charge.

The Russells made their way to Albany, then to Buffalo via the
Erie Canal, the same route of the Muirs and thousands of other
immigrants. Nancy walked on the towpath with the horses much
of the way, for even the gentle motion of the canal "line boat"
made her nauseated. The family paused near Buffalo for two years,
staying with relatives on a farm to learn the trade, living in a
small town named Westfield. Two brothers continued westward
to Marquette County, where they walked the land with a spade
until they found a wooded, fertile spot on a flat in the west-
central part of the county. Five years later a tiny hamlet named
Westfield was platted northeast of the flat. The brothers readied
the new farm in Wisconsin while the family remained in New
York. On April 15, 1850, the Russells left one Westfield for the

other: by steamboat across the Great Lakes to Milwaukee, by horse team to Watertown, and by oxen team to Westfield, arriving at their New World farm southwest of the hamlet on the morning of the twenty-eighth. Ever since, the area has been known as "Russell Flats" and has been home to descendants of Nancy's family.

The two brothers had built a crude shanty for the family near a spring in the woods. Nancy kept house, such as it was. They survived on cornmeal and wild game until the first crop of potatoes was harvested that fall. By then a log cabin had been built; windows were added by spring. Unfortunately, the cabin sat right on an Indian trail, forcing travelers to walk around the obstacle. This irritated the Indians, who would physically bump into the cabin, perhaps in protest, before sidestepping the structure blocking their way. Nancy recalled they sometimes snooped a bit about the cabin and took great fancy to a mirror she had hung outside by the washbasin. The Indians would pass the mirror around, laughing at the strange images that looked back at them.

The men worked the fields, wheat at first, and Nancy kept house. As Fran wrote, "Nancy dried apples and corn, filled crocks with lard and salt pork, and churned her own butter. Chicken and eggs were eaten sparingly as they could be sold in exchange for flour, sugar and tea. She gathered hickory nuts, blackberries, plums, and grapes, asparagus and dandelion greens. She made soap and candles, and stuffed feather pillows and straw ticks. She washed her father's shirts and battled the bed bugs that were tenants of every log cabin. Years later, when she wanted a new dress, and her husband couldn't spare the team, she left dinner in the oven, walked 12 miles through the woods to Montello to buy her dress goods, and was home in time to get supper." Pioneer life and the farm life that followed was a team effort between husband and wife, father and mother, man and woman, parents and children.

Now nearly eighty years old herself, Fran and her husband sold the last of their cropland last week, keeping just thirteen acres around the home. "It's like a death," she told me in her gentle voice. "I felt a great loss. I lost my roots; I've been cut off." Her voice quivered. They know the remainder will go soon. "I have a real affection for it," she told me. "We live on the top of a hill and have a beautiful view. Every morning when I look out I think to myself, I don't know how I can stand to give it up."

Fran lived away from Russell Flats for about fifteen years while she went to college and married. The couple returned to help her father. The farm they took over was the original Russell farm on the Flats—Nancy's home. "When I got there, I felt like I was back where I belonged," she remembered. "So I hadn't lost my bond here even in the years I'd been gone." She recalled walking in the woods where Nancy's cabin had been, and where the springs were that the Russells had depended on, and the ford where they crossed the creek. "All those things meant so much to me, and they still do," she said. "But we don't live there anymore; we moved to a different farm a few miles away."

Her brother is selling the home farm. He'll be the last Russell on it, she says. His children pursued other careers. Relatives remain in the area but the family is gradually breaking up and moving off: a sister lives in Colorado and the other in southern Wisconsin. Her other brother lives in Milwaukee and is about to move to Colorado as well. The land means less to them, Fran thinks. None share her sense of history or her emotional bond to the area. Her children have all gone their different ways too, though she's sure the farm on which they were raised remains home to them. Can people who live in cities and suburbs form the same bond to the "old neighborhood" as rural people form for their farms, I asked. "I'm sure they can," she said, "if they live in a place long enough."

We spoke while sitting on a picnic table shaded by mulberry

and black walnut trees in the rear garden of the Cochrane–Nelson House Museum. Harry Cochrane built the handsome two-story wood-framed house in 1903. His father, Robert Cochrane, was a pioneer from Westfield, New York, who built a mill in 1850 on the creek that runs past the back of the property. Robert owned the land from which Westfield, Wisconsin, was platted on the opposite side of the creek. Tomorrow I'll return for the annual Strawberry Sociable held under the trees. Fran has volunteered countless hours to the museum and the historical society. It's another of her legacies.

She remembers when there were more trees on the Flats and the tornadoes that blew many down fifty years ago. She remembers friendly Indians from nearby villages visiting with baskets. One old woman frequently visited her father's two elderly aunts, the three ladies becoming good friends. The Indian woman would stay the night, sleeping on the parlor floor, refusing a bed. "I often feel sad that their culture was wiped out so quickly," Fran confessed. "One hundred years isn't very long and there's not a sign of them around anymore, not a sign of how they lived or where they lived, just a few mounds in the woods." She remembers the Great Depression in the 1930s: putting cardboard in the bottom of their worn shoes, her parents cashing in the life insurance policy and taking out the phone, yet they always had food from the farm—sheep, pigs, chickens, beef and dairy cows, corn, alfalfa, and the big vegetable garden. Once when she needed a prom dress, her father sold a cow to buy the dress. "What a sacrifice," she said, upwelling with emotion. "A cow produces so much milk and butter, and income. When I think of the things they did like that and never said anything to me. I didn't know what it meant. It breaks my heart to think of it now." When she and her husband ran a farm later, she learned. At the end, their 160-acre farm specialized in hogs, but it wasn't a large enough operation to be very profitable. Its sale to another farmer brought relief to be free of the burden mixed with regret at giving up the land.

Do men and women have different feelings for the land, I asked. "No, not out here, not in the rural community," she replied. She never worked in the fields; some farm women do, some don't. The division of labor and gender roles vary somewhat from farm to farm and over time on a farm, although almost always within the context of teamwork. Everyone focuses on the farm and family. "Perhaps the feelings differ between men and women who live in town," she thought. "There, men and women may have different interests that take them in different directions."

I asked if she felt the sense of community had changed in the area over her lifetime. "Oh yes," she responded. "When we were bringing up our children, and before that when I was growing up, you knew every child in the neighborhood and you were free to go and visit anyone. The school was the center of the community. The whole community came there to be together, to do things together and hear things together. There was a big 4-H club on the Flats and all the neighborhood kids were in it. Today there's a 4-H club called 'Russell Flats' and it's not even on the Flats and it doesn't have a Russell Flats person in it." Other long-time residents I spoke with felt similarly. But I've heard the same lament in suburbs and cities. "The people don't know each other, the neighbors don't know each other," she continued. "In the days when we were working with horses and even early with tractors, farmers helped each other. Now they hire people to come in with the big combines to do the work and they're gone. You don't have to feed them, you don't have to socialize with them or do anything with them but pay them and let them go. It's a whole different feeling now," she said. As a result, she feels people are more disconnected from one another, from the community, and from place. One's neighbors might be newcomers who work in a variety of occupations—postal worker, truck driver, electronics business—and have little feeling for the land, from her perspective, little community pride or sense of doing things together.

Who buys your books, I asked. Local folks, she replied, mostly older ones, people looking back to childhood, people who remember the places and faces she describes. "Anybody who gets to be fifty or sixty begins to look back and then this feeling of place and history begins to take hold of them," she said. "That's how history gets passed from one generation to another." None of her children—now middle-aged adults—are interested in it, but she trusts the time will come when they'll begin to ask questions about the family, so their history will be carried on.

Most people in the area arrived in recent years. Many of the elderly newcomers also have an interest in the local history, she noted. Some are now stalwarts of the historical society and museum. Few members are native to the place; few have roots as deep as her roots.

Why is place of so little interest to most people, I wondered. Why isn't it more central to our lives? "When I look back, I didn't think much about history class in high school," she noted, "although we had a wonderful teacher who told good stories of Abraham Lincoln and others. It didn't mean much to me. I didn't listen to my teachers or my dad when he used to talk about old times. I'd heard all that before. And I thought I'd remember it." We're too busy with our lives and families for such matters, she thinks. We're too materialistic and have little direct dependency on the land. "When we depended on the land, we appreciated it more." Still, she's optimistic about people rediscovering the importance of place in the future. A local sixth-grade boy works at the museum and shares Fran's sense of time and place. His family moved to the area just a decade or so before. "When I hear our little Tim, I just hope there're more like him; but he wishes more kids in his school were interested in history. He seems to feel pretty much alone."

Fran sees time and history differently than most people, enabling her to see the ghosts of Marquette County all around her. "When I started my research twenty years ago for my newspaper articles," she said, "there were so many good old-timers to talk to; they're gone now." Thankfully, Fran was there to hear their stories.

The Sodas also know the currents and eddies of time swirling about their farm. Sixty-eight-year-old Ken is the fourth generation there. He and his wife, Eunice, live in a modern home encircled by a pine stand they planted on a knoll overlooking the property. They picked out the site for their retirement home in 1965 and began work preparing it then. Their two sons, Steve and Kevin, both live on the farm with their families. Kevin's comfortable house was built from logs cut on-site. The seven grandchildren are the sixth generation on the farm. Ken's great-grandparents homesteaded the original 160-acre quarter section on arrival from Prussia in 1862. The farm has passed from one generation to the next every forty years since great-grandfather Stefan transferred the property to his son Frank in 1875. Ken took responsibility for the farm from his father in 1955 and deeded it to his sons in 1995. "You have to let the kids leave their mark on the land instead of running the farm until you're too old and they're too old," he said.

It's a big, profitable operation now, nearly 1,200 acres in total, although several hundred acres are rented from eight nearby farms. They have a signed contract with only one owner and that's because it's a corporation. The economics currently favor renting versus buying. They can no longer justify the purchase price of additional acreage given assessed values, mortgage rates, and commodity prices. If equipment prices continue to escalate faster than income, they won't be able to depreciate the cost of new equipment the next time they need to replace it. The future is uncertain for them despite their success. But they can't imagine selling off parcels to cover costs.

The Soda farm is a model of technical prowess and innovation, and Ken has been invited to countries around the world as an agricultural adviser. He seems suited to that—he has a bit of an evangelical zeal for farming and a well-developed philosophical framework that he's eager to share. His passion and beliefs bubble forth when he speaks, his compact frame and round face alive with energy. Yet the Sodas keep untouched a 40-acre stand of valuable white pines in the middle of their property. They hunt in the stand and have thinned it a bit, but otherwise leave it alone. Why? Because Ken likes to stand among the ferns, looking upward into the swaying tree canopy, listening to the soft melody sung by the gentle breeze. "When the wind is whispering in the pines," he told me, "it's like a little heaven." Family and place, time and history, past, present, and future intertwine on the Soda farm as tightly as those white pine branches.

Great-grandfather Stefan Zoda was a tenant farmer who fled the civil wars in central Europe and came to America in search of land like thousands of displaced Germans and Poles. The family entered the New World through Quebec, since American ports were closed due to the civil war here. From there they crossed the Great Lakes to Milwaukee and made their way to northeast Marquette County. Other emigrants from their home province of Posin had preceded them to the area around the village of Princeton and had written home of its suitability. The sandy soil and the rolling, partly wooded uplands were similar to their Old World farms so they knew how to work the land. Like their countrymen, both old and new, the Zodas bypassed other more fertile places to stake a claim to land that felt familiar. They selected a vacant quarter in Section 8, Township 16, Range 11, along a southerly-facing slope overlooking a small valley with readily available water from the stream that flowed through the marshy bottomlands at the foot of the hill. A small registration payment was made according to the procedures of the Homestead Act and the Zodas set to work making a new home. Five years later, Stefan's claim was "patented"—he received clear title to the land—and changed the family name to Soda.

President Abraham Lincoln considered the Homestead Act of 1862 one of his administration's most important achievements. The act granted title to 160 acres of the public domain to anyone—man or woman, citizen, or alien—over twenty-one years of age for $1.25 per acre after six months' occupancy or for only a registration fee of about $30 following a five-year occupancy. Occupancy meant the construction of a house and the cultivation of a minimum percentage of the acreage, reflecting the deep-rooted philosophical basis of ownership founded on "occupancy" and "improvement" of the land. To people here and abroad the Homestead Act represented the essence of America—land and opportunity. Free land! For anyone! What could be more American?

The Homestead Act's impact transcended its actual effects on the land to become a part of America's western settlement mythos—homesteading became one of the central defining images of America. It remains so today. Part fact and part fiction, the mythos depicted the western settlement process as one in which hearty, intrepid pioneers set off across the endless sea of the Great Plains in fleets of "prairie schooners." It represented who we were and what we wanted to be in a romanticized, self-congratulatory way: cowboys with cattle and settlers with crops, windmills, barbed wire, and railroads, overcoming Indians and bison, prairie dogs, and big bluestem to achieve their manifest destiny. The homestead and western settlement myths told of immigrants scratching the tough, dry soils to make a living in the desolate plains of North Dakota and Nebraska. It told of humble common folk persevering over the harshness of nature, conquering the wilderness, and building a country.

Frederick Jackson Turner gave the mythos academic credibility in perhaps the most famous and influential paper ever presented by an American historian. His "Frontier Thesis" took the academic world by storm after its presentation in 1893 at the Columbian Exposition in Chicago. The thirty-two-year-old professor from the University of Wisconsin, who grew up in Portage only fifteen miles from the Muirs, proposed that this settlement process gave rise to those values and institutions that most defined and differentiated America from its European roots. Like the myth, his enticing thesis was partly true; both overlooked the story of America's eastern settlement.

President Lincoln's signing of the Homestead Act into law on May 20 represented many myths of the past: the Jeffersonian infatuation with the noble yeoman civilizing a vacant virgin paradise to create a republican nation of small farms; the perception of the West as the release valve for eastern urban tensions as the hordes of poor residents and new immigrants crowding in eastern cities find freedom, prosperity, and virtue in western landownership; and the suitability of eastern-style land settlement practices and policies for the western landscape—the Land Ordinance, row cropping, and water laws. Lincoln's action culminated a complicated political process played out over several years.

The Republicans promoted the act as a means of garnering desperately needed political support for the war effort from people who stood to benefit from more rapid western settlement. That expansion had slowed in the mid-1800s as pioneers encountered the difficulties of the plains and prairies. Many people felt additional incentives were needed to spur the process. Eastern urbanites supported the plan as a means of accommodating the shiploads of immigrants pouring into the major ports. They hoped the plan would reduce the teeming overcrowding and the resulting social problems in the urban centers by drawing off the poor to the nation's heartland. Long-standing opposition from the southern states in part out of fear that the program favored formation of "free" rather than "slave" states became moot due to their secession.

The Homestead Act's principal incentive was cost: one could acquire a quarter section nearly for free as the act dropped the minimum sales price originally established by Jefferson's Land Ordinance. Proponents argued that the spin-off revenues generated by the more rapid settlement would more than replace the federal revenues lost from discontinuing fee simple sale. Land was America's principal resource, its principal currency, and its principal wealth, and the government again used its distribution as a means to direct the nation's physical and social development. The national land survey system—the grid—remained the framework for that distribution. Its procedures continued to serve as the means of parceling the wilderness into property, perpetuating the perception of land as merely a commodity where one piece was little different from another.

Consistent with the history of land distribution, rampant abuse and land speculation plagued the Homestead Act and the land laws that followed it. Most of these laws assisted big business more than the yeoman. Generous government land grants to states and companies complicated the dispersal of the public domain, as did other, often overlapping or contradictory means of legal and illegal land acquisition. In short, the process remained a tangled mess. Government was unable or unwilling to effectively reform it. Little had changed in the seventy-five years since the Land Ordinance. While up to 90 percent of the land claims made under the various Homestead Act programs were likely fraudulent, the government's general purposes were achieved as millions of people moved west onto the plains and prairies. Unfortunately, few homesteads were patented as nearly two-thirds of the homesteaders failed and returned east due to the unsuitable conditions for eastern-style land use. New land-use practices based on western realities would eventually open the plains to more settlement, but until they did no more than 400,000 families, about 2 million people, patented their homestead claims between the 1860s and 1900s. During the same period, the total U.S. population more than doubled to 76 million. The overwhelming majority of people remained in the East and the population of major cities like New York swelled. Yet the Homestead Act worked as intended for the Sodas.

Initially they grew wheat and raised a few dairy cows. The herd size gradually increased to about twenty head by 1900, though there was little market for dairy products due to the lack of refrigeration. The products had to be used on the farm or sold in the fresh market. And milk production per cow was low and the technology for separating butterfat and making other by-products was primitive. Like most farms in the region, the Soda farm remained a "sustainable," integrated operation that required few inputs from off the farm, mostly granulated sugar or molasses. Otherwise the farm produced all the food for the family and stock and recycled all the field and barn "waste." A few products were traded or sold for cash money to satisfy household needs. Little was wasted and little was needed.

By the 1920s, changes were under way. Use of better feed crops like clover and alfalfa hay raised milk yields, and hybrid seeds raised crop yields. More widespread refrigeration and improved transportation made dairy products more marketable and a number of technological innovations made production of dairy products more economical. The Soda farm gradually enlarged its dairying operation as a result. In the 1950s, the Sodas tilled and drained the marshlands to bring them into crop production, but the farm remained very diversified: dairy cows, hogs, chickens, geese, sheep, with twenty acres of grain and twenty-five acres of corn as feed for the stock, and the remaining lowlands in hay and pasture. However, everyone else was raising the same crops and stock. Ken sensed the potential limits in this.

Adaptability, he told me, is the key to success. "You've got to do something harder than the normal farmer wants to do—more difficult—otherwise they overload the market so fast. It has got to be more specialized and harder to do. That's the way it has got to be if you want to make a go of it in this business." Mint became his niche.

It began on the advice of an agriculture professor who conducted on the farm training sessions in the mid-1950s for older farmers who couldn't go to college. Ken's GI benefits from his Korean War service paid him ninety dollars per month for the training in lieu of GI college benefits. The first year he planted just five acres. He soon found the unusual crop was two or three times more profitable than corn, though much harder to handle, requiring specialized equipment that you had to fabricate yourself to plant, harvest, and distill the crop on a commercial scale. "You have to build it in the shop and that's what we did," he said. No equipment manufacturer made it. He designed the equipment in his head and cannibalized parts from old tractors to construct it. The acreage in mint gradually expanded as he improved his mint-farming technique and jerry-rigged the required implements. Today mint has driven off the livestock. The farm is much larger and more specialized. This season the Sodas are growing 320 acres of spearmint and peppermint, 500 acres of cash corn, 150 acres of cash soybeans, and 150 acres of clover, vetch, and other crops to rebuild soil fertility on worn-out fields. Until several years ago, they also raised chickens, producing half the eggs in the county. But that market became saturated too, so they adapted again, converting the large coop to a new use: growing yellow perch.

The Sodas now raise 11,000 fingerlings in huge tanks. Nine to twelve months later the fish are marketable. With fillets selling for $9 per pound at the farm and $14 in the stores, and with depleted yields from the Great Lakes due to pollution and other causes, the market seems ripe. Part of the fish waste is recycled on the fields. It's been three years of trial and error, as it was for mint. They had to discover an optimum feeding regimen and again jerry-rig construction of the required equipment, including the huge tanks and a precise biofiltration system to remove ammonia and reoxygenate the delicate water composition. Two-thirds of the first "crop" died. Now they think they've debugged the process.

"Land is a living thing," Ken told me as we toured the impressive farm—neat, carefully organized, modern, more so than most farms I'd seen. Scientifically based. Cleverly engineered. "It's a living entity that I don't want to abuse. We take what nature gives us," he said in his bubbly voice. "I can leave the land better. I always try to make it better than the year before." He sees the land partly as a production unit and partly as a spiritual element. "Winter is the time to inhale," he said. "When springtime comes and all through the summer, we exhale. When fall comes, we start pulling back in. These are the four seasons and how they revolve and recycle. We inhale; we exhale, just like biodynamics, one of the things we also practice." We wandered through the three giant buildings that hold the shop, a collection of historical farm equipment beside the rows of huge new tractors, combines, and planters, and the mint-drying and distillation facility. Steve was at work in the shop. Kevin was driving a four-wheel ATV around the central yard with his son on his lap. The other kids played about the buildings on toy tractors. Everyone except Ken's wife, Eunice, gathered for a group photo. We would chat shortly when Ken and I joined her up the hill at their home. Ken thought they'd go dancing tonight.

I asked Kevin and Steve how they felt about the farm. Ken

stepped aside to let us talk. "Freedom," responded Kevin. "You can do what you want." Steve listened and nodded. They said they felt a longing for the farm if gone only half a day. "Why would I want to go somewhere else, Kevin continued. "I'm happy here. People today focus on possessions. They look at the land for how much money they can make from it, rather than what it can do for them. You can't put a value on the land." Do you feel the same about the land you rent, I asked. No, they responded. Do you think a fifth-generation resident of Manhattan, New York, has the same connection to place as a fifth-generation resident of a farm near Manhattan, Kansas? Does your sense of connection to the land stem from the act of farming or your legacy here, I asked. "The city person doesn't own Manhattan or make a living off the land. We do," they answered. Most everything Kevin and Steve need and want is on their property. They seem unbothered by there being few thirty-to-forty-year-old peers who farm to socialize with. They know the land intimately; it's a part of them in a way I can scarcely fathom. They buy no meat and few groceries. Each shoots three deer a year for venison from the hundreds on the farm. "The deer nip the first eight to twelve rows of our corn and we eat the deer," they said. Seems like a fair trade. They shoot wild turkeys, too, from the hundreds that threaten to overrun the place.

Eunice met Ken and me at the door of their home atop the hill. We sat on a garden bench in the yard, warmed by the glorious afternoon sun. She has a soft, quiet manner and shares Ken's passion for the land. "It's life. It's sustenance," she said, spiritual and physical. "We get our life from it, not just our livelihood." She grew up on a farm but rarely worked in the fields and never milked cows. Eunice is related by marriage to Morrie and Mary Kearns—her brother is married to Morrie's sister. All her siblings live close by and have a strong feeling for the land, she thinks. She misses the family most when they travel. Ken was the only boy in his family. His sisters moved to the city and never had any real interest in the land, he said.

Ken and I headed out across the fields in his late-model pickup. We crossed the mint fields and stopped to walk into the white pine stand. It was still and quiet. The diffused light cascading down through the canopy gave the stand an almost spiritual glow. I asked if he had any other special places on the farm. He hesitated, and asked if I'd ever seen a medicine wheel. No, I responded as we drove off toward another pine stand across the way. In the middle of the stand Ken had arranged soccer-ball-sized boulders to form a wheel sixty-four feet in diameter with an inner ring fourteen feet in diameter. The wheel had nineteen spokes radiating out from the hub, which was located on what once was an anthill. There, he told me this story, not sure how I'd respond.

"Several years ago I was in Ohio and met a Canadian clairvoyant named Ken Killick. We spoke on the phone sometime later and he started telling me all about the farm even though he'd never been here. 'Well,' Ken Killick said, 'you have a spot out there to the west of your buildings in a little grove where you can put a medicine wheel. Send me an aerial photo and I'll show you.' So I did and he sent back a professional-looking overlay to the photo that located this spot, but I didn't do anything about it.

"Several months later a friend of his, who was a dowser, came through the area. So we went out to find the spot. We walked into this stand and he said we're getting close. His two 'L' rods soon crossed atop the anthill, a 'negative' point, he called it. So with his assistance, the boys and I set up a tripod and laid out each spoke on a different compass orientation. Another dowser visited the spot with me later and explained, 'You've got energy flows coming in and out of the spot. The energy flows are the ley lines of the land.' We constructed the wheel with rocks based on those lines.

"Ken Killick later explained all this to me over the phone. He said we had one ley line that went from this spot, through the forty-acre white pine stand, to the river. But the map I gave him didn't have the river on it and I'd never mentioned the river. How'd he know that? 'Actually,' he said, 'there're six Indians who died of smallpox in 1887 buried in the woods, right over top of the line.' Oh? That was the first time I'd ever heard of them, even though those woods are right next to our property.

"Well, one day sometime later, a neighbor's mother was visiting from Florida and said she remembered when she was young that the kids used to drive cattle through those woods. She said there used to be a marker in them. Her dad told the kids not to disturb the place because Indians were buried there. So Steve, Kevin, and I went and found the place, too. We've never disturbed it."

Ken Killick believes that once the energy flows are balanced on the spot of the medicine wheel, the place will become serene; good things will happen there and radiate outward along the ley lines off into the landscape. Some people sense the serenity when they visit the medicine wheel, Ken Soda said. He does, somewhat. I wanted to, but wasn't sure whether I had. Perhaps Ken somehow senses that flow of positive energy along the ley line that passes through the forty-acre white pine stand. Perhaps that's why he finds the place so soothing. Lightning has struck the stand around the medicine wheel four times that Ken remembers, apparently attracted to the spot's negative energy before the energy flows were balanced by the medicine wheel. One tree has been struck twice, he stated. Yet, inexplicably, the twisted tree lives. Are there aspects of the landscape that our Western way of thinking blinds us to? Does our modern technology and sense of environmental dominion shield us from forces and sensations other cultures experience, including our Old World ancestors and our New World predecessors? Ken noted, "We're living things within a community. If we can keep the community going, we'll have time to grow spiritually, provided we don't get too big and lose sight of what's important in life." Connection to place forms gradually over time spent in that place, he told me. Like Fran, he showed me a sense of time and place I hadn't known before.

[14]

I drive onto the Ho-Chunk powwow grounds several miles east of Black River Falls, Wisconsin, feeling out of place and very conspicuous. I have little experience being a minority. Spectators park in a grassy field right off Highway 54. Three men, presumably Ho-Chunks, sitting on folding chairs by the gravel entrance keep an eye on traffic. Their stares follow me as I pass. Participants park their conversion vans, campers, pickups, and RVs closer to the powwow arena and the surrounding food stands and booths selling Indian crafts. Many of the vehicles have brand names borrowed from Indian words—Cherokee, Navajo, Winnebago. Others have names borrowed from words with western-related meanings—Bronco, Durango, Tahoe. Perhaps the makers feel their customers associate Indian words with a fabled free-roaming lifestyle of holiday ramblers or that customers relate in some way to imagery of the nation's romanticized western settlement myth. Turner's Frontier Thesis is alive and well with Madison Avenue advertising executives and American consumers. I find lots of ironies here. My visits with the Ho-Chunks would be filled with them. The powwow grounds stand on sandy soils at the edge of young piney woods that lend this landscape the same messy, disturbed look as the piney woods along the Atlantic coast. No admission or parking fee; everyone is welcome. I've come early, not knowing what to expect. This is my first powwow. The Grand Entry begins in an hour at one o'clock.

I left my motel at the Black River Falls interchange by the interstate around 9:00 A.M. this Sunday morning to have a look around the area before the opening ceremonies of the annual Labor Day gathering. Another gathering is held annually on Memorial Day. The Arrowhead Lodge resembles many throughout the western United States with its pseudo-Indian motif and decorations, inside and out, and quaint western or Indian names for the function rooms and restaurants. Many of the guests are whites who've come from their suburban homes for a weekend of gaming at the casino or for outdoor recreation fishing or roaring around the woods on the many nearby ATV and dirt bike trails. Do they know that the Ho-Chunks inhabited all this land for centuries before whites forcibly evicted them in the 1830s? The local white residents must know this. The tourists probably don't. They've come to play. Regardless, neither group likely cares. For most of us, the natives are invisible. They've always been to me. Indians inhabited my central Ohio homeland before white settlement cast them aside in the late 1700s. Place names recall their presence but I don't know what the names mean and never noticed any descendants of the indigenous people in the community. I've never been to their annual powwows either. For most Americans, the history of place begins when whites settled the area. The Scots speak of their medieval, Roman, Iron Age, Bronze Age, Neolithic, and Mesolithic settlement history. America has a settlement history that ancient too, except we largely ignore it.

The Ho-Chunk tribal headquarters fronts on Airport Road, about a mile from the motel. The wooded area was once a small airport catering to private planes, until the strip was relocated to the west side of town. The site retains the sparse, flat feel of an airport office park. ATV trails cross the road. A prison sits at the end. The new building has the nondescript, anonymous look of a modern office building found anywhere in America: two stories;

boxy shape stripped bare of "bourgeois" ornamentation; and a smooth brick exterior wrapped with two horizontal bands of dark glass windows that screen eyes looking in and out like sunglasses. The seal of the Ho-Chunk Nation hangs above the main entrance. Parking spaces closest to the entrance are reserved for tribal elders. A sign by the doors announces that visitors are subject to the laws and rules of the Ho-Chunk Nation and may be denied access. In some subtle ways visitors leave the regular United States when they drive onto the building's parking lot. This is tribal land, the property of a sovereign nation. I feel more alien here than I did in Scotland.

The Wisconsin Ho-Chunks are one of the few Indian nations recognized by the federal government without a reservation (a branch of the Ho-Chunks removed to Nebraska by the federal government in the 1800s lives on a reservation there). The fact that the federal government "recognizes" Indian nations, as if legitimizing their identity, strikes me as a bit strange given our past efforts to bring about their extinction as distinct societies. I understand the political and practical necessity for the designation today, though the morality escapes me. Like the Muirs, I see no resolution to the conundrum of how the predominant American culture should coexist with the Indian cultures.

Federal recognition of Ho-Chunk sovereignty and their claim to 7 million acres of tribal lands in south-central and western Wisconsin dates to the early 1800s, except the United States rarely treated the Ho-Chunk Nation as a peer. Yet the Ho-Chunks have never been hapless victims. They've always debated among themselves how best to interact with the white world and have chosen the course of action that best balanced the many conflicting circumstances and points of view at the time. The U.S. response to their sovereignty has ebbed and flowed with shifts in economic self-interest and general policies toward all Indians, especially policies promoting assimilation versus removal and relocation to reservations. At times the federal government has promoted tribal sovereignty, self-sufficiency, and self-governance, and supported the consolidation of land over which the tribe would have full jurisdiction. At other times the government has sought to displace and disperse the tribe in an effort to force their assimilation into mainstream American society, based on the assumption that Indians would eventually cease to exist as a separate people. Since the 1960s, Ho-Chunk sovereignty has been reaffirmed, although the renewed status brought with it no land to replace the millions of acres taken fraudulently by the United States. Most of the nearly 10,000 acres of land the Ho-Chunks now own they have purchased fee simple on the open market over the past decade no differently than would any other buyer.

An ironic remnant of their original land claim rests in the final line of the infamous 1837 treaty in which they relinquished the last of their land to the United States. The inconspicuous clause grants the Ho-Chunk Nation the right of first refusal to repurchase surplus federal land that the U.S. government wishes to sell if the land lies within the Ho-Chunks' ancestral territory. I suspect few whites thought the clause significant when the treaty was signed. But the Ho-Chunks' time frame stretches for generations far into the future. Perhaps they foresaw what was unthinkable to the whites at the time—that one day the whites would no longer want the land they had taken. One tribal official told me, "We were here long before the whites came and we'll be here long after they've left." That's a common belief among Indians. In the next year, the Ho-Chunks hope to double their land holdings.

Once the Ho-Chunks acquire a property, they can apply to the U.S. secretary of the interior to designate it as part of their trust. This frees the property from local and state laws and taxes. The secretary grants the designation based on need, primarily economic. Financially secure tribes presumably have no need to be relieved of paying taxes. Public input plays a role as well. Local governments often fight the designation as it removes the property from their tax rolls and places it outside their jurisdiction. Today the Ho-Chunks have little land in trust and little chance to add more. "Sovereignty" for Indian nations has its limits.

Anthropologists, ethnographers, and historians classify the Ho-Chunks as Siouan-speaking members of the Northeastern Woodland Culture Area, closely related linguistically and genetically to the three western Chiwere tribes—Iowa, Oto, and Missouri. They believe the Ho-Chunks were mostly sedentary villagers who lived in substantial rectangular structures in east-central Wisconsin near "Red Banks" (Green Bay) and Lake Winnebago around the time of the first recorded European contact in 1634. The tribe was organized into twelve clans and governed by a complex moiety system with dual chieftains, one governing civil affairs and the other governing criminal affairs and tribal security. The Ho-Chunks grew corn, beans, and squash in large productive gardens and gathered wild foods in the forests and marshes. These they supplemented with fish and game obtained from the surrounding landscape. Hunting parties of able-bodied men and sometimes women set out in dugout canoes down the Fox River and portaged across to the Wisconsin River to travel it and the connecting Black and Mississippi Rivers in search of large game.

European contact quickly changed that lifestyle. Disease decimated the Ho-Chunk population, as would wars triggered by disputes about hunting grounds resulting from the fur trade and conflicts over territorial claims as displaced bands competed for land. In a generation, the Ho-Chunks verged on extinction. To survive, they sought peace, began to intermarry with neighbors and former enemies, and adopted a new, more mobile lifestyle based on extensive fur trading modeled after that of the nearby Algonquians. During the 1700s, the new Ho-Chunks flourished.

By the early 1800s, the reinvigorated Ho-Chunks had dispersed into nearly forty small, seasonally mobile settlements housed in domed huts. They ranged over a triangular-shaped region from Green Bay west to the Mississippi River and south to Rock Island, Illinois, harvesting furs for trade, though they still planted large gardens. Villages varied in size from 100 to 300 residents. A few larger settlements perhaps contained over 1,000 people. Politically, the Ho-Chunks shifted their allegiance to whichever white nation—French, British, or American— dominated local affairs. This period of Ho-Chunk prosperity ended as a consequence of the War of 1812 between the United States and Britain.

American fur interests and settlement pressures surged into the Upper Mississippi Valley in the aftermath of the war, triggering another period of upheaval for the Ho-Chunks. Whites wanted more control of the profitable fur industry. They also discovered lead deposits and other natural resources they wanted. Then they demanded the land itself. So they took it, ostensibly legally via a series of treaties negotiated during the 1820s and 1830s in which the Ho-Chunks "voluntarily" sold their claims to their vast fertile homeland and eventually agreed to relocate westward to relatively small reservations on the Great Plains. No one reading the details of the "negotiations" and treaties today can reasonably conclude that they were fair. The Ho-Chunks were coerced into signing away their heritage, especially in the 1837 treaty that culminated in their removal. The federal government purposely pressured, misled, and lied to the Ho-Chunk negotiators in order to gain their approval of the treaty. The travesty split the tribe into two groups: one group begrudgingly accepted the treaty and the required relocation; the other rejected the agreement and remained behind. The split persists today as the basis for the tribe's two branches, one in Nebraska and the other in Wisconsin.

When the Muirs, Russells, and Sodas arrived in Marquette County, perhaps as few as 2,000 Ho-Chunks remained, most living west of the Mississippi River. Four times during the mid-1800s, the U.S. army hunted down the handful of people remaining in their Wisconsin homeland. The soldiers at times herded those they apprehended into railroad boxcars at gunpoint and shipped them like cattle to the western reservation. But refugees kept returning to their sacred sites, living as fugitives on their ancestral lands, trying to keep a low profile to avoid attracting attention. These were the Ho-Chunks who befriended Nancy Russell and the other pioneers.

In 1875 the federal government gave in, somewhat, accepting the fact of a Ho-Chunk presence in Wisconsin, when it extended the Homestead Act to all Indians if they agreed to abandon tribal affiliations. Assimilation was the goal even though the means used might have been unethical and illegal. Some Ho-Chunks did not apply for the forty-acre "allotments," thinking the plan a ruse to trap them for another removal. Others were too poor to afford construction of even the simple dwelling needed to "prove up" the claim. In 1881 special legislation supplemented the program to make it more viable for them. On the surface the program appeared generous. Each Ho-Chunk family could be granted a forty-acre allotment tax-free and inalienable for twenty-five years. In addition, an annual stipend of $25,000 for twenty-five years was created to help them establish a farm, the funds to be divided among the properties. About 650 Ho-Chunk household heads and adults eventually registered homesteads in Wisconsin.

Beneath the surface, three problems undermined the program. By the 1880s, whites had claimed virtually all the arable land in Wisconsin. Only the unwanted leftover lands—swampy bottomlands and rocky hillsides—remained for the Ho-Chunks, hardly lands suitable for farming. The parcels also lay widely scattered across ten counties, effectively dispersing the Indians among the predominant white population. However, the Ho-Chunks retained much of their traditional village-based lifestyle at the time, so the dispersal threatened those ties and their remaining cultural cohesion. The old Jeffersonian concept of integrating the Indians into the white world as farmers remained even though the concept rarely worked in practice. Lastly, the program put an end to the practice of exempting property held by a sovereign nation from taxes, a practice with constitutional and judicial bases.

Few Ho-Chunks assimilated. When the allotments appeared on the tax rolls in 1906, most Ho-Chunks were unaware or unprepared to pay. Many parcels were forfeited. An eager land company quickly bought up the better ones. When tax-free status was restored to the properties in 1934, it was too late. Most of the land had been lost to whites. Other parcels remaining in Ho-Chunk possession had been split up by inheritance into such small slivers owned by so many people that they were useless and abandoned. Determination of clear legal title on many properties became a tangled mess, and the costs of trying to untangle matters via legal proceedings to restore title to the rightful owners were too high. Today the Ho-Chunks repurchase properties that title searches show once belonged to them and were lost in this confusion.

Some Ho-Chunks in effect became homeless on their former homeland, many living in poverty where for centuries they had flourished, the vanquished in an undeclared war for land between two vastly different worlds. Perhaps that vagueness was the core of the problem. Both cultures had long histories of warfare fought for land. Both knew the old rules: to the victors go the spoils and moral righteousness, then life for the combatants returned more or less to normal. Both prized bravery and honor on the battlefield. Wars had clear beginnings and decisive ends.

But this was different—just gradual attrition with less bravery, less honor, more rationalizations, deceit, and subterfuge. False promises bred faint Indian hopes. Neither side likely relished the new rules, except the rules made "triumph" nearly a certainty for the whites. The Indians had a chance in a declared war with clear consequences fought under the old rules. The new rules, however, placed the whites in a moral dilemma: how to take control of the land legitimately. "Negotiated" treaties were the response. The conundrum made for messy moral quicksand then, as it does today.

The Ho-Chunks are a proud people who care passionately about their culture, their land, and their daily lives. They're survivors too. Buffeted by three hundred years of upheavals since the first white contact, the Ho-Chunks have found a new way after each shift in circumstance. By the 1900s, they'd developed a successful itinerant economy based on selling whites beadwork and basketry and crops grown in small gardens or harvested in the wild, and crops picked seasonally for wages: strawberries and wild blueberries in the spring; cherries in the summer; cranberries, corn, potatoes, peas, and other vegetables in late summer. In the early fall, many families gathered at campsites along the Mississippi River in the La Crosse region, hunting and trapping during the winter. And they gathered to practice the traditional ceremonial cycle, as they had for generations—medicine dances in the summer, when they danced and played lacrosse games at large social gatherings; seasonal war-bundle feasts; and special ceremonies such as wakes and ghost feasts. The cycle provided a continuing source of strength and cohesion, cultural and spiritual.

World War II offered a short period of relative prosperity earned from wage work in defense industries and servicemen's salaries, and it provided a great source of tribal pride as many Ho-Chunks served with distinction in the military, often as volunteers. Circumstances changed again after the war. Increased mechanization reduced the need for crop workers, raising unemployment and poverty. The government also resumed efforts to solve the Indian "problem," made all the more glaring as prosperity swept the rest of the nation in the 1950s, by again adopting the strategy of eliminating Indians as a distinct people. Congress sought to accomplish this using a two-pronged approach to force the Indians to assimilate into mainstream America. The government would terminate reservations and all related federal responsibilities toward the Indians, and it would relocate Indians to urban areas by providing inducements to move. The new initiative reversed the short-lived, sensitive policies established by the Indian Reorganization Act (IRA) of 1934, itself an effort to reverse the destructive effects of nineteenth-century Indian policies, particularly the General Allotment Act of 1887, which was designed to shatter tribal ties by individualizing property ownership and reducing tribal-held reservations. The IRA enabled tribes to adopt constitutions to manage their own affairs; it offered assistance in finding capital to promote economic development; and it provided protection for tribal lands and began efforts to restore reservation land that had been lost or fragmented by allotments. Unfortunately, the onset of the Depression and World War II dampened its promise. After the war, Congress rejected the New Deal ideals of the Roosevelt era and set a new national Indian policy.

The Ho-Chunks survived the latest attack, barely. Bolstered by renewed Indian activism in the early 1960s and the resulting shift in government policy of the Kennedy administration, the Ho-Chunks became the first tribe to reorganize under the IRA provisions since World War II. The reorganization enabled the tribe to acquire land and put it under trust, laying the groundwork for the tribe's current resurgence in the aftermath of a 1987 U.S. Supreme Court decision that upheld the Ho-Chunk Nation's right to regulate gambling/gaming on its property. They also began a remarkable effort to obtain government assistance and recognition of past injustices. Progress has been hard fought. Even today the Ho-Chunks live in an alien world, caught between a past way of life they can't fully abandon and a new way of life they can't fully accept. Ironically, the financial security gained from the casino profits now threatens the Ho-Chunk culture. In the past, poverty in some ways kept the Ho-Chunk people isolated from mainstream America. Now their prosperity has opened the door to the American consumer lifestyle.

There's a fundamental flaw in this historical account, a simple, inescapable flaw that rests at the core of the conundrum: Ho-Chunk culture sits upon a much different foundation than Western cultures. One culture cannot be fully explained or understood within the framework of the other. My Western social sciences classify the Ho-Chunks as "Siouan-speaking members of the Northeastern Woodland Culture Area," but the Ho-Chunks' oral history says that they are a unique people created by the "Earth-maker," not descendants of another more ancient people. They believe themselves to be the parent people of the Sioux, the Oto, the Missouri, the Iowa, and other tribes. I can categorize their language, art, lifestyle, and beliefs and tell their history based on my outsider's view, yet that is a bit unfair for it imposes a framework on them that is derived from different rules. That same analytical framework may work well when applied to another culture predicated on Western precepts, but it loses validity when applied to a culture founded on other precepts. Perhaps it's like trying to explain the Ho-Chunk language using the English language—something subtle yet significant is lost in the translation. How can I know and describe such a different culture in a way that accurately captures its essence? How can the two cultures coexist in time and place? I'm confronted with the same conundrum as the Muirs and the other white settlers 150 years ago. And like them, I see no way out. This limitation became real to me when I went before the "traditional court."

The Ho-Chunk traditional court and tribal court are housed in a low wood-framed building with several trailers attached at the rear another mile out toward the powwow grounds on Highway 54. The traditional court governs cultural matters and the tribal court adjudicates criminal offenses, reminiscent of the dual chieftains. I presented myself before the traditional court on an earlier visit. It happened quite impromptu. I'd written the court months before to introduce myself and explain my desire to speak with members of the tribe. No response. During my first visit to the tribal headquarters, several of the staff I came to meet urged me to go before the court, which happened to be in session that day. Few staff members would talk with me until I'd made that call. Off I went.

I assumed the court would have a feel similar to a city council meeting—court members seated on a dais facing the audience and a speaker's podium, with a clerk to the side. I assumed wrong. At the reception desk in the foyer, I filled out a speaker's form for the court and was told to wait since I would be last on its agenda. Half a dozen Ho-Chunks waited for their turns too. The recording secretary led me back to the meeting room about two hours later. The waiting room had long since been empty. Clan leaders make up the court; most are elders. We met in a smoke-filled trailer, the six members in attendance seated on metal folding chairs around a long conference table formed from several metal folding tables slid together. The table was bare; the room was spartan. The recording secretary pointed me to a chair at the table and briefly introduced me but not the others. He then withdrew to his desk by the door. We were alone. Dead quiet. I had much to learn about the Ho-Chunks. This was my first lesson.

No one spoke, no one moved, and no one looked at me. After an awkward silence I politely introduced myself, thanked them for the opportunity to speak with them on such short notice, and described my desire to talk with tribal members to learn about Ho-Chunk land management practices and traditional landscape values. I ended by respectfully requesting the court's advice and guidance on how I might proceed. Another silence. Still no one made eye contact with me or offered any overt recognition of my presence. Their eventual responses were as unsettling as their indifferent reception. The first to speak acted as the chair of the court, inviting each member to speak his thoughts.

They spoke of pride for their people and respect for all things. They spoke of their role as guardians of the tribe's culture and history. They told me of the complexity of that history and the impossibility of understanding it in less than a lifetime of learning. They stated they wouldn't divulge many aspects of that history to anyone because it was secret and sacred. They repeated tales of others like me who had come before them seeking access and information and how, when given, the petitioner had written lies or half-truths out of malice or ignorance. They spoke of their skepticism now about granting others such assistance.

They wondered about me and questioned my motives. Why was I really here? Did I have respect for them and all things? Did I know who I am? Was I going to make money from my book? How would the Ho-Chunks profit from sharing their story with me?

They spoke slowly as if each word was a delicacy and each phrase full of meaning to be savored. The tone seemed surly. Still no one looked at me. They spoke into the air, mostly about me, not to me. They considered my requests without asking direct questions. No guidance was offered and no decisions were made. Silence again. I waited, bewildered. The recording secretary came to my rescue, suggesting that I write another letter to the court restating my requests in much greater detail for the court to reconsider in several months. I said I would happily do so, thanked the court for the audience, and was ushered out. No one moved. No one responded.

I sat perplexed in the small gravel parking lot at the front of the building. Part of me wanted to laugh at what I assumed was pretense; part was irritated at their seemingly curt, condescending, unprofessional behavior; and part was angry at their nonresponsiveness. I'd come a long way after months of preparations making calls and writing letters to schedule appointments, to no avail. I'd written a detailed letter they hadn't seen just like the one they now requested. Had I failed my first lesson? The answer came when I returned to Black River Falls several months later. The answer came the day of the powwow.

I spent most of my morning prior to the powwow at the Majestic Pines Ho-Chunk casino, another mile or two beyond the traditional court. I wanted to see one of the profit centers financing the tribe's resurgence. The hotel/casino complex has glitz and glitter similar to those in Las Vegas or Atlantic City. Row upon row of flashy slot machines surround the blackjack tables in the center of the giant gaming room. The dealers are mostly Ho-Chunks. Even at 9:30 A.M. this Sunday morning, gamblers fill the room, car- and tour-bus-loads of retired white suburbanites by the look of them. Few Ho-Chunks. The doorman confirms my sense of the clientele. He said they come mostly from the nearby big cities—Chicago, Milwaukee, Madison, Green Bay.

I'm not a gambler. I don't even play the state lottery. Yet I felt compelled to give it a try. Background research, I told myself. Plus, my motel gave me a coupon worth $10 if I bought another $10 in tokens. So in I went armed with $20 worth of quarters jiggling in my large plastic cup. I walked around for an hour trying unsuccessfully to understand the motivation of the gamblers and the unwritten social rules governing their behavior. I also scouted for a suitable machine to play, meaning I searched for an understandable game so I wouldn't make a fool of myself and might even have some slim chance of winning. Having discovered a likely candidate, I set to work feeding quarters in its hungry mouth as fast as it could swallow. Nothing to it, I discovered. I learned to slow my frantic pace and savor the action as my supply dwindled, wisdom that came with experience. I won! Beginner's luck. I left $54.75 ahead. I'd spend my take at the powwow on lunch and some gifts for my two preschool-aged kids.

I sat in my car, nearly lost in the vast sea of parking, trying to sort out the experience. The casino runs continuously—round the clock—from Memorial Day through Labor Day. It has shorter winter hours but does just as well. More tours then and less competition from outdoor recreation, I guess. The Ho-Chunks use the profits to build homes for their people, to buy farms from whites ready to retire, to purchase properties for business sites, and to build a social infrastructure to provide quality services for the tribe. It's a daunting task given their needs. They've made amazing progress in the decade since revenues began to trickle in from the first bingo hall that stands, now shabby, by the edge of the new complex. The money pours in now seemingly by the truckload, tons of quarters accumulated one coin at a time.

A subdivision of suburban-style tract homes encircles the rear of the complex. Other small developments sit scattered in the surrounding woodland, many funded by the gambling/gaming profits. The Ho-Chunks build 200 to 300 modest new homes a year and have a backlog of 1,800. When possible, new developments abut existing subdivisions to reduce the costs of providing the needed physical and social infrastructure and to reinforce a sense of community. Finding suitable sites for expansion adjacent to existing tribal holdings challenges their land development skills and political acumen, just as it would those of any real estate developer. Their history complicates the process further. This subdivision follows conventional site design practices found

anywhere in America—it has a loop road with cul-de-sacs—
although the bland, blocky houses have a public housing project
look about them. The pastoral design imagery felt a bit con-
trived, as if forced upon the flat, sandy soils and the scruffy piney
woods. The residents appeared a bit uncomfortable with the setting too, as displayed by a type of care and use of their properties
that differs from the unwritten code of suburban conduct found
across the country. Driving around, I caught the stares of the
kids playing in the street and the yards and the adults coming
and going. I felt unwanted and unwelcome, so I moved on to the
powwow.

People gather gradually for the start of the powwow. No rush
to be seated since the festivities run several days and all the
seating in the round outdoor arena gives a good view of the
action. The arena's dirt floor is about one hundred feet wide and
sits about ten feet below grade. No fixed seating in the stands;
people spread out blankets or set up folding chairs for seating
on the concrete tiers. I find a perch on the top tier, chest height
above the walkway that circles the perimeter, shaded from the
bright afternoon sunshine by a wood overhang. The MC makes
announcements over the PA system. Participating drumming/
singing groups set up around their drums, positioning their eight
folding chairs and testing the microphone connection to the sound
system. A buzz of anticipation sweeps over the grounds in the
moments before the start.

At one o'clock, the arena fills as if by magic with spectators
and players appearing suddenly from the powwow grounds,
transforming it from a lifeless place into a stunning display of
color, sound, and motion. Flag bearers lead the categories of
dancers into the arena during the Grand Entry, the processional a
new tradition in part derived from the Wild West shows of the
late 1800s grafted onto the old social dances. Recognition of war
veterans begins the festivities. I'm drawn down to the arena floor

and stand at the edge so the sensual waves of pageantry wash over me: the pulsating drumbeats that represent the voice of God; the powerful chants sung by the chorus of masculine voices; the rhythmic spinning and swaying of the dancers—men and women, young and old.

The watchwords for the powwow repeated over and over again by the announcer are "pride," "beautiful," and "unity." "We are proud of each and every one of you," he says again and again, and "so proud of our veterans. All of our children are beautiful." A blond-haired, fair-skinned young woman wearing a full ceremonial outfit spins and twirls in the moving mass of dancers from many different cultures, enraptured by the music, embraced by the feeling of unity.

Susette LaMere meets me forty-five minutes later to help me understand the festivities and the Ho-Chunk culture. Susette manages the Cultural Resources Division for the Ho-Chunk Nation. "When I read the job description," she tells me, "I was working at the casino in an administrative job. But I was interested in the position so I asked my uncle, who is an elder in the bear clan, if he thought I'd be qualified. He'd already submitted my name." Clan connections still exert a strong influence on tribal life. Clan membership is determined by paternal bloodline, as marriages must be outside the clan. Each clan historically has had a specific function in the tribe. A person's job can still be influenced by that function. The bear clan is responsible for land management. Do clan members have personalities consistent with their traditional roles, I ask. She pauses, then responds, "Yes, I guess some do." Nothing magical or mysterious to it, she thinks, just the product of generation after generation having specific responsibilities. I ask if she feels unusual pressure to perform in her job because she's female. "Yes, I feel as if I have to prove myself every day," she replies. Traditional gender barriers break down slowly in Ho-Chunk society, just as they do in white society. Do you think men and women have different attitudes toward the land, I wonder. "No," she replies, "traditionally both worked the land—the men hunted and the women worked the fields." Both sexes had to practice stewardship to maintain their resource base. Susette says she learned respect for the land and water as a child, gifts from the Earthmaker to be used wisely and not wasted.

She wears a blue dress, simply cut and unadorned. Tasteful traditional Indian jewelry—bracelets, necklace, and earrings of silver and turquoise—add decoration. A crocheted shawl drapes over her shoulders. Susette has an elegant, graceful air and greater comfort with non-Indians than most Ho-Chunks I've met. She speaks softly and listens well, yet speaks her mind. The fact that she'll speak with me now I interpret as a result of my experience before the traditional court months earlier. She initially advised me to write the court, then to speak directly to them. She also forewarned me of the guarded reaction I'd receive from many people. Today she's arranged for me to meet an elder in the Native American Church, a friend she thinks will be willing to chat.

Powwows arose in the mid- to late 1800s, she tells me, when the Indian tribes "broke the arrow" and stopped fighting with one another. The intertribal "gatherings," as the Ho-Chunks call them, were a way for the tribes to make friends, exchange culture, and enjoy companionship. No one I spoke with knew the origins of the word "powwow." They assume it's derived from an eastern Indian word that was corrupted by whites. Powwows have always been mostly secular celebrations. Today they've become competitive events for the dancers and drummers/singers. Prize money at the large powwows can be $10,000 in a category. Some competitors tour from one powwow to another. This is a medium-sized event, Susette says. The powwow in Bismarck is the biggest in the region. Dancers compete as individuals, while drummers/singers represent a clan or village. Their songs have lyrics mixed with the patterned, melodic chants, what ethnomusicologists term "vocables" like "doo-wop." Unfortunately, fewer and fewer in the audience are fluent in the language. Apparently I'm not the only person, white or Indian, hearing the songs only as pleasing chants. Susette confesses she isn't fully fluent.

Language, I was learning, rests much more at the core of the Ho-Chunk culture than the English language does in American culture. Before the early 1900s, when the Ho-Chunks first began to use the written word, the spoken word was used to communicate their culture from one generation to the next via story, song, and poem; art and dance conveyed their culture too. If they lose their language, their culture may die. Having already lost much of their traditional way of life, language is a critical cultural lifeline and source of identity. That's one reason Susette said that many Ho-Chunks will not divulge tribal stories with non-tribe members. When those stories become public knowledge, what remains that is uniquely Ho-Chunk? Those stories are the repository of their past. Preservation of their language is a key to their future, for the stories lose subtle shades of meaning when transferred into written form or translated into another language, like English. Susette now runs a program to record the elders telling those stories in Ho-Chunk to safeguard them in their original tongue. A sense of urgency permeates the program. The number of Ho-Chunks fluent in the language is dwindling; now perhaps fewer than 225 fluent people remain and most are elderly. Another program—the Language and Culture Program—teaches the language to Ho-Chunk children at Head Start preschools. Unfortunately, many kids forget this essential foundation when they begin public primary school. There the language can be taught only in voluntary classes held after school. Attendance is poor. As is true of all kids, their interests lie in other activities.

"Language is the basis of our culture," William O'Brien told me two days later in a labored, windy voice as if speaking with his dying breath. He called O'Brien "a good Indian name" with a laugh, but didn't care to elaborate on the family history. William teaches Ho-Chunk at the Language and Culture Program with eighteen other instructors and works to reconstruct the first complete dictionary of the language; the original version they completed last year was stolen. Like other Indian tribes, the Ho-Chunks adopted the International Phonetic Alphabet about ten years ago, replacing an alphabet developed in the early 1900s. In William's lifetime, the language and culture have gone from being oral-based in Ho-Chunk to being a mix of oral and written bases mostly in English. He's not unhappy with this transformation. It makes teaching the eroding cornerstones easier. He likes anything that perpetuates them. Yet he knows the Ho-Chunk tongue must survive. The program is housed in a former meat-packing plant bought by the tribe several years earlier in a failed effort to run the business profitably. The tribe is wiser and more disciplined now in its land purchases and business ventures. The facility has since been adapted to office use.

William has a wonderful face with deep fissures and strong features. To many whites like me, it's a classic Indian face, since we grew up seeing it—William made his living as an actor in Hollywood, often playing an Indian in the cowboys-and-Indians shows. He's sixty-eight years old, he said with a chuckle, and now works at the serious job of perpetuating the Ho-Chunk language and, quite probably, the culture. He grew up near Black River Falls speaking Ho-Chunk, and only learned English in white public schools and special schools for Indians. In Ho-Chunk, William's name is "the one they ask." I came to ask him about the language. Some Ho-Chunks believe that when they die and go before the Great Spirit, he will ask who they are and expect them to give their Ho-Chunk name. William, I think, has an appropriate name.

"To really understand our culture you must know the language," he told me. "The young people don't realize this. You can call yourself a Ho-Chunk," he tells them emphatically, "but you aren't Ho-Chunk unless you speak the language and think like a Ho-Chunk." He thinks in Ho-Chunk and mentally translated his thoughts into English as we spoke. Not all his thoughts survive the translation, he said, since many Ho-Chunk words and thoughts have no direct English counterpart; others require a paragraph in English to explain. "Ho-Chunk is a descriptive language," he explained. "Everything has a name that is descriptive of the thing—what the thing is, what it does, what it looks like. That's how our language connects us to the land and our heritage. It's a beautiful and complicated language with a lot of spiritualism embedded," he continued. "It expresses the nature of the world around you better than English."

Ho-Chunk, he said, means "the people with the big voice." Until recently the white world knew the Ho-Chunks as the Winnebago people. William explained that Winnebago was a French corruption of a Chippewa word roughly meaning "dwellers of the stinking water," since the Ho-Chunks lived along what are now known as the Fox River and Lake Winnebago. He said other Indian tribes refer to the Ho-Chunk people as "Grandfather" in recognition of the fact that the Ho-Chunks are the parent people of many western tribes. I assumed my visit with William was also made possible by my appearance at the traditional court.

At the powwow Sunday, Susette introduces me to George Hindsley at his food stand facing the arena. Like the dozen other stands, his sells fry bread, Indian tacos, squaw burgers, corn soup, soft drinks, and desserts. George is a sixty-nine-year-old retired carpenter with a barrel chest, a long face, and a prominent nose. He smokes continuously, noting with a grin that the Indians introduced the whites to tobacco and the whites introduced alcohol to the Indians—each people infecting the other with a plague.

George grew up in Chicago and New York; his father was a ceremonial dancer who traveled a lot from show to show. George regrets the competitive commercialism at the powwows now. Something important has been lost in the new form, he feels. He has a deep attachment to the area and knows many stories about it dating to childhood visits, none he cares to share with me. We sit between the back of his booth and his RV on flimsy aluminum folding chairs with nylon straps woven to form the seat. I fear his chair will collapse under the strain of his large frame.

George speaks and I listen, my few questions serving as prompts that trigger his wide-ranging responses on various subjects, at times without immediate relevance to the questions. The conversation and tone are reminiscent of my meeting with the traditional court. I'm beginning to understand that the dynamic there wasn't a response to me; it was simply part of their culture. Susette later explained, "In Ho-Chunk culture, the court was being kind not to come right out and chastise you for digging once again into the private thoughts of the Ho-Chunk people." I had misinterpreted the court's actions as being unhelpful, even hostile, because of our cultural differences. "For generations," Susette continued, "Indian people have been thought to be backward for not looking the person they are addressing directly in the eye. However, it is respect for the other individual that they do not stare into the eyes of the other person. Yet in white society, it is quite disrespectful not to give direct eye contact to the person you are addressing. How differently we evaluate body language," she noted.

As the court had done, George begins by questioning my motives. Who am I, he wonders. Why am I here and what do I hope to gain? Will I make money from the book? Am I simply stealing information from the Ho-Chunks for personal profit? What will the Ho-Chunks gain by sharing their knowledge and wisdom with me? His hostility, suspicion, and cynicism toward whites are palpable. "How would you feel," he says bitterly, "if someone broke into your home and stole it from you, then made you buy it back from them?" I have trouble answering him.

Almost everything George tells me has a concept of "respect" at its core, not the sense of respect I was familiar with, but one with deeper, broader, and subtler meanings—respect for oneself, for other people, and for all things. To have respect, he says, you must first know what beliefs and values shape your life. "You must know who you are, be secure in your being, and love yourself. Only then can you have respect for other people and other things."

Traditional Ho-Chunk attitudes toward the land derive from their concept of respect. Before contact with whites, he tells me, the Ho-Chunks did not believe one could own land. People had personal possessions, but the land was a gift from the Earthmaker. They called the earth "Grandmother," and she happily provided all the tribe needed as long as they treated the gifts with respect and gave thanks for them. "Ho-Chunk teachings say we were placed on earth to care for our Grandmother, not abuse her the way it is being done," William O'Brien told me later. "We were taught not to let greed overcome our sense of trust and stewardship. I cry when I think of what some are doing to our Grandmother and her children." For the Ho-Chunks, each element in nature possessed a spirit and significance, and each had a place in the natural order, none more exalted than the others. Since white contact, many Ho-Chunks have lost their sense of respect: too much focus on money and possessions; too little understanding of self; too little concern for community and environment; too little attention to the truly important aspects of life. It's a plight suffered not just by the Ho-Chunks, George notes. Most societies suffer from it now. Stewardship suffers as a result. I've read and heard all this before—it's almost clichéd—but hearing it within the context of "respect" gives it more meaning for me.

George dislikes cities. He thinks connection to place and sense of community suffer in them. The rural landscape offers opportunities to see nature unavailable in built-up areas. "How can you feel the same about nature—the trees, the animals, the water—in a city," he asks, "when there is so little of it left?" Connection to place and community, he suggests, rests on two foundations: a stewardship ethic that derives from respect, which any person regardless of cultural background can possess; and contact with the land. He feels these connections aren't necessarily unique to the Ho-Chunks. The issue to him is whether one acts on them or becomes too focused on money and acquiring property, losing respect. I ask how he resolves the traditional Ho-Chunk attitudes toward the land with the contemporary concepts of private property imposed on them by the white world. "I can't," he replies, "they both exist." "We have to deal with both, but it's not so much a problem for the young. They don't know the traditional ways as much. They care more about getting things."

A coworker calls George back to the booth. I sit at the side counter eating my lunch of a squaw burger and corn soup (both very tasty) and watching the activity. He's busy now with other matters and other people. Our conversation is over, so I finish my soup and sandwich and wander the booths with the remainder of my casino winnings in search of gifts for my kids. I buy my daughter a silver and turquoise bracelet and necklace set similar to Susette's. I find my son a deerskin medicine pouch made of the softest, creamiest leather I've ever felt. The powwow no longer feels threatening to me.

[15]

Ritchie Brown, the manager of the Ho-Chunk Nation Division of Natural Resources, parks the giant GMC Suburban at the edge of a pasture beside a strip of young woodland overlooking the

Wisconsin River on the tribe's Bison Restoration Project property. A large fiberglass case in the back holds a mobile ground-penetrating radar system. He points to a distant farm on the hill overlooking our position which he's been trying to buy for about five years. It has a quarter-mile-long effigy mound of a bird on it, the largest one in the country, he tells me. His division manages approximately 7,000 acres of the tribe's 10,000 acres in Wisconsin, including a dozen farms for cash crops, the bison project property, elk and wolf recovery project sites, and various timberlands. Land acquisition began about eight years ago as gambling/gaming revenues accumulated. At the time, the tribe only owned a few parcels amounting to several hundred acres. Now they have nearly 150 parcels. The largest is around 1,500 acres. The buying frenzy of the first few years has now been tempered by experience and become more disciplined and professional.

Ritchie's staff also surveys and conducts environmental assessments of potential land acquisitions using all the latest computer technologies: a state-of-the-art geographic information system to construct an integrated spatial database with map layers describing the physical and legal attributes of some properties, global positioning satellite data for land survey registration, and the mobile ground-penetrating radar in the back of our Suburban to scan potential sites of burial and effigy mounds. Ritchie has a degree in land surveying. I suspect he as much as anyone in the tribe struggles to blend the old ways of the Ho-Chunks with the new ways forced upon them by the white world. The bison project illustrates the conflict between those ways.

Our ninety-minute drive south from the tribal offices in Black River Falls to the Muscoda property along the lower Wisconsin River gave us time to get reacquainted. We first met earlier in the summer just before I went before the traditional court. He'd told me how the court responds to his requests for guidance on projects: "If I have a question about can I do this or can I do that,

I can go and ask them," he said, "and if they feel inclined to tell, they'll tell me." That's the way they are, he commented with a matter-of-fact chuckle. "You can't go in and ask your question, get an answer, and leave. You go in, sit down, and listen to whatever they want to talk about. They'll tell you all kinds of stories. At the end, when they've said all they want, you can ask your question. They may answer then or they may tell you another story and such. If they feel you have a valid question and you need an answer, they'll give it to you. But if you have a question that they think you can answer yourself, then they'll leave it up to you, based on their judgment of you as a person to do what's right. They say, 'You know what you have to do, go ahead and do it.' But that's all you need. Once you've asked them and they've had the opportunity for input, basically you've got their approval and they'll back you up. It's a lot of responsibility they can put on you in a hurry." Everything's done orally, Ritchie said. I didn't appreciate what he meant then; I do now.

Ritchie has short hair, a round face with glasses, and the familiar barrel chest of most Ho-Chunk adults, male and female. A cute picture of his young daughter serves as the screen saver on his office PC. His son graduates from high school soon. Ritchie's infectious, easygoing manner can't hide his obvious professional knowledge. He seems comfortable with non-Indians and comfortable with himself—I think he has the "respect" that George described. Perhaps it comes with maturity and experience. Ritchie was a foster child raised by parents of recent Irish descent. His wife is of Italian descent and grew up in a very Italian home. Their son speaks about as much Italian as Ho-Chunk, Ritchie noted, having spent a great deal of time with the grandparents. Ritchie understands Ho-Chunk pretty well but has trouble speaking it.

He was hired in 1992 as the second member of the newly formed land department, after a dozen years of work with federal land management and planning agencies and several years with the state of Wisconsin preparing watershed plans. Too many moves for his wife, who wanted the family to settle down, since their son had just started school. They were living in Black River Falls at the time, so when the Ho-Chunk position arose, it was a perfect fit. An elder once advised Ritchie that his varied past makes him the perfect liaison to the non-Indian world needed by the tribe to grow and develop. "That's your job, that's why you're here," the elder said. The Creator gives each person a special gift, the elder believed. Ritchie's gift is his background. About ten months later, he was promoted to manager. The division now has thirty people on the staff. The growth of the tribal government in size, organization, professionalism, and breadth of services since the gambling/gaming revenues started pouring in during the early 1990s has been phenomenal.

Two weeks after Ritchie started in December, he got a call from a farmer, nearing retirement, who wanted someone to look at the mounds on his property along the Wisconsin River. The state was proposing to build a canoe landing nearby and he feared the mounds would be damaged if he sold them the land. Ritchie went to look. He found about a dozen effigy mounds intact overlooking the river. Further research revealed that the mounds were part of a major grouping that once contained nearly one hundred mounds stretching along the riverbank into the adjacent farms. A survey of the grouping done in the mid-1800s, when white settlement reached the area, showed the precise location and configuration of each mound. Someday Ritchie hopes to recall the lost mounds by outlining their former shapes with fieldstones. The Ho-Chunks believe the mounds were built by their direct ancestors, the oldest perhaps as long as 1,500 years ago—at about the same time that King Loth cast Princess Thenew off Traprain Law. They also know that a major Ho-Chunk village with perhaps 1,500 inhabitants was located on the site at the time the tribe was evicted from the state following the 1837 treaty.

Ritchie soon began work on a proposal to buy the 20 acres containing the dozen intact mounds using the new revenues from the burgeoning bingo and gambling businesses. The plan expanded to acquire the entire farm and the adjacent farms on either side—a total of 640 acres with 1.5 miles of river frontage and two islands—as more information about the site's historical significance was uncovered and the owners learned of the Ho-Chunks' interests. Both adjacent owners were retired and leased their farmland to others to work. Even though their farms had been in their families for generations, neither person had family who wanted to continue the farm. The three farm owners were white and willing sellers.

"I couldn't make my initial plan work to establish a buffalo herd on the farms and justify the purchase on economic grounds, even with a seven-year cost recovery," Ritchie told me. "But when I reworked it on cultural grounds, all the pieces fell in place." One night after he'd worked on the proposal for nine months and was still struggling with what to propose for the property, he had a dream in which he was standing in a vast western prairie, "like a scene in an old western movie where you see a cloud of dust coming at you," he said. The cloud turned out to be raised by a herd of buffalo. "The next day, I talked with a friend of mine who was an elder and I told him what happened. He looked at me and kinda smiled and said, 'Well, I guess they're coming, aren't they.' " The Bison Restoration Project resulted. Given the vast backlog of needs, it is extraordinary to me that the first major property purchased by the Ho-Chunks was justified on cultural grounds: to preserve the effigy mounds, to establish a bison herd on a prairie/native grass landscape, and to have a natural setting in which to hold a variety of outdoor educational and cultural programs for tribe members of all ages. I think the project gets at the heart of the tribe's values.

Today about 115 bison and 10 horses feed on the 500 fenced acres. Fencing continues on the remaining acreage. Ritchie hopes to expand the herd to 300 head in several years. Crops are no longer grown. The fields are being returned to native grasses and prairie. Last spring they conducted the first controlled burn needed to suppress invasive plants. During summer months, the land teems with youth programs, leadership camps, and cultural instruction programs to reintroduce tribal members to their homeland and aspects of their traditional culture in a way few have experienced.

"We're caretakers of the land," Ritchie tells me, keepers for future generations, not owners. Traditionally, everyone in the tribe shared the land, he explains. Land and most everything else was held communally or by family. Life was easier then than today, he thinks. People worked less since what they needed they obtained relatively easily from nature, so they enjoyed more time for other activities. "They weren't lazy," he says, "they just didn't have to work as much since they weren't so fixated on accumulating possessions. This left time for building mounds."

How do you merge that legacy with the functions of your division, I ask. How do you merge global positioning satellites, ground-penetrating radar, property surveys, and property boundaries with that past? "The Ho-Chunks first dealt with boundaries and ownership when given the allotments in the 1880s," he replies. Before white contact the Ho-Chunks didn't draw maps, nor did they have a word for the property in the Western sense. Places were known by descriptive names that conveyed location or other characteristics. The language had words for personal possessions but nothing meaning private ownership of land. Nor did it have a word for "wilderness." The land around them was a nurturing home alive with spiritual meaning and history, not a threatening, alien place to be subdued and conquered. Nor were their concepts of "home" and "permanence" like those of the invaders they encountered. By Western standards, the Ho-

Chunks lived their entire lives in temporary structures, never setting foot indoors or settling in a single place long enough to assume occupancy. Ironically, I think the Western lifestyle that replaced their lifestyle is less at home and less rooted to place. "The white man says this is progress," William O'Brien told me. "We accept that. We have to. We have to embrace two cultures. Which one do we embrace more? We have to abide with what the government says. We should all try to embrace brotherhood; everybody should be treated with respect—respect the other person, respect all people. If we had more respect, we'd have less conflict."

"How do we merge the past and present?" Ritchie asks. "We just do; we have too. That was a real difficult task when we started acquiring land eight years ago. It was difficult to make everything we did culturally acceptable." How do you tie the cultural concerns to the current realities, I ask. "It's an ongoing process," he says, "that forces you to think and rethink what to do with acquisitions: what is our intent; what's there; is there anything culturally significant there that needs protection, and if so what direction should we go with that." Land means responsibility to Ritchie. Adoption of the tribal land-use plan recently marked a big step forward and came as a relief to him. Now he refers to the plan when considering options. Now he relies on its goals and policies for guidance. The plan brings discipline to what before had been something of a land-grab free-for-all.

Chris Straight cochairs the tribe's land development team with him. Chris directs the Ho-Chunk Nation Planning and Development Division. He earned graduate degrees in urban and regional planning and geography from the University of Wisconsin and worked in the Dane County planning department before joining the Ho-Chunk staff about the same time as Ritchie, except Chris is white and not a tribal member.

Chris said the new land-use plan creates a more equal balance of cultural and economic concerns in determining land purchases and proposed uses than typically applied by non-Indian businesses and public planning agencies. Formulation of the plan over the past few years was very broad-based with extensive input from all tribal groups. The process followed to develop the plan, he thought, differed from non-Indian planning processes not so much in the basic approach taken as it did in the relationship to and input of people. He felt the unusual degree of public involvement shaped the plan and now shapes all aspects of the tribe's land affairs.

"The last few years or so we've been in a land acquisition mode," Chris told me. "It's really an attitude of reclaiming their lost homeland, finding lands on which they can express their sovereign power. I feel awkward talking about some of this," he said. As a non-tribe member and outsider, even after years at the core of the Ho-Chunk land planning/management team, many aspects of Ho-Chunk culture remain closed to him. He worked to choose his words carefully and struggled to express sensitively and accurately what he knows, or senses, about their attitudes. "Treating Mother Nature—Mother Earth—with environmentally sound practices is a higher priority with the Ho-Chunk," he said. "Stewardship is high among their priorities, it's central to their culture and religion."

He noted that a significant percentage of the tribal membership remains below the poverty level. "We've got all these real basic needs that would be high on a hierarchy of needs in conventional Western terms," he stated. Yet while they address these necessities, the Ho-Chunks also devote significant resources to cultural, environmental, and other concerns that would be of much lower priority in Western societies. "The structure is very different here." Those other concerns are perhaps as central to their basic needs as food and shelter. "We've got major housing needs, nearly 30 percent unemployment, yet we're spending

money on wetland restoration projects and bison/prairie restoration. It's interesting that from my perspective as a planner, I'd hit
the housing and unemployment really hard and to heck with
those other things for five to ten years until we've got those basic
needs met. But no, we're doing some other things. Great, I'm
all for it." Linkage to the land—"rootedness"—he said, is very
much a part of the Ho-Chunk culture, much more so than in the
white world. The best proof, he thought, might be seen in the
way the Ho-Chunks returned to the Wisconsin homeland after
each forced eviction in the mid-1800s. "I think that goes right to
the heart and soul of it," he said.

Ritchie and I walk into the woods among the low mounds
partly hidden by brush, some long and ridgelike, others circular.
The shapes are hard to distinguish at ground level. Filtered light
cascades down through the young canopy, setting the leaves and
ground aglow. Do the mounds affect you, I ask as he guided me
around them. "Oh yeah," he replies. In what way, I ask. "Relaxing, I guess. I feel at home here," he says. "These have been here
for eight hundred to a thousand years or more. The people who
built these mounds didn't have books or videos to tell us what
was going on then, so this is how they did it. They built these
mounds because they knew the mounds would be here. If we can
protect them, then we've accomplished something. We don't
have to know what they mean to protect them. People have different interpretations of them. I don't think there's any secret
about what you're looking at, no mystery to it. The fact that they
are here and that you can come here and be a part of them, standing on the mounds when the sun comes up, makes their purpose
and meaning real, not a thought. If you're here using them, then
the mounds have accomplished what the builders intended.
That's what they're for—continuity."

Do you think this place has the same effect on you that a
church has on other people, I ask. He paused, then with a lift in

his voice says, "I don't know. That's a good question. People react in different ways here. A busload of elders once visited the site on a beautiful day like today. Three ladies got off the bus and stood in front of me. They looked at one another smiling. I thought they were just glad to be here. But one lady said to the others, 'Do you hear it?' They could hear the drums of our ancestors." A raucous chorus showers down on us from a wedge of geese passing overhead. "This is a powerful place," he says. "I know that much. I know it's an important site and it was Ho-Chunk. The rest of it is up to the individual."

We return to the Suburban and set off around the rest of the rolling property. It's gorgeous land with stunning views of the Wisconsin River, especially on a brilliant late summer day like today. My eye can't comprehend the palette of colors painted across the folds of land and the sandbars and small islands that braid the water. The dark foliage of the trees along the river highlights the light greenish brown pastures withering at the end of the growing season. The place has an eerie stillness for someone like me, accustomed to the constant din of "white noise" in the background of cities and suburbs. Without it I feel naked, nervous, and vulnerable. No wonder the Ho-Chunks lived here for centuries, perhaps millennia.

The bulk of the bison herd grazes peacefully on an upper pasture, clustered around the dominant bull. Ritchie explains that the bull, as yet unnamed, just dethroned the former dominant male, named "Kunu." Kunu—meaning "first son"—was exiled to a remote corner of the pasture, down the hill out of sight of the others. We stop to pay our respects as he chews on a bale of hay. Kunu served the herd and the tribe well, Ritchie explains. He was the herd's first father and first leader. He weighs 2,000 pounds. "We don't control Kunu," Ritchie says. "He chooses to be here. You see, Kunu can break through our gates and escape anytime he wants to, if he wants to. Every once in a while he flings open a gate like a toy simply by bending his head down so his horns catch beneath the bars, then he raises up his head and lifts the gate off its hinges. He does that just to remind us that he isn't our prisoner, our captive." Kunu seems oblivious to our presence ten feet away. I know little about bison but Kunu projects something special, a sense of nobility in his carriage and his extraordinarily massive head and shoulders, not arrogant or defiant but proud and dignified. Ritchie suggests halfheartedly that they might fatten him up and let him have another go at his young challenger. It might be too late. Although Kunu is only six years old, Ritchie thinks he has accepted his fate. "He's just a little smarter than the rest," Ritchie says. "He knows when to retire."

On our way back to Black River Falls, we stop at a fast food drive-through for burgers and fries. Ho-Chunk attitudes toward the land focus more on stewardship than white attitudes do, Ritchie tells me, and they're changing for the better now that the tribe's basic utilitarian needs are being met. "When you're hungry and cold you worry about meeting those basic needs. We're now at a point where we can worry about other things." The land-use plan has stewardship interwoven throughout. They try to manage their properties based on a long-term, generation-to-generation perspective, not the relatively shortsighted perspective often applied by others.

William O'Brien quoted a speech he particularly liked that he thought reflected their stewardship ethic. In speaking of forests, the earth, and water, Looking Horse once said: "I do not cut my mother's hair, even if it is long. I do not scar my mother's face. I do not dirty my mother's blood." William told me the Ho-Chunks were taught traditionally to take only what was needed, no more, and all that they obtained they shared equally among all in the community. "The animals are our brothers and sisters," he continued. "When we go out to kill a deer, we ask that deer permission to kill it. We ask, 'Will you give yourself to us so we can eat?' If the deer says yes, he'll stand there for us to kill him. Then when we slay him, we give thanks. We take a piece of his heart and tongue, build a fire, and make a sacrifice. We thank the deer for giving of himself, the same way with any other animal. If the animal sees that you're hungry, he'll feed you. That's what they were placed on Grandmother Earth for, and you in turn give them respect and don't abuse them—kill them—without purpose. Ho-Chunk people can't have this sense of stewardship and community if they don't know the language," he said. "No, those who don't speak the language don't understand what stewardship and community mean. There're a lot of things to our culture and what we do that they have no inkling about if they don't speak Ho-Chunk."

I doubt that that traditional thinking and behavior is common today, but vestiges of them have been incorporated into the Ho-Chunk land-use plan, their land acquisition priorities, and their land management policies and practices. William continued, "I say to the Creator, 'Let me see the way; show me the right way.' That's why we do our fasting. Some people don't do it anymore. I hardly fast anymore. I used to do it quite a bit. It's a way of purging yourself of your bad feelings. It's a way of self-meditating and self-cleansing. I still do some of the traditional things, but not as much as I should."

Do you think the land means something different to the Ho-Chunks than to the whites living in the area, I ask Ritchie. Do you manage your land differently? "I'm sure we do," he responds. "Ho-Chunk stories have us here since the beginning," he says, "we're here and we're going to be here. Two years ago," he says, "a piece of fee land in the Oneida reservation came up for sheriff's sale. The legislators sent me to buy it with a blank check and instructions not to come back without it. The sale started at 8:00 A.M. on the steps of the courthouse. I was there and didn't know anybody else and just started bidding. It finally got down to two guys and I just kept right on going, so I ended up with it. I went in and filled out the forms, putting the land in the tribe's name. A group of people hung around to see who I was and started asking questions when I came out. The guy I was bidding against was from the Oneidas' lands department. A few weeks later their Department of Natural Resources manager calls me and asks what I was doing over there and why I was buying land on the Oneida reservation. 'Well,' I told him, 'the Ho-Chunk look at you as visitors; we were here when you came and we'll be here when you leave.' 'Oh, OK,' he said, and that was that." "What makes you a tribe," Ritchie said, "is your land base and your language; if you start losing either one of them, the tribe is in jeopardy; its identity is lost." That's why they bought the land for the bison project first. Land and language and identity are inseparable for the Ho-Chunks. Unfortunately, they never were for most of the aliens who displaced them. John Muir was an exception, I think; so are Erik Brynildson, Bessie Eggleston, Morrie and Mary Kearns, Fran Sprain, and the Soda family.

THE OLD WORLD

I caught the scent of the salt sea breeze which, although
I had so many years lived far from sea breezes, suddenly
conjured up Dunbar, its rocky coast, winds and waves;
and my whole childhood, that seemed to have utterly
vanished in the New World, was now restored. . . .
The Firth of Forth, the Bass Rock, Dunbar Castle,
and the winds and rocks and hills came upon
the wings of that wind, and stood in as clear
and sudden light as a landscape flashed upon the
view by a blaze of lightning in a dark night.

JOHN MUIR, *A Thousand-Mile Walk to the Gulf*

[16]

John Muir's decision to return to the Old World came as suddenly
as the announcement by his father forty-four years earlier that the
family was departing for the New World. He too had the idea—
the dream—for years, perhaps since his boyhood in Wisconsin,
just as his father's dream germinated in his boyhood home near
Crawfordjohn. The father dreamed of setting down new roots in
the New World; the son dreamed of rediscovering roots severed in
the Old World. What would John find there? How had the land
in East Lothian and the people of Dunbar changed? He couldn't
expect the land to have changed as much as had his adopted
homeland. Here, he and millions of other pioneers thought they
had transformed the western wilderness into a civilized, settled
landscape. That transformation had occurred centuries earlier in

the Old World. Nor could he expect the people to have changed as much as his new compatriots. Here, he'd witnessed the effects of industrialization and the formation of many institutions, social customs, and conventions. As a founder and the first president of the Sierra Club and as a champion of the national parks, he'd participated in some of those formative events. In the Old World, the effects of industrialization were now a century old and most institutions, customs, and conventions had centuries-old legacies as well. Fifty-five-year-old John Muir had matured too, like the land and the people around him. He'd risen to national and modest international fame based on his many magazine articles—some scientific, describing his landmark findings on the effects of alpine glaciers in shaping the Yosemite landscape; some journalistic, describing his wilderness adventures in Alaska and the Sierra Nevada; and some philosophical, setting forth his ideas on wilderness preservation. Perhaps like me, a search for answers prompted his return to his Scottish roots.

A telegram from a friend with whom for a decade he'd planned to travel finally sent him off from San Francisco in May 1893. "I can't wait any longer. I'm starting tomorrow," it read. Meet me in Chicago, then the site of the World's Fair, the traveling partner proposed. John followed several days later, stopping first in Portage for an impromptu visit with his mother. A note awaited him in Chicago. "Couldn't stand the crowd," his friend said, "Will wait in New York."

Muir swept through the fair, "a cosmopolitan rat's nest," he called it, although he admired some of the art on exhibit and the spectacular transformation of Jackson Park guided by the fair's designers, Daniel H. Burnham, Frederick Law Olmsted, Augustus Saint-Gaudens, and Louis Sullivan. Olmsted was an acquaintance who had been a commissioner of Yosemite State Preserve years before and like Muir was now a leading voice for the protection of the nation's scenic wonders. Muir's preservation sensibilities must have been offended by the Columbian Exposition's glorification of America's material progress and the forces that triggered it: raging free-market capitalism, technology, industrialization, and the accompanying consumer culture. Why pay homage to machines that lay waste to the nation's natural resources in an effort to quench its insatiable thirst for more material possessions, he must have thought. Why glorify the needless destruction of wilderness—God's glorious handiwork? It must have reminded him of his father's shortsighted abandonment of Fountain Lake Farm for the false promise of Hickory Hill. The belief that land was merely property, simply a commodity to fuel economic growth and development, prevailed more than ever.

Just weeks later, on the evening of July 12, Frederick Jackson Turner would deliver perhaps the ultimate expression of those prevailing attitudes. Blond, handsome, and athletic, the young University of Wisconsin geography professor from Portage redefined the nation's history and self-image as he distilled the essence of the American experience into his Frontier Thesis. He told America what it was and how it came to be in his hour-long speech titled "The Significance of the Frontier in American History." Not since Lincoln's Gettysburg Address had a single speech done so. The simple, elegant thesis tapped common dreams and noble aspirations: "Up to our own day American history has been in a large degree the history of the colonization of the Great West. The existence of an area of free land, its continuous recession, and the advance of American settlement westward, explain American development." Never mind the effects of immigration and the teeming eastern cities, or slavery, or the transfer of European traditions. Instead Turner believed that "to the frontier the American intellect owes its striking characteristics." He continued,

That coarseness and strength combined with acuteness and inquisitiveness; that practical, inventive turn of the mind, quick to find expedients; that masterful grasp of material things, lacking in the artistic but powerful to effect great ends; that restless, nervous energy; that dominant individualism, working for the good and for evil, and withal that buoyancy and exuberance which comes with freedom—these are traits of the frontier. . . .

Turner proposed that true American culture and institutions, those things truly American, arose at the frontier. There, the struggle to forge civilization out of the western wilderness forced pioneers like the Muirs to shed the values and institutions that tied them to their European heritage. America was born in the process of pushing the frontier across the continent, especially the western plains and prairies. He continued, "The stubborn American environment is there with its imperious summons to accept its conditions; the inherited ways of doing things are also there; and yet, in spite of environment, and in spite of custom, each frontier did indeed furnish a new field of opportunity, a gate of escape from the bondage of the past; and freshness, and confidence, and scorn of older society, impatience of its restraints and its ideas, and indifference to its lessons, have accompanied the frontier."

Self-serving and self-congratulatory, the thesis struck a chord with the public. It seemingly gave credence to the popular belief in manifest destiny and the other myths and illusions about America's settlement story. Scholars attacked it immediately. Its significant insights simplified a more complicated story, they said. Still, the thesis rapidly infected popular thinking, gaining acceptance not because it was accurate but because it encapsulated what Americans believed or wanted to believe. The Columbian Exposition, an unbridled affirmation of America's belief that it had ascended to the pinnacle of the Western world, was the perfect place for Turner to first present his thesis. No wonder Muir left for New York in a rush. In a western boomtown like Chicago the thesis made some sense; in New York it made no sense.

Muir hoped for a quick rendezvous with his traveling partner in New York and a prompt departure for the Old World. Unfortunately, his fame scuttled the plan. "I had no idea I was so well known, considering how little I have written," he commented in disbelief. Robert Underwood Johnson, a close friend and his influential editor at the country's leading literary magazine, the *Century*, swept him up into a whirlwind of gala parties, luncheons, and champagne receptions given in his honor.

One evening Muir was feted in grand style by former timber baron James Pinchot at his lavish Gramercy Park residence. The Pinchot family had made a fortune in forestry, clear-cutting the hardwood forests that Muir so admired. Now they were making another fortune in New York merchandising. During dinner John met James's son, Gifford, who had gone to Europe several years earlier to study forestry, since no American school taught the subject. On his return Gifford began a career as perhaps the nation's first "consulting forester," devoted to maximum use/sustained yield practices and the social philosophies of the emerging Progressive Era. Those practices arose in the Old World where timber had been a scarce and valuable resource requiring careful stewardship for generations; in contrast, American attitudes toward forest resources remained focused on removal, not replanting. Gifford acquired his utilitarian, progressive philosophy also as a result of his Old World experience—his disgust with the lingering class system of aristocratic privilege, the same system that drove immigrants like Daniel Muir to America, and the same privileges he (Gifford) enjoyed.

The meeting of John and Gifford proved fortuitous. The two began as friends, master and acolyte, but in several years would become bitter opponents in a decade-long national cause célèbre regarding the fate of a valley in Yosemite National Park and the general purpose of the national parks and forests. Muir would champion the "preservation" philosophy, advocating the protection of wild lands from damage due to human uses. Pinchot, as the head of the U.S. Forest Service and the government's principal adviser on land management, would advocate a "conservation" philosophy that emphasized the maximum production of natural resources on a sustainable basis to feed the nation's consuming appetite. The battle between the two would shape the American environmental debate from that day forward.

From New York, Johnson moved John on to Boston, Cambridge, and Concord for more glittering social affairs. It was all a bit much for Muir, but he made a host of prominent new friends, including paleontologist Henry Fairfield Osborn, preservationist Charles Sprague Sargent, naturalist John Burroughs, historian Francis Parkman, and authors Mark Twain and Rudyard Kipling. He also made a pilgrimage to Sleepy Hollow Cemetery in Concord to pay homage to the plain graves of Nathaniel Hawthorne and Henry David Thoreau and the grander grave of Ralph Waldo Emerson, authors he greatly admired. From there Muir walked the short distance—"a mere saunter," he noted—to Walden Pond, the young woodland surrounding a small lake on Emerson's property. There, Thoreau—"the blessed crank and tramp," Muir called him—lived while he wrote *Walden,* the classic story of his experiment in the transcendentalist life. The beautiful setting must have reminded Muir of Fountain Lake. The glacial pond sat "embosomed like a bright dark eye" within the luminous spring foliage. "No wonder Thoreau lived here two years," Muir wrote. "I could have enjoyed living here two hundred years or two thousand." Before leaving the area, Muir dined with Emerson's son in the family home, to which he had been invited to live years earlier by the patriarch of American letters. Muir had refused the great man's offer, preferring to remain in his Yosemite temple where he lived the transcendentalist life that Emerson, Thoreau, and the others in their Concord circle could only imagine. Yet Emerson's son told Muir that he was something of a household name during his father's last years.

Finally, on June 26, John set sail for Liverpool on the steamer *Etruria*. His friend had left about three weeks before with the faint hope that they'd meet in London or Paris. They never did. Late the evening of July 1, the *Etruria* docked, a much quicker and more luxurious passage for Muir than his first ocean crossing. But the roar of the 30,000-horsepower engines, the stench of their fumes, and the jerky shudder of the ship as it charged breakneck through the chop spoiled the voyage. John arrived in the Old World with no set plans and few specific intentions. Like his father, he often set off on adventures and allowed circumstances to guide him.

A daylong train trip took him to Edinburgh on July 3, thence to Dunbar on an afternoon train two days later. After the hourlong ride, he stepped onto the platform of the same small outdoor station he'd left a lifetime ago. The handsome T-plan Tudor station house, with hood-molded ground-floor windows and gabled first-floor windows, stood little changed since completion in 1845. Only the stains of engine smoke on the orange cast to the station's ironstone walls and the pale white limestone dressings quarried at Catcraig just a mile or two away marked the passage of time. No fanfare, no welcoming ceremony, he stood alone with his luggage. He was home.

Were his childhood memories of people and places real or merely phantoms of his imagination distorted by time and space? Can one's sense of self be complete without that confirmation? Are those memories the sustenance for our roots? I suspect he'd come to validate his past, to see the settings of his childhood memories, to revisit the ruins of Dunbar Castle, the fishing harbors and inland fields, the rocky cliffs and tidal pools, the school, the church, the shops, the gardens, and Doon Hill. How would the Old World look after he'd been so long in the New?

His first stop was 130-134 High Street, the prominent building in the heart of the town's commercial strip that had housed his father's store on the ground floor and the family flats above— the home they left in 1849. Although only four blocks from the station, the building was too far to walk to with his load of luggage in hand, so he hailed a carriage instead. High Street had changed slightly since he'd walked from the house to the station forty-four years earlier. Grandfather Gilrye's flesher business across the street from the Muir home had closed long ago. The Gilrye building had been demolished in the 1880s and replaced by a private residence. Several doors down the street, Cassars Inn had been converted into the St. George Hotel. Yet the street's general appearance and function remained little affected. The three-hundred-year-old harl-clad Town House (town hall) remained unchanged. Its stout, hexagonal clock tower still dominated the skyline, and the clock on which John learned to tell time still displayed the hour.

Lauderdale House still anchored the north end of the street. Its facade, finished in the smooth-faced, finely fitted blocks of ashlar stone popular with expensive buildings of the period, still blocked the spectacular view to the castle and sea beyond. The grand neoclassical home, originally known as Dunbar House, was begun in 1737 for the Falls, a family of wealthy merchants operating around the Mediterranean and Baltic ports. "The greatest Scottish merchants of the eighteenth century," they were called. For a century the Falls had served as public officials in the burgh, and they owned land and tenements in and around the town. Few residents likely complained openly when the imposing residence was built, interrupting the perspective down High Street to the sea.

In the mid-1700s, the Falls launched a whaling company from

the "old" harbor their new house overlooked. The company flourished briefly, at one point operating five ships weighing a total of 1,532 tons and employing 238 seamen. But the venture dwindled and ultimately failed in 1803. Dutifully the family maintained their lifestyle despite their declining fortunes. Even Robbie Burns joined the provost and his wife at Dunbar House for tea on May 19, 1787. "Riding like the devil," Burns wrote in his journal, "[we] passed through the most glorious [cropland] I ever saw, till I reached Dunbar, a neat little town." He continued, "[We] dined with Provost Fall, an eminent merchant and most respectable character." Mrs. Fall, he thought, was "a genius in painting." A year later the family fortunes collapsed and the house was sold at bankruptcy to the Duke of Lauderdale, who sought to gain greater influence in Parliament by establishing a residence in Dunbar.

His Grace quickly hired Robert Adam, the most famous architect of the day, to enlarge and remodel the renamed house. The resulting structure was the Lauderdale House that John Muir knew as a child. However, the duke's family owned other fabulous properties in East Lothian, so when laws affecting parliamentary membership were changed, they sold Lauderdale House to the War Office in 1859. The strategic importance of Dunbar's location for Scotland remained as real in the nineteenth century as it was when Dunbar Castle controlled the Firth of Forth in the fourteenth century. Troops occupied the Lauderdale House at which John Muir now looked, elegant nonetheless.

The Abbey Church still anchored the opposite end of High Street. Built in 1849 as Daniel Muir hived off for religious opportunity in America, the Free (Presbyterian) Church it housed hived off from the Kirk during the "Disruption" about a half dozen years earlier. Those two High Street anchors constantly reminded the townspeople during John Muir's childhood of the dominant forces in Scottish society: the landed aristocracy and the church. The place of the common person reflected by the town hall sat halfway between, physically and politically. The message remained unaltered in 1893 despite the change in ownership at Lauderdale House. And shops still filled the ground floor of many buildings along High Street, with the proprietors living above, although the new owner of the former Muir home converted the building into the Lorne Temperance Hotel shortly after the family departed. John would stay there. A walk around town the next day found forgotten friends amid the familiar closes and a favorite cousin living a short ten-minute walk away. John quickly moved from the Lorne to stay with her.

Did the former Muir home feel familiar to John despite the alteration? He once climbed precariously out his bedroom dormer window seeking a way to freedom from his nighttime confinement. That search for adventure was one of his most vivid Dunbar memories. Did the steep slate roof outside the window match that memory? "I have been here a week and have seen most of my old haunts and more than I expected of my boy playmates," he wrote to his wife. Were his childhood experiences and the places where they occurred around Dunbar as he remembered—were his roots real or only romanticized exaggerations? Real, I suspect.

What he saw beyond High Street had changed as little as the town's main commercial strip. Dunbar at the end of the nineteenth century remained a town of several parts: a market town centered on the high street and its adjacent closes and approaches; an active fishing harbor and a port for trade; and an agricultural center catering to the outlying farms. The burgh's population during his absence grew only from about 3,000 to 3,500 people. Rows of red sandstone town houses built in the 1880s now lined the town's two approaches, with many of the elegant Victorian homes serving as summer residences for prosperous professionals and businessmen from Edinburgh. The building of these summer homes marked the beginning of the town's gradual transformation to a commuter and recreational basis, similar to Marquette County. That trend continues today in both places.

The stifling poverty in the closes running off High Street stood in stark contrast to the influx of affluence. Logan's Close was typical. John knew it well as a child for it lay along his way to the school at Woodbush Brae, and young hooligans like him loved to clatter helter-skelter down the narrow paved walkways banging on doors and windows. Eleven tiny flats housed twenty-seven people in the short close: James Ballantyne, age eighty-five, a retired sailor, and Elizabeth Ballantyne, sixty; Mary White, eighty, Mary Darg, thirty, her daughter Mary, seven, and a month-old infant daughter; Christian Wilson, thirty, Mary Fairbairn, seventy, and Mary Shaw, seven; Alison Allan, fifty-five, an agricultural worker; Janet Hill, forty-five, a pauper, Thomas Doughty, nine, and James Mein, fifteen; George Crail, seventy, a laborer, and Christian Crail, sixty; James Dickson, eighty-five, Jemima Dickson, twenty, Janet Dickson, nine, James Dickson, four; Helen Gordon, seventy, a spinster of independent means; Henrietta Spears, sixty, a washerwoman; James Civess, fifty-five, a laborer, Mary Civess, sixty, Archibald Civess, twenty, a laborer, Robert Civess, eighteen, a laborer, and Helen Civess, twenty; and Archibald Harrier, an eight-month-old infant.

Logan's Close was a cross section of Dunbar's poor at the time—laborers and menial workers worn and twisted well before they reached middle age, ragged beggars, and sickly children. Many of the flats were merely single rooms in poorly lit, drafty, dirty, whitewashed tenements opening onto the narrow passage-way, which once served as a dumping ground for waste. Disease ran rampant. Cholera, typhus, scarlet fever, and whooping cough plagued the people as much as their poverty. Small improvements had been made in sanitation and living conditions since his footsteps last echoed off the stone pavement and walls, yet poverty remained, insidious and endemic, he noted with sadness. He couldn't turn away. Just before Christmas, after he had returned to the States, John sent his cousin a draft for fifty dollars to divide equally between her needs and those of the Dunbar poor. He would make the contribution, raised to one hundred dollars in a year or two, each Christmas for the rest of his life, the last contribution made just days before he died on Christmas Eve twenty-one years later.

Below the high ground of High Street, the harbor and its adjacent fishing community remained intact too, though lingering in a deepening twilight. In season, one could still walk boat to boat across the "new" harbor, the safe haven filled with sixty to eighty fishing *cobles*—open-hauled wooden boats that could be rowed—sheltered from the North Sea gales. For 350 years, herring was the prize catch. In times past, perhaps a thousand boats from around the North Sea rendezvoused off Dunbar during the late summer when the shoals ran so thick that their shimmering mass and motion seemingly transformed the sea from a liquid into a slithering solid. The local fleet caught cod and haddock (whitefish) the remainder of the year. In Cromwell's day, 20,000 people were reported to visit the tiny burgh over the two-month-long Dunbar *drave,* when the swarm of small boats chased the shoals just as the Plains Indians in the New World chased the vast herds of buffalo across the prairie sea. The arrival of the human throng must have transformed Dunbar as much as the arrival of the herring transformed the waters offshore. But herring yields, always uncertain, declined during the 1800s. Early on, 300 boats with 2,000 men still fished for herring from Dunbar, yielding about 35,000 barrels of the silvery catch in a season. By John's return the herring no longer ran in great shoals. Whitefish and lobster were the principal catch.

Potatoes were the principal export from the port, the crop's red-roofed warehouses still standing around the harbor. London markets paid top dollar for the staple. Business was good, but no longer booming as it had following the opening of the new harbor in the early 1840s and the end of the potato blight around mid-century. Other cargoes in or out of the once flourishing port had changed little since King David II established the Royal Burgh in 1369 with a free port at Belhaven, but the amounts varied significantly from year to year and decade to decade due to the condition of the harbor, the fleet, and the markets, all of which were routinely disrupted by storms and wars. John likely saw little evidence of Dunbar's history of maritime trade.

During the harbor's heyday in the first half of the 1800s, two dozen vessels from foreign ports and twelve-score ships from coastwise ports docked annually at Dunbar, perhaps thirty-five of which made the small harbor their home. Only a few still did. In a good year the port received 15,000 tons of coal, 700 loads of fir timber, and modest amounts of wheat, barley, and miscellaneous dry goods. Outbound ships carried thousands of barrels of fish and the bounty from the rich outlying farmland: 20,000 quarters of wheat, barley, oats, beans, peas, malt, and flour, and 200,000 gallons of whiskey. Loads of fertilizer came and went as well: "ashes" were imported; burnt lime was exported from small harbors along the coast at places like Catcraig, southeast of town, where limestone quarried nearby was reduced in giant kilns overlooking the beach. Little of these cargoes crossed the wharf when John returned to the harbor.

Here, along Lamer Street, Woodbush Brae, and the harbor area, John discovered the biggest difference between the Dunbar of his childhood and the Dunbar of his adulthood. The tight streets and landings once teemed with activity and industry— granaries and maltings, a brewery, a tannery, a soap works, dairies, coopers, fish-curing yards, warehouses and customhouses, small boatyards, and cordage and sailcloth makers. Now he found fewer businesses and slackened harbor life as the fishing yields

declined and maritime trade moved elsewhere. A drop in the stifling density of people living in the crowded tenements here may
have partly offset the gain in Dunbar's population at the fringe.
Still, the tight-knit fishing community remained strong and as
closed to outsiders as ever, its distinct customs and culture as yet
undiminished by the latest downturn. After all, they'd weathered centuries of economic storms as well as North Sea gales.
They would weather this latest tempest too.

As a member of the middle class of High Street, John would
forever be a "streetie" to the mariners. He would forever be an
outsider, an onlooker, to the "shories" who made their living
from the sea and lived along the harbor and coastline below the
market town. In between, the poor lived in the netherworld of
the closes that connected the two communities. Whether professionals, merchants, tradesmen, or farmers, people of the land
could never really know the seafolk any more than they could
know the sea itself. Nor could the shories understand life on land
the same way that those who made their livelihood from it did.
How could it be otherwise?

Perhaps this is true of coastal communities everywhere, yet
here it was part of a pervasive, long-lasting class system. Dunbar still suffered the same social stratification of John's childhood: a social hierarchy descending from the ancestral nobility to
the landed aristocracy, to middle-class gentry, professionals, and
merchants, to tradesmen, tenant farmers, fishermen, and skilled
workers, to unskilled servants and laborers, to the indigent poor.
Daniel Muir fled Dunbar in part to escape this deep-rooted
system. Perhaps he felt there was an inescapable class barrier, a
social chasm, between himself and some in the community. Perhaps they felt it too. Daniel had no pedigree, though he had risen
to the middle class as a successful merchant. Yet he wasn't born
into the middle class; even today I sense that that makes a difference to some people here—birth, not personal achievement, de-

termines one's social status. Daniel's father-in-law, David Gilrye, had worked his way up as well from an apprentice flesher to a prosperous tradesman, though he and Margaret might have considered themselves members of the middle class before, based on family lineage. Did they think Daniel below them in status at the time of his marriage to Anne, or was their disapproval based on other concerns? In the New World such things mattered less. Daniel Muir's New World homeland surely had its social stigmas, but I doubt they matched those that he left behind in the Old World. John might have had his first full taste of America's class consciousness at the champagne parties given for him by the eastern elite just before he left New York.

"Dunbar is an interesting place to anybody," John wrote home, "beautifully located on a plateau above the sea and with a background of beautiful hills and dales, green fields in the highest state of cultivation and many belts and blocks of woods, so arranged as to appear natural." Outside town he found the farms and fields little changed from those he knew as a boy. "I have had a good many rides and walks into the country among the fine farms and towns and old castles, and had long talks with people who listen with wonder to the stories of California and far Alaska," he continued. "I was on a visit yesterday to a farmer[']s family three miles from town. . . . This was a fine specimen of the gentleman farmer's place and people in this best part of Scotland. How fine the grounds are and the buildings and the people. . . . Nothing can surpass the exquisite fineness and wealth of the farm crops—while the modulation of the ground, stretching away from the rocky, foamy coast to the green Lammermoor hills[,] is charming."

The rural landscape fabric he admired had not changed substantially in over a century. The patchwork pattern of fields partitioned by dykes and hedgerows remained unaltered since it was established during the Enclosures that began around 1700 as a new agricultural system at long last replaced the centuries-old medieval system. Many triggers led to the transformation, particularly those that fostered social stability and created economic incentives for farmers to improve fields and cropping practices. Changes that lengthened the term of a lease gave tenants greater security on the land. Other changes enabled tenants to profit from the improvements they made, instead of passing on the entire benefit to the landowner. For landowners, the most important trigger was the Act of Union in 1707 and the political stability it eventually brought to the region. Intermittent warfare had stifled experimentation and innovation for centuries as a wave of destruction swept across the East Lothian landscape with each invasion. Now landowners felt free for the first time to focus attention on their land rather than on the latest political upheaval. Stability also fostered economic incentives as distant markets opened up and demand for agricultural products surged. Booming industrial centers lured workers off the fields and farms, creating demand for food while reducing the rural labor force. By mid-century, new farming practices increased yields and a new rural order fundamentally restructured fields and fostered other significant social changes. Landownership became more concentrated in the hands of a few, farms grew in size and became more well defined as separate entities tenanted by a single family, the number of farmworkers declined and they became less dispersed across the land, and the social stratification between landowners, tenants, and laborers intensified.

Nor had the agricultural commodities produced changed much over the past hundred years since the Improvements. Potatoes were still grown on the best soils, with wheat, barley, turnips, oats, beans, and peas rotated elsewhere. Cattle and sheep grazed marginal lands and the rocky slopes too steep to cultivate on the face of the Lammermuirs. Woodland was scarce, for farmland was too valuable to be left uncultivated. What little forest existed in the Dunbar area often grew on the large estates, like the 800 acres of woodland planted in the early 1700s by the sixth Earl of Haddington on his Tyninghame Estate. These estates still dominated the countryside by retaining ownership of almost all the land, shaping its physical form and its social organization just as they had for centuries.

The Duke of Roxburghe still owned the Broxmouth Estate and the adjacent farms with their associated houses and properties immediately south of town, some 80 holdings in all, including farms or cottages at Boonslie, Brandsmill, Broxburn, Brunt, Catcraig, East Barns, East Meikle Pinkerton, Kirkhill, Links, Little Pinkerton, Oswaldean, Oxwellmains, Sloebigging, and West Meikle Pinkerton. His properties roughly formed a triangle four miles on a side, stretching from the estate southeasterly down the coast to Skateraw, then inland southwesterly along the Dry Burn, then northeasterly along Spott (Brock) Burn back to the estate.

The area's other titled nobleman, the Earl of Haddington, still owned about 150 properties, including the Tyninghame Estate and the block of land to the west and northwest of town. His holdings, including farms or cottages at Easter Broomhouse, Hedderwickhill, Johnscleugh, Kirklandhill, Knowes, Lawhead, Lochouses, Tynefield, Tyninghame village, and Wester Broomhouse lay scattered about, but the core formed roughly a parallelogram running several miles along the coast between Peffer Burn to the north of the Tyne estuary and Hedderwick Burn to the south, the boundary then running inland along the burns to the parish boundary.

The wedge of land to the southwest and west of Dunbar, between the Roxburghe and Haddington holdings, still lay mostly in the hands of three landed aristocratic families. The Warrenders owned the Eweford, Hallhill, Lochend, Newtonless, and Chesterhall Farms. The Nisbets owned the Beesknowe, Biel,

Hedderwick, Howmuir, and Ninewar Farms. And the different branches of the Hays retained the Belton, North Belton, and South Belton Farms. Only a handful of other people owned more than a single small property. The inability of common people to purchase land, to gain the economic and social privileges afforded by property ownership, to gain greater control over their lives, to gain power, helped to drive Daniel Muir from Dunbar. Nothing of significance had been done since to change the situation.

John stayed in Dunbar about two weeks, then continued his tour of the British Isles, Scandinavia, and the Continent. He returned briefly to Dunbar on his way back to the New World, forever leaving his Old World home behind. Had he found his roots? Did they match his memory? Was he able to complete his sense of self? I think so. I think I must as well—I must confirm my roots here, and at home, to complete my sense of self and find my place in the landscape.

[17]

Will you be buried here, I ask John George Baillie-Hamilton, the thirteenth Earl of Haddington, as we sit on the low stone wall that traces the outline of St. Baldred's Church on his Tyninghame Estate. We face south, looking across the River Tyne's broad estuary toward his Hedderwickhill, Tynefield, and Kirklandhill Farms a mile off on the opposite side. The Lammermuir Hills stand several miles beyond in the distance. The view is stunning on this unusually warm, muggy summer day. We're both sweating from our stroll about the estate, so the brief respite allows us to catch our breath. He lights a cigarette. "Yes," he replies.

The earl doesn't look the part. He's sixty years old, affable but a bit reserved, with a large chest, a full face of reddish complexion, metal-framed spectacles, and a ring of scruffy silver-white hair around the fringe of his bald spot. He's dressed comfortably, wearing an old cotton T-shirt labeled "Borneo Divers," a wrinkled light beige linen sport coat, khaki pants, and Timberland shoes. He speaks softly with a proper English accent, punctuated by a throaty chuckle quick to erupt. He looks well worn to me, slightly frayed around the edges. The unkempt condition of his new Land Rover seems fitting.

The parish church in which we sit was built in the mid-twelfth century and named for the disciple of Saint Mungo who made his anchorite cell on the property perhaps as early as the late sixth century. Most accounts claim he died in 606. King Lothian probably launched his pregnant daughter's coracle from the mouth of the River Tyne within our view. The church remained in use for six hundred years until the parish merged with the adjacent parish of Whitekirk in 1761. The abandoned church was pulled down in large part then and the small village for estate workers that had grown up around it was relocated, perhaps to clear the view to the estuary from the house and gardens. The earl owned the village and employed the people, after all. The displaced were moved a half mile west into new housing added around the "Widow's Row" for estate retainers. A skeleton of Norman arches and shafts, the tracery wall, and the headstones are all that remain of the church now. A curious pattern of thistles and nettles in the surrounding pasture mark the former village site, their presence a faint reflection of the past human presence.

The family acquired Tyninghame in 1628 when the first earl, Sir Thomas Hamilton, bought the property from another wealthy family, who themselves had recently acquired it. For nearly a thousand years before it had been church property. Sir Thomas was a "demon" lawyer and a favorite of King James VI (James I of England) who held numerous crown appointments in the 1600s: lord clerk register, lord of session, secretary of state,

lord of Parliament, privy councillor, lord privy, commissioner of
the treasury, lord president of the Court of Session, and king's
advocate. As a reward, the king bestowed the earldom on his
trusted friend in 1627. Competent, efficient, and a bit of a
rogue—"Tam o' the Cowgate," he was called—Sir Thomas used
his considerable power and position to acquire one of Scotland's
largest fortunes at the time.

The current earl—John, as he's comfortable being called—
shows me the markers for his parents, grandparents, and great-
grandparents, headstones for generation after generation of
ancestors lying flat on the closely cropped turf. "She was really a
marvelous person," he says, standing over his grandmother's
marker. "She kept the estate going for thirty-five years after
grandfather died in 1917." A career soldier, he'd served king and
country in Africa, Asia, and India, fighting in remote theaters to
secure the empire. Unfortunately, he died at home of a war-
incurred disease three months before his father died at age ninety.

Since feudal times, the nobility composed the backbone of the
nation's officer corps, serving the crown on command as part
of the social contract. By the 1800s, military service defined
the life of many noblemen, together with civic functions, estate
management, and sports. World War I devastated their ranks,
prompting one commentator to say that the flower of the British
aristocracy perished during the retreat from Mons and the first
battle of Ypres. The feudal system vanished, the commentator
explained, as the fire of the Great War consumed the landed
class.

Taxation in the 1900s, though, proved to be the real death
knell. Popular opinion turned against landowners in the late
1800s, bringing political reforms that imposed death duties for
the first time in 1894, followed by a succession of other taxes on
property and profits. Rates were raised throughout the early
1900s, reaching a punitive level when the death duty for large

estates rose to 40 percent in 1919. Dozens of grand ancestral estates sold land to pay the bills.

The double duties due on the deaths of the earl's grandfather and great-grandfather in 1917 forced the family to sell about 10,000 acres of its 27,000-acre total holdings. Had John's grandfather died in the field, much of the duty would have been forgiven. When the earl's grandmother died in 1954, her possessions in Tyninghame were subjected to 80 percent death duties. Such punitive taxation persisted from just after World War II until the mid-1960s, forcing the sale of more estates. Apparently the postwar Labour government and popular opinion felt the wealthy should carry a heavy burden to finance the country's reconstruction. Perhaps they also felt it right to redistribute the wealth since so much of it was acquired from the land and labor of others. Perhaps they also intended the sales to break up the stranglehold the landed elite had had on landownership since feudal times. Many estates began to sell pieces from their art collections to pay taxes or finance household repairs, although creditors often permitted the art to stay in the estate as long as it was open to the public. The practice continues today, in response to many mounting economic and social pressures on the owners of estates to convert them into public attractions.

Yet when the estates sell, often they aren't broken up into many small parcels bought by commoners. Instead many sell intact or in large pieces to wealthy entrepreneurs and professionals from home and abroad, little affecting the concentration of landownership. Today Scotland retains the highest concentration of landownership in Europe. The transfer of land into many hands occurs more successfully when an estate shrinks gradually, selling off farms sequentially.

Tyninghame followed this path, dwindling by attrition. Another 1,700 acres were cast off as part of a divorce settlement in 1980. Death taxes due when John assumed the title in 1986, following his father's death, finally forced the sale of the actual estate house and 80 acres of the immediate grounds. The family's winter residence at Mellerstain became their year-round home. But in death John will return here to St. Baldred's, embosomed in the family's ancestral seat.

In life, the earl visits Tyninghame about once a month; he still owns 3,000 acres surrounding the main house and gardens. Picnics on the beach below the house remain a family favorite. He also owns a grouse moor hill farm of about 2,500 acres, used mostly for shooting, in the Lammermuirs. Do you miss the house, I ask. "I do in a way, yes, absolutely. But you have to make do," he replies with a slight chuckle. He holds no bitterness or resentment about the circumstances that forced the sale. "It's not a bad life," he says. After all, Mellerstain is one of the grand houses of Scotland, set in a storybook 8,000-acre estate overlooking the Cheviot Hills in the Scottish Borders. The family acquired the estate by marriage generations earlier. Yet the same financial necessities that forced the sale of Tyninghame House forced the new earl to place Mellerstain in a charitable trust, open most of the sprawling house to the public on a daily basis, and move the family into a "small" wing.

We walk on, through an ornate iron gate, up an overgrown path toward the family's immense home for 350 years, but no longer. "There," he says, pointing to two large windows on an upper floor of the eastern wing. "That was my bedroom." The massive rosy pink sandstone house towers over us. "The house martin nest there?" he asks himself. "We always had a house martin nest. They'd come sit on the end of my bed in the morning. Lovely," he says.

How many square feet does the house have, I ask. "I'd hate to think," he says, chuckling. "Mellerstain is smaller and it has 365 windows. Tyninghame has a much different feel than Mellerstain, you know."

We first met there on one of the earliest spring days comfortable enough to sit outside in the sun without wearing a coat. I'd previously interviewed two other nobles—dukes—at their grand estates. This meeting, though, was different, almost surreal. We shared his last beer while we spoke sitting in the courtyard of the former carriage house and stable, now just outside the dining room of the family wing. As our conversation concluded, the countess invited me to join them and four family friends for lunch. I felt the interloper until her gracious charm put me at ease. She prepared the meal from scratch in the kitchen, no servants or maids, nothing unusual. We served ourselves from the sideboard. After dessert we retired to the living room for coffee and drinks and talked all afternoon amid the family mementos. The children busied themselves playing chess, working a jigsaw puzzle, and eventually escaping to the den for video games.

The day was not what I, as a commoner from the New World, expected, although I wasn't sure what I expected. The family's mix of traditional Old World wealth, title, and privilege, with the modern-day realities that dictate their daily lives seemed bizarre. I left in a rush to make a wine-tasting party that evening hosted by a friend who lives in Oldhamstocks, a tiny village of farmworker cottages like those that once housed the workers at Tyninghame and Mellerstain. The cottages have all been renovated, making modest, quaint, and comfortable homes. The party this evening would be held in a restored old smiddy, a fitting end to the day.

Tyninghame House stands solid, stark, and rugged, romantic in a wild sense. Mellerstain appears dignified, one of the great "Adam" houses of the Scottish nobility. Refined and elegant, it was built in two stages by the famous father-and-son architects, the first stage constructed by William Adam in 1725 and the second by his son Robert Adam in the 1770s. Its library is one of the most famous rooms architecturally in the country. Do you reoccupy the full house at the end of the day when the tourists are chased away? "We don't, actually, no," the earl replies. "Too much to do in our own portion of the house to spread ourselves any further." Do you feel like a tenant in your own house? "No, not at all. We live in one wing, which is perfectly adequate for a family with three children." Did the mammoth Tyninghame and Mellerstain houses feel like "homes" to you growing up? "Absolutely," he says. "They were wonderful homes. They're very much home."

The Duke of Roxburghe, who lives in Floors Castle, the largest inhabited house in Scotland just down the road from Mellerstain, explained, "It's obviously very difficult for anybody who hasn't been fortunate, or dare I say unfortunate, enough to live in a place like this to understand how you can have the same attachment to it as you would have to a two-, four-, or six-bedroom house that has been your home all your life. The castle and park are home. The whole thing is a living entity, particularly since I was brought up in it. That's very important. You don't feel the same for a house if you recently bought it or moved into it from another residence. In that case it's not home because it's not where you have your childhood memories. You need those memories to have a love affair—and that's what it is—with a house from a young age. And I was lucky in that, for although this is a massive castle, those memories are what binds me to it." He feels the same for the land on which he's fished, ridden, and hunted since childhood at the core of his 56,000-acre estate. Connection to place comes from personal experience and memories, regardless of scale.

The earl and I walk along the gravel path toward the extensive gardens on the west side of Tyninghame House, discussing the financial circumstances that now confront many grand estates. Giant holly hedges neatly clipped and shaped for three hundred years muffle the crunch of our footfalls. Historically, owners of estates like this derived most of their income from the estate's many farms and rental properties, particularly during the profitable 1700s and 1800s. Few lairds possessed significant sources of outside income and few diversified their asset base. Their wealth rested in the opulent family homes filled with fabulous furnishings and art, and in rural land, farm buildings, and worker cottages. Maintenance of their grand homes and their corresponding lifestyle consumed most of their income. Like many estate homes and grounds during this period, Tyninghame House was significantly enlarged and the grounds redone. William Burn supervised the work in 1829, transforming "a plain old Scottish mansion of large size" into an imposing baronial structure of Tudor and Jacobean styles adorned with pointed circular turrets, large mullioned bay windows, and crowstepped chimney towers.

When Daniel Muir fled Dunbar, Tyninghame House alone employed about twenty servants, including Mary Porteous, age fifty-eight, single, housekeeper; Esther Frost, forty-six, married, cook; Dorothea Ranzen, fifty-two, single, lady's maid; Mary Edington, fifty-two, widow, laundress; Jane Dixon, thirty-nine, single, housemaid; Elizabeth Gunn, thirty-five, single, housemaid; Marion Alison, twenty-eight, single, dairymaid; Anne Moore, eighteen, single, still room maid; Elizabeth Ward, twenty-seven, single, kitchen maid; Hannah Hay, eighteen, single, scullery maid; Mary Henderson, twenty-one, single, housemaid; George Baker, fifty-three, married, butler; William Bavin, thirty-five, single, coachman; John Dickson, twenty-one, single, footman; Samuel Wade, twenty-five, single, footman; Samuel Norman, twenty-eight, single, groom; and James Prentice, sixteen, single, steward's room boy. The estate stables, grounds, and gardens employed dozens of others, as did the numerous farms. The dominance of estates like Tyninghame over the physical and social landscape persisted.

By the 1900s, the economics and politics had changed. "You can't maintain a huge house and everything that goes with the ownership of large properties like this on rental income or, indeed, on income from in-hand farms. It simply doesn't work anymore," the earl says. "So you must find other means of raising cash." Profits plummeted from the farms due to rising labor costs and declining commodity prices caused by international competition. Profits dropped as well from rental properties as the rural population declined due to mechanization and other social forces. Taxes increased too, especially on inheritance, as the public and the government became more hostile toward the wealthy estate owners. All this ensnared many lairds in an economic trap: while they now needed to diversify, many found it too late to do so without incurring a staggering loss in assets. The trap remains. For rural estates, property values are low due to the poor profitability of farming, the limited market for the sale of farmland, especially tenanted farms, and the lack of non-farm land-use alternatives. And what little revenue it receives when it sells farmland is further reduced by capital gains taxes.

Today, the earl explains, his properties are valued for tax purposes based on a 1982 assessment adjusted for inflation. If he sells a farm he rents to a tenant (and he rents most of his land), he pays 40 percent tax on the capital gains plus 40 percent income tax. And the market value of that farm is about half that of land he farms in-hand because the tenancy transfers unaffected by the sale—the new owner must accept the sitting tenant. "It's just not worth it to sell much of our land for farming," he says, "and it has little development potential, at least that which the Council government will permit." If he sells land he farms in-hand, he pays no capital gains and the land has twice the market value of tenanted land. So why not sell it and invest the profit in stocks or other properties that generate greater returns? Because often that's the land they like best, the heart of their estates. It's the land they struggle to retain. It's their home.

Yet that's just what the earl was forced to do when he assumed the title. Financial necessity forced him to choose between Tyninghame and Mellerstain. The budget could only support one, and only then if he took other measures to stabilize the family finances. "Which arm do you cut off?" he says. The family had spent summers at Tyninghame beginning when he was a thirteen-year-old in 1954, after his reclusive grandmother who lived alone in the vast house died. Only winters were then spent at Mellerstain, about fifty miles to the south. Mellerstain was always more of my home, he tells me. He preferred its wilder landscape too. Tyninghame also needed major roof repairs and other upgrades. And the property had been eyed by developers like Jack Nicklaus, the renowned golfer and golf course designer, who planned to transform the estate into a world-class golf resort with a links-style course built along the shore and the main house converted into a clubhouse/hotel complex. "I wouldn't do that," John states emphatically. "It would destroy the house and the gardens my mother worked so hard to create."

However, he would like permission to build new homes on portions of the property. The Council government won't permit it. Its land-use policies limit him to partitioning and renovating remaining estate buildings like the stable and steading into individual flats. While this preserves the historic character of the estate and the landscape, limiting low-density sprawl, it also limits his ability to capitalize on the value of his property. Individual property rights are balanced much differently against public interests here than in Marquette County, Wisconsin.

Nor would he sell the property to a single buyer. "The danger in selling the place to one person is that if he can't keep it up, he might sell to another person who would have no regard for the place. You'd have no control on the future." So he sold the house and gardens for a song (£250,000) to a specialist in the conversion of grand country homes into exclusive multiple-owner properties. The contents of the house were sold at auction for more than £4 million. The house was then broken up vertically into nine private residences, each with a separate entrance, while leaving the exterior and much of the interior virtually untouched. "Having nine people in it," he says, "is more secure. They can't all go bust at the same time, you see. It works much better—more likely to maintain the place in good order." A fund supported by the nine owners pays for the upkeep of the extensive gardens.

The plan apparently worked. The nine units sold promptly to buyers including the director of the National Gallery of Scotland and the CEO of a giant international supermarket chain. Several owners are good friends of the earl. He says he's delighted with the condition of the grounds as we explore the "secret" garden his mother made. He stops and tells me about the plants and statues, speaking with love and admiration for their beauty. "If I'd sold the place to Jack Nicklaus, would he have maintained all this?" The gardens and grounds are opened to the public twice a year, although the spring tour this year was canceled due to the foot-and-mouth disease outbreak in livestock throughout England and Scotland. The "Old Kitchen," one of the nine residences, is now on the market for offers over £325,000. The newspaper advertisement describes it as "a stunning conversion of the original kitchens of Tyninghame mansionhouse to form a charming very stylish country home in courtyard setting with right of access to approx. 30 acres of formal and wilderness gardens and woodland walks. Porch, hall, kitchen/living room/dining room, sitting room, study/bedroom four with ladder access to floored playroom, bathroom, cloakroom/laundry, principal bedroom with en suite bathroom and walk in closet, two double bedrooms and family bathroom. Patio garden. Shared tennis court. Two garages."

What do you consider your job since you assumed the title, I ask. "Perpetuating the estate; yes, I think that's really what my role is," he replies. The Duke of Roxburghe concurred. "I care for my estate deeply because it is my inheritance and it is what I have been fortunate enough to be given. And, my, it is important to me whether it is the house or the grounds. My challenge is to try and pass it on to future generations in as healthy a state as I can. The raison d'être of the estate is very much linked to the continued survival of the castle as a home and focal point for the family. We're lucky that the estate is big enough that we can afford to keep the castle going, unless we make a mess of it."

Both the earl and the duke see themselves as the chief executive of the family business—the estate. They oversee the management of the houses, the farms, and other properties assisted by a *factor,* a professional full-time estate manager. But the management isn't as cold and calculating as it might sound. Emotions complicate the calculus. What rules, your head or your heart, when you make those decisions, I asked the duke. "The heart controls the head a fair amount of the time in my case, but hopefully not too much so," he responded with a laugh. "There has to be an economic reality to things. There comes a time when you have to face up to the fact that you must make a decision that hurts your heart. But obviously there're certain parts of the estate, going back to one's memories, in which the heart has a greater role to play than the head."

The earl's estate is financially stable now, he believes, depending on how much money the family draws from it to support their lifestyle. The lavish days of the past, even as recent as his childhood, are only memories, though the family lives in their twilight. But the new balance won't support several households. The children will probably need careers that earn outside income. "Mellerstain is a place I have chosen to preserve," he says, "so I really have to make sure that everything goes well there, and that I can leave it in good state for my son. Hopefully he'll be able to live there. But I'm not convinced I'd have him as involved in agriculture as I've been. He ought to go and get another well-paying job in the city because in the future even the in-hand farms are not going to give him the income to support the place."

What will be your son's role when he assumes the title, I ask. Will he be the CEO of the estate? "Well, that depends on how things go in the future," the earl replies. "I'd rather he got a job on the outside. It'd be nice, though, to think it'll go on, somewhat like it is now. But I have my doubts—costs, politics, and economics of agriculture. Things do go in cycles and no doubt it'll bounce back again, but whether it'll come back in the same way, I don't know." It's a delicate balance to achieve before one assumes the title: developing an outside life and career while maintaining a passion, a love, for the estate. It's an even more difficult balance once the title is acquired.

How does your son feel about inheriting the title and the responsibility for the estate, I ask. Is it a curse or a blessing? "It's very much a double-edged sword," he answers. "I really haven't bothered him with it yet. The children love it there and should have a jolly childhood without worrying about such matters until they come of age." That time will come later. The practice of primogeniture for centuries has helped keep the estates intact, maintaining family wealth and power. It also entangles the eldest son in a life he may not desire. Primogeniture persisted until the mid-1960s, when a change in inheritance laws permitted greater flexibility in the naming of heirs, although the practice continues today by personal choice.

How do the other children feel about the bulk of the family inheritance going to the eldest son? How does that fact affect their feelings for the estate? I suspect the issue—siblings split by the traditions of inheritance, albeit for understandable reasons— lies shallow beneath the surface of the nobles' thinking. "It's very difficult for the siblings who are not going to inherit the estate," replied the Duke of Roxburghe. "You want them to love it as a home, like you'd want anyone to love a home; but obviously they can't have the same emotional attachment to the place because it's not going to be their future." The earl's two daughters, both younger than his son, have little sense of it yet.

The duke assumed the title and the responsibilities at age nineteen, giving him little opportunity beforehand to form a life—a career and interests—beyond the boundary of the estate. He's been able to do so since and thinks it critical that his children do so as well. The call came for the earl at age forty-five. After private schooling and university at Trinity College, Dublin, the young earl-to-be explored the Middle East and Australia before beginning a career as a photographer in London. "Making wedding pictures wasn't what I wanted to do," he tells me. "But that was the only work I could get. I wanted to photograph landscapes and such." Five years of wedding portraits and party pictures was too much, so he set off for South America in search of adventure, eventually finding work on a Bolivian ranch. A year later he returned and studied agriculture. In 1975 he took over a 400-acre farm on the Mellerstain property. "I loved it. I did all the work with two hired hands—lambing, plowing, seeding. I liked driving a tractor the best." He farmed for eleven years, until inheriting the family responsibilities. He continues to be deeply involved in their 2,200 acres of in-hand farms. He served in the House of Lords for about a dozen years as well. "I quite enjoyed that," he says, until he lost his seat as a result of recent changes in membership rules that largely banned hereditary peers. Shooting, fishing, riding, and photography remain major interests. He also publishes a biannual magazine for a charity he founded that works for the protection of songbirds. And with his noble status come numerous calls to participate in various civic and charitable activities. In effect, being the earl now defines his professional and personal life, whether he likes it or not.

"I suppose I'm most proud of having put the family holdings in good order," he tells me as we walk through Binning Wood at Tyninghame after a break for lunch and a pint of cask ale at the Drovers Inn in East Linton, just up the road from Tyninghame village. "And I'm quite pleased we were able to restore some life to the village." Those will be his legacies. In John Muir's day, Tyninghame was a reasonably self-contained rural village with nearly 275 people living in seventy-two rented cottages. The village also contained a post office, pub, school, smiddy, saw-mill, and bakery/miller. Most of the handsome red sandstone ashlar buildings with pantile roofs were constructed to replace thatched-roofed cottages between 1830 and 1850 by the estate's mason, Thomas Hannan, after renovation of the main house and the construction of a new courtyard stables, dairy, ice house, and piggery. Like the main house, the picturesque village overlooks the River Tyne valley and the Lammermuirs from its promontory on a long, low hill. Binning Woods forms its backdrop.

The village typified an English style for the properly planned estate village of the period, its neatly crafted cottages set back from the street and positioned in an orderly manner around a vil-lage green. It also reflected the predominant social order and physical organization of the prosperous eighteenth- and nine-teenth-century East Lothian rural landscape. The biggest estates controlled enough land and employed enough people in the main house and farm that a small community formed near some. Out-lying farms, usually tenanted, shared the same basic social and physical structure, although on a smaller scale, with a modest main house and a cluster of fewer farmworker cottages. On farms employing less labor still, rows of cottages lay scattered along fields near the main house.

The grand farm steading was the showcase of the farm, proudly symbolizing the farmer's and the region's agricultural prowess and profitability. East Lothian farms were famed throughout Britain and the Continent for both. The long rectangular stone barns with steep-pitched tile roofs formed an elegant quadrangle facing a central courtyard. A brick smokestack towered overhead, carrying away the steam and soot from the newfangled threshers and other mechanized implements revolutionizing the operations and reducing the need for workers. Today many abandoned steadings have been converted into attractive housing complexes. The earl hopes to do the same for the steading on Tyninghame, just as he's converted the carriage house/dairy and other historic farm buildings into rental properties.

Mechanization meant change, not just in farming technology but also in the social fabric of rural life. The effects came in phases. The rural population began to decline during the first phase of change in the early 1700s concurrent with the improvements in farming that replaced the former "infield/outfield" farming practices. Infields were expanses of open, arable land surrounding a loose cluster of perhaps a dozen or so tenant cottages and steadings that formed a *fermtoun*. The small community of tenants and *cottars* (married laborers who subleased some land from a tenant) jointly cropped and fertilized the land continuously using the run-rig method. Run-rig plowed fields into long strips (rigs) several yards wide and a yard high, progressively mounding the soil year after year to improve drainage. Manure, household waste, turf, seaweed, and later lime were applied to the rigs with loving care to sustain the yields of wheat, *bere* (a hardy form of barley), oats, and legumes grown on them. Each family worked several rigs, with responsibility rotated periodically. Leases were short, often annual, so tenants had no security. Outfields lay beyond the more fertile infields. Outfields were cropped (oats mostly) between fallow years and manured mostly by grazing stock. The least productive land, usually lying even

further out, was used communally for pasturing with little husbandry practiced on the land. Practical, adaptable, cooperative-
based, the infield/outfield system served the needs of Scotland
when farm production barely satisfied demand beyond the subsistence level. Yet throughout the 1600s, social, economic, and
population pressures grew for change in this well-worn way of
rural life. The resulting revolution in the Lowlands began by the
early 1700s.

The estates led the way. Their size and financial security gave
the lairds more freedom to experiment in improvements and
practice sound husbandry than did the circumstances confront-
ing tenants or owners of small farms. Stone dykes and hawthorn
hedges enclosed fields partitioned into individual units, replacing the open lands worked in common by many hands. New
tillage techniques and crop rotations replaced the traditional
run-rig cultivation practiced since medieval times. The sixth
Earl of Haddington personified the forward-thinking laird. Some
say he was the first person in Scotland to enclose agricultural
fields, using limestone dykes and holly hedges. In the early
1700s, he also introduced the practice of fallowing fields and the
use of ryegrass and clover.

These agricultural improvements resulted in the depopulation
of the rural landscape, shifting the distribution of people from
farms to towns to an extent approaching that of the infamous
Highland Clearances. The advent of steam-powered implements
in the mid-1800s brought another phase of improvements and
displacement. The latest phase began after World War II as tractors, combines, and other implements became commonplace.
Tyninghame village mirrored those changes.

For years the earl's mother held a Christmas party for the children from the village and the estate's seven outlying farms. In
1953, 103 children attended. One hundred years earlier, that
number might have been double. By the 1980s, fewer than 20

children could be counted. Some of the village cottages stood empty as the estate and farms supported only a fraction of the former number of people, and those cottages that were still occupied typically had fewer children per household as family size had declined. The village was withering. In 1991 the earl began efforts to reinvigorate it.

The estate still owned twenty-five of the thirty-three cottages, having sold eight in the early 1980s during the divorce settlement. To spur redevelopment, the earl proposed to sell off various buildings for conversion and a small amount of land for new construction. Council government approval of the plan was grudging. Nine new homes have been built and six converted for occupancy, giving the village today forty-eight residences, more families, and more life. The old smiddy has been converted into a successful coffee/gift shop. Cute and quaint, the village survives with a new population and a new role in the social fabric, although the physical fabric remains less affected. Few residents now work on the estate or the farms; few work the land. Commuters, retirees, and recreational residents predominate. It's the same basic change occurring in Marquette County.

Are the big estates anachronisms, dinosaurs of a time past, serving a role now nearly extinct? The earl and the duke think not. "The people who live and work on these big estates enjoy it and have a good life," the earl says. "Certainly the tenant farmers have a good deal and they have more of a personal influence than if the land belonged to a bank. But as far as the estates being an influence on the larger landscape, that's gone."

Tenanted farms enable people to begin farming with relatively little capital, people who would otherwise be financially excluded due to the cost of acquiring land and buildings. In addition, tenanted farms form a ladder of opportunity that permits farmers to gain the experience and the assets needed to move up to larger leased properties, then purchase their own.

Do the estate owners feel differently about the land than their tenants, I asked the duke. "Yes, but in grades," he replied. "It would be very strange if they all shared the same attitudes. Feelings vary between owners, long-term tenancy holders, short-term tenancy holders, workers, and those who live nearby. But mutual land interests and attitudes between the landowner and tenants have probably come closer together in the past two generations due to shared economic interests and other social changes."

The estates tend to perpetuate the region's traditional landscape character and social fabric that today attract tourists and non-farm residents. Commercial farming and new estate owners may more frequently threaten that character and fabric. Many new property owners take a more business-oriented attitude toward the land than longtime owners. Few new owners feel the same sense of responsibility for the local community than does the ancestral estate owner. And few are willing or able to accept as low a return on asset value as the longtime owner, forcing a more intensive use of the land that might well threaten long-term sustainability and environmental quality. Such uses might also change the landscape's appearance by the removal of woodlots, hedgerows, and dykes, and by the addition of new structures that contrast with the historical houses and farm buildings. The duke explained, "We have a completely different view on management of the estate, and indeed on the relationship with the local community. Ours would be much more traditional, shaped by the history of the estate, while they might look at it in much more of a business sense. We'd have much more support for the employees; if things were going bad, we'd be much more understanding and forgiving toward them."

Concern for husbandry has persisted for centuries on many estates, creating a deep-rooted stewardship ethos born of circumstances and a sense of social responsibility. Without it, the present East Lothian landscape would certainly look much different—more barren, less beautiful. Estates like Tyninghame championed reforestation and landscape design on their grounds, as well as innovations in farming practices and improvements in farm buildings. I doubt such stewardship would have occurred had these estates been broken up into many small independent farms centuries ago, although such a breakup might well have triggered other social benefits.

Despite this historical and contemporary relevancy, the earl believes the long-term fate of the estates is very much in doubt. "I can foresee the end of the estate. We have governments now that are increasingly unsympathetic toward the land and land-owners. We're also rapidly losing markets for our produce, and new countries with cheaper labor and more fertile soils are join-ing the European Union. The future of the estates is very shaky, though I'd hate to see them broken up."

We continue our walk through Binning Wood, following one of the fifteen-foot-wide paths, called *rides,* radiating out from the three circular clearings, like spokes on giant wheels. The wood contains twelve miles of rides, all open to the public by tradition. It's quiet, still, and serene. "My father was a keen forester. The wood is his legacy to us all. He was very proud of it." So is his son.

The sixth earl planted the 300-acre wood originally in the early 1700s at a time when the region was nearly devoid of trees. In total he planted about 800 acres of mixed hardwoods—oak, ash, beech, elm, sycamore, and willow—and Scots pine for tim-ber production, windbreaks, hunting, beauty, and pleasure. He also began strip-planting around fields to shelter crops from the strong coastal winds. Other estate owners followed suit. Those stands still make up most of the region's woodlands. Tyning-hame today has about 1,000 acres of woodland. Small farms and corporate farms typically can't afford to plant such stands due to the low returns and the danger of damage to the wood before har-

vest. A violent gale blew down much of Binning Wood in 1881;
replanting followed. The wood was then clear-felled in the 1940s
to supply timber needed for the war. John's father replanted
the stands after the war with the original species, carefully re-
creating the original network of clearings and rides. The original
uses remain, save for hunting. "They say you won't see sprouts
grow into trees during a lifetime," the earl says as we walk, "but
that's not true. I've seen this wood change from nearly an open
field of young saplings to become a proper wood. We'll harvest
the hardwoods when they're ready and thin until then. The wood
is very much a crop, although it's a very long-term proposition.
Hopefully, the wood won't be clear-felled again." The fifty-year-
old trees now reach perhaps five stories overhead, casting a heavy,
dark shadow on the ground beneath. The rides cut straight lines
of light through the forest masses, accentuating the geometric
forms. The effect is magical.

The earl shows me his favorite places at Tyninghame: Binning
Wood where he brought his girlfriends as a caddish young man;
the grounds he enjoyed traipsing about; the beach ridges at the
edge of the estuary where he and a keeper went with a ferret to
"pot" rabbits using a .22-caliber rifle; the chapel; the gardens;
and the small glade where he once saw a dozen fairies. "It was
about 7:00 A.M.," he recalls. "I was walking up the stream one
September morning and saw them standing there, about fifty
feet on, just there in the bush, little black monkeylike creatures
swinging from the branches. When I walked forward to get a
closer look, they dropped to the ground and vanished." The earl
tells me of other inexplicable landscape encounters he's had at
Mellerstain, in the Middle East, and at a volcanic lake inhabited
by banshees high in the mountains of Ecuador. "Every landscape
has its own special spirit. Every place has devas—spiritual entities that live in the landscape," he says. "It's a concept which is
quite hard to put over to people who have never come across this

sort of phenomenon before. There're plenty of spooks about," he says. "Mellerstain has them." He's heard them there but has never seen one.

Magic: that's it, I think. Landscapes can be magical when we form a strong sense of connection to them. The nature of that magic varies from person to person, and the connection usually takes time and a bit of work to acquire. But the rewards appear genuine. "On a glorious day, when I turn a corner on the road coming down from Edinburgh, the whole of our valley opens up before me and it's a gut-wrenching thing," the duke told me. Tyninghame and Mellerstain are magical to the earl. "They give one a great sense of history," he feels. Would you describe your feeling for them as a passion or a love, I ask. "Oh yes, a great love. I couldn't imagine what would happen if one had to move. Where would one move to? I cannot think of one place where I would really happily settle down. I love Scotland too much, though it has the most appalling weather. But it's just so beautiful in the Borders. Wonderful. And East Lothian is God's country as well." Does the countess share your feelings for the land? "Oh yes, quite so." Do you think Scots feel differently about the land, about place, than Americans? "I think they do, yes. There's a great feeling in Scotland, whoever you are, that you own a part of the country, whether you actually own it or tenant it or just share it somehow." The duke agreed. "Yes, I'm sure about that. I think it must be true because of the length of our history and association with the land." The Scottish landscape, like many ancient landscapes, *is* magical if you allow its history to seep into your soul.

[18]

Weathered and rusted, the white wrought-iron gate opens through the twelve-foot-tall stone wall into an overgrown garden filled with waist-high weeds. Vines intertwined in sensuous curves and swirls culminate with a graceful script "AR" framed in the gate's oval focal point, a faint reminder of the time when Anne Roxburghe's walled garden enchanted the senses. John Muir and his grandfather Gilrye must have gazed at the garden through the gate on their frequent walks here to Broxmouth, the dower estate of the Duke of Roxburghe, to check on the few cattle the flesher pastured in the field across the drive.

Perhaps the gate symbolized the separation between classes that drove commoners to the New World: such tantalizing beauty and plentitude for the pleasure of the dowager duchess lay just beyond their reach behind the wall and the gate. Two dozen people worked on the estate house, grounds, and gardens at the time to maintain her world. The head gardener's stone cottage guards the gate only fifty feet away. Did the gardener chase off the old man and the eager young lad or permit them a brief look?

I suspect he welcomed the walkers, for the garden was walled not to exclude people but rather to keep out deer. The high walls also blocked the wind and lengthened the growing season by about a month. Walled gardens like this one played an important role in the function of an estate, just as the estate played an important role in the life of the surrounding community. Both the walled estate and its walled garden sat clearly separate from its surroundings, yet each was closely intertwined with those surroundings, similar to the way the wrought-iron thistle and honeysuckle vines intertwined to form the gate. Fruits and vegetables for the tables of the dowager and the estate workers were grown amid the garden's parterres of flowers and clipped box hedges or in the adjoining hothouses. Surplus might have been sold in Dunbar. Townspeople traditionally enjoyed the right to walk the countryside and within limits likely enjoyed access to the estate grounds. Perhaps the many families that formed the community of estate workers had known the Gilryes and other townspeople for generations. Perhaps their children knew the

Muir children. Most families worshiped together at the Dunbar Kirk, where Grandfather Gilrye was an elder. All were equal in the eyes of God, they believed, although the dowager duchess sat in a separate pew. "The rank is but the guinea's stamp, / The Man's the gowd for a' that," wrote Robbie Burns in his beloved poem "A Man's a Man for a' That," nearly a national anthem for Scots.

> A prince can mak a belted knight,
> A marquis, duke, an' a' that;
> But an honest man's abon his might—
> Gude faith, he maunna fa' that!
> For a' that, an' a' that,
> Their dignities an a' that,
> The pith o' sense an' pride o' worth
> Are higher rank than a' that.

The democratic strain that ran so strongly through Daniel Muir's veins ran through most Scots, nobles and commoners. After all, the Scots fought bloody war after war to ensure that no bishop could rule over a congregation and no one could come between a person and God. Still, the estate and the town remained patriarchal communities, and the social separation persisted, just as a high stone wall enclosed the estate and its garden, even though large landowners often practiced noblesse oblige toward their employees, tenants, and community.

Graham White, a fifty-three-year-old environmental activist and author, lives in the head gardener's cottage at the moment, although today he purchased a partly renovated farmworker cottage fifty miles from here. He'll have much to do to make it comfortable by contemporary standards. His "short-assured tenancy agreement" for the gardener's cottage terminates in September, and the estate has been listed for sale by the current owner: "private residential estate centred on a Georgian country house set amidst parkland and woodlands within an estate wall," the sales brochure says. "113 acres. For sale as a whole or in five lots. Offers over £1.25 million for the whole." The glossy full-color brochure boasts, "The bell in the Bell Gate in the gardens of Floors Castle came from Broxmouth and until recently was used to signal the start and finish of the working day in the gardens." The estate's history features prominently in the sales pitch, proudly describing how Oliver Cromwell used the main house as his headquarters during the Battle of Dunbar in 1650, and how Queen Victoria stayed at the estate in 1878, planting a cedar tree that still stands majestically beside the current house, which replaced the former house in 1775.

"This is the most beautiful and peaceful place I've ever lived in the U.K.," Graham tells me. Toby, his brown-and-white springer spaniel, charges about the fields as we walk, a gamekeeper's gundog, stocky and muscular, bred for the hard work of retrieving. "Pedigree springers bred for show are taller and more graceful, but they are useless as working dogs," Graham explains. Toby scours the hayfield for rabbits and pheasants. "It's been a rare privilege to live here for six years. The estate has nearly five hundred acres of woods, stream, and parkland, with the biggest beech and sycamores in East Lothian apart from the Earl of Haddington's trees at Tyninghame. I live in a virtual nature reserve. Almost every day I see roe deer, foxes, herons, and owls, along with birds like curlews, merlin, oystercatchers, and shelduck. The environmental richness I experience here every day is similar to that enjoyed by a prince or duke on his estate. I've lived like a king at Broxmouth."

Graham is a commoner by birth, born into a blue-collar family that lived in the working-class city of St. Helens, outside Liverpool. "From our school roof I could count 150 giant industrial smokestacks above the glass factories and colliers," he says. "Everyone's dad worked in the glass factories, down the coal mines, or in the breweries, generation after generation. I grew up in the same house in which my father and grandfather lived and probably had fifty relatives living within a few blocks." Like many of that generation of postwar babies, he was the first in the family to win a place at university, where he earned a "first" in the history of ideas, politics, and modern literature. To get a job, though, he returned to university to earn a graduate teacher's qualification. That was in the early 1970s. Several years of community work with innovative nonprofit groups in London followed, then two years wandering in California and Central America. In 1979 he returned to the U.K. and joined the swollen ranks of the unemployed, degrees be damned. To get off the street, he took a government-funded job to organize and direct a new job-training center in Edinburgh. "I thought I'd do that for three months while I got back on my feet and decided what I wanted to do next." He left the position twenty years later, having built the nonprofit Edinburgh Environment Centre into an action-oriented organization that conducted in-school and community-based educational programs throughout the city. At its peak in the late 1980s, the Centre had a fifty-person staff and programs that annually reached thousands of children, adolescents, and adults.

Graham's path from Edinburgh to Dunbar was as accidental as John Muir's path from Dunbar to Marquette County. "One afternoon in 1979, the phone rang," he recalls, "and an American lady asked if she could visit the Centre to get some information while in town for a few days. When she stopped by, she asked if I would take her to John Muir's house in Dunbar. I knew nothing of John Muir at the time, much to her amazement. Since I was about to drive a busload of youngsters out into the countryside for a coastal adventure that day, I offered to drive her the thirty miles to Dunbar and search for Muir's house while my staff explored the beach in the new park with the kids." Much to Graham's surprise, the new park was John Muir Country Park. And much to his American guest's horror, John Muir's birthplace housed a dry cleaning business on the ground floor. Few in Scotland knew of John Muir. That first introduction to Muir, his books and his legacy, changed Graham's professional direction. Muir's social activism and environmental philosophy reinforced Graham's own beliefs and experience. In Muir he found an ethos and role model. The seeds for this were sown in his childhood.

"Once when I was nine years old," Graham recounts, "a thirteen-year-old boy from the neighborhood asked if I wanted to go to the woods with him. He had a .22-caliber air rifle and I'd never seen one, so I went along. He took potshots at birds as we walked but didn't hit any. When we reached a beautiful pond, we lay on our stomachs in the rushes watching the starling chicks that had just fledged, little soft brown-colored puffballs of feathers twenty feet away. It was late May, the hawthorn were in full bloom, and the chicks were lined up on tree branches almost ready to fly, but still being fed by their parents. Before I knew it, he was methodically picking off the chicks one by one, with a tin of several hundred pellets open at his hand. A chick with a patch of bright red blood on it fell from the tree, fluttered in agony, and died. I was absolutely shocked. He shot another and another, and each fell from the branch into the water. I finally realized he intended to shoot every chick. I'd never seen anything killed. Tears streamed down my cheeks. He kept shooting and the chicks kept plopping in the pond. Finally I grabbed the tin of pellets and flung it across the water, peppering the pond with a shower of hailstones. He burst my nose. I hit back, knocking him off his feet with a wild haymaker, and ran home." Graham has been fighting for social and environmental causes ever since.

Today a nonprofit trust owns Muir's birthplace, which is undergoing conversion into an interpretive center. An army of dedicated local residents, as members of the Dunbar John Muir

Association, work to promote Muir's memory, providing tours, publishing materials, and managing a Web site. Another non-profit group, the John Muir Trust, buys and manages wild lands nationwide to preserve Scotland's natural heritage, and it presents the John Muir Award annually to hundreds of schoolchildren and groups who work to identify, preserve, and promote that heritage. Graham White originated the award.

Frank Tindall shared Graham's passion for Muir. As East Lothian's pioneering planning director from 1950 until 1975, then as director of physical planning for the Lothian region for another eight years, and as the unpaid director of the Lothian Building Preservation Trust after "retirement," Frank shaped the current landscape as much as any individual, until his death in 1998. His proactive planning philosophy in the mold of Patrick Geddes and the postwar liberal idealism won widespread support and admiration, as he protected much of the architectural heritage and traditional landscape character that distinguishes the region today, including the Muir heritage. Frank became aware of John Muir by accident, under circumstances similar to those that awoke Graham.

In 1966 Dunbar's lady provost received a letter of introduction and inquiry from Bill and Maymie Kimes, bibliographers of John Muir from California. They asked if a local historian could guide them during an upcoming pilgrimage to the Dunbar places they knew so well from John Muir's autobiography—his home on High Street, Dunbar Castle and Doon Hill, and the outlying fields, cliffs, beaches, and tidal pools that spawned his love of nature and wild places. John who? No one knew. A quick check found no books by or about Muir either in the Dunbar library, the East Lothian library in Haddington, or the national library in Edinburgh, so books were borrowed from Plymouth, England, hundreds of miles to the south. The Kimeses' visit introduced people like Frank Tindall to John Muir for the first time, inadvertently setting in motion his rediscovery in Scotland.

Following the visit, Frank helped initiate a photographic exhibition of Muir's life that was displayed in Dunbar as part of the Royal Burgh's six-hundredth-year anniversary celebration in 1970. Stunning black-and-white photos of Yosemite National Park by Ansel Adams, donated by the Sierra Club, highlighted Muir's achievements. By the mid-1970s, Frank found the Muir cause close to his heart.

Concurrently, work on a new 1,667-acre country park planned for the River Tyne estuary and surrounding shoreline had progressed to the point where a name was needed. The proposed park would combine land owned by the crown between the high- and low-water levels with an agreement between the Council and the Earl of Haddington for public access to the top of the foreshore around his Tyninghame Estate. Other parcels would be purchased and leased from the estate for parking and park facilities.

The earl supported the plan. "I think it's a good idea to have a park that enables you to walk along the coast; definitely a good idea. It's something people like to do, to watch the birds. Great place for birds here," the earl told me. "Having it as a country park gives some control over what goes on here. In the old days you used to get people coming down here, bothering the wildlife and such, all around the bay. It became a trial for the keepers to keep an eye on things."

Frank and a colleague proposed that the new park be named John Muir Country Park since this stretch of shoreline made such an impression on young Muir and the purpose of the park paralleled Muir's preservation philosophy. The park opened in 1976 and later expanded to 1,807 acres with the purchase of another parcel from Tyninghame.

Frank Tindall continued to champion Muir's message, laying the groundwork for the preservation of Muir's birthplace. He also persuaded the national library to acquire a complete set of Muir's writings and present an exhibition on his life, and he helped persuade Canongate Press in Edinburgh to republish a series of Muir's books. Thanks to the efforts of people like Frank Tindall and Graham White, Scotland began to repatriate one of its long-lost sons and recognize the contemporary relevance of his message.

"I've become convinced that Muir became who and what he was," Graham tells me as we walk about Broxmouth, "because he was born into a place of extraordinary environmental richness. Edinburgh has nothing like this; even thirty miles from here you've got nothing like this." In Dunbar, Graham says, three environmental worlds meet: the coastline, the moorland, and the transient world of migratory wildlife.

"John Muir Country Park has a staggering 160 breeding or visiting bird species: eider ducks, oystercatchers, common shore larks, and the rare little tern. Then there are the myriad marine species of the tide pools, salt marsh, and sand dunes, with their hermit crabs, otters, and seals. Young Muir could wander down to the seashore at Belhaven and in just a half a mile from his bedroom find himself in the midst of extraordinary diversity with gannets plunging into mackerel-crowded seas, terns flashing across the waves, and gray bull seals hopping beyond the breakers.

"On another day young John might turn his back to the sea and follow a river gorge a mile or two inland to discover a totally different habitat atop the windswept world of the high heather moors of the Lammermuirs. Those hills are still coastal— lapwing and curlew fly in from the sea to breed up there. But there are other wonderful species there, inland species like the merlin, our smallest and most beautiful hawk, or the great tawny buzzards. There he could hear the curlews and the grouse, the peewits and the plovers.

"And because Dunbar's coastline straddles 56 degrees north," he continues, "Muir could experience another world, that of global migration. In winter, birds like whooper swans, Bewick's swans, pinkfoot geese, and Slavonian grebes fly down from Russia, Greenland, and Scandinavia to escape the bitter cold. Then, as soon as spring comes, they disappear back to their northern solitudes, and birds coming north from Africa and the Mediterranean fill their vacant niches. From Belhaven sands you can see 80,000 gannets carpeting the Bass Rock in a living mass; three months ago they were 8,000 miles south of here, fishing off the west coast of Africa. Swallows and swifts fly up from Morocco; pied wagtails arrive from Egypt and delicate tortoiseshell butterflies flutter more than 1,000 miles from southern France to breed here. So Muir's boyhood was spent in the vortex of this strange, shifting world, exposed to the fantastically rich environments of the seashore and moorland, and seasonal swings in migratory species. Few places in Europe offer such richness.

"I've been privileged to live for six years with the same influences that affected Muir," Graham says. Is Broxmouth your home, I ask. "Yes, it is, in a sense, but I'm about to leave it," he replies with a laugh. "My family home will always be St. Helens. But I don't have a single home landscape. That home is all over, in whatever touches one most deeply: in Wordsworth's Lake District, in the Burns country of Dumfries, in Yosemite and the High Sierra, in New Zealand, in Tonga; it's not in any one place, though East Lothian will always be the core of my 'home range' in Britain. Whenever I top the crest of the hill at Gladsmuir and I look down towards Traprain Law, I have a sense not only of coming home but of something deeply significant having happened here, knowing that people kept watch on top of that hill fort two thousand years ago when the Roman legions marched past.

"Similarly, the Bass Rock always has been a deep emotional

trigger. To me it's one of the great centers of life on earth: to have about 250,000 living beings nesting within a single square mile, that disperse every year all over the world, and then return again, year upon year, century on century. That island has something biologically and spiritually very powerful about it. And quite apart from that, it's staggeringly beautiful.

"I think we all have some sensitivity to the mystical side of landscapes, if you open up to it," Graham tells me. "We all have a romantic, mystical side as well as a scientific one." He recites a portion of "The Debtor," a favorite poem written by Edwin Muir (1887–1959) while standing in an ancient Iron Age hill fort on Orkney:

I am debtor to all, to all am I bounden,
Fellowman and beast, season and solstice, darkness and light,
And life and death. On the backs of the dead,
See, I am borne, on lost errands led,
By spent harvests nourished. Forgotten prayers
To gods forgotten bring blessings upon me. . . .

Like John Muir, Graham isn't rooted to a single landscape. He's too restless spiritually to be content with only one. I think he shares that trait with Muir. And like his mentor, he makes every landscape his home. "I feel a connection to the ancestors who hunted and plowed here long before us, reaching back thousands of years to the Anglo-Saxons, the Picts, and the Celts. I'm fascinated by history, by place names and maps and standing stones that evidence their passing," he explains. The East Lothian landscape, like all ancient places, is alive with history for those willing to look.

The duke has little memory of the Broxmouth Estate, although the estate belonged to the family for about 350 years and the family historically was the leading nobility of Dunbar parish.

"My memories of Broxmouth are very, very faint," he told me. "I was born in 1954 and my father sold the estate in the early 1960s. I remember going there as a child, but we never lived there and never went there, although my father lived there at certain times in the past. I have a vague memory of going there once, walking about the grounds, and going into the house, but I wasn't more than eight or ten years old. I went back about three years ago. I happened to be up in that part of the world on a drive with my wife and we did a 'sweeper'—nipping in the drive, looking, and going out again." With little memory of the place, His Grace also has little concern for it. "To a certain degree I care for the place, yes," he said. "It was the dowager's house to the estate and my grandmother lived there. But my feelings for it are completely different than they are for Floors Castle. Broxmouth is fifty miles away from Floors, the center of the family holdings. I have far less an emotional attachment to it than I do for here. And I've lived here for nearly fifty years. Broxmouth has never really been a feature in my life."

The duke's father sold the estate and all the family's surrounding properties in a complicated set of transactions centered on the development of a giant cement plant and limestone quarry at Oxwellmains and Catcraig adjacent to the estate. I suspect the duke seized the convenient opportunity to sell the properties at a good price in an effort to consolidate the family holdings around their Floors Castle home in the Borders, while raising capital for other business needs. Again, Frank Tindall led the way. Flexing his powers as the Council planning director and stretching the authority given the position by planning law and practice, he negotiated a plan for the immense project that was acceptable to all involved.

Sir Patrick Geddes applied the same proactive approach in the early 1900s when he led the redevelopment of Edinburgh's Old Town closes to remedy the horrid, inhuman conditions found in many. Geddes redefined the practice of town planning, steering it away from its prevailing focus on grand schemes for beaux arts layouts of urban centers and housing estates and refocusing it on more socially responsible schemes achieved through incremental steps. "Survey—Analysis—Plan Leading to Action" was his motto. Geddes rejected the seat-of-the-pants approach to planning practiced by elitist thinking architects, in favor of decisions made on the basis of sound physical, economic, and social data. He rejected the demolition of existing buildings and urban forms simply to make way for the latest fad in architectural taste, preferring instead to retain and restore buildings and forms possessing architectural, historical, and cultural significance. Practical, humane, and progressive, the Geddes philosophy guided British planning in the post–World War II era. Frank Tindall read Geddes' approach while at Cambridge University studying history, then studied it at the School of Planning in London, and experienced it firsthand as a junior planner in offices immediately after the war. He then implemented it as the planning director in East Lothian, where he was hired and mentored by Sir Frank Mears, Geddes' distinguished son-in-law.

The Town and Country Planning Act of 1947 revolutionized planning in the U.K., embracing many aspects of the Geddes philosophy. The act established for the first time that the community as a whole, acting through democratically elected local authorities, determines what use people can make of their property— individual landowners would no longer have the unfettered right to do whatever they wished with their land. Later clarifications ruled that no compensation would be paid for property values reduced by plans, and no taxes would be levied on increases in value. While various forms of planning preceded those empowered by the act, the new act greatly expanded their scope. It remains the foundation of British and Scottish land-use planning, remarkably unaffected by dramatic swings in national politics.

The act arose during the war as the nation prepared to rebuild once peace was won, a time when an extraordinary wave of liberalism engulfed political thinking and public opinion. Many people considered reconstruction an opportunity to remedy long-standing social and economic inequities and environmental problems. A host of reforms, including nationalized health care and welfare, redefined the role of government. Land-use planning in cities and the rural countryside—town and country planning—followed suit.

The act created a hierarchical planning process in which the national government—Parliament—sets general goals and guidelines, then allocates responsibility for implementation to lower levels of government, although the European Union now sits at the top of the hierarchy for a small number of planning issues, such as environmental quality. Today land planning in Scotland is a devolved function granted by Westminster to the Scottish Parliament, which serves as the ultimate policymaker. Beneath it, thirty-two Council governments then prepare general policies and specific local plans in accordance with the national policies. Public consultation plays an important role in the review of drafts.

An intermediate level of planning, such as that done by Frank Tindall at the Lothian Regional Council, was conducted by nine regional councils from 1975 until 1996, when that function was returned to the local councils. The resulting "structure" plans address regionwide issues such as the allocation of future growth, greenbelts, and infrastructure improvements. The Scottish secretary of state (now the first minister) approves each plan, with the authority to change it as he sees fit without public inquiry. Structure plans take several years to develop and approve, making the preparation of local plans agonizingly slow—requiring up to a decade to complete—since the structure plans precede draft local plans.

Once the regional structure plan and the local plan are completed, a specific development proposal for a parcel of land is considered in light of them. Typically a private individual or company submits the actual proposal. The Council planning department reviews the application, negotiates details and changes when warranted, then makes a recommendation for approval or rejection to the elected Council representatives, who grant or deny permission to proceed.

This approach results in land development being more of a privilege based on negotiation than a right based on adherence to a set of preexisting zoning ordinances, subdivision regulations, and building codes made at the local level, as in America. It also makes land-use planning in the U.K. far more responsive to social and environmental issues than in the United States, because governing policies are made at a national level, free from the pressures imposed by locally dominant people and the possible effects on individual properties.

These key distinctions result from historical differences between the Old World and New. Traditionally, the British are more willing than Americans to subordinate individual property rights to broader community interests. This willingness derives in part from the history here of higher urban and rural densities and the resulting need to organize spaces to provide for municipal services, to lessen sanitation problems and fire risks, and address other health, safety, and social issues. American cities have rarely approached the crowding seen in cities that formed centuries before around the world. Today New York City has a density of about 23,000 people per square mile, making it by far the densest American city. Most U.S. cities have densities well below 10,000 people per square mile. In contrast, most major cities in the Old World have densities greater than New York, often several times greater. The same difference exists in the rural landscape. The Land Ordinance and the timing of initial settlement west of the Appalachian Mountains after laborsaving improvements in agriculture saw to that.

The legacy of the feudal system in the U.K. also contributes to this willingness. Someone has always controlled the land, usually the laird. After centuries of this practice, people became accustomed to having a very small minority dictate land-use decisions and many other aspects of daily life, promoting an acceptance of centralized authority not traditionally found in America. Combined with other forces, this dependency created a deep-rooted social welfare tradition expressed in the reforms after World War II, including the Town and Country Planning Act.

And although the bases for planning in both the Old World and New share roots in the effort to protect public health and safety in the teeming city cores suffering under the strains imposed by industrialization in the nineteenth century, land planning gained acceptance in America under much different circumstances a generation before it did in Great Britain. Those circumstances help explain Americans' curious acceptance of land-use controls,given our historical obsession with unencumbered property rights, twenty-five years before similar controls appeared in Britain.

Comprehensive land-use planning, implemented by zoning controls, became popular in the United States during the 1910s and 1920s, gaining Court approval as constitutional and becoming commonly used in the years of prosperity before the Great Depression in the 1930s. People accepted the new restrictions on the use of their land, in part, as a means to protect the property value of their suburban homes from threats posed by incompatible neighbors and nuisances. Americans were flooding to the suburbs at the time, buying single-family detached homes with large mortgages. Zoning offered a way for homeowners to safeguard their investment from potential physical and social changes in the neighborhood that might diminish its value. Hence land-use planning to this day occurs most commonly at the local level—in the municipality or rural township—where homeowners can most readily dictate the type of community they desire, seemingly in a democratic way. Regional, state, and federal roles are minimal, often visible only indirectly through funding grants for infrastructure improvements. In contrast to Great Britain, planning in America tends to be "bottom-up," not "top-down," and it tends to focus more on the protection of individual property rights and less on serving larger social functions.

The result: East Lothian has no lines of large-lot houses strung along farm fields fronting country lanes, like Marquette County. It has crisp boundaries between villages and the surrounding countryside. It has little low-density suburban sprawl spreading outward from towns. And it maintains the traditional architecture and landscape character by requiring the renovation and reuse, or the preservation, of suitable buildings and sensitive lands. This also means the Earl of Haddington can't build homes around Tyninghame as he might wish, and that to renovate his steading or cottages he must follow detailed guidelines; or that the current owners of Broxmouth can't build a housing development as they want. Certainly land-use plans and controls in the States can and do place such restrictions. The difference between Old World and New is a matter of degree. The hot land-use issues in East Lothian today are very similar to those in Marquette County, but the planning outcomes have been much different to date.

Those outcomes in East Lothian haven't always been accepted without controversy, including many championed by Frank Tindall. The provision of public access to the coast was one of those areas of occasional conflict, and the John Muir Country Park was one of the last parts of that jigsaw puzzle. It took time to persuade some private owners to enter into access agreements, the Earl of Haddington among them. Frank considered it his role—

his duty—to advise the Council on how best to protect the public good from private profit interests. A profound sense of history informed his socialism, allowing it to be inventive and pragmatic. But the wave of liberalism that swept in the extraordinary social reforms after the war dissipated in the 1950s as conservative policies returned. After all, the act called for a fundamental redistribution of power in land-use control, granting more to the public and less to the landowners who before had exercised almost total control. The balance has since ebbed and flowed with swings between Labour and Tory governments, but remains shifted far more in favor of the public than it has been historically, or as balanced in the United States.

Uncertainty clouds the fate of Broxmouth since the duke sold it, just as haar often envelops the estate in a misty veil. The property became the focus of golf course/housing development interests during the economic boom of the late 1980s. Investors from around the world took early options on a deal with the cement company, but an economic downturn soon scuttled the plan. As a result of that interest, the Council's draft local plan in the mid-1990s designated the estate for golf-based leisure and hotel development, provided the design minimized adverse effects on the historical character of the grounds. The local plan supported that scheme also because those uses reinforced other planning objectives for the area.

Surprisingly, in 2000 the cement company circulated a proposal to build eighty houses in a portion of the estate "deer park," even though the scheme violated the local plan that designated Broxmouth for golf-related development and marked the former Lochend Farm about a mile away as the primary site where new housing can be constructed to meet the community's future needs. Late last winter, an offshore development company bought the estate from the cement company and submitted an application for the same proposed housing development. The Council refused the application. The new owners appealed. Meanwhile they placed the estate proper on the market. The fight over its fate continues as Graham prepares to move.

Graham hasn't always appreciated landscapes like Broxmouth. Few young people do. History for most is too abstract—something distant and of little immediate relevance, something to be read, not seen firsthand. Graham's epiphany occurred after he hitchhiked across America and experienced a land with so little history recorded in it, at least a history that most people are willing to recognize. "America is the most transient culture I've ever experienced," he tells me as we explore the "folly" overlooking the coast toward the rear of the estate. Perhaps the dowager escaped to the small stone retreat during balmy summer evenings to read Byron and have tea. The windows frame dramatic views of the links (now a golf course), the rocky shoals at Dunbar, and the Bass Rock beyond. "I felt anxious the whole time I was there." Too little sense of community and too little connection to place for his comfort, I suspect. Only after he returned home did he realize how culture and history molds and shapes us.

"A trucker dropped me off on a triple-decker overpass on I-80 before sunrise just outside Omaha, Nebraska. I'd never seen such a bridge. It shook every time a truck went by. Eventually a local man picked me up on his way to work. As we drove we passed two road signs: 'Ogalalla' and then 'Council Bluffs.' I got goose bumps, for I had just read *Bury My Heart at Wounded Knee*. I said to the driver, 'Oh my God, this is where *it* happened.' And he asked, 'Where what happened?' I said, 'Where Sitting Bull held the War Council of the Ogalalla Sioux in the last battle of his war with the U.S. cavalry.' The driver said, 'Is that right? I didn't know that. I've only lived here twenty years.' "

On his return to England, Graham bought an old Volkswagen microbus and toured the country with some friends for the first time, drawn to one ancient historical site after another. Late one evening, they arrived at a medieval cathedral near the town of Wells in Dorset. The door lay wide open. Inside, a choir of fifty schoolboys dressed in red surplices with white ruffs rehearsed Christmas carols, singing exquisite harmonies in the timeless setting. One of Graham's companions turned to him and asked if he knew how long it took to get something like this together. "No," Graham responded. "Seven hundred years," his friend replied. "That's when I realized that I was heir to a much different landscape than you have in America—a landscape drenched in five thousand years of history, a land with a truly developed culture. That history had never affected me until I had spent two years in a country where there was so little connection with place. I was moved to tears." The sense of being involved in an endless national pageant—a culture—is the most valuable thing one can possibly have, Graham believes. "If you have culture, you don't need money. If you don't have culture, you fill the void with money and possessions," he says.

We finish our walk around Broxmouth. Graham returns to the gardener's cottage, perhaps to begin packing his possessions for the pending move. He has enough to fill a small rental van or two, but the vast piles of books will need a lot of sorting. I visit the garden a last time to photograph the field of spear thistles, the common weed used so frequently as the national symbol, representing the Scots' fierce sense of independence. The motto *Wha daur meddle wi' me?*—Who dares to meddle with me?—sometimes surrounds the symbol. A dense tuft of purple fibers forms a flower that sits atop the seed head like a sculpted crown. Toby barks from outside the wrought-iron tracery, calling me. The hundred-year-old rusty gate creaks as I close it and leave.

[19]

"Bind us together, Lord, bind us together with cords that cannot be broken," we sing, accompanied by the electric piano and the breeze blowing through the gaping windows and entryway of the

Dunglass Collegiate Church. The Reverend Anne Lithgow suggested we fetch our "woolies" just before beginning the service. I brought none so I shiver, hesitant to raise my off-key voice as a means of raising my body temperature. Unfortunately, little of the August morning sunlight outside warms the cold stone walls and gravel floor inside the circa 575-year-old ruin.

Large landowners in the 1400s and 1500s built and endowed nonmonastic "collegiate" churches like this one to ensure masses would be said for the souls of the dead, usually the donor's ancestors, and to enable the living to hear more ornate masses and services than would be possible in parish churches. The bishop of St. Andrews approved Alexander Home's church in 1443, giving his consent for three "perpetual chaplainries" to be in continuous residence along with a choir of "four singing boys." Each of the three priest positions was endowed with a salary and housing near the church, complete with a garden containing fruit trees. The agreement even prescribed the vestments to be worn by the priests—long surplices with sheepskin-lined hooded capes. A hundred years later an inventory of the church's valuables, provided mainly by the Homes, included "a list of altar cloths and priests' garments—albs, chasubles, copes, and surplices—in velvets, cloth of gold, satins, silks and camlet (a rich mixture of silk and wool), some edged in lace." The intense colors and textures of the adornments must have been stunning in contrast to the structure's stark gray stonework.

Dunglass parish of the Church of Scotland now holds service in the stripped hulk once a year. What little ornamentation that once graced the small church was removed long ago. The church ceased to exist as an institution in 1644, when the Homes sold the estate. The buyers were probably believers in the new Presbyterian faith of post-Reformation Scotland and shared the prevailing disdain for the papacy. That same year an act of Parliament stated that the "use and form of divyne service of the collegiat kirks is noways now necessar efter the reformatioune of religion, the institution and exercise therof being ane superstitious will-worship and human inventione, whylk and the lyk ar become in desuetude and ought to be abolished."

In the early 1700s, the owner converted the abandoned building for use as a coach house, stable, granary, and pigeon loft. A case of Calvinist practicality, I suppose, which met considerable condemnation, particularly from the Homes for the removal of family graves. The tall east window and part of the surrounding wall behind the chancel were knocked out to form the coach entrance, and floors were added about the nave. Later the north transept was used as a potato store and the sacristy as a carpenter's workshop. No stained glass remains in the windows and much of their stone tracery has been knocked out. The original wood doors and interior ironwork are gone, too.

Yet the Gothic cruciform design remains in remarkably good condition today. The massive walls of ashlar stone blocks, the barrel-vaulted ceiling, the stout square tower, and the roof of large overlapping stone slabs stand nearly oblivious to the passage of time and the hand of man. Perhaps eighty worshipers, mostly middle-aged and older, sit on folding chairs in the nave, our backs to the ragged entrance ripped in the chancel wall below the window's pointed-arch head. A tennis court surrounded by a chain-link fence added by the current owner sits 100 feet from the jagged opening.

The church stands atop a small knoll of closely cropped grass in the middle of the famous Dunglass Estate, overlooking potato, wheat, barley, sprout, and turnip fields that descend 150 feet toward the North Sea about a mile east. The estate dates to the 1200s, changing hands and configuration from one private owner to another: the Pepdies held the estate for over a century until the Homes (or Humes) acquired the property by marriage around 1390, and subsequently held it 254 years until 1644, when it passed in quick succession through the hands of several short-term owners—the Ruthvens, Sharps, and Callenders; the Halls acquired the estate in 1687 and held it for 232 years, until they sold it in bankruptcy to the Ushers in 1919. Frank and Merilyn Usher own it now. Over the centuries the estate was the site of a significant share of Scottish history due to its strategic location along the Dunglass Dean, and its owners have been among the country's most distinguished families, especially the Homes and Halls.

Francis James Usher, a keen sportsman and master foxhunter, bought the 9,000-acre property for £153,000, primarily so he could shoot partridges. Later the family trained racehorses on the property, his grandson Frank told me. He too enjoys shooting and other sports to occupy his time. Frank's great-grandfather and a great-great-uncle made fortunes distilling blended Scotch whiskey and distributing it worldwide. The brothers rode the rise of whiskey from relative obscurity to the national drink in the 1800s, as the "wee dram" replaced French brandy and wine as a favorite spirit, joining a pint of hearty ale. New government policies promoted the rise as leaders sought to stamp out illicit whiskey making and smuggling by licensing many new distilleries, with the full support of the lairds. The Ushers pioneered and profited from the increased production and export perhaps as much as any family (early on they controlled all the output of the famous Glenlivet Distillery).

By the turn of the century, though, overproduction flooded the market, consumer tastes were changing again, and the government imposed heavy duties. World War I devastated demand as well, as did mounting pressures for Prohibition in the United States. In the midst of this, the Ushers sold their distilleries and distribution businesses in 1918 to Scottish Malt Distillers Ltd., leaving Francis with the wealth to pursue his sporting interests full time. He and his wife, Catherine, redecorated the century-old Dunglass mansion, then moved the family from fashionable Belgrave Crescent in Edinburgh to their dramatic rural residence that stood only three paces from the brink of the dean. *Country Life* magazine featured the restored hundred-room home in a 1925 issue.

However, Francis and his son had little interest in the estate's farms, allowing all to be let to tenants and leaving the estate's management to a factor. Profits from family investments subsidized their lavish country lifestyle. In late summer, Frank remembered, his grandfather, followed by his father, would rent a private train every year to take the entire household and a score of guests to the Highlands for an eight-week grouse-shooting holiday. World War II interrupted the tradition, although it resumed briefly afterward.

The government requisitioned the mansion for the war effort, as it did Tyninghame and Mellerstain. Donaldson's School for the Deaf moved out of Edinburgh to avoid the risk of being bombed and its 360 children occupied the mansion. Frank, his mother, and his nanny moved into the laundry cottage. Later the family moved into the renovated stable block. "They wrecked the house," Frank said. "It was beyond repair." Plus the house had simply become a dinosaur after the war: it couldn't be heated; it required extensive repairs and upgrades; and it needed a large staff to maintain it. It was all too much and too expensive. Rather than make the repairs and fight the property's possible compulsory sale for conversion to a police college, Frank's father removed the massive lead-clad roof and stripped the interior in 1946. The house went to complete ruin. In 1958, four years after inheriting the estate, Frank blew up the skeleton. Three years later, he moved into a much more modest contemporary-style house he built on its site. Do you miss the old mansion, I asked. "No, blowing it up was the best thing I ever did," he replied.

At the same time, Frank assumed partial responsibility for

four farms, raising 200 beef cattle and 1,600 ewes on 3,500 acres. "But I got too big," he told me. "And I borrowed money to do it and you just can't do that these days. So I sold our Townhead and Morehouse hill farms to pay off debts. They were remote and Morehouse had no steading." Though less involved with the farms than in the past, he continues to take an interest in the Home Farm as well as the Springfield, Birnieknowes, and Old-hamstocks Main Farms. In addition, the estate still owns the Cove-Linhead, Pathhead, Redheugh, Cambus East, and Cambus West Farms, and some of their cottages; 6,000 acres in total. An estate management company handles the details for all the farms and rental properties. Financial necessity has forced the sale of other farms and properties, including Chapelhill Farm, Cove cottages, and many houses in Cockburnspath. Other properties have been renovated or developed, including the beachfront at Pease Bay, which Frank converted into a large caravan park. He sold the park four years ago. "No regrets," he said. Each year he sells a few properties, although he doesn't foresee selling any more farms. "It's a way to get just a little capital," he told me as he listed the mounting costs he faces: insurance, the estate agent's fee, workers' wages, and general maintenance.

The estate will most likely come to an end as a definable property on the deaths of Frank and Merilyn. I suspect the remaining farms and cottages will be sold off then, ending nearly 800 years of history. Perhaps the "policies" on which the church and several other historic buildings sit immediately around the house might remain intact, but the sprawling estate will cease to exist. The Ushers agree, though they note that the fate of the property remains uncertain, depending on local land values, government policies, global economics, and the wishes of their adult-aged children. Despite their best efforts to provide for death duties and corporation taxes with life insurance, trusts, and other measures, "it's probably not enough," Frank admitted. Nor have the children shown an interest in settling on the estate. "They're not really interested in it," he said. Their son is a professional musician—a rock drummer—working in Edinburgh, and their daughter lives in Kansas City. Perhaps circumstances will change; perhaps the property and its heritage will become of greater interest to them.

The parents' passion for the place has waned as well. Frank and Merilyn enjoy the beauty and serenity of the land immediately around the house, but the estate has become a bit of a burden for them. The bother of estate management and the worsening economics of agriculture have dampened their enthusiasm for the property. And they see the government becoming increasingly hostile toward rural landowners with proposals to ban foxhunts and fishing, and other plans to expand the rights of ramblers. Threats to the estate and complications in its maintenance seem unending.

Historic Scotland now cares for the nationally significant— "A"-listed—ruin standing several hundred yards from Frank and Merilyn's front door. Like the passing of the Catholic collegiate church it once housed, due to changes triggered by the Reformation, perhaps the day of the grand estates has passed too. Recent reforms may have seen to that.

Sheepshank, granny, bow—Anne holds up the large drawings one by one, showing each to the congregation to name the knot—surgeon's knot, slipknot, fisherman's knot. She speaks deliberately with impeccable enunciation of clear, crisp, fully formed words. Her friendly, pleasing voice befits her ministerial personality. A baptism has brought several families with young children to the service; the fussing of infants and the antics of toddlers provide a welcome distraction for they foretell of desperately needed rebirth in the parish congregation.

Has the parish structure become a dinosaur too, perhaps like the grand estates? For nearly a thousand years the church parish has served as the principal organization of the local community and landscape, linking people to one another and to place generation after generation. Partly geographical, partly ecclesiastical, the parish defined a person's physical and liturgical place in the world. Certainly other layers of religious, social, and political organization existed parallel to or above the parish, but parish functions were the primary focus of daily life. Perhaps this extraordinary continuity in one's sense of belonging to a specific place explains in part the deep-rooted Scottish love of the land. Even the new Calvinist religious life triggered by the Protestant Reformation as Scotland cast aside Catholicism continued the parish system, which provided a critical source of stability in the midst of profound change.

The changes that most affected the daily life of commoners occurred in the local parish church. Beginning in 1560, the Presbyterian Church of John Knox rapidly cleansed parish churches nationwide of their Catholic liturgy, look, feel, and form. Altars, screens, and statues of saints were removed, walls were whitewashed, and the interior layout was refocused on the pulpit, but the church building and the parish organization were kept.

The content and conduct of worship services changed as well. Sunday assumed a greater focus as the day of worship, and services emphasized the sermon and participation in prayer, psalm singing, Bible reading, and the catechism. The number of sacraments dropped from seven to two (baptism and the Eucharist) and their form of celebration changed. Communion became a congregational act, linking people to community and place in the shared experience.

People were further linked to place by the exercise of Kirk "discipline" at the parish level. One's moral behavior was reviewed in the local Kirk session by one's peers. Elders examined the ecclesiastical knowledge and behavior of those parishioners in their "quarter" before approving their participation in communion. And to move from one parish to another and find a job, people usually needed a "testificate" obtained from the local Kirk session attesting to their moral standing. Hence one's identity was inextricably connected to the parish—to a geographical place on the land and a community of neighbors.

Sermons and church doctrine likely had much less of an effect than the parish structure on people's attachment to the land and their attitudes toward it. Perhaps the Protestant "work ethic," to the extent that it existed, arose in part as a response to pastoral urgings to demonstrate one's worthiness for election, despite the Presbyterian belief in predestination. Perhaps Calvinist tendencies toward moderation, hard work, and striving shared similar roots. The Kirk downplayed religious holidays, including Christmas, probably contributing to the stereotype of the dour, stoic Scot. More importantly, though, parish life reflected a common-sense perception of the land and its stewardship, since most parishioners farmed or lived in intimate contact with the land until the Industrial Revolution. The Kirk approved of farmwork necessary on the Sabbath. Thoughts of "dominating" nature or "conquering" wilderness likely had little relevance for subsistence farm communities until technology gave them greater control over their environment. Most likely pastoral messages said little about one's relationship to the land: no need to state the obvious, no need to tell farmers to care for their land and stock. Sermons focused on more important spiritual matters.

Still, the Kirk divorced the agricultural year from the liturgical year, which had been married since medieval times. For centuries festivals and celebrations shared both agricultural and religious significance. The Reformation disconnected ecclesiastical celebrations from the seasons and rhythms of the land because agricultural-based festivals lacked scriptural bases. The week, culminating in the Sunday Sabbath, rather than the year became the focus of liturgical time. Yet many of the agricultural events and festivals such as hiring fairs continued because they fulfilled community needs.

Today the importance of the local parish in people's lives has diminished, declining gradually over decades. So too has the role of the Kirk. Perhaps a growing sense of disconnection from community and place has accompanied that decline.

Anne ties together the theme of the hymn and the quiz on knots in her "talk" on the loving bond that links people to their faith, to their family and community. Is it the same bond that links us to place? Anne cuts short her talk, recognizing the discomfort of her listeners. As the service concludes and we move outside into the warm sunlight, Graham White's story about stumbling upon the choir rehearsal in the medieval church and the seven hundred years needed to create what he witnessed runs through my mind. A parish picnic follows on the grounds around the ruin. Jane Hood of Cove-Linhead Farms offers me a ride back to my house in the square of Cockburnspath. I decline, preferring to walk the mile to reflect on the service and enjoy the stunning scenery of the sea, the coastal cliffs, the fields, and the hills.

The Hoods have been tenants of the Dunglass Estate for over 250 years, likely tenanting at Townhead and other local farms when fields were first enclosed and farms formed in the mid-1700s, and even earlier they leased land in the area under the prior infield/outfield system from the Homes (Humes). Family lore holds that a Hood helped the Earl of Hume escape the slaughter at the Battle of Flodden in 1513: "Of a' who fought at Flodden Field, Rab Hood alane cam' bame," the poem proclaims. Jimmy and Jane Hood now live in one of the houses at Cove Farm. They bought the houses, but not the farm, from Frank Usher about twenty years ago. They then sold one house to a nephew and another to an architect from London. A niece lives in the converted corn barn. Their son Peter lives with his family in the Linhead farmhouse a quarter mile up the road toward Pease Bay. He assumed the tenancy for the combined Cove-Linhead Farms from his parents seventeen years ago as they began to retire.

The Hoods hold an old-style lifetime tenancy, which is inheritable and gives them the right of first refusal to purchase the farm should the landlord wish to sell. Rents are negotiated every three years or so. The tenancy can be terminated only three ways. The holder can be evicted if the landlord proves negligence or similar breach of contract. If the landlord wishes to sell the property, the tenant can purchase it for about half of the market value. If the holder wishes to terminate the tenancy, a settlement price would be negotiated with the landlord for the value of improvements made by the tenant. The tenant's discounted purchase price for the property reflects the difference in property value between land held in-hand by the landlord and tenanted land. The difference constitutes a form of paper equity for the tenant, becoming real when the holder either buys the farm or gives up the tenancy. I suspect landlords promoted the move away from lifetime tenancies so as to restore greater control over and value for their properties.

Jimmy and I sipped his homemade sloe gin from tiny liqueur glasses as we spoke, bathed in the bright warmth of sunshine flooding through a large window. His recipe for the rose-colored cordial: to a pint of good Gordon's gin add six ounces of whole sloe berries gathered from wild bushes in the autumn, lance the berries to release their juice and put them in the bottle; to this add five ounces of sugar (six ounces if you prefer a sweeter flavor), one clove, and a bit of almond essence; then let the mixture set for three months. By Christmas the spirit is ready to warm you through the frequent dreich days and long nights.

Jimmy remembered the squads of seasonal workers who used to gather potatoes plowed out by hand or "spun out" with a digger. Now machines do it all without a hand ever touching the crop. He grew about 300 acres of cash crop potatoes and barley, and turnips, oats, and hay to feed stock. Sheep and cattle were pastured on 150 acres of rough grazing and *sea braes,* dangerous land at the cliff face overlooking the North Sea. Sheep that fell over the cliff to the rocky beach a hundred feet below were placed in a cloth bag loaded with stones and carried out to the low-water mark where the sea, crabs, and lobsters did the burying. He recalled a six-foot-high wall of seaweed across the beach below the farm, and how farmers made a mound of it to rot for use with manure as fertilizer on their fields. "It smelled to high heaven," he said, "but it was a good healthy smell." The region's famed "ware barley," which resulted from the enrichment provided by the "seaware," made the best sweet malt and commanded a £20 per ton premium price from brewers, bakers, and distillers. Trawling destroyed the seaweed beds.

And he remembered when the farm employed a dozen people, most with large families that lived on the farm as a tight-knit community. Now the farm employs nil. No more *kirns:* every year after harvesttime the farmers in the area held a communal celebration, moving it from one farm to another each year. Everyone came; all the farmworkers and families attended the thanksgiving. No sense of community remains on the farms. Few people who actually work the land now live in the farmhouses and worker cottages. Have attitudes toward the land changed as well, I ask. Do people care less about it? "Yes, very much so," both Jimmy and Jane said. "You get people moving out to the country from the city who don't really care about the country. It's sad, but it's happening everywhere. To be a farmer once was something, even to people in Edinburgh. Now it doesn't matter. It's just a business," Jimmy said. On the other hand, history of the place permeates his life.

Tell me about your relationship with the laird, I ask. "At one time they were the Lord's anointed, now they're just ordinary people," he replied. "In some cases, they've not earned the money at all and merely fallen heir to it." "It's about time tenants have the ownership of the land," Jane interjected, "like the crofters are gaining in the Highlands." The relationship between a laird and a tenant differs from case to case and over time, making generalizations dangerous. "Old family lairds do take an interest in the long-term future of the land," Jimmy thought, "though not as much as they used to." By implication, he suggested newer owners are perhaps less involved. A touch of resentment tinged his comments as well as Jane's.

"I'd like to see my son farming more or less as I did," Jimmy said, "with the long-term future of putting something back into it. But I realize now that with modern taxation, you can't do it. You've got to live hand-to-mouth, day to day, year to year." "It's different now," Jane said, even though they farmed the same land as Jimmy's father, grandfather, and great-grandfather. Their son Peter no longer farms himself; he leases the land to contractors. "It's very hard for him," Jane felt. He and his wife both work off the farm and run a "B&B" to earn supplemental income. Jimmy and Jane wish Peter had chosen another career. He attended an exclusive preparatory school in Edinburgh without enthusiasm, perhaps always more interested in the farm than in law, medicine, or business. Agricultural college followed. The Hoods are well educated and well traveled, hardly the parochial image of a farm family. In times past, farming paid handsomely, even for tenants. "Farming is a business now," Jimmy noted again. "I'm sorry we have to farm the way we do but economics has forced us into it." "And we're not helped by this government," Jane added.

Jimmy never had a choice to not farm: his two older brothers had left the land and gone to sea when he came of age during the Depression. The farm meant a job and an income. So he stayed. Would you have bought the farm if given the chance, I asked. "It would all depend on economics, very much so," Jimmy said. At the moment economics favor tenancy over ownership with rental payments amounting to about one-third of corresponding mortgage payments. Yet he'd prefer to own the farm. Would you feel different about the land if you had owned it, I wondered. "No, I don't think I would very much," Jimmy replied. Jane agreed. Tenants aren't like short-term renters. Tenants had rights and status. They made their living from the land and had a direct financial stake in it, so they had much the same motivation to manage it wisely as did the owner. Perhaps the change under way in Scotland from tenanted family farms to corporate-owned and -run farms won't be an improvement over the earlier system being replaced of lairds and tenants. At what price, social, economic, environmental, should "progress" come? It's a complicated equation. Jimmy was never offered the chance to own the farm, nor was his father or grandfather, although he thinks they would have declined. They loved the land but had lives that took them away, allowing other family to work it in their absence. Jimmy loves it too. "I used to enjoy very much walking around the sea braes because you had the fields on one side and the sea on the other." Jimmy no longer walks well.

Peter's face lit up when he described what he liked best about farming as I walked out the door at Linhead. We'd just finished a conversation in the kitchen, and finished several imported lager beers too. I'd asked the question earlier; the answer came to him as I was leaving. "It's magic, you know, the colors of the crops in the autumn and the way the colors change in the light and weather as the wind blows across the fields, making waves in the crops. It's always different," he said. His fields reach inland about a half mile from the seaside cliffs, rising several hundred feet and affording spectacular panoramic views: a tapestry of rolling fields with lush crops in shades of dark green and golden beige, neatly partitioned by dykes and hedgerows, with the dramatic cliffs and sea beyond. It's breathtaking in the low light of dawn and dusk, with a deep blue sky and blue-green sea as backdrops. "Once one bright, sunny December day—the type where the air and sky are crisp and clear and a light frost covers the ground—I was plowing at about four in the afternoon with the tractor visor down because of the low sun glowing red, and the field was red. The whole farm was red, absolutely red, from the color of the sand coming out in the sun. I stopped the tractor and got out to look, standing there for ten minutes. The sea was calm. There was no wind and no noise. I'd never seen anything like it, before or since. That was magical." He misses plowing the fields.

Peter Hood has one of those fascinating, friendly faces—handsome, expressive, with prominent cheekbones, a lively voice, a big smile that spreads from a small mouth, and deep creases around bright eyes, all beneath a thick growth of black hair. He has a slight frame, standing perhaps five feet eight inches tall with a trim build, and seems a bit shy about his upcoming fortieth birthday. Don't tell anyone.

The farm is slightly smaller now, a highway project having eaten some of the acreage. Peter grows 210 acres of spring barley, 70 acres being a rare variety on contract to a distillery for a premium price. The rest of the barley has been placed with a local grain merchant. Another 30 acres have been set aside, for which he receives a subsidy, according to a government requirement that he lay down 10 percent of his arable land. Rough grazing and sea braes account for 60 acres, and a small amount of additional set-aside land for the remainder. He stopped raising sheep several years ago because it wasn't profitable. At about the same time a drop in grain prices due to world markets shrank profit margins. With the long-term prospects as bleak as the short-term situation, he was forced to change the farm operation to stay financially afloat. So he sold all his equipment and hired outside contractors to do the work. Peter continues to manage the opera-

tion but works full time in an agricultural supply store twenty-
five miles away.

"It broke my heart to do it. I didn't want to do it," he told me.
He loves farming and holds faint hopes of returning to it full
time. "It's not a job to a farmer," he said. "You've got everything
out there. You plow it; you sow it; you look after the crops; you do
everything. You clean your ditches; you cut your hedges; you
clean your sheds. You try to keep it the best it can be. It's your
life." He still holds the tenancy, though the end of that looms
ahead. "I'm pretty sure the Hoods' relationship with agriculture
will end when I retire," he said. "It'll make me sad but not sorry."
His two kids don't feel the same about the land. Neither wants to
farm, nor does he want them to. Yet he would buy the farm if
given the chance, to keep the land in the family for sentimental
reasons, whether or not future generations would choose to actually work the farm or let it. "I always wanted to farm," Peter said.
"Mum and Dad didn't want me to farm. I think Dad saw a dim
future for the small family farm, and he was right. Every year it
becomes more and more agribusiness. But the farm means everything to me. I've been here my entire life; I know every inch of it."

Like other family farmers in area, Peter knows his fields on a
first-name basis. They all have names, just as houses do. He likes
that, much better than merely numbers. Does a field have a personality, I ask. "Not as such," he responded. Do you like some
fields better than others? "Oh yes. There are some I can't stand
and some I know will be sot every year, and when it rains certain
fields will be horrible." Each field is unique, and each responds to
weather and working differently. He has fields named "Bang the
Wind," "Cat Hole," "Faughill," "Kippie," and "Hawkheugh,"
each with a meaning related to place, some names dating back
hundreds of years. I like that too.

"It's good to get away, though," Peter told me. He's traveled to
the Continent and to the States repeatedly. New York City is his

favorite place. "I just fell in love with it," he confessed. "It's so different from here, like day and night. But a week there is enough for me, and after two weeks away, I'm ready to get back. The best part of traveling is coming home."

Peter sees no shortcut to forming a linkage to the land and a connection to place. It just takes time, whether for those who work the land or for those with other jobs. A bit sentimental, nostalgic, and romantic, he regrets the changes in farm life and farm communities and the way of life rapidly being lost. "I sometimes sit and think, Boy, I wish I had lived back then. It just seems farming was so much more fun because everybody was born and brought up here," he said. "There weren't any incomers; it was all families who had lived in the village for years. They'd all been born and bred here. They all knew one another. Some hated each other and others didn't get on well, but there was always that sense of community. You don't get that now. A lot of it's gone now and it'll never return to what it was before. And it's still changing. Farms will get bigger; small farms will disappear; farming families will disappear, and so on. The new people who'll work on farms won't feel the same for the land as those in the past. It'll be a job. You do what you're told to do. And that's it."

[20]

The *Fisher Lassie* set to sea from Dunbar harbor late this summer morning—7:30 A.M. rather than the usual 6:00 A.M. or earlier. Gordon Easingwood and his hand, Ian, made a quick trip twenty miles down the coast to Eyemouth to buy four boxes of mackerel and flatfish from his cousin's trawler for use as bait in their lobster pots. A box costs £5 there, versus £8 here. But his brother docked last among the boats that were out overnight, delaying our departure today. Gordon tries to catch his own bait during the summer season. He or Ian takes the *Fisher Lassie* out many evenings to fish for mackerel. When their supply runs out, they go to Eyemouth.

Conditions are good this morning: mild sea and moderate breeze, low sixties, some sun. I've worn a heavy wool sweater (it's cooler at sea than onshore) and my "wellies"—Wellington boots—and I swallowed a Dramamine just in case. Ian has already changed into his work clothes: heavy yellow oilskin bib pants that nearly come up to his armpits, matching hooded jacket, knee-high rubber boots, and heavy rubber gloves. He's at work preparing the bait, slicing a half-inch cut in the back of any fish still living; lobsters and crabs prefer freshly dead meat. Gordon steers the thirty-foot boat through the narrow throat of the harbor entrance blasted into the ruins of Dunbar Castle, past the rocks gaping above the surface—Wallace's Head, Scart Rock, the Gripes—and heads west-northwest across the bay of the River Tyne and John Muir Country Park to the first of his fourteen "fleets" of lobster pots scattered from here about eight miles up to the small islands off North Berwick.

He shows me the gadgets in the tiny cabin, two ship-to-shore radios, radar, global positioning map display, and sonar. I think he likes the high-tech tools. It must run in the family. His father was the first in the area to install radar in his fishing boat, which he bought new back in 1963. It had hydraulics too. The locals referred to the radar as "Easingwood's toy." "The generation before me saw the most changes," Gordon says. Machinery replaced some of the old manual tasks, displacing hands. Engines replaced oars and sails early in the century; power winches then replaced pulleys, block and tackle, and heaving arms. "I'm one of the few who can remember when you navigated using triangulation of landmarks and set a course and time because you only had a compass and watch," he says. Most boats in Dunbar traditionally were bought secondhand until his generation (which began fishing in the 1950s) because fishing wasn't seen as a business.

"I've seen 'em sitting in the cabin at the three-corner table," he tells me, "having just been given the gross earnings of the boat that week, counting out the pay for the hands—one for you, one for you, one for you, like dealing cards, because they couldn't say, 'Well we made £100, so the four of us each get £25, minus the running costs.' But as things progressed people realized that fishing had changed with computers and technology." Tradition gives way slowly, though. Gordon fishes within sight of land.

The sea has a thousand faces, like the land, a thousand forms, textures, and colors, a thousand personalities. I've learned that living along the Scottish North Sea coast in Cockburnspath. It came as no surprise, confirming what I intuitively knew before. Yet my knowledge of those faces remains as shallow as the pools I search at low tide among the rocks at the mouth of the Dunglass Dean and Cove Harbor. I'm mostly an observer, a voyeur looking with longing for the hidden treasures. I envy people like Gordon who know the "moods, secrets, and seasons" of the sea and shore intimately just as I envy those who hold that knowledge of the land. Having lived my life five hundred miles from the shore, it has always been an alien world to me with tantalizing sights, sounds, and smells. Annual family vacations as a child to the south New Jersey coast whet my curiosity. Ever since, the shore has held an inexplicable attraction for me. Or is it an innate attraction?

Gordon gives me a glimpse of this world, his world. He's one of the few people in the Dunbar area who still works the sea for a living, fishing for lobsters and crabs just offshore in the Firth of Forth. About a half dozen boats work from the harbor; most trawl for prawns. Afternoons, he volunteers at the tiny Dunbar historical museum in the dungeonlike base of the Town House (town hall). "Most Americans who go in there are looking for something to hold on to; they're looking for their roots," he says. Dunbar has filled with incomers over the past forty years, changing the sense of community. Yet many incomers are mainstays for civic groups like the historical society, just as they are in Marquette County.

Gordon is an incomer in the small remaining fishing community—he's only fished for about forty years. "In some fishing quarters, we're still looked at as interlopers," he says. Gordon's grandfather was an English salvage diver who moved to Dunbar before World War II to strip nonferrous metal from the many wrecks around the rocky coastline. Gordon's father and uncles gradually started fishing in the early 1950s to earn supplemental income during downtime in the winter when there wasn't much salvage work or when conditions weren't right for diving. Gordon can't swim.

The family boat prospered. Yields were good during much of the 1950s and 1960s. As each Easingwood boy reached his teens, he went to work on the boat. Gordon began at about age fifteen. He's fifty-three now. They worked for a "half-deal" at first—paid half a hand's share—although they could do the work of a man. "That's how it was done then," he tells me. "The work didn't do any harm," he says. "It brightened your outlook." They trawled for prawns and scampi and set pots for lobsters and crabs. "You serve an apprenticeship when you have a fishing family—you're out on weekends and holidays; life revolves around the harbor area." He grew up in a house at the base of Woodbush Brae. During storms, the surf crashed over their rear garden wall. He's lived near the harbor ever since.

The boat supported three brothers, two of whom were married. Eight or nine lobster boats and fifteen to twenty trawlers for prawns and whitefish, plus visiting boats from other local ports, worked from Dunbar then. During the stormy winter months, some of the boats went up the Firth of Forth to pair-trawl, working out of harbors nearer to Edinburgh. Two boats together would trawl with a ring net to ensnare an entire shoal of sprats (small herrings). Times were good and they made a good living, plus the winter trawling meant they didn't have to set pots that would get lost or damaged in storms. The pots were kept safe on the pier, awaiting summer use. The winter work also earned them steady wages due to the sheltered water and more reliable catch. "The Forth Bridge was under construction then," Gordon remembers. "I loved watching the work progress." Eventually the government clamped down on pair-trawling to protect stocks from being depleted.

In the late sixties, Gordon joined an older brother who had just bought his own boat, the first of its type in Scotland to have a Gardner engine—the Rolls-Royce of marine engines. About five years later, in late 1973, Gordon bought his own boat, a traditional Northumberland coble with a double keel. He fished for lobster and poached a bit of illegal salmon with monofilament nets, as did others. "It was just slaughter," he admits. It was a fun time, though. He bought the *Fisher Lassie* in 1986 and fishes every day with one mate, weather permitting, year-round. Early on he had a relief skipper who would take the boat out and trawl for prawns in the evenings. "I hated the prawns because it was long hours of boring trawling," he says, "where lobster fishing is short hours and physically demanding but you're finished at lunchtime." The combination got the boat on its feet financially. "I made a lot of money with little effort," he says. "You have to work hard and profit during the good times because the cycles will reverse. The tide always turns."

Eighteen months ago it did just that. Lobster and crab yields dropped, together with prices. His cousin used to captain a seventy-foot boat from Eyemouth with four hands. Now it's just him and a deckhand. Stiffer international competition and EU fishing policies make matters worse. Gordon pays income tax as a "share fisherman" on his daily pay and corporate tax on the boat's profit as the boat owner. Unlike farmers, fishermen receive no government subsidies. In good times, they can make a good living. In bad times, they're left alone. Hands are hard to find now as people take better-paying jobs onshore. "There're always peaks and troughs in fishing; 'seven good years and seven bad,' the saying goes. I'm a great believer in cycles," Gordon tells me. "Fishing nowadays is poor. The old men will tell you the job's done, it's finished. Traditionally," he said, "you could set your clock by it—times of the season and what to expect and where to go; it was up here [pointing to his head]." But he believes a major change is under way: no cycles or discernible pattern in yields, and no clear reason for the change. "Everybody blames something. I dunno. You can blame global warming, you can blame this, blame that, but worldwide something seems to be happening. Tradition has gone out the window the past five or six years."

We've reached the first fleet. A yellow flag bobs as a buoy to mark the start of the line. Gordon slips his oilskin over his heavy cotton pants, knit shirt, and wool sweater, transforming himself from a cap-topped person seemingly just off the links to a fisherman. Ian's blue knit hat has a marijuana leaf embroidered on it. He joined Gordon this past winter, preferring to work rather than collect unemployment benefits after having been made "redundant" at the Torness Point nuclear power plant. He's an engineer. Already he moves with practiced precision, setting up the bait box on the metal frame he attaches to the boat's gunwale a bit forward of amidships. Gordon pulls the port side of the boat beside the buoy, standing on a two-foot-wide swath of deck alongside the cabin and reaching through the porthole to the wheel and throttle. The boat's design reflects the well-honed routine of lobster fishing. A lever at his right elbow works the winch in front of him. Overhead hangs a pulley. He snags the buoy with a grappling hook and strings the thick rope line through the pulley. He then runs the rope around the winch wheel and engages the drive to pull the 35 pots attached to the rope on board one by one. The buoy comes up first, followed by the twenty-pound weight that anchors the buoy to the bottom some fifteen to twenty-five feet below. He passes them back to Ian to store on deck. The pots appear every forty-five seconds or so, spaced six to seven fathoms apart.

Gordon and Ian work in a careful choreography to keep up with the pots coming aboard. Gordon opens the flap of net across the top of the pot, removes the catch, if any, and throws it into plastic bins mounted just in front of him. He then passes the pot back to Ian, who cleans out the unwanted catch—sea urchins, small crabs, dog whelks, "mermaid's purses" (the milky egg sacs of dogfish), and an occasional cod or wrasse—and places two mackerel as bait in the noose suspended atop a round pancake-shaped concrete weight in the middle of the trap, closes the flap, then stacks the readied pot in proper order on the boat's long rear deck. They work in tandem with little wasted motion, attentive to the sequence of steps. Today they'll check ten of his fourteen fleets—350 pots—which yield twenty-seven lobsters, four boxes of crabs, and a small basket of velvet crabs.

Prime lobster season begins in several weeks when the water temperature warms to over 50 degrees and lasts until late autumn when the water again cools. Winter storms and cold water—44 to 46 degrees—keep the creatures lethargic most of the year. When the water is cold, Gordon usually leaves the pots to set two days, instead of checking them every day, so he checks about 250 pots each day off season. The gauge indicates the water temperature is 48 degrees today. The lobsters are just beginning to emerge from their rocky crevices to scavenge on the bottom. Changes in lobster behavior brought about by constant changes in water temperature and marine conditions, combined with knowledge of the seabed terrain, make the effective placement of pots an art learned from years of experience. Two pots this day came up with basket-sized octopuses, the despised enemy that eat the catch. Gordon twisted each slithering creature across his knee, ripped it apart with his giant hands, and flung the halves overboard in disgust.

The local wholesale buyer happens to be Gordon's brother-in-law. He has a warehouse neatly tucked into the ground floor of a handsome red-roofed building of flats overlooking the old harbor renovated by Cromwell. From the street you don't notice the warehouse entrance. Inside, tiers of holding tanks for lobsters line a wall running the length of the building, thousands of creatures destined in a day or two for diners in London and on the Continent. Some lobsters are held for weeks to play the fluctuation in market prices. Crabs are shipped live in Styrofoam boxes, lying beneath a layer of newspaper covered with ice. Velvet crabs are shipped to Asia, a welcome new market developed in the past few years for what before was an unwanted catch. Too bad whelks and urchins have no market. Gordon is paid weekly by the weight of his catch. Each box of crabs, filled with individuals about as big as your hand, will earn him around £25. His twenty-seven lobsters today will yield around £140, he guesses. By the end of the season, he might get up to £250 for the same number. The lobsters will have gained up to 50 percent more weight and prices traditionally rise around the Christmas holidays due to increased demand and less supply. Many days, though, he catches only a dozen, while in season he might catch one hundred or more. The minimum legal size is 9½ inches head to tail, or about a ten-year-old creature. No need to measure each; in a quick glance Gordon can tell with uncanny accuracy.

He and Ian have the full fleet aboard. I tried to stay out of the way, standing aft, while Ian filled the deck with stacks of pots. Gordon has already decided where to replant the pots and steers the boat about fifty yards further out. Once in place, he sets the global positioning navigation system to record the boat's precise location and nods to Ian to begin casting the pots overboard as the boat moves along the desired course and the fleet line feeds out. Five minutes further on, the buoy for the next fleet waves in the gentle swells, and they repeat the process, again and again. After the fourth fleet, they break for breakfast while we run twenty minutes on to North Berwick. Gulls glide along beside the boat, as if suspended in the air, motionless, riding the wind. Bold ones try to steal a meal from the bait box. Ian lights the small propane stove in the cabin to make coffee and fry fat slices of bacon to make bacon rolls.

What does the sea mean to you, I ask as we eat. Does it mean the same as the land to a farmer? "Yes," Gordon replies. "If you're not interested in this job, it's laborious and very repetitive. But last Monday there wasn't enough water to come into the harbor and I saw something I'd never seen in fifty years. The water was clear and I could see down to the sea urchins, kelp, and everything, and I saw a ridge in the rocks below. Every day when I come in I sail over it but didn't know it. If you're interested in the job and the sea, there's something different in it every day. Sometimes you may not like the difference, like a downpour, but, oh, I have an affinity for it." Sunrise and sunset are the most amazing times. "Every night is different—the clouds, the fields, the sunlight highlighting a field, all these things, and the sunset, it's unbelievable."

I witnessed the wondrous display, accompanying Gordon one evening on a casual outing to catch mackerel with my family and some friends. We caught the silvery fish a half mile beyond the harbor mouth with four-hook lines baited with simple lures. Once atop a shoal, the kids reeled them in as fast as we could cast a line, filling two boxes in less than an hour. But the sea and shore made the real display. The sky and fields on that calm evening were just as Gordon had described them. The boat swayed gently, rhythmically, on the sensuous swells of satin water. The warm air was still and scented with the raw smell of salt, seaweed, and fish.

The white clouds overhead, adrift in the light blue sky, changed to orange and pink, then to deep purple and midnight blue, as the sun set. The colors of the cliffs and fields ashore changed as well, intensifying the reds, greens, beiges, and ambers, as beams of light broke through parts in the clouds and focused on one spot after another. Doon Hill stood in the background, behind Dunbar Castle and the town, the silhouette of Traprain Law visible to the west.

"I did exactly the same things in the rock pools and alike as John Muir did growing up, only 110 years later," Gordon tells me. "Down at the back of the castle, where Muir played, we used to take a wee bit of cork and stick it on the dorsal fin of a stickleback [the fin sticks up and has spikes on it]. The secret was to use the right amount—too much and the fish couldn't submerge, which was cruel, but just right and it would pop up every time it stopped swimming. I imagine John Muir did things like that. We'd play in the kelp tangle whenever it got washed up and used the stalks as a club, like a medieval club, when we'd play *conkers* on the way to school." History means a lot to Gordon; place and community too. They're inseparable.

After breakfast Gordon and Ian check six more fleets, and we head in. It's about 1:00 P.M., a later finish than usual after the later than usual start. Gordon lets me steer the boat to the dock while he looks over my shoulder and works the throttle. It's fun and makes me feel useful. On the way Ian hoses down the rear deck and sweeps the fish parts overboard. He then sets to work banding the lobsters' claws. He sits on a box, grabs one lobster at a time and sets it in his lap, and pops a rubber band around each claw. I'm amazed at the lobster's deep blue, speckled color and the delicate feathery fringe to their fanlike tails. Gordon has stripped off his oilskin, restoring his shore appearance, and leans out the cabin door in what I think is his favorite position: his feet just inside the threshold, his shoulders wedged in the frame, and his head extended outside, the back of his cap against the upper frame as he's a wee bit over six feet tall.

The fishing community was always somewhat suspect to the "proper" folks of the Dunbar market town that sat above the harbor. Gordon knows. Many streeties looked askance at the crude shories. Even to other fisherman, the Dunbar crew was a bit unusual since they often worked on Sunday, contrary to the normal practice of observing the Sabbath by God-fearing fishermen up and down the coast. Little of the fishing community remains by the harbor. Gordon and a few others still live there, but the gang of men who used to frequent five or six pubs has dwindled to only enough to fill one pub. Historically, each fisherman created sufficient work for seven land-based jobs. "There'll always be boats running out of Dunbar," Gordon thinks. "Crabs and lobsters aren't like herring. Once you scoop out shoal fish, that's it. But if crabs and lobsters are overfished, it becomes unviable financially, so the effort drops in balance with the yields. Between here and the Bass Rock is six miles; today another chap and I work the area. He works 600 creels and I work 500. When I first got my boat in 1973, I had 350 to 400 pots, my oldest brother had 450 to 500 pots, my dad had 450 to 500 pots, Orlando had 250 to 300, Jimmy had maybe 300, and Zander had maybe 300, all working the same area." Eventually he believes the stocks will increase when they're not being overfished—when a new equilibrium is reached.

He's begun looking for someone to carry the boat forward, although it's too early for him financially and physically to retire. Yet the years of hard work have taken a toll. He'd like to cut back. His son decided as a teenager that he didn't want to fish because of the hard work. He's a test engineer working in Sweden now, the first in the family to attend college. Gordon wasn't sad when his son chose another career. "It's been a good life for me, but I saw how things were going." The boat and the business will probably pass from the family just as many of the local farm families I've met will end their legacy on the land and likely disperse in search of opportunity.

Ben and Jill Tindall think crabs are the perfect food. Ben sits on a chair outside their stone cottage at the shore end of the seaward breakwater, overlooking the dry sand and shingle bottom of Cove harbor twenty feet below, hard at work mixing the delicacy for their annual crab party tomorrow. When the tide comes in, the three-acre harbor fills to a depth of fifteen feet at its mouth. The rubble cottage once was one of five built end-to-end in the 1700s and 1800s, the row housing over forty people. The two cottages on the ends have been removed, and of the three remaining, only their cottage has occasional occupants. Perhaps one hundred friends will come for tomorrow's noontime feast, some driving several hours. A heavy overcast tonight has brought darkness prematurely to the tiny harbor—his harbor. He bought it in 1991, acquiring with it the august title of "harbormaster," he notes with a chuckle in a proper accent that tends to tail off into a quick mumble at the end of sentences. He certainly looks the part: short, well proportioned, wearing wellies, old rumpled pants, and an old wool sweater, with a jolly face behind a long beard laced with gray and a bald head fringed with wild hair topped by a hat. Jill's voice and demeanor are soft, slow, and melodic. Both voices and personalities instantly convey friendliness and warmth. Thick clouds muffle the air, breathless, silent save for the gentle lapping of the tide against the breakwater and rocks. Pungent sea smells flavor the stillness. A light mist diffuses the forms, transforming them into ghostly apparitions.

Ben purchased the place following a systematic search for a retreat from life in Edinburgh, somewhere by the sea where he could keep his boats along the Firth coastline in Fife or East Lothian. He considered dozens of places and made several offers, though Cove was special: he'd played in the harbor during family

picnics as a child, and hosted several memorable parties here as a
student. And this entire stretch of coast with little, out-of-the-
way bays and harbors has always fascinated him. "There're lots of
wonderful places along this coast, secret crags, and this is just
one more of them," he tells me. "It's amazing how many incredibly beautiful places there are within easy reach of Edinburgh that
people really don't bother visiting. To be able to buy one seemed
quite extraordinary."

He came to Cove initially to look at a house for sale across the
harbor—the former fish-curing station—but they wanted too
much for it so he looked elsewhere. The local Council owned the
harbor at the time, minus its two habitable houses. Frank Usher
had donated it to them in 1974 because he couldn't afford to
maintain the breakwaters. The Council then spent £106,000
repairing the harbor over the next dozen years, eventually decid-
ing to sell it to rid itself of a management problem and to escape
the liability. In 1990 the Council accepted an offer from a development company intending to convert the historic harbor into a
marina with additional housing built around the shore. Notice to
quit was given the fishermen. Local folks were aghast. Luckily
the deal collapsed. Ben then made an offer that was rejected.
He reformatted the proposal and resubmitted, successfully. "I
bought Cove to prevent it from being developed," he says.

For £50,000 he bought everything from the gate and the fence
along the cliff top above the hidden harbor down to the low-
water mark, only excluding the two privately owned houses at
the base of the sea braes, though as their "feudal superior" he
owns the land beneath them. He owns the breakwaters with the
"pier cottages" that sit on the seaward wall, and the harbor the
seawalls enclose, a small boathouse, and the crude access road
that winds a quarter mile down the outside cliff face to the
seaward breakwater from the village of Cove one hundred feet
above. He formed a limited-liability company to protect himself

in case he's sued beyond the sums covered by his public liability
insurance, and signed a public access agreement that gives people
the right to visit. Bit by bit, he and Jill are slowly conserving the
property, within the regulations associated with its "B-listing" as
a place of regional architectural and historical significance.

"I have few responsibilities or obligations as harbormaster but
a huge number of powers," he says with a laugh. "I can search any
vessel; I can arrest anyone in a vessel; I can impound the vessel; I
can do almost anything." He permits the two remaining fishing
boats free use of the harbor, contrary to the usual practice of
charging a docking fee. "I wouldn't dream of charging them," he
says, though he charges recreational boats that moor in his harbor
a very modest fee of £9 per week. "It's a pleasure to have the fishermen; it remains a real harbor with them here," Jill adds. "And
the way they look after the harbor is worth more than money,"
Ben notes. He's not in it for the money.

We work in tandem by the hissing glow of an old oil lamp set
on the makeshift table—Ben and Jill and their seven dinner
guests this evening. Earlier we grilled kebabs of aubergine, cour-
gette, onion, and red pepper, and sausages of pork and apple,
pork and leek, and lamb and mint. The small charcoal grill sat
outside the door of their dilapidated stone cottage, which the
Council declared "unfit for human habitation." No gas. No electricity. No running water. No telephone. "Keep Out, This Building Is Dangerous," the large ivy-engulfed sign on the corner of
the cottage proclaims. No one pays attention to it. I love the
irony: Ben's a nationally prominent architect from Edinburgh.
Jill's a noted artist. They retreat on weekends to Cove to refresh
and reinvigorate themselves. What does the harbor mean to you,
I ask. Is it what you'd hoped it would be when you bought it?
"Oh yes," he replies. "It's become a home. Jill and I got engaged
here. The rock formations that surround the harbor are beautiful.
It's a place where we come to relax. The tide and the way of life

are incredibly restorative." Simplicity. Clarity. "He often resolves nagging design problems here," Jill notes. She finds inspiration in the tranquillity for her art as well. "Our weekends here improve our quality of life," Ben continues. "They reconnect us with real life: we actually catch crab, kill crab, cook crab, eat crab, and dispose of the shells ourselves. We collect driftwood for the fire, and we collect sand and stone for rebuilding—we deal directly with nature. That makes us feel a lot better. We always go back thinking we've been away for a week or two."

We enjoyed the sausages and kebabs together with glorious multigrain bread and several bottles of good wine, huddled around the table in the cottage's cozy main room, warmed by a coal fire with oil lamps and candles for light. Every nook and cranny in the room holds artifacts of Cove's fishing heritage, nothing fake, no clutter, not a museum. Genuine. The room, the cottage, the harbor, share the patina of age, weathered and well-worn, landscape and people forming a perfect harmony over the centuries of interaction. The pier cottages and part of their breakwater appear to have grown out of the underlying rock formation that rises up from the sea at a thirty-degree angle to blend organically into their foundations. I wonder if the many tourists who now visit the place sense the harmony, or are they simply attracted to its rugged beauty and quaint charm. Scenes in several movies have been filmed here because of its character. A hundred years earlier, the "Glasgow Boys" found the harbor and the spectacular local landscape to be wonderful subjects. The group of renowned artists advocated a more naturalistic approach to painting called *en plein air,* as opposed to landscapes painted in studios, and lived part time in Cockburnspath a half mile inland. A cluster of artists still lives in the area, Jill among them. I think they sense the harmony. I think the locals sense it too. For generations the harbor has been a favorite destination for walks from Cockburnspath. Dinner completed, we nine diners set to work to earn our meal: Ben and Jill; Larry and Anne, friends from America who arrived yesterday to begin a holiday; Graham, a local friend; and my wife, Marie, our kids Katie and Ed, and me.

Larry and I remove the claws and legs with quick snaps and sort them into the Styrofoam boxes that the fresh, cooked *partans* came in this morning from the wharfside fish market at Eyemouth. Katie and Ed help. We're the novices so we do the simple part. Marie and Graham finish "dressing" the crabs, using their thumbs to pop off the body. Then they remove the mouthparts and any remaining gills. Ben scoops out the meat from the seventy palm-sized shells, filling two large plastic bowls. Jill and Anne work in the cottage preparing other ingredients. When we've completed the process, Ben adds a half cup of English mustard, the juice from a half dozen lemons, a cup of vinegar, breadcrumbs made from two loaves of the best Dunbar bread, and chopped parsley to complete the pâté. The crab shells and discarded parts are left to the tide and gulls to recycle. Nothing remains by morning.

Nothing remains either of the natural sea-carved cave from which Cove probably takes its name. *Cowe, coaue,* or *coif,* in ancient Scots, means a recess in a rock, a cave, or a cavern. Such a den opened onto the harbor between the low- and high-tide levels, extended slightly upward about twenty feet into the soft sandstone, until a nervous Council government sealed it with thousands of tons of cliff-top rock in 1981. For centuries the cave's seclusion and twelve-foot-wide mouth made it perfect for smugglers to store barrels of French brandy and wine, and for bathers from Cockburnspath who used it as a changing room. Generations of local children learned to swim in the safety of the harbor's calm water. Fishermen have used Cove for generations as well. For perhaps five hundred years they've accessed the small C-shaped harbor through the "Gutt"—a long, narrow natural channel between bands of ragged rocks called "the Shore Goats and the Hurkers" that sit just below high-tide level.

As early as 1603, the Cockburnspath postmaster collected customs on the catch and goods arriving by sea, with the income applied to the maintenance of "Quhytecoifl" (Whitecove). By mid-century the laird of Cockburnspath assumed responsibility for the natural harbor, collecting customs and anchorage duties during the late summer herring draves. The average daily catch in 1660 was five hundred fish—brill, cod, dab, eel, flounder, gurnet, haddock, halibut, herring, ling, mackerel, mullet, plaice, salmon, skate, smelt, sole, sprat, thornback, trout, turbot, and whiting, as well as crabs, lobsters, mussels, oysters, and prawns. The Halls acquired the property in 1692, incorporating it into their Dunglass Estate, where it remained until Frank Usher disposed of it 282 years later.

In the 1700s, over one hundred cobles used Cove during the annual herring drave. A century later, the Halls made a number of improvements to the harbor, building sound breakwaters in 1831 after winter storms destroyed earlier attempts. By the 1860s, twenty-five boats harbored here, supporting well over one hundred people as fishermen, gutters, packers, net makers, coopers, and vendors. The curing station alone employed fifty-five men and women baiting lines and processing the catch—splitting, smoking, salting, and extracting cod-liver oil.

The village above the harbor was begun in the early 1800s to house the rising population of fishing families and farm families on the Dunglass Estate. The Halls built ten cottages on the cliff top in 1809, based on a plan focused on a central cultivated area with a well, and gradually expanded the hamlet as the population grew. Over twenty families with fifty children still lived in Cove as late as the 1920s, a fine example of an east coast *heugh heid* village built at the cliff edge overlooking the sea. But circumstances changed. Fishing yields declined together with the number of fishermen, and more mechanization reduced the number of farmworkers. The Ushers began to sell off the Cove cottages in the late 1920s and the village began to gradually transform into retirement and holiday home use. A line of new houses have been built in recent years on land Frank Usher sold adjacent to the village, adding a few permanent residents to the population, though the sense of Cove as a distinct community has been lost. Little remains to tie the permanent and seasonal people to the place or to each other. Today thirty-some residents live there year-round and two fishing boats operated by cousins from a longtime family of Cove fishermen work from its harbor.

Ben and Jill see Cove and their Edinburgh home mostly from the heart, not the head. Their urban home a mile from the center of Edinburgh was a ruin with no utilities when Ben bought it, a picturesque Scottish Georgian house built in 1734 on the city's south side. Once a country villa, it now stands surrounded by urban growth. "It has a beautiful atmosphere," Jill says, "it's a very friendly house, you never feel on your own in it." His restoration of the home, like his concern for Cove, reflects Ben's holistic view of architecture. "I'm interested in landscape down to product design and color," he tells me. "I don't see architecture as just magazine photos of buildings; that's not my style at all. It's the whole thing. I suppose I view architecture as a small part of life as a whole, and it's all about quality of life." No stark and sterile modernism or postmodernism in his work. No isms at all, really. Ben doesn't impose "style." The firm of "Benjamin Tindall—Architects" has ten staff members, completing a wide range of project types throughout Britain, from new commercial and civic buildings to residential properties and the restoration of historic structures and landscapes. The firm could be larger if they wished.

"The landscape has so many layers that you see at once," he explains. "You think of Stone Age hunters, the Romans, the Normans, the Border raiders and the Covenanters, the agricultural improvers and industrialists. That's why the landscape is so amazingly rich. It doesn't take a lot to read it. Little in the landscape is accidental. People have used most everything for centuries. You can look at the landscape purely in visual terms and it's very, very, very beautiful. But it's more than that, more complex, and I think that's very exciting."

His approach to architecture and landscape and life were influenced by a year's study in the design school at the University of Pennsylvania in 1976–77. There he gravitated toward the landscape architecture faculty with an ecological and humanist-oriented view, which he found more natural and sympathetic than the prevailing architectural orientation. "I found landscape to be a much more rigorous, rational basis for architecture than accepted contemporary theory," he says. His experience in Philadelphia and America made him more appreciative of the British landscape and its extraordinary depth of history, and more of a rebel in that he found new bases of design beyond those he'd learned in the U.K. Ben believes the nature of people, culture, and landscape are intertwined. He rides a bike to his office in a renovated building in the Old Town, just below the castle and the Royal Mile, only one hundred feet from the "Patrick Geddes Steps."

"My father (Frank) was very forceful and quite a character," Ben says. "His successors kept to his rules, not realizing that he never kept entirely to his rules himself," he says with a chuckle. Frank was strongly socialist in his support of centralized planning to achieve societal goals and benefits. Like father, like son. Unfortunately, many of those "rules" or planning principles, based on a Geddes-like progressive socialism, have been overshadowed or forgotten since the halcyon days in the postwar years when his father worked. Planning in many places has lost its luster and much of its power and influence. Ben sees it as being too often punitive, negative, and reactive, rather than positive, proactive, and progressive. Development pressures dominate. As a result, landscapes in Scotland run the risk of losing their distinctive historical character—their traditional harmony between people and place. He tries to maintain that harmony in his work and his life. For ten years he served as a trustee of the John Muir Trust and championed the creation of the John Muir Award with Graham White.

The weather has worsened since the night before as Marie, Katie, Ed, and I descend the gravel road from the village to the harbor for the Tindalls' crab party. The overcast now drips a steady drizzle. Fortunately, the temperature is mild and the wind is calm. Guests gather around a makeshift serving table made of driftwood planks covered with seaweed atop overturned fish boxes. The setup sits in the sand in front of the boathouse on the inland side of the harbor, opposite the pier cottages and the seaward seawall. The diners use small beach stones to crack open the crab legs and, when those are consumed, the claws. No one seems to mind the wet. Another cluster of people stand in the boathouse, where three other makeshift tables hold the crab pâté, breads, salads, beverages, and desserts. Everyone brought something. The drizzle becomes a steady rain. No one moves, no one minds: academics, artists and authors, businessmen and -women, scientists, and professionals from various disciplines, a fascinating array of local and faraway friends drawn to the place and the people. Kids play in the sand and the shallow water. Adults crack away at the crab. Other guests climb the breakwaters and explore the cellars chiseled into the cliff face. The rain becomes heavy so Katie, Ed, Marie, and I join a group going to see the cellars.

While there are no records of how the man-made vaults were used in the 1700s and 1800s, circumstantial evidence and the long history of smuggling in the area suggests that much of their use was illegal. A strong door guards the entrance now. Several of us help Jill light dozens of small candles to place along the chambers to light the absolute blackness of the interior. The temperature is cool inside, perhaps 55 degrees, and the air is very moist.

We can see our breath in the faint glow of candlelight. The soft sandstone walls easily yield virgin sand with a gentle scrape. Carvings of initials and figures decorate some walls, and carved niches for candles and lanterns are inset in others. It's an eerie place. The echoes of the past are as audible as the echoes of our footsteps.

The main chamber of the cellar extends 100 feet into the cliff face, ascending about 25 feet from its mouth at the beach. The 9-foot-wide opening enabled horse-drawn carts to enter. Four side chambers perpendicular to the main chamber, the largest 45 feet deep and 10 feet wide, open about every 25 feet on the right-hand side. The walls and roof are carefully pick-dressed with even surfaces. The caverns were cut in 1751–52 at the Halls' expense, probably by Northumberland miners who enlarged a natural cave formed when sea level was once higher.

At the same time they cut a 120-foot-long tunnel parallel to the main cellar shaft through the hillside to improve harbor access from the cliff top via a new road scoured around the outside ridge. Before, a crude cart path zigzagged precariously down the unstable foreshore slope. The new tunnel opened 30 feet above the beach; a wooden bridge was built to make the final drop. A path long ago replaced the bridge. When the Halls built the harbor breakwaters, they also had a tight 20-foot-long passage cut connecting the tunnel to the back of the first side chamber in the cellar to improve ventilation in the vaults. That connection is now the only entrance to the cellars. In 1981 the Council sealed the natural mouth, already partly blocked by recurring rock falls from the headland above, after a sloppy effort to solve the problem resulted in another landslip. The mishap prompted the Council to close off the entrance to the harbor's other cave at the same time.

Local legends say that smugglers used the cave and cellars to hide barrels of brandy. Perhaps even the Halls profited from the operation. Small, secluded beaches and harbors indented in the cliffs, some with natural caves, dot this stretch of coastline, but none are better suited for clandestine landings than Cove—perfect for nefarious activities late on stormy nights during low tide, save for the dangerous rocky shoals around the Gutt. Other man-made caves, all very small, are cut in the cliff face near the opposite mouth of the tunnel. Some people believe a long passage used by smugglers runs from one to the White Swan cottage or Sparrow Castle in Cockburnspath, at the back of the medieval church and cemetery just behind the house we let. It is doubtful that the tunnel exists; it would have been uneconomical to dig one that long. Perhaps the legends refer to a medieval *cundie.* Constructed of large stones that lined an underground tunnel up to several feet wide and high, these drains made perfect hiding places for people or contraband. In 1792 a "tide-waiter" inspected suspect vessels and watched for suspicious landings at Cove. Eyes have scanned the coastline for smugglers ever since, keeping a lookout for drug smugglers most recently. I suspect fact underpins much of the Cove lore.

The rain has let up when we leave the cellars. The warm, fresh air feels good. The feast continues late into the afternoon, by which time the tide has once again filled the harbor. Water now engulfs the legs of the serving table in front of the boathouse. No bother; people still stand in the wet cracking the few claws that remain. Several guests swim; others row around in Ben's fifteen-foot skiff, *Jeanie.* We say our goodbyes and leave through the tunnel, up the road to Cove village, to our car parked in a paved lot that was once the community's garden.

I return to Cove the next day to reflect on the place, its current caretakers, and my stay in Scotland. No trace of the party, save for a small pile of crab shells in front of the boathouse, just above the high-tide level so they haven't been washed away. They'll be gone in a day or two; birds and shore animals, wind, rain, or a storm tide will see to it. No sign of yesterday's wet weather either. The sun has returned, bringing a brilliant blue sky, a gentle breeze, and wonderful warmth. I'll take some pictures. It's late August and we leave for the States in three weeks. No rush to get home for Marie, or for Katie and Ed, or for me. No homesickness. We've not missed the place—the landscape—though we'll all enjoy the familiar comforts of home and our friends. I'm beginning to sense more and more that we'll leave something special behind: a much stronger sense of landscape and connection to place than what we'll return to. Like the Muirs and millions of other immigrants, we'll leave behind a landscape alive with layers of history as we depart from our adopted Old World home. I suspect our pleasant New World suburban landscape will seem more shallow and unsatisfying than before. The Spanish philosopher José Ortega y Gasset once said, "Tell me the landscape in which you live and I will tell you who you are." It's not always true, although in the case of Ben and Jill Tindall and Cove Harbor, it certainly is. Cove couldn't be in better hands and hearts, landscape and people in perfect harmony. I wonder how the thought applies to me.

Epilogue

A place is not a place until people have been born in it,
have grown up in it, lived in it, known it,
and died in it—have both experienced and shaped it,
as individuals, families, neighborhoods,
and communities, over more than one generation.

WALLACE STEGNER, *Where the Bluebird Sings
to the Lemonade Springs*

[21]

Autumn envelops my suburban subdivision in the American Midwest. Fifty-some years before, crops grew where houses now stand. A deep blue sky brought by an arctic high descended from Canada has displaced the milky haze of summer humidity. Crisp. Clean. Clear. Days are noticeably shorter. Darkness comes just after dinner rather than just before bedtime. And sunshine brings pleasing warmth to the coolness. I relish its radiance, unlike the hot glare of the sultry summer sun. The bright greens of spring and summer have given way to the empty, hollow beiges and browns of desiccation and dormancy. Only a few late season flowers brighten gardens. Even mums are past their prime. Most herbaceous plants have withered, saving energy for the coming winter and the following spring renewal, except those stimulated by fertilizer and irrigation. For deciduous plants, though, the growing season ends with a bang, not with a whimper. Their ostentatious display of dazzling color mocks the coming cold, gray starkness. For a brief moment, the foliage flashes fiery crimson, gold, and yellow, then falls to the ground like fireworks, the color extinguished as suddenly as it appeared in the brilliant outburst. The cycle of life and death is most apparent now.

The pattern of suburban life has changed with the season as well. School has resumed and fall sports have begun, including both the Old World and New World forms of football. Preparations are under way for Halloween and trick or treat. Pumpkins, apple cider, and ghostly costumes fill the stores now. Thanksgiving and Christmas soon follow. I wish I could say I was happy to be home, but I can't.

I miss our adopted home in Cockburnspath. I miss the way of life. It seemed a bit less cluttered with less background "noise." It seemed less focused on unimportant "stuff" and more focused on meaningful matters—personal relationships, simple pleasures and joys. The first night back, as I lay in bed wide awake at 3:00 A.M., a comfortable breeze blowing in through the open windows, the din of noise outside seemed deafening to ears recently accustomed to the stillness of country life. I rarely noticed the constant background noise before, oblivious to this by-product of my suburban lifestyle.

The audible sound of cars, trucks, trains, and planes is indicative of other forms of suburban "noise" that too often drown out the real music of life. Marie and I discovered this in Cockburnspath. Daily life there was stripped bare of much of that racket, not by choice. The decision to live in Cockburnspath was as much accidental as deliberate. While we wanted to live in East Lothian so I could research material for the book, and we searched the region for a residence via the Internet, we chose the converted schoolhouse in the 250-person village, located miles from the nearest "city" (Dunbar), because it was the only reasonably sized and affordable option we had as our departure date rapidly approached. Neither Marie nor I had lived before in a small rural village. We were worried. Would we be welcomed?

Would we miss the conveniences of our contemporary suburban lifestyle?

Gone were most of its trappings and what before we might have considered near necessities. Much to our surprise we never missed them, not for a moment. No fast food restaurants, movie theaters, theme parks and play places, shopping malls, big-box superstores, or strip commercial centers within almost an hour's drive. Unwanted ads, news, and information were easily avoided. Gone were the constant assault on our senses and the relentless invasion of our privacy, mental and physical. No traffic lights or traffic jams, and few streetlights, either. There, we found time to be quiet and recover. Night was black, just outside the village. And it was silent. When the wind blew from the east, across the North Sea, the salty smells of surf, sand, and rotting seaweed enticed the senses. When it blew from the west, across the Lammermuir Hills, it carried the bleating of lambs together with the rich scent of turned earth, manure, and crops. No dirty industrial sounds or smells, no vehicle exhaust, just a natural sweetness. Views of wondrous sunrises and sunsets were unobstructed by buildings and trees. Sheep pastures and barley fields lay a minute's walk from the quaint square on which our house fronted. Just beyond lay Dunglass and Pease Deans. Cove Harbor sat indented in the dramatic North Sea coast, a ten-minute walk from our door, and the Lammermuirs rose just behind the village, rising like ocean swells. Single-track country lanes lined with dykes and hedgerows extended into the surrounding landscape, and a public pathway edged the rugged cliff top along the sea braes. It was a landscape of staggering beauty and charm in nice weather, and a place of dramatic character somehow in harmony with the all-too-common windy, cold, and damp conditions.

Our landlords had intended to let the recently renovated house unfurnished, and kindly consented to partly furnish it before our arrival at no additional rent. Compared with the home we left, our new home was spartan. Rooms had less furniture and fewer fixtures. The sitting room had one tiny TV and no VCR or stereo, although we bought the cheapest VCR we could find. The small kitchen was equipped with a convection oven and electric cooker, a seventeen-cubic-foot refrigerator/freezer, and little storage. No microwave. No dishwasher. No disposal. A small-capacity clothes washer that worked wonderfully was built in beneath the counter, but with no dryer; we draped the wet laundry over the radiators around the house and hung it on lines outside when the weather permitted, as did many neighbors. The one small bathroom had no vanity or mirror. A wall-mounted "geyser" trickled warm water for the shower. The Franklin stove in the dining room supplemented the "heat slave" boiler and hot-water radiator system. A call to the local coal merchant in the morning would bring fifty-weight bags of clean hard coal and soft (starter) coal delivered to our door by afternoon. I loved the smell of the coal fire but never mastered stoking the stove so it could burn overnight. Katie and Ed had fewer toys; Marie and me, too. We bought a small, well-worn car that even new was a throwback to the 1950s—a twelve-year-old diesel Ford Orion with 135,000 miles, a stick shift, and no power or electronic anything. We parked the car unlocked in the square, beside the five-hundred-year-old mercat cross, amid a half dozen other cars. European cars, like most homes and consumer products, are a bit smaller than their American counterparts, yet of comparable quality. We found less conspicuous consumption in Cockburnspath, compared with our New World home; less excess; less wastefulness, too.

Cockburnspath has nestled on the side of a gentle slope above a small burn, sandwiched between Dunglass Dean and Pease Dean, for perhaps a thousand years. A generation or two ago, the self-sufficient village still contained several groceries, a dairy, a post office, an inn/hotel, a sweetshop, a saddler, dressmakers, several joiners, builders and masons, a butcher, a bakery, a shoemaker, a smiddy, and a mill. Today the village no longer lives in isolation. Local bus service links the village to the broader world beyond every two hours, and the A-I, the major highway between Edinburgh and England, passes nearby. Several new subdivisions have added homes, but the overall population has changed little as the number of people per residence has declined. Homes are comfortable and contemporary, despite the fact that many still occupy stone shells hundreds of years old. Many huddle together, sharing walls and shaping narrow lanes, to form a tight-knit physical and social fabric. New homes sit on tiny lots, still a part of the fabric yet just slightly separate. Only two businesses remain: the "shop" next door, in the girls' half of the Old Schoolhouse, which serves as post office, newsstand, confectionery, grocery, video rental, and liquor store (we let the boys' half); and the car repair garage from which we bought our red saloon for £750. A fishmonger and butcher visit the village weekly, selling fresh product from their vans. Unfortunately, the village pub closed several years ago, to the disappointment of many. Pubs serve much more than a wee dram and a pint: they're often the village sitting room—the community lounge, the communal hearth. Efforts were under way to develop a new pub just off the square. Cheers.

The village population remains a broad cross section. Some residents are retired, others work in small nearby towns, and some commute to larger cities like Berwick and Edinburgh. A handful of farmers and fishermen live on the outskirts. The village hall sits a hundred yards up a narrow lane on the opposite side of the square from our door, with the community football pitch behind, an adjacent playground, and the ninety-student elementary school across the lane. On school days, a small flock of mums and a few dads gather by the school to see their wee ones off or to welcome them back, often lingering to chat while the kids play in the playground. Katie and Ed knew almost every child in the school and many of the village teenagers who attended high school about twenty miles away, forming as large a circle of friends whom they saw regularly there as they have in our 35,000-person community here. St. Helens Church stood just over our rear garden wall, surrounded by a cemetery. Portions of the current structure may date to the 1300s. Perhaps twenty-five parishioners, mostly elderly, attended Sunday service.

"No place is a place until things that have happened in it are remembered in history, ballads, yarns, legends, or monuments. Fictions serve as well as facts," wrote Wallace Stegner. His landmark works of nonfiction and fiction in the latter half of the 1900s shed new light on the American West and American culture. "Some are born in their place," he said, "some find it, some realize after long searching that the place they left is the one they have been searching for. But whatever their relation to it, it is made a place only by slow accrual, like a coral reef." Cockburnspath and the surrounding landscape have been accruing for millennia. It shows. In many ways, I felt more at home there than I do in my suburban home here.

I miss the people of Cockburnspath too, though we returned to kind and caring family and friends. Every few weeks the village gathered for some communal event, usually at the village hall. Disco nights with a disc jockey commanding a booming sound system attracted families with young children and the grandparents early in the evening. Teenagers came later, and adults often socialized until after midnight. The annual flower/craft show, sports day, and various holiday celebrations, like *Hogmanay* (New Year's), brought neighbors together for little reason other than to be together. Most events included a raffle for inexpensive prizes. Many had a cash bar.

"Beetle Drive" is typical. Simple. Silly. Even corny. Fun,

nonetheless. More than fifty people of all ages gather in the hall several times a year to play the game. Admission is 50 p. for adults. Kids pay 25 p. The first player each round to draw a complete beetle wins the round, with the overall winner determined by total score after twelve rounds. Eleven parts compose the bug: body, head, two eyes, two antennae, four legs, and a tail (so, it's not anatomically correct). Each body part corresponds to a number on a dice. To draw a part, you must roll the corresponding number; however, you must first roll the head and body to draw the parts attached to each. Four players sit at a table and share one dice, which is passed from player to player after each roll. Be careful that you don't toss the dice off the table in the excitement. "Beetle Drive!" shouts the winner. Players then add up their score, one point for each body part. Prizes are given at the end for the highest and lowest scores and runners-up, by gender and age group, so almost everyone wins something. Snacks follow, then a raffle for prizes that as often as not are donated back for the next raffle. Proceeds are used for the church vestry project, or to secretly purchase a watercolor portrait of the village square for a family of wayward Americans living in their midst.

However, mostly I miss the place. I miss the landscape. I feared I might. Why would I fear this? Two reasons, I think. To miss it might mean that my suspicions about the importance of possessing a sense of "rootedness" to place and continuity between the past, present, and future were correct. If so, I would be learning that for years I *had* missed something of importance, something that enriches, something that deeply satisfies. What a shame. Worse, how could I then find in my suburban landscape what I had missed when that landscape is so devoid of history and the principal source of the problem? I also feared the changes in my life that I might want to make in response to what I had learned, and doubted my courage to make them. If I genuinely missed a sense of connection to the landscape and community in my American home, would I be willing to do something about it? Would I be ready to move to another place where I could find it, or to change my lifestyle to better embrace it?

Perhaps it was just *me* and not really a function of the place. Was I simply ready for such an escape with a change of pace and place, as if on an extended vacation? Was my reaction temporary, rather than permanent? If I were to live there longer, would the infatuation wear thin as the novelty wore off? Perhaps I was having a nostalgic, romantic reaction as I anticipated a return to the routine of work and suburban life. Perhaps I can experience the same lifestyle, the same satisfactions and fulfilling joys here, if I choose. Certainly America has cozy rural communities, maybe even tight-knit suburban neighborhoods. Mine enjoys an extraordinary sense of community for a place its size. Perhaps all that's required for me to realize the missing benefits is a change of attitude. Simple.

I wish I believed these alternative explanations were true, but I don't. While they may be true in some small part, I fear I found a place, a landscape, perhaps even a lifestyle, more to my liking. Landscape is key. It shapes people and their lifestyle in a thousand minute ways. American geographer Peirce Lewis knew it. "If we want to understand ourselves," he said, "we would do well to take a searching look at our landscapes." Now I understand what he meant. The Old World landscape of my adopted home in Cockburnspath shapes its residents and their lifestyle differently than my New World landscape shapes me. The effect is inescapable and can't be duplicated in the adolescent-like American landscape. While I might find communities in America with a similar sense of closeness as Cockburnspath, I cannot find them set in a landscape where the past, present, and future form so seamless a fabric. Time matters. Place matters. History matters. People in Wisconsin told me: Erik, Bessie, Morrie and Mary, Fran, and Ken. The Ho-Chunks tried to teach me too: Susette,

George, William, and Ritchie. And many of the Scots showed me. John Muir's story said it all along. "When we try to pick out anything by itself," he noted, "we find it hitched to everything else in the universe." Time, place, and history are cumulative, not linear like most Westerners believe. Look at a map. It'll tell you. Compare a 1:25,000 scale Ordnance Survey map of East Lothian to a 1:24,000 scale USGS topographic quadrangle map of Marquette County, Wisconsin. You'll see it.

The East Lothian map carries the imprint of human occupancy that reaches back millennia. Ancient standing stones, Iron Age hill forts, medieval castle ruins, and feudal doocots litter the landscape, the faint echoes of past people. Place names recall the many cultures that have settled the land, leaving another lingering record of distant time. And the landscape patterns of past and present interweave to form a complicated plaid, like a Highland tartan. The map guides the traveler through time and place. So does the Marquette County map, though the map has far fewer remnants of the past to serve as markers and milestones. Their scarcity stands in striking contrast to the plentitude of markers and milestones in the Old World map, testimony to the "placelessness" of my New World culture.

"We have made a culture out of the open road, out of movement without place," wrote Wallace Stegner. "Freedom, especially free land, has been largely responsible. Nothing in our history has bound us to a plot of ground as feudalism once bound Europeans. In older, smaller, more homogeneous and traditional countries, life was always more centripetal, held in tight upon its center," he continued. "Indifferent to, or contemptuous of, or afraid to commit ourselves to, our physical and social surroundings, always hopeful of something better, hooked on change, a lot of us have never stayed in one place long enough to learn it, or have learned it only to leave it.

"It is probably time we settled down," Stegner said. "It is

probably time we looked around us instead of looking ahead. We have no business, any longer, in being impatient with history," he noted. "History was part of the baggage we threw overboard when we launched ourselves into the New World. We threw it away because it recalled old tyrannies, old limitations, galling obligations, bloody memories. Plunging into a future through a landscape that had no history, we did both the country and ourselves some harm along with some good. Neither the country nor the society we built out of it can be healthy until we stop raiding and running, and learn to be quiet part of the time, and acquire the sense not of owning but of belonging." Where do I belong? "Only in the act of submission," he concluded, "is the sense of place realized and a sustainable relationship between people and earth established."

[22]

Can a person possess an innate attraction to place—to landscape— as if we were preprogrammed in our genetic code to somehow sense our ancestral home? Scientists have long speculated about a genetic-based predisposition for savanna-like landscapes stemming from the origins of human evolution. I mean a different attraction, one related to our more recent family roots. Might my reaction to the landscape around Cockburnspath have such roots?

I puzzled over that a lot during my nine-month stay in Scotland, remembering that my direct ancestor, John "the Scot" Simpson, emigrated from the Old World to the New in 1677. Perhaps he lived in East Lothian near where we lived in Cockburnspath. I found one Simpson buried in the St. Helens cemetery just over our rear garden wall. Simpson (or Simson, Simsone, Symson, Symsone) is a traditional Scottish name, especially in East Lothian, where George Brent might have recruited John the Scot to work on his properties in the fledgling Virginia colony.

However, it is nearly impossible to trace John the Scot in his homeland because we don't know his parents' names and parish records indicate several dozen John Simpsons were born in Scotland in the 1640s, the time we know John the Scot was born. Still, it's a tantalizing thought that my reaction to the place was in some subtle way a response to the area being my ancestral homeland. Perhaps that's also why I've always felt some special attraction to the sea, even though I've lived my entire life over 500 miles from it. Landscape, I learned, does matter; roots do matter in many more ways than I initially suspected.

Late on the evening of Saturday, September 8, just days before we left Cockburnspath to return to our New World home, I received a startling e-mail message. The next day, we hosted a goodbye party for our many friends in the village and I shared the news with them, after I told them the story of John the Scot. With an emotion-choked voice and teary eyes, I read the message:

On October 14, 1649, there was christened in Cockburnspath, Berwickshire, Scotland one Johne Symson. His parents were Johne Symson, father, and Alison Bookles, mother.

BIBLIOGRAPHIC NOTE

The Wisconsin interviews were conducted in June and September 2000. The Scottish interviews were conducted between January and September 2001. Material from an interview is accurate as of the time of the interview; material was not updated to make it all accurate as of a single date. All interviews were tape-recorded, by permission. Quotes obtained from the interviews have been edited to improve the wording and clarify the meaning. In some cases, the sequence of the conversation has been changed to better interrelate content.

The literature on and by John Muir is extensive. I've relied most heavily on general biographies by William Frederic Badè, *The Life and Letters of John Muir* (2 volumes; Houghton Mifflin, 1924); Frederick Turner, *Rediscovering America: John Muir in His Time and Ours* (Viking, 1985); and my favorite, Linnie Marsh Wolfe, *Son of Wilderness: The Life of John Muir* (Knopf, 1945). Millie Stanley's *The Heart of John Muir's World: Wisconsin, Family, and Wilderness Discovery* (Prairie Oak Press, 1995) provides a wonderful glimpse into his Marquette County landscape and life. Additional insight on Muir was drawn from Michael P. Cohen, *The Pathless Way: John Muir and American Wilderness* (University of Wisconsin Press, 1984); Richard F. Fleck, *Henry Thoreau and John Muir Among the Indians* (Archon Books, 1985); Stephen Fox, *The American Conservation Movement: John Muir and His Legacy* (University of Wisconsin Press, 1985); Steven J. Holmes, *The Young John Muir: An Environmental Biography* (University of Wisconsin Press, 1999); and Thurman Wilkins, *John Muir: The Apostle of Nature* (University of Oklahoma Press, 1995). Of Muir's actual writings, *The Story of My Boyhood and Youth* was most useful. See as well *John of the Mountains: The Unpublished Journals of John Muir,* edited by Linnie Marsh Wolfe (University of Wisconsin Press, 1979). The Muir archives at the University of the Pacific Holt-Atherton Library provided me with a copy of portions of his unpublished writings and the Dunbar John Muir Association shared with me its archives on his childhood in Scotland. Background on the John Muir Memorial County Park and the National Historic Landmark in Wisconsin were obtained from the U.S. Department of the Interior, National Park Service, Midwest Region, "Management Options for the John Muir Memorial County Park and Boyhood Home—Wisconsin" (1990); and the nomination application for the national historic landmark designation (1987). Background on John Muir Country Park (Scotland) was obtained from the East Lothian Council's "John Muir Country Park: Descriptive Management Plan" (1976) and "John Muir Country Park: Management Plan, 2000–2004" (2000).

The literature on the general development of the American landscape, including landscape values and land management practices, is vast as well. I've relied primarily on Daniel Boorstin, *The Americans: The Colonial Experience* (Random House, 1958); Michael Conzen, *The Making of the American Landscape* (Unwin Hyman, 1990); William Cronon, *Changes in the Land* (Hill and Wang, 1983); Donald Meinig, *The Shaping of America,* volume 1, *Atlantic America, 1492–1800* (Yale University Press, 1986); Gregory Nobles, *American Frontiers* (Hill and Wang, 1997); and John Warfield Simpson, *Visions of Paradise* (University of California Press, 1999). See also Daniel Boorstin, *The Americans: The National Experience* (Vintage, 1965); Hector St. John de Crèvecœur, *Letters from an American Farmer* (Dutton, 1945); Timothy Flint, *The History and Geography of the Mississippi Valley* (E. H. Flint, 1833); Emily Foster, ed., *The Ohio Frontier* (University Press of Kentucky, 1996); John Opie, *The Law of the Land* (University of Nebraska Press, 1987); and Donald Worster, *The Wealth of Nature* (Oxford University Press, 1993).

An overview of Scottish history was obtained from T. M. Devine, *The Scottish Nation: A History, 1700–2000* (Viking, 1999); and J. D. Mackie, *A History of Scotland,* 2nd ed., revised and edited by Bruce Lenman and Geoffrey Parker (Penguin, 1991). Magnus Magnusson's and Graham White's *The Nature of Scotland: Landscape, Wildlife and People* (Canongate, 1997) provided a valuable overview of the country's environmental history. The *Sunday Mail*'s 1988 yearlong series "The Story of Scotland" proved a valuable source with a wealth of illustrations. A detailed description of Scottish landownership was obtained from Robin Callander, *How Scotland is Owned* (Canongate, 1998); and Andy Wightman, *Who Owns Scotland?* (Canongate, 1996). Ian Burdon's *Automated Registration of Title to Land* (Registers of Scotland Executive Agency, 1998) explained the complicated feudal history of Scottish land records.

For background on the history of the Scottish landscape, R. N. Millman, *The Making of the Scottish Landscape* (Batsford, 1975); R. J. Brien, *The Shaping of Scotland* (Aberdeen University Press, 1989); and Leah Leneman, *Fit for Heros? Land Settlement in Scotland After World War I* (Aberdeen University Press, 1989), were critical starting points. Although the English and Scottish landscapes developed differently, an examination of the literature detailing England's landscape history provided valuable context. W. G. Hoskins's classic *The Making of the English Landscape,* as updated (Hodder and Stoughton, 1988), was the obvious starting point. Alan Everitt, *Landscape and Community in England* (Hambledon, 1985); Oliver Rackham, *The History of the Countryside* (J. M. Dent, 1987); and Tom Williamson and Liz Bellamy, *Property and Landscape: A Social History of Land Ownership and the English Countryside* (George Philip, 1987), were of additional usefulness. Context on and details of land planning policies were obtained from Barry Cullingworth, ed., *British Planning: 50 Years of Urban and Regional Policy* (Athlone, 1999); and J. B. Cullingworth, *Environmental Planning,* volume 1, *Reconstruction and Land Use Planning, 1939–1947* (Her Majesty's Stationery Office, 1975).

Background on Wisconsin was drawn from Robert C. Nesbit and William F. Thompson, *Wisconsin: A History,* 2nd ed. (University of Wisconsin Press, 1989); Dennis Boyer and Justin Isherwood, eds., *A Place to Which We Belong: Wisconsin Writers on Wisconsin Landscapes* (1000 Friends of Wisconsin Land Use Institute, 1998); August Derleth, *The Wisconsin: River of a Thousand Isles* (Farrar & Rinehart, 1942); and Wisconsin Cartographers' Guild, *Wisconsin's Past and Present: A Historical Atlas* (University of Wisconsin Press, 1998).

Details on Marquette County were obtained from Fran Sprain, *Places and Faces in Marquette County, Wisconsin,* 3 volumes (Isabella Press, 1991, 1993, 1998); and U.S. Department of Agriculture, Soil Conservation Service (Keith O. Schmude), *Soil Survey of Marquette County, Wisconsin* (Washington, D.C.: USDA Soil Conservation Service, 1975). William Rudolph Smith's *Observations on the Wisconsin Territory* (Arno Press, 1975; originally published in 1838) and Increase Allen Lapham's *Wisconsin: Its Geography and Topography,* 2nd ed. (Arno Press, 1975; originally published in 1846), provided historical accounts of the region circa the time of Muir's arrival.

Information on the Ho-Chunk people was drawn from Paul Radin's classic, *The Winnebago Tribe* (University of Nebraska Press, 1970); Robert E. Bieder, *Indian Communities in Wisconsin, 1600–1960: A Study of Tradition and Change* (University of Wisconsin Press, 1995); and Nancy Oestreich Lurie, "Winnebago," in *Handbook of North American Indians,* volume 15, ed. Bruce G. Trigger (Washington, D.C.: Smithsonian Institution, 1978). Autobiographies were also useful. These included Muriel Blackdeer, *An Eagle Blessed Our Home* (Skandisk, 1994); *Mountain Wolf Woman,* ed. Nancy Oestreich Lurie (University of Michigan Press, 1961); and *Crashing Thunder,* ed. Paul Radin (University of Nebraska Press, 1983). The three-part video *Indians of the Upper Mississippi,* produced by the Ho-Chunk and Menominee Nations, provided other useful insights.

Historical background on the Dunbar region, including East Lothian and the Borders, included David Dick, *A Millennium of Fame of East Lothian: 200 Lives of Achievement* (Clerkington, 2000); Dunbar John Muir Association, *John Muir's Dunbar* (DJMA, 1998); Charles E. Green, *East Lothian* (William Green, 1907); Historic Scotland, *Rural Buildings of the Lothians: Conservation and Conversion; A Guide for Practitioners* (Crown, 2000); James Miller, *The History of Dunbar* (William Miller, 1830); Eric Rankin, *Cockburnspath: A Documentary History of a Border Parish* (T. T. Clark, 1981); John Sinclair, ed., *The* [First or "Old"] *Statistical Account of Scotland* (William Creech, 1791–99); Sally Smith, *Cockburnspath: A History of a People and a Place* (Dunglass Mill Press, 1999); Catherine P. Snodgrass, *The*

Third Statistical Account of Scotland: The County of East Lothian (Oliver and Boyd, 1953); Alexander Somerville, *The Autobiography of a Working Man* (MacGibbon and Kee, 1967); Robert Somerville, *General View of the Agriculture of East Lothian* (Richard Phillips, 1805); *The* [Second or "New"] *Statistical Account of Scotland* (no author or publisher, 1834–45); and Frank Tindall, *Memoirs and Confessions of a County Planning Officer* (Pantile Press, 1998). The account of Cromwell and the Battle of Dunbar was based primarily on John D. Grainger, *Cromwell Against the Scots: The Last Anglo-Scottish War, 1650–1652* (Tuckwell Press, 1997). Background on the Tyninghame and Broxmouth Estates was found in articles contained in the topic files of the Haddington Local History Centre. Material on place names was drawn from David Dorward, *Scotland's Place-names* (Mercat Press, 1998); W. F. H. Nicolaisen, *Scottish Place-Names: Their Study and Significance* (Batsford, 1989); and William Patterson, "East Lothian Place-Names: Some Clues and Challenges" (unpublished paper, 1999). Details of Cove Harbor's history were found in Angus Graham, "Cove Harbour," in *Proceedings of the Society of Antiquaries of Scotland,* session 1963–64 (Edinburgh: National Museum of Antiquities of Scotland, 1966). Maps also provided important insights, including Blaeu's Atlas map of East Lothian (1654), Roy's Military Survey map of Scotland (1747–55), Forrest's map of East Lothian (1799), the Ordnance Survey map of East Lothian (1853) and the Explorer Series Ordnance Survey map of Dunbar and North Berwick (2001).

American attitudes on nature and wilderness, including sections on John Muir, were explored in Roderick Nash, *Wilderness and the American Mind,* 3rd ed. (Yale University Press, 1982); and Max Oelschlaeger, *The Idea of Wilderness: From Prehistory to the Age of Ecology* (Yale University Press, 1991). Peter Coates, *Nature: Western Attitudes Since Ancient Times* (University of California Press, 1998), provided a general overview while Keith Thomas, *Man and the Natural World: Changing Attitudes in England, 1500–1800* (Oxford University Press, 1983), focused specifically on English attitudes.

Changing concepts of property and environmental stewardship in the New World, and to some extent in the Old, were detailed in Eric T. Freyfogle, *Bounded People, Boundless Lands: Envisioning a New Land Ethic* (Shearwater/Island Press, 1998); Harvey Jacobs, ed., *Who Owns America?* (University of Wisconsin Press, 1998); John Hanson Mitchell, *Trespassing: An Inquiry into the Private Ownership of Land* (Addison-Wesley, 1998); and Theodore Steinberg, *Slide Mountain: or the Folly of Owning Nature* (University of California Press, 1995). See also Norman Cantor, *Imagining the Law* (HarperCollins, 1997); John Opie, *The Law of the Land* (University of Nebraska Press, 1987); Rutherford Platt, *Land Use and Society* (Island Press, 1996); and Donald Worster, *The Wealth of Nature* (Oxford University Press, 1993).

Primary sources on the Land Ordinance include Daniel Boorstin, *The Americans: The National Experience* (Vintage, 1965); Michael Conzen, *The Making of the American Landscape* (Unwin Hyman, 1990); R. Douglas Hurt, *The Ohio Frontier* (Indiana University Press, 1996); J. B. Jackson, *Landscapes,* ed. Ervin Zube (University of Massachusetts Press, 1970); Hildegard Johnson, *Order upon the Land* (Oxford University Press, 1976); Donald Meinig, *The Shaping of America,* volume 1 (Yale University Press, 1986); Janet Mendelsohn and Claire Marino, producers, *Figure in a Landscape* (a film by Direct Cinema, 1988); Carolyn Merchant, ed., *Major Problems in American Environmental History* (Heath, 1995); John Opie, *The Law of the Land* (University of Nebraska Press, 1987); John Reps, *The Making of Urban America* (Princeton University Press, 1965); John Stilgoe, *Common Landscape of America* (Yale University Press, 1982); and Norman Thrower, *Original Land Survey* (Rand McNally, 1966). Major sources on land speculation and distribution and the Homestead Act, in addition to those above, include Goodwin Berquist and Paul Bowers, *The New Eden* (University Press of America, 1983); Paul Gates, *The Jeffersonian Dream: Studies in the History of American Land Policy and Development* (University of New Mexico Press, 1996); and Christopher Tunnard, *The City of Man* (Scribners, 1970). Marion Clawson, *The Federal Lands Revisited* (Johns Hopkins University Press, 1983), and *America's Land and Its Uses* (Johns Hopkins University Press, 1972); Gregory Nobles, *American Frontiers* (Hill and

Wang, 1997); Donald Worster, *The Wealth of Nature* (Oxford University Press, 1993); and Dyan Zaslowsky and T. H. Watkins, *These American Lands* (Island Press, 1994), provide additional insight on general American land use and land policy.

Descriptions of general European immigration to North America included Bernard Bailyn, *Voyagers to the West: A Passage in the Peopling of America on the Eve of the Revolution* (Knopf, 1986); Oscar Handlin, *The Uprooted,* 2nd ed. (Little, Brown, 1973); and Marcus Lee Hansen, *The Atlantic Migration, 1607–1860: A History of the Continuing Settlement of the United States* (Harvard University Press, 1940). General descriptions of emigration from the United Kingdom included Barbara De Wolfe, *Discoveries of America: Personal Accounts of British Emigrants to North America During the Revolutionary Era* (Cambridge University Press, 1997); Charlotte Erickson, *Leaving England: Essays on British Emigration in the Nineteenth Century* (Cornell University Press, 1994); and William E. Van Vugt, *Britain to America: Mid-Nineteenth-Century Immigrants to the United States* (University of Illinois Press, 1999). Sources on Scottish emigration included Ian Adams and Meredyth Somerville, *Cargoes of Despair and Hope: Scottish Emigration to North America, 1603–1803* (John Donald, 1993); Jeanette M. Brock, *The Mobile Scot: A Study of Emigration and Migration, 1861–1911* (John Donald, 1999); David Dobson, *Scottish Emigration to Colonial America, 1607–1785* (University of Georgia Press, 1994); Marjory Harper, *Emigration from North-East Scotland,* volume 2, *Beyond the Broad Atlantic* (Aberdeen University Press, 1988); Douglas Hill, *Great Emigrations,* volume 1, *The Scots to Canada* (Gentry Books, 1972); James Hunter, *A Dance Called America: The Scottish Highlands, the United States and Canada* (Mainstream, 1994); and William C. Lehmann's *Scottish and Scotch-Irish Contributions to Early American Life and Culture* (Kennikat, 1978).

Descriptions of sailing ships and ship and harbor life were drawn from Robert Greenhalgh Albion, *Square-Riggers on Schedule: The New York Sailing Packets to England, France, and the Cotton Ports* (Princeton University Press, 1938), and *The Rise of New York Port, 1815–1860* (Northeastern University Press, 1939); Terry Coleman, *Passage to*

America: A History of Emigrants from Great Britain and Ireland to America in the Mid-Nineteenth Century (Pimlico, 1992); Carl C. Cutler, *Queens of the Western Ocean: The Story of America's Mail and Passenger Sailing Lines* (United States Naval Institute, 1961); and Edwin C. Guillet, *The Great Migration: The Atlantic Crossing by Sailing-ship Since 1770*, 2nd ed. (University of Toronto Press, 1963). For detail on the design of nineteenth-century merchant sailing ships, see Robert Gardiner, ed., *Sail's Last Century: The Merchant Sailing Ship, 1830–1930* (Conway Maritime Press, 1993); and David R. MacGregor, *Merchant Sailing Ships, 1815–1850* and *Merchant Sailing Ships, 1850–1875: Heyday of Sail* (both Conway Maritime Press, 1984).

Background on the Reformation and religious history was drawn from Sydney E. Ahlstrom, *A Religious History of the American People*, 2 volumes (Image Books, 1975); Jon Butler, *Awash in a Sea of Faith: Christianizing the American People* (Harvard University Press, 1990); Owen Chadwick, *The Reformation* (Penguin, 1972); Justo L. González, *The Story of Christianity*, volume 2, *The Reformation to the Present Day* (Harper & Row, 1984); and Martin E. Marty, *Protestantism in the United States: Righteous Empire*, 2nd ed. (Scribners, 1986).

Acknowledgments

Thanks to Jean Thompson Black, Howard Boyer, Harry Foster, John Glusman, Susan Rabiner, Hal Rothman, and John Stilgoe for wise counsel on and support of my writing wants and wishes. Their help led to this work.

Dozens of wonderful people have assisted my research for *Yearning,* especially those who generously shared with me their personal stories. In the New World, these people are Ritchie Brown, Erik Brynildson, Bessie Eggleston, George Hindsley, Maurice and Mary Kearns, Susette LaMere, William O'Brien, Ken and Eunice Soda and family, Fran Sprain, and Chris Straight. Other kind people shared with me their valuable time and knowledge, including Debbie Daniels, Mary Falz, Janene Ford, Patrick Kilbey, Mark Koziol, Robert Kravick, Willard Lonetree, Nancy Oestreich Lurie, Mark Martin, Ardith McDowell, Daryl Morrison, Tom Onofrey, Jeff Remling, Millie Stanley, Allan Turner, Keith Vander Velde, and Bernice Wegner.

In the Old World, those who graciously shared with me their personal stories are Gordon Easingwood, the Earl and Countess of Haddington, Jimmy and Jane Hood, Peter Hood, the Duke of Roxburghe, Ben and Jill Tindall, Frank and Merilyn Usher, and Graham White. Other people who assisted my research include David Anderson, Calum Bannerman, Simon Bell, Bill Brown, Stephen Bunyan, Sally Butler, Dan Cairney, Jackie Clark, John and Judy Cockburn, Will Collin, Pete Collins, Jane Dawson, Gary Donaldson, Tom Dykes, Ian Fraser, George Gretton, the Duke and Duchess of Hamilton, Marion Lauder, the Reverend Anne Lithgow, Margaret Mackay, Alison McGachy, Alastair Milligan, John Murray, Alan Ramage, Jenny Sheerin, Duncan Smeed, Alastair Smith, Sally Smith, Margaret Stewart, Ian Thompson, Catharine Ward-Thompson, Andy Wightman, and Paul Zochowski.

Special thanks as well for a thousand acts of kindness to Richard, Margaret, Lindsey, and Lorna Copland, Jim Thompson, Ben and Jill

Tindall, Graham White, and my many friends not listed above in Cockburnspath, Oldhamstocks, Dunbar, North Berwick, and Edinburgh.

A host of readers have lent portions of the manuscript their careful editorial eyes: among them in the New World are Jean-Marie Cackowski, Jack Nasar, and Nancy Oestreich Lurie; in the Old, they include David Anderson, Pete Collins, Jane Dawson, Anne Lithgow, and Paul Zochowski. Every person I interviewed and quoted in the text was given a draft of the corresponding portion of the manuscript for review and comment. Thanks to all who responded. Of course any faults in the text are entirely the result of my own failings.

I was quite pleased when Jane Garrett, my editor, acquired the proposal for Pantheon Books. *Yearning* owes its being to her. It has been a pleasure to work with Jane and the Pantheon production team.

And, finally, thanks to my family and friends who shared in some way my nine-month sabbatical in Scotland during which most of the work on the manuscript was completed. It was a grand adventure indeed.

J.W.S.
Dene Vue
Cockburnspath, Berwickshire
September 2001

About the Author

John Warfield Simpson received a B.S. in landscape architecture from the Ohio State University, an M.L.A. from Harvard University's Graduate School of Design, and an M.A. from Duke University's School of Forestry and Environmental Studies. Since 1983 he has taught at Ohio State, where he is currently professor of landscape architecture and natural resources. In 2001 he was visiting research fellow at Heriot-Watt University in Edinburgh, Scotland. He is the author of *Visions of Paradise: Glimpses of Our Landscape's Legacy* (1999) and numerous articles.

Pooh Invents a New Game

By the time it came to the edge of the Forest
the stream had grown up, so that it was
almost a river, and, being grown-up, it did
not run and jump and sparkle along as it used
to do when it was younger, but moved more
slowly. For it knew now where it was going,
and it said to itself, 'There is no hurry.
We shall get there some day.' But all the
little streams higher up in the Forest went
this way and that, quickly, eagerly, having
so much to find out before it was too late.

There was a broad track, almost as broad as a road, leading from the Outland to the Forest, but before it could come to the Forest, it had to cross this river. So, where it crossed, there was a wooden bridge, almost as broad as a road, with wooden rails on each side of it. Christopher Robin could just get his chin on to the top rail, if he wanted to, but it was more fun to stand on the bottom rail, so that he could lean right over, and watch the river slipping slowly away beneath him. Pooh could get his chin on to the bottom rail if he wanted to, but it was more fun to lie down and get his head under it, and watch the river slipping slowly away beneath him. And this was the only way in which Piglet and Roo could watch the river at all, because they were too small to reach the bottom rail. So they would lie down and watch it . . . and it slipped away very slowly, being in no hurry to get there.

One day, when Pooh was walking towards this

bridge, he was trying to make up a piece of poetry about fir-cones, because there they were, lying about on each side of him, and he felt singy. So he picked a fir-cone up, and looked at it, and said to himself, 'This is a very good fir-cone, and something ought to rhyme to it.' But he couldn't think of anything. And then this came into his head suddenly:

> Here is a myst'ry
> About a little fir-tree.
> Owl says it's *his* tree,
> And Kanga says it's *her* tree.

'Which doesn't make sense,' said Pooh, 'because Kanga doesn't live in a tree.'

He had just come to the bridge; and not looking where he was going, he tripped over something, and the fir-cone jerked out of his paw into the river.

'Bother,' said Pooh, as it floated slowly under the bridge, and he went back to get another fir-cone which had a rhyme to it.

But then he thought that he would just look
at the river instead, because it was a
peaceful sort of day, so he lay down and
looked at it, and it slipped slowly away
beneath him . . . and suddenly, there was his
fir-cone slipping away too.

'That's funny,' said Pooh. 'I dropped it
on the other side,' said Pooh, 'and it came out
on this side! I wonder if it would do it
again?' And he went back for some more fir-
cones.

It did. It kept on doing it. Then he
dropped two in at once, and leant over the

bridge to see which of them would come out first; and one of them did; but as they were both the same size, he didn't know if it was the one which he wanted to win, or the other one. So the next time he dropped one big one and one little one, and the big one came out first, which was what he had said it would do, and the little one came out last, which was what he had said it would do, so he had won twice . . . and when he went home for tea, he had won thirty-six and lost twenty-eight, which meant that he was—that he had—well, you take twenty-eight from thirty-six, and *that's* what he was. Instead of the other way round.

And that was the beginning of the game called Poohsticks, which Pooh invented, and which he and his friends used to play on the edge of the Forest. But they played with sticks instead of fir-cones, because they were easier to mark.

Now one day Pooh and Piglet and Rabbit and Roo were all playing Poohsticks together. They

 had dropped their sticks
in when Rabbit said
'Go!' and then they had
hurried across to the
other side of the bridge,
and now they were all
leaning over the edge, waiting to see whose
stick would come out first. But it was a long
time coming, because the river was very lazy
that day, and hardly seemed to mind if it didn't
ever get there at all.

'I can see mine!' cried Roo. 'No, I can't.
It's something else. Can you see yours, Piglet?
I thought I could see mine, but I couldn't.
There it is! No, it isn't. Can you see
yours, Pooh?'

'No,' said Pooh.

'I expect my stick's stuck,' said Roo.
'Rabbit, my stick's stuck. Is your stick
stuck, Piglet?'

'They always take longer than you think,'
said Rabbit.

'How long do you *think* they'll take?' asked Roo.

'I can see yours, Piglet,' said Pooh suddenly.

'Mine's a sort of greyish one,' said Piglet, not daring to lean too far over in case he fell in.

'Yes, that's what I can see. It's coming over on to my side.'

Rabbit leant over further than ever, looking for his and Roo wriggled up and down, calling out 'Come on, stick! Stick, stick, stick!' and Piglet got very excited because his was the only one which had been seen, and that meant that he was winning.

'It's coming!' said Pooh.

'Are you *sure* it's mine?' squeaked Piglet excitedly.

'Yes, because it's grey. A big grey one. Here it comes! A very—big—grey—Oh, no, it isn't, it's Eeyore.'

And out floated Eeyore.

'Eeyore!' cried everybody.

Looking very calm, very dignified, with his legs in the air, came Eeyore from beneath the bridge.

'It's Eeyore!' cried Roo, terribly excited.

'Is that so?' said Eeyore, getting caught up by a little eddy, and turning slowly round three times. 'I wondered.'

'I didn't know you were playing,' said Roo.

'I'm not,' said Eeyore.

'Eeyore, what *are* you doing there?' said Rabbit.

'I'll give you three guesses, Rabbit. Digging holes in the ground? Wrong. Leaping from branch to branch of a young oak-tree? Wrong. Waiting for somebody to help me out of the river? Right. Give Rabbit time, and he'll always get the answer.'

'But, Eeyore,' said Pooh in distress, 'what can we—I mean, how shall we—do you think if we—'

'Yes,' said Eeyore. 'One of those would be just the thing. Thank you, Pooh.'

'He's going *round* and *round*,' said Roo, much impressed.

'And why not?' said Eeyore coldly.

'I can swim too,' said Roo proudly.

'Not round and round,' said Eeyore. 'It's much more difficult. I didn't want to come swimming at all to-day,' he went on, revolving slowly. 'But if, when in, I decide to practise a slight circular movement from right to left— or perhaps I should say,' he added, as he got into another eddy, 'from left to right, just as it happens to occur to me, it is nobody's business but my own.'

There was a moment's silence while everybody thought.

'I've got a sort of idea,' said Pooh at last, 'but I don't suppose it's a very good one.'

'I don't suppose it is either,' said Eeyore.

'Go on, Pooh,' said Rabbit. 'Let's have it.'

'Well, if we all threw stones and things into the river on *one* side of Eeyore, the stones would make waves, and the waves would wash him to the other side.'

'That's a very good idea,' said Rabbit, and Pooh looked happy again.

'Very,' said Eeyore. 'When I want to be washed, Pooh, I'll let you know.'

'Supposing we hit him by mistake?' said Piglet anxiously.

'Or supposing you missed him by mistake,' said Eeyore. 'Think of all the possibilities, Piglet, before you settle down to enjoy yourselves.'

But Pooh had got the biggest stone he could carry, and was leaning over the bridge, holding it in his paws.

'I'm not throwing it, I'm dropping it, Eeyore,' he explained. 'And then I can't miss—I mean I can't hit you. *Could* you stop turning round for a moment, because it muddles me rather?'

'No,' said Eeyore. 'I *like* turning round.'

Rabbit began to feel that it was time he took command.

'Now, Pooh,' he said, 'when I say "Now!" you can drop it. Eeyore, when I say "Now!" Pooh will drop his stone.'

'Thank you very much, Rabbit, but I expect I shall know.'

'Are you ready, Pooh? Piglet, give Pooh a little more room. Get back a bit there, Roo. Are you ready?'

'No,' said Eeyore.

'*Now!*' said Rabbit.

Pooh dropped his stone. There was a loud splash, and Eeyore disappeared . . .

It was an anxious moment for the watchers on the bridge. They looked and looked . . . and even the sight of Piglet's stick coming out a little in front of Rabbit's didn't cheer them up as much as you would have expected. And then, just as Pooh was beginning to think that he must have chosen the wrong stone or the wrong river or the wrong day for his Idea, something grey showed for a moment by the river bank . . . and it got slowly bigger and bigger . . . and at last it was Eeyore coming out.

With a shout they rushed off the bridge, and pushed and pulled at him; and soon he was standing among them again on dry land.

'Oh, Eeyore, you *are* wet!' said Piglet, feeling him.

Eeyore shook himself, and asked somebody to explain to Piglet what happened when you had been inside a river for quite a long time.

'Well done, Pooh,' said Rabbit kindly. 'That was a good idea of yours.'

'What was?' asked Eeyore.

'Hooshing you to the bank like that.'

'*Hooshing* me?' said Eeyore in surprise. 'Hooshing *me?* You didn't think I was *hooshed*, did you? I dived. Pooh dropped a large stone on me, and so as not to be struck heavily on the chest, I dived and swam to the bank.'

'You didn't really,' whispered Piglet to Pooh, so as to comfort him.

'I didn't *think* I did,' said Pooh anxiously.

'It's just Eeyore,' said Piglet. '*I* thought your Idea was a very good Idea.'

Pooh began to feel a little more comfortable, because when you are a Bear of Very Little Brain, and you Think of Things, you find sometimes that a Thing which seemed very Thingish inside you is quite different when it gets out into the open and has other people looking at it. And, anyhow, Eeyore *was* in the river, and now he *wasn't*, so he hadn't done any harm.

'How did you fall in, Eeyore?' asked Rabbit, as he dried him with Piglet's handkerchief.

'I didn't,' said Eeyore.

'I was BOUNCED,' said Eeyore.

'Oh,' said Roo excitedly, 'did somebody push you?'

'Somebody BOUNCED me. I was just thinking by the side of the river—thinking, if any of you know what that means—when I received a loud BOUNCE.'

'Oh, Eeyore!' said everybody.

'Are you sure you didn't slip?' asked
Rabbit wisely.

'Of course I slipped. If you're standing
on the slippery bank of a river, and somebody
BOUNCES you loudly from behind, you slip.
What did you think I did?'

'But who did it?' asked Roo.

Eeyore didn't answer.

'I expect it was Tigger,' said Piglet
nervously.

'But, Eeyore,' said Pooh, 'was it a Joke,
or an Accident? I mean—'

'I didn't stop to ask, Pooh. Even at the very bottom of the river I didn't stop to say to myself, "*Is* this a Hearty Joke, or is it the Merest Accident?" I just floated to the surface, and said to myself, "It's wet." If you know what I mean.'

'And where was Tigger?' asked Rabbit.

Before Eeyore could answer, there was a loud noise behind them, and through the hedge came Tigger himself.

'Hallo, everybody,' said Tigger cheerfully.

'Hallo, Tigger,' said Roo.

Rabbit became very important suddenly.

'Tigger,' he said solemnly, 'what happened just now?'

'Just when?' said Tigger a little uncomfortably.

'When you bounced Eeyore into the river.'

'I didn't bounce him.'

'You bounced me,' said Eeyore gruffly.

'I didn't really. I had a cough, and I happened to be behind Eeyore, and I said "*Grrrr—oppp—ptschschschz*".'

'Why?' said Rabbit, helping Piglet up, and dusting him. 'It's all right, Piglet.'

'It took me by surprise,' said Piglet nervously.

'That's what I call bouncing,' said Eeyore. 'Taking people by surprise. Very unpleasant habit. I don't mind Tigger being in the Forest,' he went on, 'because it's a large Forest, and there's plenty of room to bounce in it. But I don't see why he should come into *my* little corner of it, and bounce there. It isn't as if there was anything very wonderful about my little corner. Of course for people who like cold, wet, ugly bits it *is* something rather

special, but otherwise it's just a corner, and if anybody feels bouncy—'

'I didn't bounce, I coughed,' said Tigger crossly.

'Bouncy or coffy, it's all the same at the bottom of the river.'

'Well,' said Rabbit, 'all I can say is— well, here's Christopher Robin, so *he* can say it.'

Christopher Robin came down from the Forest to the bridge, feeling all sunny and careless, and just as if twice nineteen didn't matter a bit, as it didn't on such a happy afternoon, and he thought that if he stood on the bottom rail of the bridge, and leant over, and watched the river slipping slowly away beneath him, then he would suddenly know everything that there was to be known, and he would be able to tell Pooh, who wasn't quite sure about some of it. But when he got to the bridge and saw all the animals there, then he knew that it wasn't that kind of afternoon, but the other kind, when you wanted to *do* something.

'It's like this, Christopher Robin,' began Rabbit. 'Tigger—'

'No, I didn't,' said Tigger.

'Well, anyhow, there I was,' said Eeyore.

'But I don't think he meant to,' said Pooh.

'He just *is* bouncy,' said Piglet, 'and he can't help it.'

'Try bouncing *me*, Tigger,' said Roo eagerly. 'Eeyore, Tigger's going to try *me*. Piglet, do you think—'

'Yes, yes,' said Rabbit, 'we don't all want to speak at once. The point is, what does Christopher Robin think about it?'

'All I did was I coughed,' said Tigger.

'He bounced,' said Eeyore.

'Well, I sort of boffed,' said Tigger.

'Hush!' said Rabbit, holding up his paw. 'What does Christopher Robin think about it all? That's the point.'

'Well,' said Christopher Robin, not quite sure what it was all about. '*I* think—'

'Yes?' said everybody.

'*I* think we all ought to play Poohsticks.'

So they did. And Eeyore, who had never played it before, won more times than anybody else; and Roo fell in twice, the first time by accident and the second time on purpose, because he suddenly saw Kanga coming from the Forest, and he knew he'd have to go to bed anyhow. So then Rabbit said he'd go with them; and Tigger and Eeyore went off together, because Eeyore wanted to tell Tigger How to

Win at Poohsticks, which you do by letting
your stick drop in a twitchy sort of way, if you
understand what I mean, Tigger; and
Christopher Robin and Pooh and Piglet were
left on the bridge by themselves.

For a long time they looked at the river
beneath them, saying nothing, and the river said
nothing too, for it felt very quiet and peaceful
on this summer afternoon.

'Tigger is all right, *really*,' said Piglet lazily.

'Of course he is,' said Christopher Robin.

'Everybody is *really*,' said Pooh. 'That's what *I* think,' said Pooh. 'But I don't suppose I'm right,' he said.

'Of course you are,' said Christopher Robin.